1950s "Rocketman" TV Series and Their Fans

1950s "Rocketman" TV Series and Their Fans
Cadets, Rangers, and Junior Space Men

Edited by

Cynthia J. Miller and
A. Bowdoin Van Riper

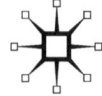

1950S "ROCKETMAN" TV SERIES AND THEIR FANS
Copyright © Cynthia J. Miller and A. Bowdoin Van Riper, 2012.

All rights reserved.

First published in 2012 by
PALGRAVE MACMILLAN®
in the United States—a division of St. Martin's Press LLC,
175 Fifth Avenue, New York, NY 10010.

Where this book is distributed in the UK, Europe and the rest of the world, this is by Palgrave Macmillan, a division of Macmillan Publishers Limited, registered in England, company number 785998, of Houndmills, Basingstoke, Hampshire RG21 6XS.

Palgrave Macmillan is the global academic imprint of the above companies and has companies and representatives throughout the world.

Palgrave® and Macmillan® are registered trademarks in the United States, the United Kingdom, Europe and other countries.

ISBN: 978–0–230–37731–8

Library of Congress Cataloging-in-Publication Data

    1950s "rocketman" TV series and their fans : cadets, rangers, and junior space men / edited by Cynthia J. Miller, A. Bowdoin Van Riper.
      p. cm.
    ISBN 978–0–230–37731–8 (hardback)
    1. Science fiction television programs—United States. 2. Television programs—Social aspects—United States—History—20th century. 3. Popular culture—United States—History—20th century. I. Miller, Cynthia J., 1958– II. Van Riper, A. Bowdoin.

PN1992.8.S35A615 2012
791.45′6150973—dc23   2012011371

A catalogue record of the book is available from the British Library.

Design by Newgen Imaging Systems (P) Ltd., Chennai, India.

First edition: September 2012

10 9 8 7 6 5 4 3 2 1

Printed in the United States of America.

*To all those who looked
at fishbowls, and saw space helmets
at cable reels, and saw rocket controls
at muffler pipes, and saw ray guns
at the stars, and saw the future*

Contents

List of Illustrations and Tables — ix

Foreword: To Infinity and Beyond! — xiii
Henry Jenkins

Acknowledgments — xxiii

Introduction — 1
Cynthia J. Miller and A. Bowdoin Van Riper

Prologue: When Our Story Began...

1. Where It All Began: The Flash Gordon Serials — 17
   Roy Kinnard

I Learning to Be Rocketmen

2. "A Commotion in the Firmament": *Tom Corbett* and the Lost Boys — 33
   John C. Tibbetts

3. Boy's Wonder: Male Teenage Assistants in 1950s Science Fiction Serials and Cold War Masculinity — 53
   Robert Jacobs

4. Girls and "Space Fever" — 67
   Amy Foster

II Reaching for Tomorrow

5. Space Fever: From Fantasy to Reality — 85
   Howard E. McCurdy

6. Shooting for the Stars: Captain Video, the Rocket Rangers, and America's Conquest of Space — 97
   Patrick Lucanio and Gary Coville

7. Space Opera TV: Seeing the World of Tomorrow — 115
   J. P. Telotte

III As Seen on TV

8. The Sky Is the Limit: Advertising and Consumer Culture in "Rocketman" Television Series of the 1950s — 133
   Lawrence R. Samuel

9. Creating a Sense of Wonder: The Glorious Legacy of Space Opera Toys of the 1950s — 149
   S. Mark Young

10. *Space Patrol*: Missions of Daring in the Name of Early Television — 163
    Jean-Noel Bassior

IV Looking at the Earth

11. Making the Universe Safe for Democracy: *Rocky Jones, Space Ranger* — 181
    Wheeler Winston Dixon

12. "Justice through Strength and Courage": *Captain Midnight* and the Military-Industrial Complex — 193
    Mick Broderick

13. "To Learn from the Past...": Becoming Cold War Citizens with Captain Z-Ro — 213
    Cynthia J. Miller and A. Bowdoin Van Riper

Epilogue: The Twenty-First Century and Beyond

14. Confessions of a *Commando Cody* Addict (or, How the Flying Suit Changed My Life) — 231
    Gary Hughes

Notes on Contributors — 249

Index — 255

Illustrations and Tables

Illustrations

0.1	Ralph Kramden and Cadet Ed Norton on the *Honeymooners*	xiv
0.2	The cast of *Dennis the Menace* in "Innocents in Space."	xvii
0.3	The cast of *Dennis the Menace* with "Captain Blast"	xvii
0.4	Buzz Lightyear and Sheriff Woody of *Toy Story*	xix
1.1	Buster Crabbe as Flash Gordon	19
1.2	Buster Crabbe, Jean Rogers, and Donald Kerr in *Flash Gordon's Trip to Mars*	24
1.3	Flash and Dale Arden (Carol Hughes) in *Flash Gordon Conquers the Universe*	26
2.1	Fischer's Buttercup Bread end seal collector's album	35
2.2	*Airship Andy* cover (Frank V. Webster, 1911)	37
2.3	The crew of the *Polaris*	40
2.4	Tom Corbett and rocket ship at a Chicago parade	43
2.5	Frankie Thomas Jr. and Ed Kemmer at a fan convention	48
3.1	Bobby (Robert Lyden) picks a lock to save the crew of *Rocky Jones*	56
3.2	Captain Video (Al Hodge) and Video Ranger (Don Hastings)	60
3.3	Captain Z-Ro (Roy Steffens) and Jet (Bruce Haynes)	63
4.1	Rocky Jones, Vena Ray, and Bobby	69
4.2	Osa Massen in *Rocketship XM*	71
4.3	Rockets paraded through the city on the planet Anthenia in the episode "Power Failure" from the series *Space Angel* (1961); CIA photograph of an R-12 rocket in Moscow's Red Square (1959–1962)	75
4.4	NASA astronaut Shannon Lucid	77
4.5	NASA astronaut Mae Jemison	79
5.1	The cover of *Science and Invention*, August 1923	87
5.2	Jules Verne's *From the Earth to the Moon*, 1865	89
5.3	*Destination Moon*, 1950	92
5.4	Wernher von Braun and Walt Disney inspect a spaceship model	94
6.1	Rocky Jones and Vena Ray sign autographs for fans	99

6.2	*Rocky Jones, Space Ranger* Calculator	103
6.3	Advertisement for *Chris Conway, Rocket Ranger*	105
6.4	Don Herbert of *Watch Mr. Wizard*	108
6.5	Tom Corbett meets his fans	110
7.1	Captain Video and his Remote Carrier	118
7.2	Buzz Corry markets a ray gun to viewers	120
7.3	Tom Corbett, T. J., and Astro	122
7.4	Rocky Jones and Space Ranger Winky	124
8.1	*Captain Midnight* 1957 Secret Squadron Official Manual and Code Book	135
8.2	Rocky Jones ad for Silvercup Bread	136
8.3	Captain Video Picture Ring	137
8.4	Tom Corbett and Pep "the Solar Cereal"	140
8.5	*Captain Midnight* Code Room instructions	145
9.1	Examples of *Captain Video* Toys	153
9.2	The Superior Space Port	154
9.3	*Space Patrol* Toys	155
9.4	The *Space Patrol* Rocket Lite	155
9.5	The Marx *Space Patrol* Atomic Pistol Flashlite with Original Box	156
9.6	The *Tom Corbett* Space Academy	159
10.1	Lyn Osborn (Cadet Happy), Ken Mayer (Major Robertson), Virginia Hewitt (Carol Carlisle), Ed Kemmer (Commander Buzz Corry), and Nina Bara (Tonga)	165
10.2	The cast of *Space Patrol* signs autographs for their fans	169
10.3	Ricky Walker Day in Washington, Illinois, January 12, 1954	171
10.4	Lyn Osborn and Ed Kemmer	173
11.1	Vena Ray in need of rescue	183
11.2	*Rocky Jones* cast members: Professor Newton, Vena Ray, Rocky Jones, Cleolanta, and Winky	186
11.3	Rocky and villain Pinto Vortando (Ted Hecht)	189
12.1	Secret Squadron preparedness montage 1 from *Captain Midnight*	201
12.2	Pacific Atoll evacuation and bomb-test montage from *Captain Midnight*	203
12.3	Secret Squadron preparedness montage 2 from *Captain Midnight*	206
12.4	Atomic testing-ground montage from *Captain Midnight*	207
13.1	Captain Z-Ro (Roy Steffens) taping at KRON-TV	214
13.2	Captain Z-Ro and Jet in the studio	215
13.3	Atlas Television Corporation Ad for Captain Z-Ro's syndicated series	217
13.4	Captain Z-Ro, Jet, and Leonardo da Vinci	219
13.5	Captain Z-Ro and Jet examine their futuristic technology	223
14.1	Ad for Captain Sacto on KCRA-TV	232
14.2	Gary Hughes and family in the Willows Lamb Derby Parade, 1966	234

14.3	Ruben Contreras, Ed Irvin, David Brunette (in robot costume), Nikki Hughes, Gary Hughes, Victor Contreras, Vic Hughes, and TV Horror Host, Mr. Lobo	237
14.4	Shooting a scene with the robot in North Hollywood	245
14.5	Gary and Vic Hughes test the flying rig	246

TABLES

9.1	Examples of *Captain Video* Toys and Merchandise	153
9.2	Examples of Space Patrol Toys and Merchandise	156
9.3	Examples of Tom Corbett Toys and Merchandise	157
9.4	The Marx Space Playsets	159

Foreword: To Infinity and Beyond!

Henry Jenkins

The happy-go-lucky Ed Norton (Art Carney) sits down in front of the television set he shares with his loud-mouthed downstairs neighbor, Ralph Kramden (Jackie Gleason), and begins pulling things out of a large cardboard box. He replaces his familiar pork-pie hat with a massive space helmet and tucks a disintegrator gun into his belt, as he eagerly awaits the start of his favorite television program, *Captain Video*. This is the day that Captain Video takes off for Pluto, and as a loyal fan, he has to be there, fully equipped, and ready to "join" the rocketman's adventures. Ralph returns to the room, just in time to see his adult friend leaning way back in his chair, as if trying to absorb the gravitational pull of the blast off. The astonished Ralph holds his tongue, with increasing difficulty, as he watches Ed take his space-cadet oath:

> "I, Edward Norton, Ranger Third Class in the Captain Video Space Academy, do solemnly pledge to obey my mommy and daddy, be kind to dumb animals, help little old ladies in and out of space, not to tease my little brothers and sisters, and to brush my teeth twice a day and drink milk after every meal."[1]

Finally, the blustering Kramden explodes, ordering Ed from the apartment, resulting in a knock-down, drag-out argument over control of the set: "For three nights, I have listened to nothing but space shows, Westerns, cartoon frolics, and puppet shows. Tonight I am watching a movie and if you dare to make a sound while the movie is on, I will cut off your air supply."[2]

After a short truce, they are soon changing channels on each other, resulting in amusing juxtapositions between the highly melodramatic dialogue of the romantic movie Ralph wants to watch ("Your hair is like golden sunflowers") and the equally hyperbolic space opera Ed desires ("a giant crater full of boiling lava.")

Aired on October 1, 1955, "To TV or Not To TV" holds a special place in the history of the American sitcom—the first episode of *The Honeymooners* produced as a stand-alone series, as opposed to as a recurring skit on *The Jackie Gleason Show*. By fall 1955, *Captain Video and His Video Rangers* had just ended its six-year run on the DuMont Network, the same network that aired *The Honeymooners*. As this book

Image 0.1 Ralph (Jackie Gleason) loses his patience with Ed's (Art Carney) "Space Fever"

suggests, *Captain Video* was one of a cluster of serials in the first half of the 1950s that targeted America's youth with larger-than-life adventures of "Cadets, Rangers, and Space Men."

This selection of essays offers us a rich and diverse account of these programs and what they meant to the generation that came of age in the mid-twentieth century. The chapters connect the programs backward in time to the pulp magazines, the space operas of Doc Smith and Robert Heinlein, B-movies and big-screen serials, the comic strips of Alex Raymond, popular discourses around science and space, and even *Peter Pan*. We learn here about how these programs addressed social debates about the nature of masculinity, the place of women in science, the global role of the United States during the Cold War, and the appropriate goals and methods for educating young citizens for the Space Age. We learn here about the ways that the "space craze" represented a key step toward serialized programming on American television at a time when dominant trends still pulled toward more episodic structures. These stories sometimes leaped off the small screen and ended up at the local movie theater (not to mention vice versa in the case of the old movie serials repackaged for early television). They were highly self-reflexive about the nature of television as a new and emerging medium. There were complex interplays between the fictional narratives and the brands attached to them. These space operas spawned a succession of licensed and tie-in merchandise that encouraged young fans to actively participate in their imaginary worlds. Each writer has his or her own reasons for reexamining these too often neglected (but fondly remembered) programs, but collectively, this book sheds remarkable insights into the social, cultural, and economic life of the 1950s. These chapters combine a fan's respect for particular detail and the academic's attention to context and implication.

Unlike many of this anthology's contributors, who write with nostalgia about programs that loom large in their childhood memories, I was born in 1958, too late to have had a direct experience of these shows when they first aired. Nevertheless, I have often encountered the "memory traces" they left behind. I listened to old records and read picture books handed down to me by older cousins. And so, in this introduction, I want to look not at the programs themselves (which are well covered elsewhere in this book) but at the ways these programs were represented in other popular texts, at the time and subsequently, which brings us back to *The Honeymooners*.

"To TV and Not To TV" is an amazing time capsule of attitudes toward television as a technology, a domestic practice, and a set of genre conventions. (Television historian Lynn Spigel [1992] draws on this same episode heavily in her book, *Make Room for TV: Television and the Family Ideal in Postwar America*). I often use this episode to get my students, who have grown up in the era of networked computing and mobile telephones, to imagine a time when television was a new and disruptive technology. The episode makes it easy to link television with new media technologies: Ralph, challenged by Alice to explain why he has not bought her a television set, finally falls back on, "I'm waiting for 3D television." So are many of my students, who are now being sold 3-D as the latest innovation in home entertainment.

By 1955, the country could look back nostalgically at a period of social viewing, where neighbors gathered together to watch programs because there might only be one set on their block. Today's generation has grown up in households where there were often more television sets than people, and the really hip ones have gotten rid of their consoles to stream pirated television content through computers and game systems. *The Honeymooners* depicts a world of conflicting tastes and clashing expectations about the medium. Alice wants Liberace to brighten up her housework drudgery, while Ralph wants home entertainment so he can relax at the end of the work day.

At the center of this farce is the image of the adult fan of children's space programs. Everything about Ed's relationship to *Captain Video*, starting with his awestruck tone every time he mentions the program, suggests age-inappropriate tastes. While the actual pledges on these action-adventure serials allow their young viewers to signal their eagerness to enter the adult realm, Ed's oath was written for someone still dependent on his "mommy and daddy" for support and protection. There certainly were adult fans of these programs—as several of the contributors here note—and science fiction fandom, having taken root in the 1920s and 1930s, had achieved a solid institutional footing by the 1950s.[3] The production of genre entertainment was being shaped by a generation of men who had grown up through fandom with its expectations about participatory culture and now were exerting influence on the media around them. But, the program treats fandom as a form of arrested development.

Ed's childlike enthusiasm, innocence, and imagination contrast with Ralph's aggressive masculinity. Ralph's own tastes would have seemed more than a little gender inappropriate by the standards of 1950s America—most of what Ralph watches are romances and musicals, both historically aligned with the female spectator. In his 1986 book *No Sense of Place*, Joshua Meyrowitz described the ways in which television viewing often scrambles traditional divisions between the genders or across generations, exposing domestic viewers to practices that once would have occurred behind closed doors. We might link the 1950s adult fans of children's space opera with mature fans today who have fallen under the spell of *Harry Potter, Twilight, Hunger Games*, or a range of other series focused on young-adult readers, while Ralph's taste for soaps would have existed in the 1950s alongside the sizable number of women who became active fans of television wrestling.[4]

Captain Video also stands here for a particular relationship with television content. The images of Ed Norton, thrown back in his chair by imaginary thrust, embody an immersive engagement with the medium. The rituals Ed performs—reciting the oath, saluting the screen before putting on his helmet—all represent a kind of ersatz interactivity: the viewer is responding to direct address from the program announcer, who often assigns specific identities and tasks to perform, but the announcer cannot respond to the participant, anymore than the host of the then-current *Winky Dink and You* program really knew what the little boys and girls drew on their "magic" plastic screens. Here, *Captain Video* embodies fantasies of television as a more responsive medium, one that extends the space of fantasy and adventure directly into the everyday lives of its viewers. William Uricchio (2005) tells us that as early as the mid-nineteenth century, people imagined television as a technology that could connect us to distant places in real time, often coupled with the telephone, to ensure actual conversations across continents. Early audiences had been disappointed with cinema, Uricchio suggests, because it was "canned" and not "live" entertainment. The space rangers' promise to show us what is happening "right now" at the outer limits of known space is just a fantastical embodiment of the same thrills contemporary audiences got when news programs showed them the East and the West Coast on screen at the same moment or took us live to Wrigley Field or to the opening of a Broadway play. And this desire for a more interactive medium has been a central promise of the digital age, one my students easily recognize when watching Norton's intense efforts to pretend he is traveling through the stars.

A 1959 episode of *Dennis the Menace*, "Innocents in Space," still uses the children's space-adventure program—represented here by the fictitious *Captain Blast*—to explore the ways in which people interact with the television medium.

Here, again, we see the fan boys gather around the set for a "special event"—in this case, the day Captain Blast and his simian sidekick, Lt. Peep, land on Mars. When the Captain is captured by the Martians, he appeals to the young fans to participate actively in his adventures. In order to convince the Martians that he actually commands a large army on Earth, the space man urges his young fans to go outside at 7:30 each night and fire glowing ping-pong balls, sold to them for this purpose, into the night sky. As the episode continues, Dennis wins a program contest, and the reward is a visit by Blast and Peep to his home. All of the local boys gather in the Mitchell living room to meet the space rangers and hear their stories firsthand.

The episode remains highly sympathetic to the boys and their active imaginations, though, as is typical for *Dennis the Menace*, the incident becomes the focus of intergenerational conflict. The camera cuts from the Dennis and Tommy watching *Captain Blast* with rapt attention to a frustrated Mr. Wilson, also watching

FOREWORD   xvii

Image 0.2   Dennis and his friends gather for an episode of *Captain Blast*

Image 0.3   Dennis wins the biggest prize of all: a rocketman in his own living room

but outraged by the show's scientific misinformation. An amateur astronomer, Mr. Wilson tries to convince the local boys that it is more fun to visit other planets through a telescope than via television.

Mr. Wilson's claims of expertise are undercut when he confuses the glowing ping-pong balls for an actual satellite being launched from Cape Canaveral. When

Mr. Wilson learns of Captain Blast's visit, he stomps over to the Mitchell's house and actively challenges the television performer's claims that, for example, Titan is a moon of Jupiter (rather than Saturn), or that he went without a space helmet on the surface of Mercury. Mrs. Wilson, on the other hand, suggests that the space stories, however fanciful from a scientist's perspective, are really no different from the fairy tales she heard as a child. As such, "Innocents in Space" stages the debates among 1950s-era parents and educators over the balance between pleasure and pedagogy, entertainment and enlightenment.

If "To TV or Not To TV" (1955) aired when children's space-adventure series were at their peak, "Innocents in Space" (1959) is decisively post-*Sputnik*, produced at a time when real world developments around space exploration outpaced "that Buck Rogers stuff." If *Captain Video* and its counterparts had just left the air when "To TV or Not To TV" was first broadcast, these series had given way to Walt Disney's *Man in Space*, *Our Mister Sun*, and *Mr. Wizard* by the time *Dennis the Menace* dealt with the phenomenon. The adult astronomers are celebrating a new "age of discovery," but they also respond with mixed feelings to the prospect that they will soon know what lies on the dark side of the moon, each adult clinging to the "sense of wonder" associated with earlier space fantasies. If "To TV or Not To TV" questions whether adult men remain "boys" at heart, "Innocents in Space" wonders, given the urgency of the Cold War and the race to space, whether young boys should be fed science fantasy or science fact. Here, again, the stunt with the glowing ping-pong balls, the space host who comes off the screen and into Dennis' living room embody fantasies about immersion, interactivity, and participation through television.

Given their enormous influence, we should not be surprised by how often the space-cadet programs surfaced as a reference point in the surrounding culture—often framed in terms of a competition between the Rocketmen and the Cowboys for the heart and soul of American boys. Consider, for example, the 1962 propaganda film *Red Nightmare*, which feels like it should have been an episode of *Twilight Zone*. A more down-to-earth version of Rod Serling, Jack Webb tells the audience that he is going to give the film's protagonist, an average American who takes his democratic birthright too much for granted, a "nightmare" he won't soon forget—showing him and us what will happen when the Communists take over the U. S. of A. The "normalcy" of suburban life is summed up by two sequences of the father interacting with his children. In the first, we see the son, dressed in full "redskin" regalia (a feathered headdress, buckskin, face paint, and tomahawk) threaten to tie up his father atop "a hill of red ants." By the film's closing sequence, the same boy is begging his dad to buy him a space helmet, as the daughter, who translates between the world of children and adults, explains, "He's gone from wide open spaces to outer space."[5]

Both the space man and the cowboy are depicted as the kind of fantasies All-American boys *should* have. The son's shifting taste implies the freedom to choose between competing consumer options as fundamental to the nation's democratic (and capitalist) heritage. Billy Wilder's *The Seven Year Itch* (1955) opens with a similar situation, as a baffled father tries to navigate his son's over-active fantasy life. Here, the boy refuses to take off his space helmet to kiss his father goodbye as he heads off for the summer, accusing Dad of "cutting off my air supply," an appropriate metaphor in a Thurburesque comedy about the battle of the sexes and the wandering attention of the American man.

Space fantasies play a remarkably similar role in Pixar's *Toy Story*, one of the most popular animation franchises of the past decade, which starts on the traumatic day when Space Ranger Buzz Lightyear displaces the Cowboy (Sheriff Woody) from his place of honor in Andy's Toy Room. This struggle between the Western and the space opera surely means much more to the baby-boomer filmmakers than to their young viewers, who have grown up in a world dominated by science fiction and almost entirely devoid of Westerns. Gags certainly link Buzz Lightyear to some contemporary franchises, starting with heavy breathing (intended to evoke Darth Vader) or references to "Stardates" (the legacy of *Star Trek*). But, there are also hints here of a much older vocabulary of Space Rangers, Evil Emperors, and Galactic Alliances, straight from the space operas of yesteryear, whose viewers would certainly have recognized the spirit behind Buzz's vow to take us "to infinity and beyond."

On one level, we should not be surprised that the space men were depicted as somehow superseding the cowboy mythology: space opera represented a force of modernity, a rereading of America's manifest destiny as the new nation accepted its obligations as a world power, or perhaps, soon, the most powerful force in the universe. Read less sympathetically, the space men represented the loss of American manliness, as the idea of the rugged individual gave way to a more corporatized conception of working well on teams, the same shift that occurs within the genre between mad scientists going where human society forbids them to go and government agents going where their national duty dictates they travel. Historically, at least on American television, the space shows came first, with children's television turning to the Western in the mid-1950s as it sought to capitalize on the success of Disney's

Image 0.4   Buzz Lightyear and Sheriff Woody vie for top hero status

Davy Crockett series, but popular memory reverses the two, assuming that the space programs were a product of the Space Race, rather than an anticipation of it.

Either way, these depictions assume that there is some kind of sharp line to be drawn between the frontier mythology of the American West and our fantasies about space as "the final frontier." Such rigid boundaries break down quickly enough in *Toy Story*, when the assembled toys are cast and recast into a variety of different adventures across the trilogy, and where Buzz and Woody discover they have a friend in each other. Our modern sense of popular genres emerged from the pulp magazines, which often sought to structure publication priorities and readerships by distinguishing among different and competing kinds of fantasies. Most of the genres that have dominated popular fiction since (and a few which have disappeared almost entirely) took shape on the pages of these magazines, and in the process, each developed particular reading protocols and genre expectations among their most hard-core fans. Yet, a closer look at the pulps shows how genre distinctions were blurred from the start. Many pulp writers moved between different publications, reworking stories that were not sold to fit into alternative genres, resulting in a constant exchange of themes and plot devices across genres. Feeding into the modern space opera, then, were other currents. The rocketeer stories were the descendants of "flyboy" dramas. The space academies owed much to boys' school stories. The battles in space were inspired by military dramas. Captain Video and the others were galactic policemen. The space opera protagonists often found themselves yielding swords (or perhaps prototypes for *Star Wars*' light sabers) as they struggled with the rulers of imaginary kingdoms and their seductive daughters. And, yes, some elements of the Western got mapped onto Mars' dusty red deserts. So, perhaps in the end, there should be no competition between Buzz and Woody, the space man and the cowboy. Ultimately, they come from the same cultural roots and serve many of the same functions for their young fans.

Today, the space-men dramas of the 1950s are likely to be the object of nostalgia and camp, as they have resurfaced via online video platforms or been reissued on DVDs. A networked culture is kind to retro-consumers, who go on eBay to buy the toys their mothers gave to the Salvation Army. In that sense, the computer is very much a time machine, where everything new is old again, and science fiction, once a genre relentlessly pursuing a future which, as visitors of the 1939 World's Fair were told, was where we would be experiencing the rest of our lives, has become fascinated with yesterday's tomorrows, futures that never quite arrived. The Steampunk movement has revitalized interest in the technological fantasies of the Victorian era, even as other works have sought to rekindle our fascination with mid-century modernism. So, something of the spirit of the space opera informs retrofuturist films such as *The Rocketeer* or *Sky Captain and the World of Tomorrow*, television series such as Hulu's *Mercury Men*, or comics such as Dean Motter's *Terminal City* and *Mister X*.[6]

Over the past few years, the Green Lantern has remerged as one of the top-selling superhero characters. Dramatic increases in comic book sales around titles associated with the Green Lantern Corps inspired the production of a blockbuster in the summer of 2011, a film that disappointed those somewhat inflated expectations, but nevertheless brought this vintage character to a much larger public. Comic-book historians are apt to link Green Lantern back to E. E. "Doc" Smith's Lensman series, and the connections there are strong.[7] They note that DC's publisher, Julius Schwartz, who was responsible for the 1959 relaunch of the Green Lantern, had been an active science fiction fan in the 1940s and 1950s, helping to organize the first Worldcon and editing some early fanzines. If the superheroes of the Golden Age were often associated with hard-boiled detective stories, those of the Silver Age were much more closely aligned with the themes and tone of space opera. DC had tested the waters with a series of space-men adventures, with titles like *Mysteries in Space* and *Strange Adventures*, which sold briskly on newsstands over the same years that young readers were racing home to watch *Captain Video*. Soon, Schwartz put a sci-fi spin on DC's classic characters such as The Flash, Hawkman, the Atom, and Green Lantern, each of whom was treated as a "man of science" and placed in space opera settings, while new characters like the Martian Manhunter continued this same tradition. Much like the television rocketmen, these superheroes were designed to be aspirational figures for their boyish readers, occupying a space somewhere between adolescence and adulthood, forming partnerships with each other that took them where no man had gone before.

In *DC: The New Frontier* (2009), Darwyn Cooke draws heavily on Tom Wolfe's *The Right Stuff* (1979) to situate Hal Jordan first in relationship to other test pilots who were commanding national attention in the late 1950s—most notably Chuck Yeager—and later, to tie him in with the "Rat Pack" in Las Vegas and with the Mercury 7 astronauts, until the Green Lantern embodies everything that was cool about the early 1960s. But, look beneath the surface, and Green Lantern continues the same genre traditions that defined 1950s television space operas. While there is only one Green Lantern on Earth, he belongs to a police force—the Green Lantern Corps—whose members function as the Guardians of the Universe. The origin story sees Jordan get recruited by a dying alien and spirited away to a space academy, where he gets to clown around with other cadets and recruits, in the process of learning how to use his power ring to exert his will on the matter around him. His mentor, Sinestro, soon becomes his greatest rival, which motivates many academy stories in order to provide the necessary backstory. Hal Jordan has to repeat an oath each time he recharges his battery: "In brightest day, in blackest night, no evil shall escape my sight—let those who worship evil's might beware my power, Green Lantern's light."[8] There is no smoking disintegrator gun that allows us to connect the Green Lantern comic to any of the specific programs this book discusses. Perhaps Captain Video and the Green Lantern simply draw on similar generic roots as the legacy of the pulps and serials were passed along to the postwar generation. But the recent success of the Green Lantern, in comics, on television, on direct-to-video DVDs, if not on the big screen, suggests that contemporary audiences are still feeding off the sagas that thrilled boys and girls in the early 1950s.

So, if you, like me, didn't live through the period this book describes, and you were not a young space cadet or rocket ranger, have no fear. This story still matters to you. These series, whether you know it or not, still shape the popular culture we consume today—even if, in an era of digital effects, we can now create far more convincing representations of these fantastical worlds than could be conveyed by sparklers attached to the backside of toy rocket ships. The promises of television as an immersive and interactive media are now more fully realized through contemporary computer games, yet these games may still depict battles in space and flights beyond the stars. We still have much to learn from the era of the Rocketmen.

NOTES

1. *The Honeymooners* "TV or Not TV" Episode 1, Season 1, 1 October 1, 1955, CBS.
2. *Ibid.*
3. Andrew Ross. *Strange Weather: Culture, Technology and Science in the Age of Limits.* London: Verso, 1991.
4. Chad Dell. *The Revenge of Hatpin Mary: Women, Professional Wrestling, and Fan Culture of the 1950s.* New York: Peter Lang, 2006.
5. *Red Nightmare*, directed by George Waggner (1962; GI Studios, 2011), DVD.
6. Henry Jenkins. "'The Tomorrow That Never Was': Retrofuturism in the Comics of Dean Motter." In *Comics and the City: Urban Space in Print, Picture and Sequence*, ed. Jorn Ahrens and Arno Meteling, 63–83 (London: Continuum, 2010).
7. Gerard Jones and Will Jacobs. The Comic Book Super Heroes: The First History of Modern Comics Books—From the Silver Age to the Present. (New York: Prima, 1996).
8. *Showcase #22* (September-October 1959), DC Comics.

BIBLIOGRAPHY

Cooke, Darwin. *DC: The New Frontier.* New York: DC, 2004.
Dell, Chad. *The Revenge of Hatpin Mary: Women, Professional Wrestling, and Fan Culture of the 1950s.* New York: Peter Lang, 2006.
Jenkins, Henry. "'The Tomorrow That Never Was': Retrofuturism in the Comics of Dean Motter." In *Comics and the City: Urban Space in Print, Picture and Sequence*, ed. Jorn Ahrens and Arno Meteling., 63–83. London: Continuum, 2010.
Jones, Gerard, and Will Jacobs. *The Comic Book Super Heroes: The First History of Modern Comics Books—From the Silver Age to the Present.* New York: Prima, 1996.
Meyrowitz, Joshua. *No Sense of Place: The Impact of Electronic Media on Social Behavior.* Oxford: Oxford University Press, 1986.
Ross, Andrew. *Strange Weather: Culture, Technology and Science in the Age of Limits.* London: Verso, 1991.
Spigel, Lynn. *Make Room for TV: Television and the Family Ideal in Postwar America.* Chicago: University of Chicago Press, 1992.
Uricchio, William."Storage, Simultaneity and the Media Technologies of Modernity." In *Allegories of Communication: Intermedial Concerns from Cinema to the Digital*, ed. John Fullerton and Jan Olsson, 123–138. Stockholm: John Libbey, 2005.
Wolfe, Tom. *The Right Stuff.* New York: Farrar, Straus, and Giroux, 1979.

Acknowledgments

BETWEEN THE COVERS OF THIS BOOK, THERE IS A GREAT deal of love, wonder, and inspiration. Rocketmen have that effect on people. While neither of us was among the generation of children who grew up with rocketmen in the 1950s, we both are captivated by their legacy. The flying suits, spaceships, and fantastic technology—and the heroes who used them to explore the universe—are, for us, more than just charming and nostalgic, they are a critical part of our cultural history. We believe they are important, not just as products of early television, but for the impact they had on the world *outside* the box—what audiences young and old did with them—the imaginative play, the merchandizing, the fan clubs, the dreams of space. And it was that belief that brought this volume into being.

This project might never have happened, had it not been for Cindy's involvement with J. P. Telotte's and Gerald Duchovnay's volume *Science Fiction across the Screens* (2011). Her research for that chapter did more than just capture her imagination; it also demonstrated just how broad-reaching the rocketmen's impact was on American youth and their families in the 1950s, and how much was still to be written on these Cold War heroes' relationships with their fans. So, Cindy would like to thank Jay and Gerry for creating the opportunity that ultimately led to this volume.

Several of our contributors also played a role in the book's initial spark, by writing books of their own that demonstrated how cultural history, production history, and fandom could be productively intertwined. For that reason, we invited them to be part of this project, and for that reason, also, we thank them now. They, and the rest of our talented colleagues featured here, gave unselfishly of their time and talents—often, simply because these interstellar heroes had touched their lives in ways that inspired them. They, in turn, inspired us. So we would like to extend our deepest thanks to each of our gifted authors.

The journey from inspiration to page was richer thanks to many other individuals as well: Cadet Ed Pippin of the Solar Guard was among the first to offer support and assistance with the project; Roy Trumbull, a former studio engineer at KRON-TV, generously shared stories, images, and insights about television's early days and KRON's *Captain Z-Ro*; and Wade Williams offered similar generosity of spirit in his willingness to share his collection of images and artifacts from rocketmen series. Likewise, Tim Hollis, Roger Freedman, and Tom Noel generously shared their images, thoughts, time, and support. And while we are already grateful to Gary Hughes for his contribution to the volume, Cindy would also like to say an additional "thank you," for the flying suits, giant ray guns, and vacuum cleaners-turned-rocketships that made their way into her world when she least expected it.

Our thanks also go to Samantha Hasey and Robyn Curtis at Palgrave Macmillan for their support, and to our anonymous reviewers for their enthusiastic comments. Last, but not least, a final, grateful thank you to all of the folks in both of our lives who wished us "Spaceman's luck!" as the project blasted off, took up the slack and often settled for less as we ventured into the unknown, and celebrated with us when we finally declared "mission accomplished."

Introduction

Cynthia J. Miller and
A. Bowdoin Van Riper

In roaring rockets they blast through the millions of miles from Earth to far-flung stars and brave the dangers of cosmic frontiers, protecting the liberties of the planet, safeguarding the cause of universal peace in the age of the conquest of space.[1]

ROCKETMEN: BOLD ADVENTURERS IN SPACE, DEFENDERS OF DEMOCRACY, MASTERS of science, icons of Cold War heroism. Each week, they blasted their way into the living rooms, imaginations, and hearts of children in 1950s America, equipped with jet packs, paralyzing ray guns, viewing screens, and other fantastic technology, their exploits in time and space animating the new medium of television in ways that would pave the way for science fiction entertainment for decades to come. While long ago replaced by new heroes, their names still resonate in American cultural history: Captain Video, Tom Corbett, Rocky Jones, Commando Cody, and of course, the interstellar hero whose adventures started it all, Flash Gordon.

As offspring of the weekly movie-house serials that began in the 1920s, televised rocketmen series of the mid-twentieth century have largely been considered as diminished adaptations of their cinematic predecessors. Scholars have documented production histories, discussed the challenges of special effects in the early years of television, and offered in-depth examinations of individual series, but few have explored the complex relationships between these series, as a body of media texts, and their audiences.[2] This volume does just that, focusing on the roles, influences, and relationships that existed between televised rocketmen and their fans. The 14 chapters included here shed new light on the culture of childhood in an era that was more innocent in some ways—and more fraught in others—than our own, and reveal the complex, often unexpected ways in which the rocketmen led the children of Cold War America into the Space Age.

Rise of the Rocketmen

Rocketmen were born in the pulp magazines of the late 1920s, and even as they spread to other forms of popular entertainment they retained the marks of their pulp origins. They were uncomplicated, unreflective characters designed to serve the needs of the action-filled stories favored by the pulps' mostly young, mostly male readership. Like the pulps' other hero-figures—ace pilots and jungle explorers, steely-eyed sheriffs and wisecracking detectives—they were drawn in bold, simple strokes and behaved in predictable ways. Their strengths were many and prominent, their weaknesses few and (unless the plot demanded it) carefully hidden. They were strong, smart, brave, and—above all—morally incorruptible.[3] In a fictional world much like that of the already familiar Western genre, where good and bad were both unambiguously defined and prominently labeled, their metaphorical hats were always a bright, shining white.[4]

The very first rocketman—Richard Seaton, hero of E. E. Smith's 1928 novel *The Skylark of Space*—can stand, in this respect, for all those who came after. A scientist-adventurer as brave as he is brilliant, Seaton has a handsome face, a "powerful body," and an unwavering moral compass. He invents a new method of interstellar propulsion, installs it in a spaceship built by his millionaire-industrialist best friend, and makes plans to explore the galaxy. When the ship is stolen and his fiancée, Dorothy Vaneman, kidnapped by Marc "Blackie" DuQuesne—an unscrupulous fellow scientist in league with gangsters—Seaton wastes no time, building a new ship (the *Skylark* of the title) and giving chase. He returns, at the end of the story, having caught the villain, married the girl, been named overlord of a distant planet, acquired alien technology that makes the *Skylark* virtually invincible, and become wealthy beyond measure. Seaton remains a Boy Scout at heart, however, content to capture rather than kill DuQuesne and given to pronouncements like: "We can outrun you, outjump you, throw you down, or lick you; we can run faster, hit harder, dive deeper, and come up dryer, than you can."[5]

The planet-hopping adventures of the omnicompetent Seaton—a hero "comfortingly bigger than life," in the words of critic Damon Knight[6]—established a subgenre of science fiction that became known as "space opera." The name, retrospectively coined (in 1941) by Wilson Tucker as a parallel to the use of "horse opera" for Westerns, was meant to evoke formulaic shallowness, but readers, delighted by the stories' fast action and its "feeling that adventures are waiting everywhere," clamored for more.[7] Within months of *Skylark's* serialized publication in Hugo Gernsback's *Amazing Stories*, the first pulp magazine devoted solely to science fiction, space opera had spread to the comics pages of newspapers, where author Philip Francis Nowlan and artist Dick Calkins began a strip chronicling the adventures of Anthony "Buck" Rogers. Nowlan had introduced Rogers to the world in a pair of novellas—"Armageddon 2419 AD" and "The Airlords of Han," both published in *Amazing Stories*—portraying him as a World War I veteran who, after spending five hundred years in suspended animation, awakens American resistance forces into battle against ruthless, technologically advanced Asian overlords.[8] The daily comic strips, published, beginning in January 1929, under the title *Buck Rogers in the 25th Century*, kept the futuristic setting but eliminated the military plot line and the violence. Buck became, like Richard Seaton, an interplanetary adventurer: a righter of wrongs, scourge of evildoers, and tireless defender of the Earth. A Sunday-only color strip, with separate story lines, began in 1930, and inspired artist Alex Raymond to introduce his own Sunday rocketman strip, *Flash Gordon*, in 1934.[9]

Buck Rogers and Flash Gordon brought space opera—and the rocketman hero—to the masses. Both comics were adapted into radio serials, Buck Rogers in 1932 and Flash Gordon in 1935, and were reprinted in comic books and Big Little books. A novel, *Flash Gordon in the Caverns of Mongo,* and a pulp, *Flash Gordon's Strange Adventure Magazine,* failed to excite interest in 1936, but a twelve-chapter film serial titled simply *Flash Gordon* drew enthusiastic audiences the same year and spawned sequels in 1938 and 1940. Larry "Buster" Crabbe, already famous for playing Tarzan of the Apes in the movies, starred as Flash in all three serials, and Buck Rogers in another, released in 1939. The 1933–34 World's Fair in Chicago featured a ten-minute film of *Buck Rogers in the 25th Century: An Interplanetary Battle with the Tiger Men of Mars,* and the 1939–40 Fair in New York allowed visitors to become rocketmen themselves on a Flash Gordon thrill ride.

Sheer ubiquity, and a broad fan base, made Buck Rogers and Flash Gordon household names by the end of the 1930s. Like other larger-than-life fictional heroes who made their first mass-media appearances during the decade—Batman and Superman, The Shadow, The Lone Ranger, Captain Midnight, and Tarzan of the Apes—their names and reputations were increasingly familiar even to Americans who did not actively follow their exploits. The trappings of space opera—the spaceships that the rocketmen rode, the alien races that they met, and the ray guns that they wielded against evil overlords—filtered into the public consciousness in similar ways. The vast majority of Americans may not have been able to tell the Tiger Men of Mars from the Lion Men of Mongo, but they knew that such beings were fixtures of science fiction, as the Apaches and the Cheyenne were of Westerns. Those who were not science fiction fans may not have known how Flash Gordon's ray gun worked, but they knew that it fired a magical beam of light just as surely as the Lone Ranger's six-shooter fired silver bullets. Above all, the general public learned, through the adventures of Buck and Flash, to associate rockets with the future, and with trips to distant worlds.

Space travel, of course, was nothing new in science fiction. Jules Verne had sent a trio of heroes *From the Earth to the Moon* in 1865 and *Around the Moon* in 1870, Edward Everett Hale had sent construction workers into orbit around the Earth (albeit inadvertently) in "The Brick Moon" (1869), and H. G. Wells had chronicled a lunar landing in *The First Men in the Moon* (1901). Those space voyages, however, had been the focus of the stories in which they appeared—ends in themselves, monumental and challenging, even though they reached no further than Earth's own moon. Space opera, by contrast, took rocket ships and interplanetary travel virtually for granted, and allowed them to fade into the background of the stories it told. To Richard Seaton and the rocketmen who came after, space travel was not an end in itself but simply a means of going someplace: reaching the next exotic planet, the next alien race, the next undiscovered wonder. To the fans who turned the pages of the newspaper to the latest installment of Buck Rogers and Flash Gordon, or settled into their theater seats waiting for the next chapter of a rocketman serial, spaceships were like the horses in a Western: essential to the story without being central to it.

The space operas of the 1930s and 1940s added outer space, with its infinity of alien species and strange planets, to the growing list of stock adventure-story settings, and rocketmen to the ranks of stock adventure heroes. And the early rocketmen *were*, first and foremost, adventurers. Richard Seaton, Buck Rogers, and Flash Gordon went to the stars for the same reason their fictional counterparts traveled to the uncharted corners of the Earth: for excitement, for the challenge, for the hell of it. It was only in the aftermath of World War II, when rocketman characters became staples of early children's television, that their adventures took on a new sense of purpose.

Days of Wonder

This volume takes readers back to that moment—to the days before astronauts like John Glenn, Alan Shepard, and Neil Armstrong were household names; before the "one small step" that left America's national footprint on the Moon; and before the wonders of science fiction became the wonders of science *fact*—to the heyday of the televised rocketman.[10] It was a time when battles were fought with Para-Ray guns and Cosmic Vibrators, Opticon Scillometers scanned through walls, heroes in jet-packs soared through the skies, and the universe was full of wonder.

Television itself was something of a wonder. Newly making its way into homes across America, it seemed not too far removed from the futuristic technology it depicted. To those behind the scenes, it was something of a wonder, as well, a wonder that they were able to accomplish the productions at all. Live productions, small soundstages, and smaller budgets challenged the creative and technical abilities of producers, engineers, and cameramen alike, who often relied on paint, cardboard, and audience's imaginations to conjure effects that seldom approximated what movie studios could create. But, as retired KRON-TV engineer Roy Trumbull reminisced, "the directors managed to make do with what they had available."[11] While often dismissed for their low production values, the series were, as a writer for *TV Forecast* noted in a review of the *Captain Video* series, feats of ingenuity: "The program is a triumph of carpentry and wiring, and the entire action takes place primarily in the headquarters of the Video Rangers—a room equipped with flashing bulbs, microphones, panels, dials, telephones which have been given names from electronic double-talk."[12] Even the hero's fantastic weaponry required imagination. The Captain's futuristic Opticon Scillometer was cobbled together from parts found in Wanamaker's automobile accessories department: a combination of a spark plug, a muffler, a rear-view mirror and an ashtray. The series' first director, Charles Polachek, recalled with amused pride, "I made it with my own two hands."[13]

Televised rocketmen series brought the thrills and chills of movie-house adventure into American living rooms, one chapter at a time. The series format, adapted from cinematic serials, was a natural fit for the new domestic medium, as well as for the attention spans of juvenile audiences. Young viewers, who often watched together with their parents, would also become the primary consumers of the advertising messages aired by series' sponsors, as a dynamic new commercial culture emerged around these, and other, television programs, targeting juvenile audiences.

Captain Video and his Video Rangers were the vanguards of the rocketmen's transition from big screen to small in 1949, ushering in these series, which were among the earliest contributions to science fiction television.[14] While criticized for its low-budget sets and juvenile simplicity, the series ignited the sparks of Space

Fever among the country's youthful viewers, a cultural phenomenon that grew in intensity over the next decade, prompting stations and sponsors to scramble for their own rocketmen. ABC's Commander Buzz Corry led his crew on *Space Patrol*; Tom Corbett kept the universe safe on *Tom Corbett, Space Cadet*, on CBS; and a few seasons later, NBC's heroic Commando Cody did the same on *Commando Cody: Sky Marshal of the Universe*. Some rocketmen, like Rocky Jones, began their adventures in syndication and only held viewers' attention for a season or two, while others, such as Captain Z-Ro, were local heroes who rose to national fame, their exploits continuing for several years. These televised series became so popular that, by 1954, one of the most popular, *Space Patrol*, ranked consistently in the top ten shows broadcast on Saturday.[15]

Like their predecessors in other media, in particular, *Flash Gordon* and *Buck Rogers*, these televised rocketmen were champions of truth and justice in a time of rapid postwar social, cultural, and political change. Fearless, loyal, resourceful, and determined, they calmed fears, preserved values, and thwarted enemies—on Earth and throughout the universe—defending humanity and democracy against the forces of evil, while fans watched in wonder. The introduction to *Captain Video*, like the opening lines of other space-hero series, sets the stage for the futuristic struggle to keep the world safe:

> Fighting for law and order, Captain Video operates from a mountain retreat with secret agents at all points of the globe. Possessing scientific secrets and scientific weapons, Captain Video asks no quarter and gives none to the forces of evil. Stand by for Captain Video and his Video Rangers!

A departure from their wartime and interwar counterparts, these were distinctly Cold War heroes—"Electronic Wizards," "Research Explorers in Time and Space," "Guardians of the Safety of the World"—representing a range of heroic masculinities that emphasized their Atomic Age scientific know-how as much, and in some cases more, than their combat skills. From the feisty Rocky Jones to the cerebral Captain Z-Ro, the rocketmen served as role models and mentors for their young audiences, and reinforced their teachings through codes, pledges, and Ranger Messages, all designed to create a new generation of Cold War Americans.

While televised rocketman series lacked the high production values of their cinematic counterparts, they offered their youthful fans something that movie-house heroes could not: intimacy. These fantastic heroes blasted directly into the living rooms of their young audiences, bringing the universe close enough to touch, creating personal relationships with their youthful cadets, and making knowledge of the fantastic "a part of home life rather than any kind of special event."[16]

This integration of science fiction series into the lives of young viewers propelled the entire family, and domestic life itself, into the electronic age, as heroes that formerly animated children's imaginative play were pushed aside by futuristic rocketmen. *Collier's Magazine* reported, "All over the air waves, the Wide Open Spaces are being traded in for the Wide Upper Spaces. The trend may be away from horses and up in the heavens for keeps."[17] And of course, no self-respecting young cadet could do without uniforms and accessories modeled after those of his or her favorite space hero. Youthful American viewers needed a "new wardrobe, new gear, and a whole new language" to keep pace with the space fever that was sweeping the nation.[18] The cover of *American Weekly* (May 10, 1953) depicted a youthful "space man" proudly clad in his new Atomic Space Suit and helmet, handing down his outmoded cowboy boots and chaps to a dismayed younger brother, and a few months later, *Woman's Day* (August 1953) proclaimed that "A new supersonic generation is putting its cowboy suits in mothballs and encasing itself in space helmets."[19]

Domestic schedules were arranged to accommodate programming schedules; mothers became wardrobe and prop masters in order to properly outfit their young rangers; siblings consumed countless bowls of "Pep: the solar cereal" and snacked on Nestlé's Caramels, for the prizes and souvenirs hidden inside or awarded for labels and box tops; and businessmen were overheard wishing each other "Spaceman's Luck!" Even family pets dined on Walter Kendall's "Fives," the multicolored "5-Course Dinner in One!," in allegiance to the sponsor of their young masters' Atomic Age heroes. Rocketmen had, indeed, taken American family life by storm.

The success of the rocketmen's collective efforts to recruit cadets, rangers, and junior spacemen was further reflected in the countless public appearances, contests, promotions, and Ranger clubs that emerged across the country, as well as in the booming merchandizing campaigns that allowed young fans to join in on the interstellar action, creating what Hugo Gernsback termed the new *"third dimensional world of science-fiction"*—"toys, games, gadgets, scientific instruments of all kinds, wearing apparel for youngsters, and countless other constantly-evolving, ingenious devices."[20] Supermarkets and department stores boasted official series merchandise, including space suits, cadet uniforms, and ray guns, which were highly coveted by viewers. A 1952 *Life* magazine photo spread illustrated a dazzling array of these pop-culture artifacts, from cosmic generators to "paralyzers," all emblazoned with the *Space Patrol* label, predicted to net $40 million in sales that year.[21]

Fan culture, however, was not limited to the collection of these fantastic space toys and costumes, or the cachet they bestowed. To be a rocketman's fan was to be part of something much bigger—a Cold War identity that united knowledge and imagination, discipline and ingenuity, nation and individual—all wrapped in fantastic science and the promise of a universe waiting to be explored. Allegiance to a favorite space hero was often formalized in official or unofficial fan clubs that served as an extended "crew" of the members' favorite rocketman: earthbound members of the Solar Guard, Video Rangers, or Space Rangers. United by their admiration for their heroes and adherence to the spaceman's code, in one of its many forms, these terrestrial cadets wrote letters to their icons and each other, organized member events, and, if a group of fans had true "spaceman's luck"—or a very active chapter—might have been left breathless by a visit from their favorite interstellar hero, as he paused at their local store en route to his next adventure.

And although the heyday of the televised rocketmen was brief—nearly all had discontinued production by 1956, and were off the air by 1960[22]—many fans' affection for their interstellar heroes has continued. These adult fans, now in their 60s and beyond, are still bound together as members of the Solar Guard and other groups, holding annual gatherings where, joined by those often too young to remember, they share and preserve memories and memorabilia, and pay homage to a golden age before manned space flight.[23] For these intrepid cadets-come-of-age, the flying suit, the jet pack, and the ray gun are hallmarks, not only of their youth but of halcyon days in American cultural history, when "smokin' rockets" signaled the romance of technology and served as a call to missions of daring in the name of early television.[24]

THE ROCKETMEN AND THEIR FANS

The adventures of the rocketmen were larger than life—played out against a backdrop as big as the galaxy—even when viewed on television's small screen. They drew their young audiences, and the adults who watched with them, into a world that surpassed their wildest imaginings, full of adventure, danger, and of course, wonder. It all began with none other than Flash Gordon, the character who leaped from the pages of newspaper comics to the screens of neighborhood movie houses in the 1930s, and set the stage for postwar rocketmen to blast through space and into American homes.

Roy Kinnard's chapter "Where It All Began: The Flash Gordon Serials" examines the three movie serials that brought rocketmen to the screen beginning in 1936 and kept them there for decades afterward. It traces the serials' history from their initial high-prestige theatrical releases in the 1930s, through their television rebroadcasts in the early 1950s, to their distillation into made-for-television movies in the 1960s, and onward into the DVD era. Along the way, it explores how the serials' blend of dramatic action, vivid characters, and sophisticated-for-the-time production values enabled them to become, for multiple generations of young viewers, a gateway into the exciting world of the rocketmen.

Our first section, Learning to Be Rocketmen, explores the ways in which rocketmen passed the torch to future generations, serving as larger-than-life role models and mentors for Cold War youth. John C. Tibbetts' chapter, "'A Commotion in the Firmament': *Tom Corbett* and the Lost Boys," begins the section with a look at the ways in which the adventures of rocketmen taught their young male fans to dream. His chapter explores what he sees as the mythic resonance between Tom Corbett and another childhood hero who inspired fantasies of flight in young audiences: Peter Pan. Like two sides of a coin, the pair of fantastic heroes inspired America's youth to flight. Whether building makeshift spaceships or leaping fearlessly into the great beyond of the backyard, flying—"jumping on the wind's back"—was a touchstone for children of the 1950s. On one hand, as Tibbetts relates, notions of flight served as an escapist leap into fantasy, but on the other, they also symbolized a tentative step toward maturity.

In "Boy's Wonder: Male Teenage Assistants in 1950s Science Fiction Serials and Cold War Masculinity," Robert Jacobs contrasts those "flights of fancy" with one of the rocketmen's more practical roles in the lives of their young male fans—serving as mentors and role models of Cold War manhood—teaching them to grow into leaders, thinkers, and Cold War heroes. Poised on the edge of the Atomic Age, with its shifting notions of successful leadership and masculinity, rocketmen such as Rocky Jones and Captain Z-Ro and their crews presented their youthful audiences with an array of heroic masculine traits, ranging from rugged independence to spunky ingenuity to corporate intellect. Through their relationships with their young charges—the cadets, rangers, and junior spacemen featured in their crews—the interstellar heroes modeled, tutored, and gently directed American boys along the path to the manhood of the future.

But what about the girls? Space, in the 1950s, was typically portrayed as a male frontier. But while the primary audience for juvenile science fiction in the mid-twentieth century may have been boys, rocketmen series of the 1950s had countless female fans, as well. In her chapter "Girls and 'Space Fever,'" Amy Foster explores the answers to questions about the relationship between young girl viewers and the male-dominated adventures of the rocketmen. Foster's work is among the first to examine this facet of the series, as she examines the female role models—from clever scientists to tyrannical rulers—present across series such as *Flash Gordon*, *Rocky Jones*, *Clutch Cargo*, *Space Angel*. Foster's work demonstrates that the rocketmen's female fans were a generation of young women shaped by Space Race rhetoric, many of whom pursued careers in science and engineering, despite the educational and workplace hardships they would face in the 1960s and 1970s.

The volume's next section, Reaching for Tomorrow, explores the ways in which the rocketman series gave fans a glimpse of the future and, by doing so, helped make that future real. Rockets capable of touching the edges of space were still brand new when *Captain Video*, the first of the rocketman series, premiered in 1949. The idea that humans might soon ride such rockets to the Moon, Mars, and beyond seemed, to most Americans, outright fantasy: "Buck Rogers stuff." Over the course of the 1950s, however, skepticism gave way to cautious interest and, for some members of the public, to all-consuming fascination. Howard McCurdy's chapter "Space Fever: From Fantasy to Reality" traces that transformation, which led Americans to see space travel as plausible even before the October 1957 launch of *Sputnik I* made it an established fact. The adventures of the rocketmen, McCurdy shows, combined with the writings of real-world rocketeers like Wernher von Braun and the day-after-tomorrow speculations of Walt Disney's animators to convince Americans that the conquest of space was both inevitable and desirable.

The young fans of the rocketman series, of course, were already convinced. Drawn together by a shared belief that adventure awaited them in space, they joined national fan clubs devoted to their heroes, but also formed less formal, local clubs whose members enacted their own space adventures in playgrounds, parks, and backyards. These clubs, which Patrick Lucanio and Gary Coville collectively dub the "Rocket Ranger" movement, allowed fans to share the experience of being—like their heroes—a member of an elite group of space adventurers, and to practice for the future, using simple props and boundless imagination to rehearse their roles in humankind's next great adventure. Lucanio and Colville's chapter, "Shooting for the Stars: Captain Video, the Rocket Ranger Movement, and America's Conquest of Space," shows how the clubs primed the Rocket Rangers of the 1950s to become supporters of the real-world space program of the 1960s.

Rockets were, as J. P. Telotte notes in his chapter "Space Opera TV: Seeing the World of Tomorrow," not the only startling technology on display in the early rocketman programs. Television itself—like rockets, still in its infancy in 1949–50—was a pervasive presence in the early rocketman series, which were acutely aware of and sensitive to their role as examples of a brand-new medium. Telotte shows that, from the moment that Captain Video, the first of the television rocketmen, turned on his "remote carrier beam" to observe his far-flung agents in the field, technologies of observation and remote viewing pervaded the world of the rocketmen. The series presented their young fans lessons about the televisual technology of tomorrow, but also "lessons in watching," allowing them to participate in the future even as it entertained them.

The chapters in our next section look at the active creation of fan culture, through the magic of marketing, promotion, and the active "recruitment" of junior rocketmen. As Seen On TV explores the creation of a consumer and fan culture that was woven through each exciting episode of the various rocketmen series, inextricably linking them to the social and economic frameworks of the wider American culture. In "The Sky Is the Limit: Advertising and Consumer Culture in Rocketman Television Shows of the 1950s," Lawrence R. Samuel examines the commercial advertising embedded in the rocketman series and discusses its social impact. These promotional messages, for products such as Kellogg's and Chex cereals, PowerHouse Bars, Nestlé's Caramels, and other products, encouraged young audience members to join the ranks of American consumers and to wield their influence on their parents, as well. Consumption, they suggested was a means to demonstrate that one was a valued member of society, and under the tutelage of their favorite space hero, the pursuit of commodities was framed as an essential part of young people's civic responsibility. Looking to the future, Samuel argues that rocketman advertising helped to plant the seed of limitless possibilities among baby boomers, conveying the notion that, both metaphorically and literally, "the sky is the limit."

S. Mark Young continues this discussion in "Creating a Sense of Wonder: The Glorious Legacy of Space Opera Toys of the 1950s." The world of commercially produced space toys was not new to the era of the rocketmen, but as Space Fever spread throughout the country in the mid-twentieth century, it received its fullest – and most dazzling – elaboration. Ray guns, space helmets, uniforms, flying suits, roller skates, badges, puzzles, pop-up books, playing cards, lunch boxes, and more filled department store shelves as toy companies, seizing a golden opportunity, went wild creating every type of space-related item imaginable—many serving as the "official" merchandise for series such as *Space Patrol*, *Tom Corbett, Space Cadet*, and *Rocky Jones, Space Ranger*. The imagination and innovativeness that went into the design and production of these early space toys has never been equaled, and in this chapter, Young explores their legacy and social significance.

The section closes with Jean-Noel Bassior's intimate and in-depth look at what was arguably the most popular of the rocketmen series in "*Space Patrol*: Missions of Daring in the Name of Early Television." Bassior's chapter takes readers along on a journey in search of those who made the magic and memories that captivated a generation, and the loyal fans who still remember. Recollections of the heroes, the episodes, the toys, and even the mighty Ralston Rocket—the larger-than-life prize in the "Name the Planet Contest"—shared by those who recall the era's sense of fascination and wonder, animate the chapter. These are memories, as one "cadet" tells her, of a time when spaceships "flew to the planets on the fuel of imagination and hope." Bassior seeks to preserve those memories, before they vanish from the collective unconscious.

The rocketman series made their way into American living rooms during the first years of the Cold War, when the atomic bomb was still new and the United States was still coming to grips with its role in a bipolar world. The fictional worlds of the rocketmen reflected the social and political realities that lay beyond their young fans' living-room walls, and the political assumptions that framed Cold War—the value of spreading democracy, the righteousness of intervention, the value of persuasion as an alternative to force—often underlay their adventures in space and time. The fourth and final section of the book, Looking at the Earth, investigates the social and political messages woven through the series' tales of interplanetary adventure.

Rocky Jones, Space Ranger depicted, as did many other rocketman series, a future in which not just nations but entire planets had united under a single government. Rocky, like his counterparts Buzz Corry and Tom Corbett, acted as an agent of that government, fighting space pirates and pursuing criminals. As Wheeler Winston Dixon illustrates in his "Making the Universe Safe for Democracy," however, Rocky's principal role was not judicial but diplomatic. *Rocky Jones* presented viewers with a series of Cold War morality plays, in which Rocky and the crew of the *Orbit Jet* defended the rights of the oppressed, thwarted the expansionist dreams of tyrannical conquerors, and reinforced democratic values wherever they were threatened. The series' defining vision, Dixon concludes, was a hopeful one: a portrait of a galaxy in which peace and harmony were possible, and diplomacy could be the most powerful weapon of all.

Mick Broderick, in "'Justice through Strength and Courage': *Captain Midnight* and the Military-Industrial Complex," considers a Cold War hero who, though his experimental rocket-jet aircraft never left Earth, was every inch a rocketman in spirit and in style. From his remote mountain headquarters, the square-jawed, stern-faced Captain Midnight, leader of the Secret Squadron, took a darker view of the Cold War than did Rocky Jones. He urged young viewers to enlist in the Secret Squadron, but warned them that, as members, it was their sworn duty to remain alert, prepared, and ready for instant action if danger threatened. The series thus reinforced the message of civil-defense films and pamphlets: catastrophe—war or natural disaster—may strike at any moment. Broderick's chapter traces, through studio and Pentagon archives, the complex relationship between the military and the show's creators, who viewed each other warily despite their shared interests in maintaining an alert citizenry in an uncertain Cold War world.

Unique among rocketmen, Captain Z-Ro presented a heroic figure more complex than his military-modeled counterparts. He was, as the series' announcer intoned, a "research explorer in time and space." Armed with books and a time machine, in addition to ray guns and physical prowess, this swashbuckling scientist-adventurer transported his crew—and the audience—to critical moments in history, intervening when necessary to ensure that history unfolded as intended. In "'To Learn from the Past...': Becoming Cold War Citizens with Captain Z-Ro," Cynthia J. Miller and A. Bowdoin Van Riper argue that Captain Z-Ro offered young fans a new kind of hero in the Cold War era: a hero whose intellect matched his bravery. As he guided his young cadet, Jet, through adventures in the past, the Captain demonstrated to the new generation of Cold War Americans that knowledge was the key to a successful—and powerful—Atomic Age future.

Televised rocketmen's heyday came and went in the 1950s. Fascination with their interstellar heroics has lived on, however, and the series, preserved initially in reruns and recordings, have once again come into their own in the age of new media. Single series and compilation DVDs are widely available, and Internet releases of excerpts, commercials, and entire episodes can be found on fan sites, social media, YouTube, and in cultural history archives. Above all, the golden age of the rocketmen is preserved in the memories of once-young fans who grew to adulthood without ever losing their fascination with the sense of wonder that the rocketmen and their adventures inspired.

Gary Hughes is one such fan, and in the book's final chapter, "Confessions of a Commando Cody Addict; or, How the Flying Suit Changed My Life," he narrates the saga of his 50-year fascination with *Commando Cody, Sky Marshal of the Universe*. He traces how a chance after-school discovery in 1961 gave rise, with the passage of time, to the creation of a popular Commando Cody website, the construction of an accurate replica of Cody's famous flying suit, and eventually to his first-time production of a four-chapter serial based upon exploits of the rocket-propelled guardian of the globe. Hughes' experience, like those related by so many other cadets, rangers, and junior spacemen, suggests that the iconic figure of the rocketman still retains its significance for fans. Over half a century later, the many changes that accompany the passage of time have added new layers of meaning to their now-adult relationships with these space heroes, but neither time nor age has lessened their desire to "keep watching the skies."

NOTES

1. Voiceover introduction to *Tom Corbett, Space Cadet* (1950–1955).
2. For a comprehensive history of the Flash Gordon serials, see Roy Kinnard, Tony Crnkovich, and R. J. Vitone, *The Flash Gordon Serials, 1936–1940* (Jefferson, NC: McFarland, 2008). For discussion of adaptation issues, see J. P. Telotte, ed. *The Essential Science Fiction Television Reader* (Lexington: University of Kentucky Press, 2008). For discussions of the series, cultural history, and fans, see Jean-Noel Bassior, *Space Patrol: Missions of Daring in the Name of Early Television* (Jefferson, NC: McFarland, 2005), Patrick Lucanio and Gary Coville, *Smokin' Rockets: The Romance of Technology in American Film, Radio, and Television 1945–1962* (Jefferson, NC: McFarland, 2002), and Cynthia J. Miller, "Domesticating Space: Science Fiction Serials Come Home," in *Science Fiction Film, Television, and Adaptation: Across the Screens*, ed. J. P. Telotte (London and New York: Routledge, 2011), 3–13.
3. On the pulp science fiction of the 1920s and 1930s, see Mike Ashley, *Time Machines: The Story of Pulp Science Fiction Magazines from the Beginning to 1950* (Liverpool: Liverpool University Press, 2001).
4. See, for example, Peter Stanfield, *Horse Opera: The Strange History of the 1930s Singing Cowboy* (Urbana and Chicago: University of Illinois Press, 2002).
5. Edward E. Smith, *The Skylark of Space* (Providence, RI: Hadley Publishing, 1946), 301. Like many science fiction novels of the pre-1945 era, *Skylark* was revised and expanded for book publication years after its initial magazine serialization.

6. Damon Knight, "In the Balance," *If,* December 1958, 110–111.
7. Ibid. On the changing definition of "space opera," see David G. Hartwell and Kathryn Cramer, "How Shit Became Shinola: The Definition and Redefinition of Space Opera," *SFRevu,* August 2003, http://www.sfrevu.com/ISSUES/2003/0308/Space%20Opera%20Redefined/Review.htm.
8. The original versions of both novelettes are available on Project Gutenberg. They were later edited into a single novel (but not updated) by Robert A. W. Lowndes, and published as: Philip Francis Nowlan, *Armageddon 2419 A.D.* (New York: Avalon Books, 1962).
9. On the emergence of serialized adventure stories in the comics, see William H. Young, Jr., "The Serious Funnies: Adventure Comics during the Depression, 1929–1938," *Journal of Popular Culture* 3:3 (Winter 1969): 404–427.
10. On Americans' attitudes toward space travel in this era, see Howard McCurdy, *Space and the American Imagination*, 2nd ed. (Baltimore: Johns Hopkins University Press, 2011): 33–59.
11. Personal communication, January 22, 2012.
12. "The Electronic Age of Captain Video," *TV Forecast* (Chicago: Television Forecast, June 10, 1950), 6.
13. Jeff Kisseloff, *The Box: An Oral History of Television, 1929–1961* (New York: Penguin, 1997), 453.
14. See Miller, "Domesticating Space."
15. Bassior, 238–242
16. John Ellis, *Visible Fictions: Cinema, Television, Video*, rev. ed. (London: Routledge, 1992), 113.
17. Murray Robinson, "Planet Parenthood," *Collier's Magazine,* January 5, 1952, 31.
18. Bassior, 8.
19. "Four Flight-Tested Space Helmets You Can Make," *Women's Day,* August 1953, 25. For more, see Miller, "Domesticating Space."
20. Hugo Gernsback, "The Science-Fiction Industry: A New Industry in the Making," *Science-Fiction Plus* 1 (May 1953): 2.
21. *Life,* uncredited photograph of *Space Patrol* merchandise, September 1, 1952, 83.
22. Final broadcasts: *Rocky Jones, Space Ranger,* 1954; *Tom Corbett, Space Cadet,* 1955; *Space Patrol,* 1955; *Commando Cody: Sky Marshal of the Universe,* 1955; *Flash Gordon,* 1955; *Captain Midnight,* 1956; *Captain Z-Ro,* 1960.
23. See the Solar Guard website: www.solarguard.com.
24. In honor of and in gratitude for the inspiration provided by Patrick Lucanio and Gary Coville's *Smokin' Rockets: The Romance of Technology in American Film, Radio, and Television 1945–1962* (2002) and Jean-Noel Bassior's *Space Patrol: Missions of Daring in the Name of Early Television* (2005).

Bibliography

Ashley, Mike. *Time Machines: The Story of Pulp Science Fiction Magazines from the Beginning to 1950.* Liverpool: Liverpool University Press, 2001.
Bassior, Jean-Noel. *Space Patrol: Missions of Daring in the Name of Early Television.* Jefferson, NC: McFarland, 2005.
"The Electronic Age of Captain Video," *TV Forecast.* Chicago: Television Forecast, June 10, 1950.
Ellis, John. *Visible Fictions: Cinema, Television, Video*, rev. ed. London: Routledge, 1992.
"Four Flight-Tested Space Helmets You Can Make." *Women's Day,* August 1953, 21–26.

Gernsback, Hugo. "The Science-Fiction Industry: A New Industry in the Making," *Science-Fiction Plus* 1 (May 1953): 2.

Hartwell, David G., and Kathryn Cramer. "How Shit Became Shinola: The Definition and Redefinition of Space Opera," *SFRevu*, August 2003, http://www.sfrevu.com/ISSUES/2003/0308/Space%20Opera%20Redefined/Review.htm.

Kinnard, Roy, Tony Crnkovich, and R. J. Vitone, *The Flash Gordon Serials, 1936–1940.* Jefferson, NC: McFarland, 2008.

Kisseloff, Jeff. *The Box: An Oral History of Television, 1929–1961.* New York: Penguin, 1997.

Knight, Damon. "In the Balance," *If,* December 1958, 110–111.

Life, uncredited photograph of *Space Patrol* merchandise, September 1, 1952, 83.

Lucanio, Patrick, and Gary Coville, *Smokin' Rockets: The Romance of Technology in American Film, Radio, and Television 1945–1962.* Jefferson, NC: McFarland, 2002.

McCurdy, Howard. *Space and the American Imagination*, 2nd ed. Baltimore: Johns Hopkins University Press, 2011.

Miller, Cynthia J. "Domesticating Space: Science Fiction Serials Come Home." In *Science Fiction Film, Television, and Adaptation: Across the Screen*, ed. J. P. Telotte, 3–13. London and New York: Routledge, 2011.

Nowlan, Philip Francis. *Armageddon 2419 A.D.* New York: Avalon Books, 1962.

Robinson, Murray. "Planet Parenthood." *Collier's Magazine*, January 5, 1952, 31.

Smith, Edward E. *The Skylark of Space.* Providence, RI: Hadley Publishing, 1946.

Stanfield, Peter. *Horse Opera: The Strange History of the 1930s Singing Cowboy.* Urbana and Chicago: University of Illinois Press, 2002.

Telotte, J. P., ed. *The Essential Science Fiction Television Reader.* Lexington: University Press of Kentucky, 2008.

Young, William H. Jr., "The Serious Funnies: Adventure Comics during the Depression, 1929–1938," *Journal of Popular Culture* 3:3 (Winter 1969): 404–427.

PROLOGUE

WHEN OUR STORY BEGAN...

CHAPTER 1

WHERE IT ALL BEGAN: THE FLASH GORDON SERIALS

ROY KINNARD

"THE GOLDEN AGE OF SCIENCE FICTION," IT'S SAID, "IS TWELVE."[1] It inspires a sense of wonder well suited to the hearts and minds of youth. This is particularly true of space opera—interplanetary adventure-melodrama layered with tales of outsized heroes, diabolical villains, and aliens from a hundred improbable worlds. It was established, in print, by stories that ran in 1930s pulp magazines like *Amazing Stories* and *Astounding Science Fiction*. But on movie screens, its iconic form was defined by the interstellar adventures of none other than Flash Gordon. These serials—three in all—based on Alex Raymond's successful comic strip, offered viewers a potent mixture of wild imagination and exotic spectacle, portraying not just spaceships and ray guns—the hallmarks of space opera—but Hawkmen, Sharkmen, evil princesses, and other glittering interplanetary wonders.

The Flash Gordon serials influenced, directly or indirectly, virtually every cinematic space opera that followed them, from *Forbidden Planet* (1956) to *Star Wars* (1977) and its five sequels. Before that, however, they were brought to television in the early 1950s, and so into the hearts and minds of a new generation of 12-year-old fans experiencing science fiction's "sense of wonder" for the first time. The fans who had watched Flash on the big screen now rediscovered him, alongside their own wide-eyed children, on the small screen. This chapter, then, is a look back at the improbably long career of the serials that started it all.

The movie serial (20-minute weekly installments of action-oriented stories, usually presented in 12 to 15 episodes) is totally forgotten today, an outdated screen format gone for more than a half-century, superceded by television programs offering the same type of fare. Produced for over 40 years, beginning in the 'teens with silents like *The Perils of Pauline*, and ending with a Western, *Blazing the Overland Trail*, in 1956, film serials covered a wide range of genres.[2] Mystery, Western, adventure, and science fiction stories were all offered to an appreciative, and almost exclusively juvenile audience, for the lowly movie serials were shown only at matinee screenings and aimed squarely at the kids. They were seldom reviewed in the general press, and rarely seen by adult viewers. Cheaply produced (the average budget for an *entire* serial was $100,000, cheap even for 1930s and '40s Hollywood); they were TV shows before television even existed, and no one over the age of 12 would have wanted to be caught dead watching one.[3] It is easy to see why movie serials have not endured in the public's consciousness in the way that film classics like *Gone With The Wind* and *The Wizard of Oz* (both 1939) have, yet there are, as with many things, exceptions to the rule, and in this case, there are three very noteworthy exceptions.

Many film serials, appealing as they did to young audiences, drew their subject material from popular radio dramas, pulp magazines, and comic books. Pop-culture figures like The Green Hornet, The Shadow, The Lone Ranger, The Phantom, Batman, and Superman all had their first live-action, flesh-and-blood incarnations in movie serials, long before their later resurrection on television and in theatrical movies. One such character was outer-space hero Flash Gordon, whose interplanetary heroics offered Depression-era newspaper readers a welcome escape from that era's daunting realities. With his beautiful girlfriend, Dale Arden, and resourceful scientist-ally, Dr. Zarkov, Flash's breathtaking adventures on another planet were certainly preferable to the average newspaper reader's further contemplation of mass unemployment and breadlines.

The creation of artist/writer Alex Raymond, the comic strip *Flash Gordon* had been conceived for the Hearst newspaper chain as competition for the already-established *Buck Rogers* strip, which had been running since 1929. Making its debut in January 1934, *Flash Gordon was* an immediate hit with newspaper readers, and soon eclipsed *Buck Rogers* in popularity.[4] Both strips were ostensibly science fiction, drawing partial inspiration from the sci-fi pulp magazines of that era, but whereas *Buck Rogers* was science-heavy and rather crudely drawn, *Flash Gordon* appealed more to the reader's imagination and emotions, with Alex Raymond's florid artwork (the artist sometimes drew his figures from live models) transporting the reader into (literally, as well as figuratively) another world. And Flash had something else that Buck didn't have: a sex life. Raymond's women were as impossibly beautiful as his protagonist was impossibly heroic—and his villain, Ming the Merciless, unspeakably evil. The strip's romantic angle was an important factor that kept readers interested and coming back for more.

This material was a natural for Hollywood, and two years after its print debut, Raymond's *Flash Gordon* was filmed as the first of three movie serials produced by Universal Pictures, with Olympic swimming-champion-turned-actor Larry "Buster" Crabbe, his hair bleached blonde for the role, as Flash Made from 1936 to 1940, these three serials, totaling forty 20-minute weekly episodes, were an immediate hit with the public, and are virtually the only movie serials to escape the pop-culture dustbin and live on in the public's memory, with the original 1936 serial, *Flash Gordon*, designated a cultural treasure and included in the National Film Registry.[5]

Like many baby boomers, this writer first saw these films on television in the 1950s. They seemed awesome at the time, even though already a couple of decades

Image 1.1   Buster Crabbe as Flash Gordon, in *Flash Gordon's Trip to Mars* (1938).

old, and were actually somewhat better-produced than many similar TV shows of the era such as *Rocky Jones, Space Ranger* (1954), and *Captain Video* (1949–1955). The three Flash Gordon serials were a staple of *Chicago Tribune*-owned local TV station WGN in Chicago, and were run constantly across the country during the 1950s and '60s.[6] Retitled *Space Soldiers* to avoid confusion with a newer, cheaply produced and vastly inferior (not to mention quickly forgotten) *Flash Gordon* syndicated series (1954–1955) starring Steve Holland, the Buster Crabbe serials drew consistently high ratings, and were popular with both adults who remembered seeing them in theaters, and children who were discovering them for the first time. The serials certainly made a huge impression on at least one viewer who would later have an impact on popular culture: George Lucas, whose original intention had been to film a big-screen remake of *Flash Gordon*, but who, after finding that the cost of acquiring movie rights from the copyright owner, King Features Syndicate, was prohibitive, altered his plans and embarked on the project that eventually became *Star Wars*.[7]

By the 1960s, the *Flash Gordon* serials were entangled in a legal battle between King Features Syndicate and Universal Pictures, with King Features claiming ownership of the films as creator and copyright holder of the property, and Universal (despite the lapse of its contractual rights) asserting that it had a controlling interest as the original producer of the films. King Features won, Universal lost control of the three serials, and the 40 episodes of the Flash Gordon serials were pulled and went into the vaults while the legal dust settled.[8]

The serials returned in the late 1960s, distributed by A.B.C. Films, and riding the wave of pop-culture nostalgia sweeping the nation, were more popular than ever, making headlines in *Variety* with the consistently high ratings they drew. After further legal wrangling, ownership of the serials was finally transferred to Hearst's King Features, which continued television distribution into the *Star Wars* era, with the serials (having themselves inspired *Star Wars*) drawing greater fan interest due to the popularity of Lucas' films.[9] Pop culture feeds on, and perpetuates itself, and the *Flash Gordon* movie serials have lived on and endured, while nearly all other film serials have been forgotten. As the nostalgia craze fades with the aging of baby boomers and with the inevitable generational shift, Golden Age Hollywood, and interest in it, has receded, yet interest continues in certain films of the 1930s and '40s, the *Flash Gordon* serials among them. The three serials (and their reedited feature-length versions as well) have been released on DVD, and there are Internet websites devoted to these films, the first of which is now 75 years old.

Why do certain classic films continue to exert a hold on many people? I recall attending a nostalgia convention in 1974, at which Buster Crabbe was the celebrity guest. Crabbe, who had become a successful businessman after his film career ended in the 1950s, made appearing at these conventions a profitable sideline in his later years, and had worked up an entertaining routine on the making of the serials that was usually followed by a question-and-answer session with the audience. The convention was held at Chicago's Playboy Hotel, and aside from the usual memorabilia dealers, there was quite a large crowd in attendance. The year 1974 was a cynical time (Richard Nixon had just resigned his presidency the day before the convention!), and I think that a partial reason for the nostalgia craze of the period was due to the (presumed) innocence of "Golden Age" entertainment. In the 1970s—as in the 1930s—the general public was tired of social upheaval, and sought escape in simpler and ostensibly more appealing entertainment. But I believe that the *primary* continuing appeal of films like the Flash Gordon serials, the original *King Kong* (1933), and the classic Universal Pictures horror movies of the 1930s and '40s lies in their *emotional* as well as their artistic content.

It is true that some viewers are drawn to these movies because of what they perceive as their "camp" value—some viewers are amused by the frequent bad acting, contrived scripting, or, as in the Flash Gordon serials, crude and obvious special effects. I once attended a screening of the 1933 *King Kong* during which the viewers responded with howls of laughter and derision at the acting in the film; practically every scene was almost cruelly ridiculed by the audience. This point of view exists, and people are certainly entitled to whatever reaction they care to express in response to what they see as a film's creative shortcomings and ineptitude, but I don't agree with this, nor do I believe that it is by any means the *majority* opinion. Most fans of classic horror and science fiction movies don't watch the films to ridicule them, but enthusiastically accept the movies at face value and enjoy them on that level. I think this is because of the films' emotional connection with the viewer, reinforced by the classical photographic styles and the very basic, direct storytelling and acting techniques of the period.

In 1970, Chicago's now-defunct Esquire Theatre, located north of the Loop, offered a month-long program of first-rate movie classics, including titles like Jean Cocteau's *Beauty and the Beast* (1946), *Citizen Kane* (1941), and *King Kong* (which, thankfully, unspooled to a respectful audience on this occasion). The films were presented in double-feature programs, with the bill changing every three days, and interspersed between each feature was a chapter of the original 1936 *Flash Gordon* serial, with the entire 13 episodes of the serial run during the month of the festival. I was already familiar with all three of the serials from earlier television viewings, but in this case I was seeing the film on a large screen in the form of a beautiful 35mm print, with nothing cut or altered, and uninterrupted by television commercials. I was highly impressed by the serial's production and overpowering innocence, as well as its straightforward faithfulness to Raymond's original comic strip, and resolved to research the Flash Gordon serials (about which very little had been written at that point). I wanted to know more about them, how they were made, and what had happened to the people who made them, and over the next few years, as I began to write about movies, I researched the films, interviewed Buster Crabbe and Jean Rogers (Dale Arden in the first two serials), and eventually wrote the recently published book *The Flash Gordon Serials*. Along the way, what I discovered was that the Flash Gordon movies, aside from their status as early science fiction film classics and top-of-the-line serials, were unique films; they were hardly run-of-the-mill low-budget fare, and they were hardly even typical *serials*.

Sound-era movie serials were primarily made by three studios: Universal, Columbia, and Republic. There had been a few scattered independent producers in the early sound era, but they had been driven out of business by 1937.[10] Prestigious studios like Paramount and MGM wouldn't touch the serial format, although RKO did make *one* serial, 1933's *The Last Frontier*, a Western starring Lon Chaney Jr. Each of the three serial-making studios' products had strengths and weaknesses: Universal's serials were heavy on plot and character development, with frequently tacky special effects and an over-reliance on stock footage. Republic's serials were slickly produced, with excellent cinematography and believable miniature work by Howard and Theodore Lydecker, but, although the Republics are highly praised by their fans, scripting was often flat and contrived, with characterization almost nil. In Republic serials, the actors often tended to be little more than one-dimensional cardboard cutouts. Columbia was generally considered to produce the worst serials (and if not exactly the *worst*, they were certainly the *cheapest*), with the scripters frequently resorting to intentional humor in order to enliven the proceedings. It was Columbia that first brought Superman to the screen as a live-action character, in, first, a 1948 fifteen-chapter serial, *Superman*, and then a fifteen-chapter 1950 sequel, *Atom Man vs. Superman*. These two films, although somewhat enjoyable on their own terms, were so impoverished that whenever Superman (Kirk Alyn) flew, he turned into a flat animated cartoon. A brief revival of interest in serials, provoked by Columbia's 1965 reissue of their 1943 *Batman* serial and the popular Adam West *Batman* TV show, occurred at the same time as the rising nostalgia craze, and in later years many of the Republic serials were later available on VHS video.[11]

The original 1936 *Flash Gordon* was produced by Universal Pictures in 1936, and released, beginning in April of that year, in 13 weekly chapters. Universal at that time was run by Carl Laemmle and his son Carl Jr. Founded by Laemmle Sr. in 1915, it was a "bread-and-butter" studio, producing a steady output of low-budget Westerns and serials, with an occasional "prestige" film added to the release schedule in order to enhance the studio's image.[12] The major studios that are still in business today—MGM, Paramount, Warner Bros., Fox (later 20th Century Fox), Universal, and Columbia—were all in place by the 1920s, before the arrival of sound. Universal was one of the smaller production companies, but even though its product was run-of-the-mill, the studio was occasionally willing to gamble on something different. It was at Universal that iconoclastic talents like Erich von Stroheim and Lon Chaney made their mark in the silent era, and in the early sound period, the studio released *Dracula* and *Frankenstein* to both critical acclaim and box-office success.

The short-subject department at Universal was under the supervision of producer Henry MacRae, a Laemmle associate and crony dating back to the beginnings of the studio. MacRae was the producer of the first sound serial, *The Indians Are Coming* (1930), the success of which revitalized the serial format. In 1935, Universal purchased the film rights to a group of newspaper comic strips for serial adaptation, among them Raymond's *Flash Gordon*, for which they paid King Features $10,000.[13]

Buster Crabbe was not initially considered for the lead; he told me in our 1981 interview that, having followed the strip like most newspaper readers, he had read about the serial's production in the trade papers and gone to Universal out of curiosity. When MacRae spotted Crabbe watching from the sidelines as other actors (including Jon Hall) tested for the role, he offered Crabbe the part and arranged for a "loan-out" deal with Crabbe's home studio, Paramount.

The serial was filmed in six weeks during December 1935 and January 1936, at a reported cost of $350.000.[14] If this amount seems miniscule in comparison with modern film budgets, it should be remembered that this was during the Great Depression. Also, as previously mentioned, most serials cost around $100,000—the first *Flash Gordon* was something special by comparison, and if any degree of fidelity at all to Raymond's comic strip was to be maintained, the budget had to be higher than usual. Even so, corners were cut, with standing sets from *The Hunchback of Notre Dame* (1923) and *Bride of Frankenstein* (1935) reused, and preexisting music scores lifted from earlier movies like *The Invisible Man* (1933) and *Werewolf of London* (1935).

After unforgettably hammy character actor Charles Middleton was cast as Flash's evil nemesis, Ming, the rest of the cast was rounded out with studio contract talent (Jean Rogers and Priscilla Lawson) and veteran character actors like Frank Shannon (Dr. Zarkov), Richard Alexander (Prince Barin), and former silent-movie Tarzan, James Pierce (Thun, king of the Lion Men). Jean Rogers cast as Dale Arden, and Priscilla Lawson, as Ming's daughter, Princess Aura, were both stunningly beautiful young starlets, and the feminine pulchritude on display was duly noted in contemporary reviews. Rogers, unlike the comic strip Dale—a brunette—was very blonde, but this departure from the source material helped to differentiate her from Lawson's Princess Aura).

Direction was by Frederick "Fritz" Stephani, also chief writer of the screenplay, and was his first directorial effort (he soon fell behind schedule, and was given an uncredited assist from serial veteran Ray Taylor). Primarily a writer, Stephani had contributed an early outline for Universal's *Dracula* in 1930, and after leaving

Universal to work at other studios, was nominated for an Academy Award for one of his later screenplays. Stephani later wrote the treatment for an (unfilmed) sequel to *Casablanca,* and did not return to direction until helming a few episodes of TV series like *Waterfront* and *My Friend Flicka* in the 1950s.

Flash Gordon was co-photographed by Jerry Ash and Richard Fryer, with Fryer handling most of the dramatic scenes involving actors, and Ash concentrating on the wobbly rocket ships and the miniature shots. Ash's career went back to the silent days; he was one of the cameramen on Universal's 1925 *Phantom of the Opera*. The look of the film, in terms of the sets and costumes, was perfectly in line with Raymond's strip as it was drawn at the time—these serials are among the most faithful live-action movie adaptations of comic strips ever made.

The first serial opens as the planet Mongo, guided by mysterious forces, hurtles toward Earth on an apparent collision course, its gravitational influence throwing the Earth into chaos. Flash Gordon, (en route home to his scientist/father) is aboard a plane with other passengers, and bails out with a beautiful young girl, Dale Arden, when the aircraft, buffeted by turbulence, spins out of control. In the countryside below, they encounter Dr. Zarkov, who plans to fly his nearby rocket ship to the onrushing planet in an attempt to prevent its collision with Earth.

Boarding the futuristic craft, they take off, hurtling through space toward the approaching planet, eventually landing in a desolate rocky valley on its surface. They are attacked by huge carnivorous reptiles, but the monsters are slain by death rays fired from the sky by another rocket ship. The alien ship lands, and an armored guard, accompanied by two armed soldiers, confronts them, telling the three Earth people that they are under arrest and are now prisoners of "Ming, emperor of the universe."

They are taken before Ming in his opulent throne room, and the evil despot immediately declares that Dale Arden is to be his bride, while Ming's daughter, Princess Aura, openly expresses her interest in Flash (poor Zarkov, too old to be included in any romantic entanglements, is made a prisoner and sent to Ming's laboratory to conduct experiments for the emperor). When Flash rebels against Ming's tyranny, he is condemned to fight three beast-men in Ming's arena. As the battle rages, Princess Aura rushes to Flash's defense, and they both plummet to their apparent doom when they fall through a trap door, hurtling down a shaft. Ming, attempting to save his daughter, activates a safety net, which catches Flash and Aura. Leaving the pit through a secret door, they escape into a maze of caverns below the palace.

After Mongo's impending collision with Earth is averted, and Zarkov is freed from Ming's palace by Prince Barin, the rightful ruler of Mongo, the three Earth people are reunited, form an alliance with Prince Barin, and find themselves in a protracted life-and-death struggle against Ming and an array of other kingdoms and races subservient to him, including the Sharkmen and Hawkmen. Complicating matters are the romantic entanglements involving Ming's relentless pursuit of Dale, and Aura's obsession for Flash, but eventually, they finally defeat Ming (who apparently commits suicide by sacrificing himself to Mongo's "Great God Tao") and, the threat to Earth ended, return home safely.

On its release, *Flash Gordon* was wildly popular with the general public, garnering favorable reviews (most serials were scarcely reviewed at all!), and unlike the usual serials, was screened for adult filmgoers at evening performances in first-run theatres. Universal Pictures, though, had changed management only a few days before the release of *Flash Gordon*, with the founding Laemmle family (as well as studio veterans like *Flash Gordon* producer MacRae) forced out and replaced by new personnel. *Flash Gordon* reaped considerable profits for the incoming studio management (a reedited, feature-length version, entitled *Rocket Ship*, was also released in 1936), and in late 1937 a sequel to the first serial, *Flash Gordon's Trip to Mars*, was produced by Universal for release in March of the following year, with the four principal actors—Crabbe, Rogers (now a brunette), Shannon, and Middleton—returning in their familiar roles. Direction was by veteran serial hands Ford Beebe and Robert F. Hill. Fifteen chapters in length, the follow-up was filmed in four weeks during November and December 1937, and produced at a cost of $182,000, a little more than half the first serial's budget—but still an impressive sum for a serial, the expenditure mandated by *Trip to Mars'* extravagant plot.[15]

Ming, having inexplicably survived after taking his own life at the end of the first serial, travels to Mars and forms an uneasy alliance with the red planet's Queen Azura, who controls her domain through the power of a magic sapphire she wears. From Mars, Ming focuses a powerful beam of light on the Earth, drawing "nitron" from the Earth's atmosphere and disrupting global weather patterns.

Image 1.2 Buster Crabbe, Jean Rogers, and Donald Kerr in a scene from *Flash Gordon's Trip to Mars* (1938).

In an effort to prevent this, Flash Gordon, Dale Arden, and Dr. Zarkov travel to Mars in Zarkov's rocket ship, with a newspaper reporter, Happy Hapgood, stowing away aboard the ship. On Mars, they are confronted by the Clay People (bizarre, gnome-like subterranean outcasts—placed under a curse by Queen Azura—who literally ooze from cavern walls), the Tree People (forest-dwelling savages), and other minions of Azura and Ming, before Ming (having betrayed Azura and successfully plotted her death) is overthrown once again when he is trapped in his own disintegrating chamber. The dead Azura's curse is lifted from the Clay People, and Flash, Dale, and Zarkov return to Earth and a heroes' welcome.

Flash Gordon's Trip to Mars, like the first serial, was a tremendous hit with filmgoers. Universal tricked at least some of the release prints up by printing the film on green-toned stock, and the serial was promoted with a series of pictorial articles in *Look* magazine.

In many ways, *Flash Gordon's Trip to Mars* was even more enjoyable than its predecessor, avoiding some of the character development, as well as the romantic entanglements, of its predecessor, but relying instead on more action and an even more bizarre plot than the original. Despite the sometimes rushed, crude technical work, the film was, at the time—and remains today—one of the best of its type. As Universal had done with *Flash Gordon*, a recut feature version of *Flash Gordon's Trip to Mars*, entitled *Mars Attacks the World*, was released later that same year.

Flash Gordon's Trip to Mars is a favorite with many fans of the trilogy. Although the plot's mixture of sci-fi and magic seems like a preposterous concept, it somehow works on the serial's basic, comic-strip level. The gadgets and gimmicks are more plentiful here, too, with Franz Waxman's great score for *Bride of Frankenstein* reused to maximum effect. The romantic element so vital to the first serial *is* downplayed in *Trip to Mars*; Ming's only interest in Dale here seems limited to using her as bait to trap Flash, although Queen Azura (well-played by Beatrice Roberts) *does* seem to take an inordinate amount of interest in Flash.

After *Flash Gordon's Trip to Mars*, Universal cast Crabbe as *Buck Rogers* in a 12-chapter serial released in April 1939. Also featuring Constance Moore (as Wilma Deering) and Jackie Moran (as Buck's juvenile sidekick, Buddy Wade), *Buck Rogers* was a solid, well-produced serial, one of Universal's best in terms of physical production values, but it was only a lukewarm success with the public. Although Universal had purchased the rights to make a second Buck Rogers serial, they opted instead to produce a third Flash Gordon. *Flash Gordon Conquers the Universe* was filmed in late 1939, and released in 12 chapters in April 1940.[16]

This third entry is one of the glossiest, most beautifully photographed sound serials ever made, with producer MacRae returning to supervise and going all out to bring Flash Gordon's screen incarnation into line with Raymond's comic-strip artwork, which had matured in style and overall detail in the years since the first serial. This is the serial that inspired artist Al Williamson, Raymond's successor on the strip, to become an artist.

For this last sequel, Crabbe, Middleton, and Shannon returned, but Carol Hughes replaced Rogers (who was then under contract to another studio and unavailable) as Dale, with Roland Drew playing Prince Barin and Shirley Deane cast as Princess

Aura. These changes in the cast are jarring to some fans, but the new actors (with the exception of Shirley Deane—hardly as colorful, or as beautiful—as Lawson in the first serial) are good in their roles, with Hughes, a cute 29-year-old brunette, a more than adequate substitute for Rogers as Dale. *Flash Gordon Conquers the Universe* involves the further efforts of Ming (who has, again, inexplicably survived his death at the end of the previous outing) to conquer the Earth by means of a virulent "death dust"; Flash, Dale, and Zarkov return to Mongo, and, teaming up with Prince Barin and Queen Fria, ruler of Mongo's frozen region, Frigia, neutralize Ming's death dust with the mineral polarite. After narrowly escaping death at the hands of savage Rock Men in Mongo's "Land of the Dead," they thwart Ming's nefarious schemes a third time, and the ruthless tyrant dies when Flash parachutes out of an exploding rocket ship that he crashes into Ming's palace.

Some fans of the series feel that *Flash Gordon Conquers the Universe* is the least effective of the three serials, but that may be due to its radical departure from the look and style of the other two, in addition to the cast changes noted. But, as previously mentioned, Raymond's comic strip had shifted in tone and artistic style also, and MacRae apparently felt that the serial had to reflect the evolution of Raymond's strip. Although *Flash Gordon Conquers the Universe* is the shortest (at 12 chapters, compared to 13 for the original and 15 for *Trip to Mars*) and the cheapest of the three films (it was produced in four weeks for only $177,000),[17] it looks far more expensive than it is.

Image 1.3 Carol Hughes as Dale Arden, with Buster Crabbe in *Flash Gordon Conquers the Universe* (1940)

After World War II, there was talk at Universal of filming a fourth Flash Gordon serial, but before this could be approved, the studio, again in financial difficulty, merged with International Pictures in 1946 to become Universal-International, and, in a bid to upgrade its public image, cancelled production on B-grade movies and serials. Although the movie serials would go on for another decade, still made by Columbia and Republic until 1956, Universal-International fell back on reissues of their former product to exploit the waning serial market, rereleasing both *Flash Gordon* and *Flash Gordon's Trip to Mars* in the late 1940s.

The three Flash Gordon serials went to television soon thereafter. As previously mentioned, there had been two contemporary theatrical-feature versions recut from the first two serials, *Rocket Ship* (from *Flash Gordon*) and *Mars Attacks the World* (from *Flash Gordon's Trip to Mars*). Although these two features were distributed to early television, at less than 70 minutes each they were too short for the two-hour movie time slots that later became popular with TV programmers. In 1966, four new feature versions were reedited from the serials for distribution to local television stations. Running 90 to 100 minutes each, these were *Spaceship to the Unknown* (derived from *Flash Gordon*), *The Deadly Ray from Mars* (cut from *Flash Gordon's Trip to Mars*), and two features that were reedited from *Flash Gordon Conquers the Universe*, *The Purple Death from Outer Space* (covering events in the first half of *Universe*), and *Perils from the Planet Mongo* (which, after a brief recap, wrapped up the story).

In 1980, producer Dino De Laurentis (who had remade *King Kong* with Jessica Lange in 1976) released a $30 million theatrical remake, *Flash Gordon*, starring Sam J. Jones as Flash, Melody Anderson as Dale, and Max Von Sydow as Ming. Directed by Mike Hodges, and with music by the rock group Queen, the film, although intentionally campy, was full of eye-popping color and production design, imparting an epic quality to the material that did full justice to Raymond's creation, with the somewhat inappropriate rock score its only real flaw. Fittingly, the movie was distributed by the studio that produced the original serials, Universal. With so many science fiction movies in release at the time, though, the De Laurentis *Flash Gordon* was lost in the shuffle, although it did enjoy a resurgence in popularity when later released on DVD.

Adequate home video releases of Universal's Flash Gordon serials were a long time in appearing, due to a variety of legal and merchandising factors. *Flash Gordon Conquers the Universe* and the first serial's theatrical feature version, *Rocket Ship*, were in the public domain and legally continuously available in copies of varying quality, but all three serials (and the four previously mentioned 1966 featurizations) did not appear in definitive versions until Image Entertainment released them, first on laserdisc, then on DVD.

With the rise of home video, the Flash Gordon serials, along with the other classic movies that were once staples of late-night local TV programming, vanished from television stations, replaced by more profitable game shows and infomercials. Cable stations like American Movie Classics and Turner Classic Movies filled this void to a degree, and, in many cases, virtually entire studio libraries were released on VHS cassettes, laserdiscs, and DVD.

While there is still enough interest in "Golden Age" Hollywood, and in classic movies like these serials, *King Kong*, *The Wizard of Oz*, and *Casablanca* to support their commercial value and current availability, interest in classic films as a whole has waned in recent years. This is particularly true in science fiction, where fans are actively wooed by corporate-controlled Hollywood studios, via viral digital marketing and celebrity-packed conventions, in their efforts to promote the latest comic book superhero adaptations and futuristic epics brimming over with spectacular digital effects. Fans who care about "the old stuff" are definitely in the minority. There is, however, a new film version of *Flash Gordon* in on-again, off-again preproduction as of this writing. Hopefully, the film will be made, with all the digital resources modern film production can provide, and Alex Raymond's vision will be revitalized for a new generation of fans.

Notes

1. David G. Hartwell, "The Golden Age of Science Fiction Is Twelve," in *Visions of Wonder: The Science Fiction Research Association Anthology,* ed. David G. Hartwell and Milton T. Wolf (New York: Tor Books, 1996), 81–96.
2. For more on this, see Kalton C. LaHue, *Continued Next Week: A History of the Moving Picture Serial.* (Norman: University of Oklahoma Press, 1964); Roy Kinnard, *Science Fiction Serials* (Jefferson, NC: McFarland, 1998); Anthony Fletcher, *Don't Dare Miss the Next Thrilling Chapter* (Minneapolis: Mill City Press, 2009); Ron Backer, *Gripping Chapters: The Sound Movie Serial* (Duncan, OK: BearManor Media, 2010).
3. Kinnard, *Science Fiction Serials*, 6.
4. For more, see Roy Kinnard, Tony Crnkovich and R. J. Vitone, *The Flash Gordon Serials, 1936–1940* (Jefferson, NC: McFarland, 2008).
5. *Flash Gordon* was selected for inclusion in the National Film Registry in 1996.
6. See Kinnard, et. al., *Flash Gordon Serials*.
7. Kinnard, *Science Fiction Serials*.
8. Eagan, Daniel. *America's Film Legacy: The Authoritative Guide to Landmark Movies in the National Film Registry* (New York: Continuum, 2009), 241.
9. Kinnard, et. al., *Flash Gordon Serials*, 58.
10. See Fletcher, *Don't Dare Miss*; Backer, *Gripping Chapters*.
11. For more on Superman, Batman, and others, see Kinnard, *Science Fiction Serials*.
12. Carl Hirshorn, *The Universal Story: The Compete History of the Studio and All Its Films* (London: Hamlyn, 2001).
13. Ibid.
14. Kinnard, et. al., *Flash Gordon Serials*.
15. Kinnard, et. al., *Flash Gordon Serials*, 16.
16. Kinnard, et. al., *Flash Gordon Serials*.
17. Kinnard, et. al., *Flash Gordon Serials*, 19.

Bibliography

Backer, Ron. *Gripping Chapters: The Sound Movie Serial*. Duncan, OK: BearManor Media, 2010.

Eagan, Daniel. *America's Film Legacy: The Authoritative Guide to Landmark Movies in the National Film Registry*. New York and London: Continuum Publishing, 2009.

Fletcher, Anthony. *Don't Dare Miss the Next Thrilling Chapter*. Minneapolis: Mill City Press, 2009.

Hartwell, David G. "The Golden Age of Science Fiction Is Twelve." In *Visions of Wonder: The Science Fiction Research Association Anthology,* edited by David G. Hartwell and Milton T. Wolf, 81–96. New York: Tor Books, 1996.

Hirshhorn, Carl. *The Universal Story: The Compete History of the Studio and All Its Films.* London: Hamlyn, 2001.

Kinnard, Roy. *Science Fiction Serials.* Jefferson, NC: McFarland, 1998.

Kinnard, Roy, Tony Crnkovich, and R. J. Vitone. *The Flash Gordon Serials, 1936–1940.* Jefferson, NC: McFarland, 2008.

LaHue, Kalton C. *Continued Next Week: A History of the Moving Picture Serial.* Norman: University of Oklahoma Press, 1964.

PART I

LEARNING TO BE ROCKETMEN

CHAPTER 2

"A COMMOTION IN THE FIRMAMENT": *TOM CORBETT* AND THE LOST BOYS

JOHN C. TIBBETTS

> I believe I am rather a fine fellow when I am flying!
> —J. M. Barrie, *Tommy and Grizel* (1900)

THE DECADE OF THE 1950S KICKED AWAY GRAVITY FOR A new postwar generation of baby boomers. Buoyed up on Icarus' wings, Galileo's dreams, and Mephistopheles cloak, we flew, as the poet sang, "into that uncharted gulf and abyss where no bird-song or shout of man could follow..."[1] Things seemed to be happening all at once—and just for us.... Almost every day the newspapers reported rocket launches and flying-saucer sightings. Science fiction stories about young spacemen flooded the libraries. Even the tail fins of Dad's family car rivaled the spaceship designs of the movies *Rocketship XM* and *Destination Moon*. Best of all, though, were the "live" telecasts of space adventures that were flying into our living rooms via the eight-by-ten-inch Motorola television sets.

And it is of these latter flights of fancy—"commotions in the firmament," as J. M. Barrie put it—that I speak. *Tom Corbett, Space Cadet* (1950–1955) had all the scientific realism of the best scientific speculation of the day and all mythic resonance of Barrie's immortal child, Peter Pan. Indeed, it can't be just coincidence that the Walt Disney and Mary Martin revivals of *Peter Pan* coincided with the arrival of our new space hero, Tom Corbett. Corbett and Pan seemed like brothers. Indeed, as I shall demonstrate, the resemblances between them border on identity. So intimate, so real were they both to the "extravagant gaze" of my own boyish eyes, that I was either down in the basement building my own spaceship with Corbett or up on the roof leaping into space with Pan (with predictable results!).[2] Nothing else mattered, neither the atomic science of Corbett's cosmos nor the melodramatic claptrap of

Pan's Neverland. It was the *flying* that stole the show.³ "I'll teach you how to jump on the wind's back," cried Pan, speaking for all of his flying brethren, "and then away we go...saying funny things to the stars!"⁴ It was a potent seduction for those of us just on the verge of puberty, when the timelessness of youth was first threatened by the terrors of impending adolescence. Flight represented, on the one hand, an escapist leap, and, on the other, a tentative step toward maturity.

Just as Pan abducted Wendy and her brothers away from the nursery to Neverland, Corbett plucked his viewers away from the cozy living rooms of the 1950s to his own cosmic Neverland. I don't use the term "abduction" lightly. It has been charged that fantasies like these "stole" the lives of children, fixing them forever in their texts. An amusing newspaper cartoon at the time illustrated the point: while two children are watching a television image of a rocket in flight, their parents exclaim: "They think nothing of a trip to some planet, but just try to get them to go to the corner store!" (Wade Williams archives). In her controversial *The Case of Peter Pan*, Jacqueline Rose darkly hints that this is an adult desire to arrest the child's development: "The child is used (and abused) to represent the whole problem of what sexuality is, or can be, and hold that problem at bay."⁵ In any event a few of us never returned from those Neverlands, as it were, "lost boys" trapped in the unrelenting grip and nostalgia of youth. However, those of us who did, admits Rose, have found that a childlike sensibility could remain a vital and healthy component of our maturity—"something which we endlessly rework in our attempt to build an image of our own history."⁶ Underlying it all is a profound ambivalence, best expressed by Barrie—who was in a unique position to know—in his novel, *Margaret Ogilvey*: "I knew a time would come when I also must give up the games, and how it must be done I saw not.... I felt that I must continue playing in secret."⁷

LEARNING TO FLY

The stories of Peter Pan and Tom Corbett are modern-day fairy tales. They embody the archetype of the Eternal Child. As Harold Schechter notes, "They are part of a mythological symbol of the *puer aeternus*—the 'divine youth,' the indestructibly childlike parts of the human personality. They are crucially important qualities too easily forgotten in our intense focus on the world of getting and spending...whose purpose is to compensate for the extravagances of the conscious mind."⁸ In a recent letter to the author, Schechter confirmed: "I love the notion of Tom Corbett as a space-age *puer aeternus* and definitely think it's a subject worth exploring. I agree that we boomers have maintained a deep allegiance to Neverland, though I'm starting to think that, in comparison to the current crop of American man-boys, we seem to be models of maturity."⁹ Consider: Pan in his costume of leaves and cobwebs, and Corbett in his silver space suit hover weightless over the mundane world.¹⁰ Their Neverlands are fairy realms where time and direction are meaningless, where strange creatures threaten, but death has no meaning. If Pan always returns to the Darling nursery and Corbett to the Space Academy, they ultimately recoil from worldly mortality and fly away again. Pan is essentially androgynous, and traditionally portrayed by a girl. Corbett is oblivious to the charms of his female

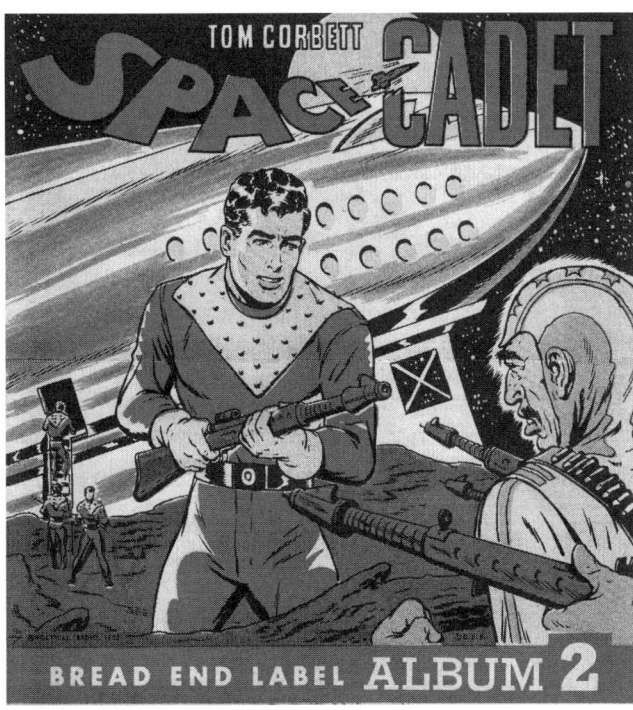

Image 2.1 Tom Corbett, keeping the galaxy safe from evildoers on the cover of a collector's album from Fischer's Buttercup Bread. [Credit: Wade Williams Enterprises]

colleague, Dr. Joan Dale, Doctor of Space Medicine, and prefers the company of his fellow Cadets. Indeed, declared producer Allen Ducovny, sex had no place in space opera—although Space Cadets may be permitted to pat lovingly the nose of the *Polaris* on occasion.[11] Pan avoids human contact and demands he is "never to be touched." Corbett wields his "paralo-raygun" as a safeguard against unwanted intrusion.

Moreover, as fairy tales, they seem to come from nowhere and everywhere at the same time. The origins of both Pan and Corbett are typically as diverse as they are obscure. Obviously, developments in the technologies of flight spawned them both. *Peter Pan* arrives on the heels of the English craze for ballooning and the new heavier-than-air experiments; *Tom Corbett* at the dawn of modern rocketry. But from there, tracing back to their respective genealogies is more difficult. Barrie is generally credited as the author of *Peter Pan*, but the fact of its creation, the precise nature of the play's appeal, and the question of its target audience—adult or children—seems to have eluded him all his life. At times, during the numerous revisions of the play, characters came and went, scenes were deleted or added, and the ending was revised and re-rewritten dozens of times.[12] When he finally got around to publishing the play, 25 years after it was first staged in 1904, he declared in the preface that he couldn't remember having ever written it![13] Indeed, the story seems to have found *him*.

Pan's story existed before Barrie in tales of those mythic figures of youthful excess, such as Dionysus, Icarus, and Hermes. In Ovid's *Metamorphosis*, for example, Dionysus is described: "He is young, this god/A boy forever, fairest in the Heaven."[14] In her study of the Pan myth, Ann Yeoman writes, "Many of the attributes of the gods we have discussed are readily identifiable as character traits of Peter Pan. His habit of crowing like a cock links him to the *other* mythic Pan and Dionysus, as does his piping. His impetuosity, magic, sudden appearances and ability to move between two worlds (Neverland and Edwardian London) are qualities of the mythic Pan, Hermes and Dionysus; spring is the season when we may expect Peter Pan to alight on our windowsill, and his association with springtime, renewal, youth, joy and spontaneity connects him to the dying and resurgent young gods of fertility and vegetation cults, as does Barrie's description of him as a type of the Green Man of Nature: 'a lovely boy, clad in skeleton leaves and the juices that ooze out of trees.'"[15]

Barrie first encountered the Pan myth, as it were, through his strange and—according to some—tragic relationship with the five boys of the Llewelyn Davies family.[16] Their adventures together became the basis for the closing chapter of his novel *The Little White Bird* (1902), and were expanded in subsequent versions for the play in 1904, another novel called *Peter and Wendy* in 1911 (which Rose contends is Barrie's *only* attempt to target a specifically youth readership), a movie scenario in 1920 (more on that presently), and the first published play script in 1928. Throughout, his many versions and rewrites reflect his own ambivalence on the matter. This is reflected, explains Yeoman in detail, in his ever-shifting authorial stance: "He is now inside, now outside, of the action," she explains, referring to the novel *Peter and Wendy*. "He contradicts later what he, or the narrative, affirms earlier, changes his authorial mind in mid-paragraph, and then writes as though he, with the reader, is discovering the narrative as he proceeds..."[17]

The origins of *Tom Corbett, Space Cadet*, while extending the precedents that had inspired *Peter Pan*, involve a variety of additional sources. Not long after the first appearances of Peter Pan's aerial antics on the London stage—and the concurrent Wright Brothers' heavier-than-air flights at Kitty Hawk—dozens of "boys' books" about flight flooded the market and invaded the homes and imaginations of their readers. Series such as "The Airship Boys" and "The Airplane Boys" (both 1910–1915) by Harry Lincoln Sayler led the way, with the "Bird Boys" books by John Luther Langworthy, and the "Tom Swift" books, principally written by Howard R. Garis as "Victor Appleton," soon to follow.[18] The spectacular success of Charles Lindbergh's solo flight across the Atlantic to Paris in 1927 immediately spawned yet another series, the "Ted Scott Flying Stories." The pulp magazines soon followed. The 1920s and 1930s saw a spate of entries, such as Hugo Gernsback's *Air Wonder Stories*, which advanced an imaginative vision of the future of aviation. "Exclusively male," reports Fred Erisman in his estimable *Boys' Books, Boys' Dreams, and the Mystique of Flight*, "as befits the protagonist of a series directed toward adolescent boys, the pilot figures become potent role models, offering a model of manhood for a technological age.... The air, for them, is at once a medium of adventure, exaltation, and commerce."[19] The vision of flight in these stories, comments Erisman, "gave to mankind—and the American citizenry in particular—the opportunity and

Image 2.2   *Airship Andy* (1911) was one of many tales of flight and adventure for boys.

the means to rise above itself, to become higher, greater, and finer than ordinary life permits." And, as it had for Peter Pan, it extended for those who gave themselves over to flight, a chance "to become somehow larger than life, somehow more than human, a 'birdman' in the largest and most evocative sense of the term."[20].

Howard Garis' "Rocket Riders" series and Carl H. Caudy's "Adventures in the Unknown" (both 1933–1934) first used rocketry as their books' central technological model, and the possibility of alien contact as a prime subject. After 1947, the further development of rocketry, along with reports of "flying discs" and the possibility of alien visitation provided dramatic possibilities for Tom Corbett and his brethren to come. An advertisement in *Aviation Week* in 1950 blared out the promise of the flying man in bold capital letters:

> AS YOU WATCH HIM, YOU KNOW HE IS NOT WITH YOU AT ALL. HE IS PILOTING A PLANE THROUGH WIND AND CLOUDS TO THE STARS. HE IS NO LONGER EARTH-BOUND—BUT A MAN WITH WINGS…ONCE YOU STOOD SOMEWHERE—IN A WINDOW, AT A SCHOOL DESK, ON A HILL—AND HAD THE SAME DREAM OF GLORY.[21]

Science fiction writer Robert A. Heinlein played his own role in the development of what became *Tom Corbett*. At first reluctant to take on "juvenile" stories, Heinlein was persuaded by his friend, filmmaker Fritz Lang, that writing for young readers could be more important than writing for adults—a chance to shape the attitudes of the next generation. Heinlein was advised not to write "boys' books" but, as he put it, books "that you know boys like to read."

> Nevertheless, such was my lack of confidence, that my first step was to go to a book store and buy more than a dozen books which the shopkeeper assured me were ones that were popular with the present-day kids. Most of them concerned aviation and were heavily filled with cops & robbers sort of adventure.[22]

From 1947 to 1958, Heinlein wrote 12 juvenile space adventures for Scribner's publishers that were set in a "Near Future" that was not very far removed from the present day, propelling their readers on flights to a cosmic Neverland. A recurring theme was how the challenges of space flight contributed to the young spacemen's coming of age. "Heinlein offered a vision of a future," writes Erisman, "in which the implications and advances of science, technological progress, and space travel permeated every level of society."[23] At the same time, contends Brian Aldiss in his *Trillion Year Spree*, Heinlein's vision was that of a "magic-inducing not-growing-up which marks so many SF writers."[24] First came *Rocket Ship Galileo* in 1947, which drew upon Heinlein's boyhood memories reading "Tom Swift." In the plot three boys work, guided by the scientist-uncle of one, on an atomic-powered rocket capable of flying to the Moon, where they encounter a cell of renegade Nazis bent on bombarding Earth with nuclear weapons. Its spare and swiftly paced narrative, supported by a carefully researched scientific background, was a success and quickly called for more books like it. *Galileo*, meanwhile, attracted film producer George Pal, and eventually came to the screen in 1950 in highly altered form as *Destination Moon*.[25]

Heinlein immediately moved on to *Space Cadet* (1948), wherein a youth trains for the Interplanetary Patrol: a multinational military force maintained by the United Nations to sustain world peace. Here we can see Tom Corbett's counterpart in "Matt Dodson," Roger Manning in "Girard Burke," and Astro in "Oscar," a colonial from Venus. "Arkwright," the commander of Corbett's Space Academy bears the same name as the Commodore in *Space Cadet*. And the pledge that Corbett and the Cadets take upon enrolling in the Space Academy is virtually the same as that of the Patrol Academy in *Space Cadet*: "[You are charged] to keep the peace of the System and to protect the liberties of its peoples... [and] possess a sense of honor, self-discipline... respect for the liberties and dignity of all creatures."[26] Heinlein was dubious about the role he played in *Tom Corbett*—"I don't want an air credit on that show," he said—but he did appreciate the royalty checks![27]

Meanwhile, one Joseph Lawrence Greene had already worked on a comic strip and radio script called "Space Academy" and the character of a young space man named "Tom Ranger." The character's name went through several changes before finally appearing on television as "Tom Corbett." The "Space Cadet" of the title was licensed from Heinlein.

> I met with them briefly on a Friday in the early afternoon and was introduced to Al Markim and Jan Merlin, neither of whom I knew. At four that afternoon, they phoned me at the Lambs Club with the news that the part was mine if I would do

it. The Rockhill group then decided to make their central character more of a take-charge type. The name "Cris Colby" was changed to "Tom Corbett," and two weeks later we were first televised in what became our regular time slot, 6:30–6:45 pm., Monday, Wednesday, and Friday.[28]

"MAKING US *FEEL*..."

Those first young audiences who came to Pan and Tom Corbett knew nothing, and cared probably less, of their immediate historical and cultural contexts, during moments when their respective postwar eras were undergoing rapid social and political changes: Pan's very first appearance on the British stage came just after the turn of the century when England's stiffly traditionalist Victorian culture was yielding to the revisionist spirit of the post–Boer War Edwardian era, when Britain's imperialist identity was being severely questioned.[29] Tom Corbett and the Mary Martin *Peter Pan* revivals appeared during the immediate post–World War II years, when an emerging Cold War culture challenged America's place in the newly drawn map of the world. They coincided, as Teresa Jones reports, "with an emerging cultural, social, and political rebelliousness of the American middle class in which prescribed gender roles were challenged, normative sexual identities were resisted, and high camp was appropriated by dominant culture. And all was packaged for the largest and savviest consumer group in American history: the baby boomers."[30] As a result, says Frankie Thomas, they all flew "westward—to the stars!"

What really appealed, of course, were the powerful emotional resonances of their mythic structures: the shaping "logic of emotional intensification," as Henry Jenkins puts it. The shows were "less interested in making us think than...in making us *feel*."[31] Both Corbett and Pan were infused with the joy of *release* from mundane realities and freedom from mortal constraints. "I am joy, I am youth!" exulted Pan. "Blast my rockets, Tom is invincible!" declares Thomas. Indeed, the optimism throughout *Tom Corbett* contrasted greatly with the more absurdly cartoonish antics of its contemporary rivals, *Space Patrol* (1950–1955) and *Rocky Jones* (1954), and the dour paranoia of the anthology series, *Tales of Tomorrow* (1951–1953).[32] In its positive emphasis on science and space travel and its constructive attitude toward the possibilities of peaceful engagement with extraterrestrial life, *Tom Corbett* belongs more in the company of another contemporary series, *Science Fiction Theater* (1955–1957).[33]

Tom Corbett, Space Cadet, like its rival, *Space Patrol*, ran from 1950–1955 on four networks, first CBS, then ABC and NBC and DuMont. Both shows, reported *New Yorker* correspondent Thomas Whiteside, reflected a change in the nature of standard puppet and nickelodeon entertainment offered to youthful viewers: "A new element has been added—space. Now we have a vogue for dramas dealing with interplanetary travel centuries hence—shattering episodes involving screeching rockets, crackling ray guns, and plastic-helmeted adventurers." Significantly, Whiteside noted one element in particular that attracted viewers: "On occasion, untrammeled by the force of gravity [the spacemen] gambol upside down in the heavens themselves."[34] Frankie Thomas boasts that he was television's first man in space: "True, *Captain Video* began earlier on the DuMont network in late 1949, but as it was first conceived, the Captain was *not* a spaceman. The title was descriptive: Captain Video, from his mountain hideaway, contacted agents in the field via video and his operatives, played by Johnny Mack Brown and Tom Tyler. It wasn't until several months of success in space on the part of Tom and the *Polaris* crew that Captain Video joined the space race in his rocket, the *Galaxie*."[35]

Tom Corbett premiered at 6:45 pm on CBS on October 2, 1950, when Corbett and his fellow cadets enrolled in the Space Academy, and ended on June 25, 1955, with their graduation. Their adventures are set four centuries in the future, 2350–2356, when Mars and Venus have been colonized, and the Solar Guard, founded in the twenty-second century, protects the peace of the Solar Alliance, a unified society of billions of inhabitants throughout the universe. Young Tom Corbett enters the Space Academy as a cadet in the Solar Guard, where he meets fellow cadets Astro and Roger Manning. Produced by Mort Abrahams and directed by George Gould, the "live" 15-minute programs were telecast on CBS thrice weekly, on Mondays, Wednesdays, and Fridays, at 6:45–7:00 p.m. Each episode begins with shots of the Space Academy. A rocket launches off the pad; streams of stars hurtle toward the screen.[36] Announcer Jack Beck's voiceover introduces the cadets: "2350 A.D. In roaring rockets they blast through the millions of miles from Earth

Image 2.3   Tom Corbett (Frankie Thomas Jr.), Astro (Al Markim), and Roger Manning (Jan Merlin) aboard Polaris. [Credit: Wade Williams Enterprises]

to far-flung stars and brave the dangers of cosmic frontiers, protecting the liberty of the planets, safeguarding the course of universal peace in the age of the conquest of space." Thomas played Corbett, Jan Merlin was Manning, and Al Markim was Astro. Ed Bryce was Captain Steve Strong, and Margaret Garland was Dr. Joan Dale. Jack Beck was the announcer. The writers were Albert Aley, Willie Gilbert, Stu Byrnes, and Thomas.

All the shows were telecast "live," reports Thomas. "Other shows shot their technical trickery in advance of the broadcast and integrated that footage during the broadcast. With *Space Cadet* when the red light on Camera One went on, it was sink or swim. The West Coast and other outlets beyond the reach of direct transmission were serviced by kinescopes which were no more than pictures taken of the live show as it was done."[37] *Corbett* quickly initiated a boom in advertising and related merchandising. Within the first six months, comic strips, comic books, and a host of toys, clothing, and other paraphernalia flooded the market. The first sponsor was Kellogg's cereal, and the cast members frequently delivered commercials. Typical ad slogans exploited the space themes, such as, "By Jupiter, you've got the favorite [cereals] of the whole universe." Sales skyrocketed. The wide array of Tom Corbett memorabilia, action figures, and space equipment included space helmets, decoder rings, and something called a "magnetic electroscope." Subsequent sponsors included Red Goose Shoes and Kraft Caramels ("the favorite candy of cadets at Space Academy").

In the first television episode, Captain Strong stands before the cadets and proclaims: "A hundred years ago the Solar Alliance was created. The Solar Guards were formed to ensure the liberty and freedom of all peoples. You, as space cadets, will now start training to become officers in the Solar Guards. Your responsibilities are great, men. You hold the future of the Solar Alliance in your hands. There are people to be met and understood. But remember this—you will meet them as men of peace. You'll deal with them in honor and trust. You'll fight only for freedom and for liberty." Cadet Roger Manning, the astrogator, cynically responds that it's a lot of "space gas. Only suckers will fall for that stuff about peace and freedom." Astro introduces himself as a Venusian, whose grandparents were among the first Earth colonists. He brings to the Space Academy lots of experience as a "rocketeer," or propulsion specialist. Tom Corbett (the pilot) is, by contrast to them both, quiet and serious, and inexperienced as a space man.

Standing before the *Polaris*, Astro enthuses to Corbett, whose shining face is held in tight close-up: "One day if you're ready, you'll be the master of such a ship as this. You'll walk her decks a million miles out in the void, stare out of the viewports at the majestic blackness of outer space, and you will see planets, asteroids, and worlds dead and worlds still unborn. Then, by all the satellites of Jupiter, you'll know what it means to be a spaceman!" This echoes Heinlein's descriptions of the allure of space flight in his juvenile novels: "[He stared] into this remove and solitary depth," Heinlein writes of the experience of his young hero in *Rocketship Galileo*, "vast and remote beyond human comprehension, until he was fascinated by it, drawn into it. He seemed to have left the warmth and safety of the ship and to be plunging deep into the silent blackness ahead."[38]

In succeeding episodes, a runaway rocket crashes at the spaceport. We learn that the Mercurians from the "twilight zone," or habitable region of that planet, are gathering a space fleet to threaten the Solar Alliance. Corbett and the crew of the *Polaris* rocket to Venus where they encounter the aliens. In the ensuing struggles, Corbett is kidnapped, Manning goes in search of his pal, and both find themselves tied up by the Mercurians on board their ship. Potential violence is averted when Captain Strong arrives to parlay with the chief Mercurian (Tom Poston). They agree to trust each other instead of resorting to war. "When nations start on a basis of mutual trust and honor," says Strong, "they're well on the way to permanent friendship. And that applies to people, too." Thus, the first three-week cycle of programs affirms a hope for peace, rather than the anxiety of Cold War paranoia.

Subsequent episodes included the Cadets rocketing via "hyperdrive"—a device reluctantly suggested by science advisor Willy Ley to sidestep the barriers against faster-than-the-speed-of-light travel—to Alpha Centauri, quelling a revolt on Venus, and exploring Jupiter. There were lost ships, dangerous asteroids and meteor showers, engine malfunctions, rescue missions, alien encounters, and cadet rivalries (particularly the ongoing feuds between the bragging and cynical Manning and the more idealistic Corbett and Astro). In "Asteroid of Death" (August 4, 1951) Corbett and his crew rescue an endangered space man from a comet. "Target: Danger" (October 10, 1953) features a dangerous rivalry between the troublesome Manning and a gunnery mate (Frank Sutton) during space maneuvers aboard a ship about to explode. In "Assignment: Mercury" (February 21, 1955), the cadets almost perish in the seven-hundred-degree surface heat of Mercury. In this episode Manning has been replaced by the bumbling T. J. Thistle (Jack Grimes). A particularly elaborate sequence involved a trip to an Earth-like planet hundreds of million years behind in its evolution, where dinosaurs still roamed.[39]

After 13 weeks at CBS, the show moved to ABC, where the network secured space on a two-floor area on West 57th Street that had formerly been a gymnasium. The increased space allowed the show's permanent sets to remain standing and proved to be an advantage for the special effects. Thomas began writing some of the episodes with his writing partner, Ray Morse. Soon, the show was a hit and extended to two half-hour shows on Tuesdays and Thursday. Thomas estimates that the merchandising blitz numbered 135 products bearing the Corbett name. He and the rest of the cast were kept busy making personal appearances all over the country. The audience base grew to include an impressive 25 percent of adult viewers.

This may be attributed, in large part, to the presence of Willy Ley as technical adviser. Ley had been a founding member of the German Rocket Society before leaving Germany in 1935, and had made a career as an author of popular-science books like *Rockets* (1944) and *The Conquest of Space* (1949). Realism, not unchecked fantasy, mattered. "The action is within the limits of physical possibility," insisted producer Allen Ducovny. "It has believability.... It is our policy to show the process of interplanetary travel, and the condition on the planets we travel to, as accurately as science can today."[40] "If the boys are thinking of flying through the tail of a comet, they check with Willy to make sure that it's possible to do so without serious damage to the rocket ship by stellar debris." Ley added: "The writers are always wanting their ship to *hit* something out in space. Thank God I've got them to stop hitting asteroids for awhile!"[41]

Image 2.4 Tom Corbett and his ship make a personal appearance at a Chicago parade in the early 1950s. [Credit: Wade Williams Enterprises]

Ley was even on hand to assist Thomas and other *Corbett* cast members with technical details during public appearances.[42] Thomas remembered him as "dedicated to make our stories deal with scientific possibility. He was an intimate friend of Werner Von Braun, who thought we were set too far in the future, that regular space travel was only 150 years ahead.[43] I must admit he took a dim view of the Cadets' Paralo-Ray, which froze victims into immobility with non-fatal results.[44] He isn't with us any more, but he lived to see his prediction come true. When I saw the astronauts take that giant step and walk out on the moon, their space regalia bore a remarkable resemblance to the outfits we wore on the show when operating in 'free fall' and on planetary surfaces. It was old home week."[45]

Flight

Alas, matching the dream of flight to its practice is never easy. Douglas Adams once defined flight as simply throwing oneself to the ground—*and missing*. Both Barrie and the producers of *Tom Corbett* had to resort to other methods. Although Peter Pan's first stage flights in 1904 had been convincing enough to his first stage audiences, Barrie himself was all too aware of the limitations of contemporary stagecraft. He groused at the trappings of harness and wires—not to mention the "think wonderful thoughts" device—and yearned for more effective ways to contrive the illusion. Things would significantly improve with the flying apparatus for the Mary Martin television revival in 1953. Although broadcast "live," her Pan profited greatly from the superior wire work. Indeed, in an interview with this writer, Martin admits she got so caught up in the illusion that sometimes she barely stopped herself from launching into space prematurely, *before the wires were hooked up!*[46]

As for Barrie, he astutely prophesied in 1920 that only the film medium would ultimately realize his dreams of flight. He knew that Peter's first appearance on the Darling rooftop and his teaching the children to fly in the nursery were possible only through the effects possible on film. Accordingly, his scenario for Paramount, written in December 1920, demonstrates considerable cinematic savvy. In the opening stage directions, for example, he declares:

> Vast practice and rehearsal will be needed to get the flying beautiful and really like a bird's. The flying must be far better and more elaborate than in the acted play and should cover of course a far wider expanse. [It] should show at once that the film can do things for *Peter Pan* which the ordinary stage cannot do. It should strike a note of wonder in the first picture, and whet the appetite for marvels.[47]

Later in the scenario he notes, that scenes should be "done in the manner which is so effective on the films."[48] The flying sequence with Wendy and the twins is quite extensive and described in detail: they first soar over the Thames and the Houses of Parliament, across the Atlantic (stopping for a moment on the Statue of Liberty), across America, over the Pacific and on to Never, Neverland.[49] Alas, reports Roger Lancelyn Green in his *Fifty Years of Peter Pan*, "The film was never made, but we may rest assured that he would infinitely have preferred the Walt Disney cartoon to the Paramount picture of 1924."[50]

Indeed, there is little doubt that Barrie would have been delighted with the flying effects of Disney's animated version. Appearing in theaters in 1953 when *Tom Corbett* was flying high, it rivaled—and surpassed—Barrie's prophecy. We should not assume, however, that the artist's pencil could easily create the effect of flying. To the contrary, the challenge was to convey *weightlessness*, of figures hovering in the air—something that could not be achieved, explain Disney animators Frank Thomas and Ollie Johnson in their seminal book, *Disney Animation: The Illusion of Life*, by merely drawing from real-life models.[51] "The film's introduction of Peter Pan," explains Susan Ohmer in her exhaustive production history, "exemplifies Walt Disney's belief that animation could illuminate the possibilities of Barrie's texts."[52] That memorable first flight across London by Pan, Wendy, and her brothers, accompanied by the choral rendition of "You can fly, you can fly, you can fly" lasts five minutes—seven percent of the 75-minute running time. The *Monthly Film Bulletin* greeted the results enthusiastically: "The time and care devoted to this sequence underscore the crucial role it plays in celebrating the possibilities of animation and the opportunities cartoons offer to celebrate the freedom and joy of childhood.[53]

We startled viewers of *Tom Corbett* were likewise dazzled by the rocket launches, near-encounters with comets, touch-downs on alien planets, and weightless cadets flying in space. It is of no consequence that the flying effects look crude to us today; it is enough to know that for viewers at the time—like those who could see the wires that were "flying" Peter Pan on stage—the results were nonetheless convincing. Early in its first season, innovations in "process" video effects aroused considerable attention, as reported by illustrated newspaper and magazine articles. For example, during a flight back to Earth, the *Polaris* was trapped in a violent "space storm." The automatic pilot, gyroscopic stabilizer, and gravity generator were disabled, rendering cadets weightless. The "live" telecast forced some ingenious strategies, as reported in *Newsweek*:

> To create the Tom Corbett episode in which gravity had been suspended, a dual set of the rocket-ship control room was built, the second one tipped on its side so that the room's walls and ladder were parallel to the studio floor. Photographed through a prism over the shoulder of an actor lying on a table, the scene reached home receivers right side up, with a space cadet walking on the walls.[54]

"Free fall" effects were done simply by painting the studio floor with stars and positioning the Cadets on small dollies that could be pulled away from the camera by stagehands with invisible ropes. Frankie Thomas admits that sometimes the actors could not "see" the effects until they later viewed the kinescopes. "The impossible took a little time," admits Thomas:

> Remember, this was live television. Actually, on one set was a miniature *Polaris*, a three-foot wooden rocket that was magnified. We were on another set, shot in miniature, and we were superimposed over the model shot. There was a problem here, since, with one film running on top of the other, there was a depth distortion. Our director, George Gould, and our control-room group developed the matting amplifier with which an electronic void was created in one film and the other picture was placed inside it. This technical advance, which we originated, allowed us to branch out into elaborate sequences with Tom, Captain Strong, and the boys floating around the control deck when the artificial-gravity generator would break down.... Later in the run, Dr. Joan Dale invented Hyper-Drive which allowed the *Polaris* to journey into the galaxy and we had quite a time on the planet inhabited by dinosaurs and other giant reptiles. We had great effects, and I'm proud of them.[55]

GROWING UP

Aside from Pan and the space cadets' identities as Eternal Youths, implicit in these stories is the inevitability that the rest of the characters—and us—would *grow up*. The threshold marking the transition between youth and maturity must be crossed. When Pan returns at the end of *Peter and Wendy* to find his Wendy now an adult with a child of her own, she tells him she can no longer fly: "When people grow up they forget the way."[56] And Neverland vanishes when you find yourself having to *look* for it. Likewise, the numerous actors portraying Pan, including notables such as Maude Adams, Margaret Lockwood, and Jean Arthur all grew up, only to be replaced by generations of new, younger players. Similarly, the passing years gradually brought *Tom Corbett* back to Earth. When after the third year the show parted company with Kellogg's, the show moved to the DuMont network and a new sponsor, International Shoes. The show's director and the writing team of Jack

Weinstock and Willie Gilbert went over to CBS' rival program, *Rod Brown of the Rocket Rangers* (1953–1954), which featured a young Cliff Robertson in the title role. *Tom Corbett* eventually returned to NBC in half-hour weekly adventures sponsored by Kraft. "This marked Tom's last flight," says Thomas. "But four sponsors and four networks must set some kind of record."[57] Thomas, Jan Merlin, and Al Markim had only limited acting opportunities after *Corbett*'s demise in 1955. They were quickly replaced by the casts of *Corbett*'s progeny in subsequent series such as *Men into Space* (1959–1960), *Lost in Space* (1965–1968), and *Star Trek* (1966–1969). Thomas, in particular, went on to other careers: "After the show went off the air in 1955, I put it behind me and settled into a successful career advocating, teaching, and publishing what had been a lifelong hobby, contract bridge."[58] It was only in his last years that the ageing Thomas would reunite with his buddies in public, and in character.

However, hints Barrie, perhaps we can still keep a connection, after all, tenuous though it may be, with the memory of our youth. Like the character of Wendy, we might momentarily *remember* what we have forgotten. Numerous cultural commentators in our own time consider the consequences of either forgetting or remembering our Neverlands. As Barrie's exact contemporary, G. K. Chesterton confirmed, "It's an old story, and for some a sad one, that in a sense these childish toys are more to us than they can ever be to children. We never know how much of our imaginations began with such a peep-show into paradise."[59] The importance of retaining this link is stated by another of Barrie's contemporaries, Robert Louis Stevenson: "We advance in years somewhat in the manner of an invading army in a barren land; the age that we have reached, as the phrase goes, we but hold with an outpost, and still keep open our communications with the extreme rear and first beginnings of the march. There is our true base; that is not only the beginning, but the perennial spring of our faculties…the green enchanted forest of his boyhood."[60] It is a quirky, tricky kind of balance to maintain. On the one hand, reports Henry Jenkins, "Nobody wants a world in which children never reach maturity, a kind of 'never-never land' where one can act infantile forever"; on the other, "we must be cautious that in furthering the development of our children, we do not push too hard toward the rationalization of all experience, destroying within them those qualities that make them most human: their capacity to play, to find pleasure, to be creative."[61]

WESTWARD THE STARS!

Today, still lured by the longing for the simplicity and guilelessness of childhood, we return Tom Corbett's "space man's salute" and follow Peter Pan's advice to sing "funny things to the stars." Their flights continue in the numerous revivals and sequels of *Peter Pan* in books and on stage and screen and in the many space series of recent years: *Babylon 5* (1994–1998), *Firefly* (2002–2003), *Battlestar Galactica* (2004–2009), and four sequel-series to *Star Trek*. Even the original 1950s adventures we boomers grew up with of Pan and Corbett are still with us. The original Mary Martin telecasts that had mysteriously disappeared after the 1973 broadcast have now been retrieved and restored.⁶² Likewise, the kinescopes of *Tom Corbett*, once thought lost, are now available. Thomas explains the circumstances of his own "resurrection:"

> In August 1979, I received unexpected communications from a publisher named Joe Sarno, whose *Space Academy Newsletter* was keeping the Corbett name alive. Fans were coming up with things I never knew about the show! But it was in August 1979 that I got a real jolt. A letter arrived from Wade Williams of Kansas City, who had been a dedicated Corbett fan. He posed some interesting questions about the show and I guess I replied with the magic answers. Two days later, Wade was on a plane to New York and... he went to Stanley Wolfe and bought the kinescopes of all the *Tom Corbett* shows. I've seen three hours of them, a sampling from all of the networks, and the quality is great. Those kinescopes had been used only once and then carefully packed away so they did not suffer the fate of so many of the other shows that were scrapped for the pittance of silver in them. They will soon be in re-release. Blast my rockets, Tom *is* invincible!⁶³

Williams, who had first seen the telecasts as a boy in 1951, was one of those Lost Boys who, in a benign sense, never returned:

> I was hooked. Tom Corbett was thrilling, like the boy next door riding a rocketship. Maybe that was to be my future? I wanted to be an astronomer, a space man. I was the youngest member of the Astronomy Club; I ground a telescope lens with the help of my grandfather. I entered a spacesuit contest at the local museum and made a satellite out of an old innertube. The stories were like the serials; they continued episode to episode. You had to watch them all to follow the storyline. At Macy's a line of Tom Corbett merchandise appeared—a plastic space helmet, ray guns, space suits. Kelloggs had pictures on cereal boxes. I had dreams and fantasies I was on the show. I sent a quarter and box top for a rocket flash light and green goggles. I had found my calling.⁶⁴

Williams went on to buy up all the rights to the show, and they are now in release through Englewood Films. Once again, viewers young and old have been enticed into the cosmic Neverland.

Scientists, astronauts, and fantasy and science fiction writers attest to the impact the show had on them. Writer T. E. D. Klein, for example, confirms that as a child he had been an avid fan and went on to read the eight "Tom Corbett" books that appeared from Grosset & Dunlap by the mysterious "Carey Rockwell." He too finds parallels with Peter Pan convincing: "I'd always thought of spaceships as essentially boys' clubhouses, made all the cozier by the contrast to the desolate void surrounding them"⁶⁵ (March 2, 2011). Late in life, Thomas and his Cadet buddy Jan Merlin received a special tribute from a professional astronomer, who sent them a bundle of photographs taken by the Hubble telescope of an exploding nova. Along with the photographs was a note stating that watching episodes of *Tom Corbett* as a kid had influenced the scientist's career choice. And in 2006, astronaut Stephen Robinson showed off his Tom Corbett lunch box during a space mission.⁶⁶

Image 2.5 Frankie Thomas Jr. (Tom Corbett) and Ed Kemmer (Commander Buzz Corry of Space Patrol) at a fan convention. [Credit: Wade Williams Enterprises]

In 1982, Williams produced a documentary film, *They Went to the Stars*, which reunited Tom Corbett with his former *Space Patrol* rival, Commander Buzz Corey (Ed Kemmer). Here they are, still trim, again clad in their flying togs, Corbett in his gray-and-blue uniform, and Buzz in his scarlet tunic. Maturity and hindsight provide a wistful note to their look back at the Golden Age of Rocketmen.

> "Programs then offered something that just isn't around anymore," declares Thomas, "even though today's programs are certainly more elaborately produced."
>
> "We did shows that were completely devoid of cynicism or pessimism," responds Kemmer. "People today seem suspicious of heroics."
>
> "You know, it was comforting to believe that science had all the answers. And we were seen so frequently—as many as six times a week on television, radio, the comics. People—kids particularly—began to think of us as real friends."
>
> "Real *heroic* friends!"
>
> Thomas salutes his space buddy: "Space man's luck, Commander."
>
> Kemmer returns the salute and turns to the camera, *to us*: "So long, Space Patrollers."[67]

They're flying still. Thomas recalls Tom Corbett's promise to the crew of the *Polaris* at the end of the last episode as they prepare for another flight (in words that would be echoed years later by *Star Trek's* Captain Kirk): "We're going farther than we've ever gone before!"[68] Indeed, both he and Peter Pan are continuing their journeys—to "the second star on the right, and then straight on till morning."

NOTES

1. Ray Bradbury, "Icarus Montgolfier Wright," in *A Medicine for Melancholy and Other Stories* (New York: HarperCollins, 2001), 305. The story was first published in 1955.
2. In *Peter and Wendy*, Barrie writes that "there was a commotion in the firmament" on the night Peter Pan steals away the Darling children (17). In the preface to the first and only play script of *Peter Pan*, Barrie noted the hazards of impressionable youngsters emulating Pan's admonition to fly: "After the first production I had to add something to the play at the request of parents... about no one being able to fly until the fairy dust had been blown on him; so many children having gone home and tried it from their beds and needed surgical attention" (6).
3. Mary Martin's *Peter Pan* was first telecast "live" on NBC in March 1955, at the same time that *Tom Corbett* was roaming the spaceways on the same network. Disney's *Peter Pan* was released in 1953. Playing on the big screen at the same time were those two seminal space-flight movies from 1950, Kurt Neumann's *Rocketship X-M* and George Pal's *Destination Moon*.
4. James M. Barrie, *Peter Pan*, in *The Plays of J. M. Barrie* (New York: Charles Scribner's Sons, 1929), 35.
5. Jacqueline Rose, *The Case of Peter Pan* (London: Macmillan, 1994), 4.
6. Rose, 12.
7. Rose, 18.
8. Harold Schechter, *The Bosom Serpent: Folklore and Popular Art* (Ames: University of Iowa Press, 1988), 136.
9. Harold Schechter, letter to author, March 2, 2011.
10. Corbett's space suit was "borrowed" from the film *Destination Moon* (1950).
11. Thomas Whiteside, "No Lobster Men from Neptune," *The New Yorker,* March 1, 1952, 38.
12. See the exhaustive history in Roger Lancelyn Green, *Fifty Years of Peter Pan* (London: Peter Davis, 1954).
13. "I cannot remember doing it," Barrie admitted. "I remember writing the story of *Peter and Wendy* many years after the production of the play, but I might have cribbed that from some typed copy. I can haul back to mind the writing of almost every other assay of mine... but this play of Peter, no" (4).
14. Ovid, 46.
15. Ann Yeoman, *Now or Neverland: Peter Pan and the Myth of Eternal Youth* (Toronto: Inner City Books, 1998), 62–63.
16. Chronicling Barrie's relationship with the Davies family is a long and complicated story heavily shadowed by Barrie's apparent obsession with the boys. The most complete account can be found in Andrew Birkin's classic *J. M. Barrie & the Lost Boys* (1979), which was the basis for a BBC film starring Ian Holm as Barrie. Two recent accounts—Jacqueline Rose's *The Case of Peter Pan* (1984) and Piers Dudgeon's *Neverland* (2009)—view the relationship as nothing short of a case of psychological "molestation." The most recent biography of Barrie, Lisa Chaney's *Hide-and-Seek with Angels* (2005), takes a more balanced and compassionate view. Johnny Depp's film *Finding Neverland* avoids any viewpoint on the matter whatsoever.
17. Yeoman, 81.
18. For an affectionate overview of the Stratemeyer Syndicate, see Carole Kismaric and Marvin Heiferman, *The Mysterious Case of Nancy Drew & the Hardy Boys* (New York: Simon & Schuster, 1998).

19. Fred Erisman, *Boys' Books, Boys' Dreams and the Mystique of Flight* (Fort Worth: Texas Christian University Press, 2006), xv-xvi.
20. Erisman, 295.
21. Erisman, 296–297.
22. Heinlein, quoted in William H. Patterson Jr., *Robert A. Heinlein: In Dialogue with His Century* (New York: Tor Books, 2010), 380.
23. Erisman, 283.
24. Brian Aldiss, *Trillion Year Spree* (New York: Athenaeum, 1986), 268.
25. For the background on the transition of *Rocket Ship Galileo* from novel to screen, see Patterson, 449, 463–468.
26. Robert A. Heinlein, *Space Cadet* (1948. Waterville, ME: Thorndike Press, 2002), 77.
27. Quoted in Lisa Yaszek, "Adapting Print Science Fiction for Television," in *The Essential Science Fiction Television Reader*, ed. J. P. Telotte (Lexington: University Press of Kentucky, 2008), 45.
28. Thomas, Frankie, "Westward the Stars!" *American Classic Screen*, 4.2 (Winter 1980), 49.
29. Second Star to the Right, 113.
30. In Allison B. Kavey and Lester D. Friedman, *Peter Pan in the Popular Imagination* (New Brunswick, NJ: Rutgers University Press, 2009), 245.
31. Henry Jenkins, *The Wow Climax* (New York: New York University Press, 2007), 3.
32. See John Tibbetts, "The Watchers: *Tales of Tomorrow* on Television," *Journal of the Fantastic in the Arts*, 19, no. 3 (2008), 379–398.
33. Wheeler Winston Dixon hails *Science Fiction Theater* (1955–1957) as "an attempt to break out of the mold of the space opera and produce more adult science fiction…exploring the wonders of science …." See Dixon, "Tomorrowland TV," in *The Essential Science Fiction Reader*, ed. J. P. Telotte (Lexington: University Press of Kentucky, 2008), 105–107.
34. Whiteside, 32.
35. Thomas, 48.
36. The shots of the launch of the *Polaris* were actually appropriated footage of V-2 launchings.
37. Thomas, 50. See my "The Watchers" for details on the procedures of "live" broadcasts in the early 1950s.
38. Robert A. Heinlein, *Rocket Ship Galileo* (1947. Waterville, ME: Thorndike Press, 2002), 167.
39. See Thomas Whiteside's detailed account of the planning and shooting of the dinosaur sequence.
40. Whiteside, 34.
41. Quoted in Whiteside, 34–36.
42. During Frankie Thomas's public appearances, Willy Ley would be concealed behind a partition in order to whisper in Thomas' ear the scientific answers to questions put by eager fans. "I might be okay out in space," said Thomas, "but I'd sure be lost in those quizzes without Willy. You can't bluff your way through." See Leslie Lieber, "Whispering Willy," *Milwaukee Wisconsin Journal*, June 25, 1955.
43. Patterson's authorized biography of Heinlein reports (p. 438) a rather different story. Heinlein's relationship with Wernher von Braun, who had not only formerly been a member of the Nazi Party but had been an SS officer, was decidedly cool.
44. *Newsweek* reported, in an article titled "Hi-you, Tom Corbett!" published in its April 2, 1952 issue, that Willey Ley questioned the feasibility of the Paralo-Ray gun: "Knocking victims out without killing them, the gun was adopted by scripters

to provide the Cadets with a means of self-protection. Ley considers such a weapon doubtful."
45. Thomas, 50.
46. Mary Martin, interview with author, April 8, 1988. Mary Martin began her role as Peter Pan on stage on October 20, 1954, and recreated it for "live" television on NBC on March 7, 1955. For a detailed study of the Mary Martin performances of Peter Pan, see Teresa Jones, "Peter and Me (or How I Learned to Fly)," in *Peter Pan in the Popular Imagination*, ed. Allison B. Kavey and Lester D. Friedman (New Brunswick, NJ: Rutgers University Press, 2009), 243–263.
47. Quoted in Roger Lancelyn Green, *Fifty Years of Peter Pan* (London: Peter Davis, 1954), 172.
48. Green, 215.
49. Green, 182.
50. Green, 168.
51. Frank Thomas and Ollie Johnston, *Disney Animation: The Illusion of Life* (New York: Abbeville Press, 1982), 331.
52. In Kavey and Friedman, 169.
53. Quoted in Ohmer, in Kavey and Friedman, 169.
54. "Hi-yo, Tom Corbett!" *Newsweek*, April 2, 1951, 80.
55. Thomas, 50.
56. Barrie, *Peter and Wendy*, 109.
57. Thomas, 52
58. *They Went to the Stars*. Wade Williams, director. 1982.
59. Quoted in Maisie Ward, *Gilbert Keith Chesterton* (New York: Sheed and Ward, 1943), 261.
60. Richard Holmes, *Footsteps: Adventures of a Romantic Biographer* (New York: Vintage, 1996), 47.
61. Jenkins, 184
62. "The caution with which NBC approached the miraculous rediscovery and potential rebroadcast of the original [*Peter Pan*] videotape," reports Teresa Jones, "attests to the network's initial appraisal of the production as just too outdated, in both its cultural and production values, to attract an audience. When the decision was finally made to air it again in January 1989, the timing likely proved critical in that the country was once again floating on an illusory wave of economic prosperity and conservative family values..." (Jones, 254).
63. Thomas, 52.
64. Personal communication, March 2, 2011.
65. Personal communication, March 2, 2011
66. See the website Thunder Child: http://thethunderchild.com/RadioDrama/TomCorbett/FrankieThomas.html.
67. *They Went to the Stars,* directed by Wade Williams, 1982.
68. Frankie Thomas died in 2006 and, at his request, he was buried in his Space Cadet uniform. The words to the Space Academy oath were recited over his grave. Ed Kemmer died two years earlier.

BIBLIOGRAPHY

Aldiss, Brian W. *Trillion Year Spree*. New York: Atheneum, 1986.
Barrie, James M. *Margaret Ogilvy*. London: Hodder & Stoughton, 1897.
———. *Peter and Wendy*. Bath: Robert Frederick Publishers, 2010.

———. *The Plays of J. M. Barrie*. New York: Charles Scribner's Sons, 1929.
Bradbury, Ray. "Icarus Montgolfier Wright." In *A Medicine for Melancholy and Other Stories*, 303–307. New York: HarperCollins, 2001.
Dixon, Wheeler Winston. "Tomorrowland TV." In *The Essential Science Fiction Reader*, edited by J. P. Telotte, 93–110. Lexington: University Press of Kentucky, 2008.
Dudgeon, Piers. *Neverland*. New York: Pegasus Books, 2009.
Erisman, Fred. *Boys' Books, Boys' Dreams and the Mystique of Flight*. Fort Worth: Texas Christian University Press, 2006.
Green, Roger Lancelyn. *Fifty Years of Peter Pan*. London: Peter Davis, 1954.
Heinlein, Robert A. *Rocketship Galileo*. 1947. Waterville, ME: Thorndike Press, 2002.
———. *Space Cadet*. 1948. Waterville, ME: Thorndike Press, 2002.
"Hi-yo, Tom Corbett!" *Newsweek*, April 2, 1952.
Holmes, Richard. Footsteps: Adventures of a Romantic Biographer. New York: Vintage, 1996.
Jenkins, Henry. *The Wow Climax*. New York: New York University Press, 2007.
Jones, Teresa. "Peter and Me (or How I Learned to Fly)." In *Peter Pan in the Popular Imagination*, edited by Allison B. Kavey and Lester D. Friedman, 243–263. New Brunswick, NJ: Rutgers University Press, 2009.
Kavey, Allison B., and Lester D. Friedman. *Peter Pan in the Popular Imagination*. New Brunswick, NJ: Rutgers University Press, 2009.
Kismaric, Carole, and Marvin Heiferman. *The Mysterious Case of Nancy Drew & the Hardy Boys*. New York: Simon & Schuster, 1998.
Lieber, Leslie, "Whispering Willy," *Milwaukee Wisconsin Journal*, June 25, 1955. Wade Williams Archives.
Patterson, William H. Jr. *Robert A. Heinlein: In Dialogue with His Century*. New York: Tor Books, 2010.
Rose, Jacqueline. *The Case of Peter Pan*. London: Macmillan Press, 1994.
Thomas, Frankie, "Westward the Stars!" *American Classic Screen*, 4, no. 2 (Winter 1980): 47–52.
Thomas, Frank, and Ollie Johnston. *Disney Animation: The Illusion of Life*. New York: Abbeville Press, 1982.
Tibbetts, John. "The Watchers: *Tales of Tomorrow* on Television. *Journal of the Fantastic in the Arts*, 19, no. 3 (2008): 379–398.
Ward, Maisie. *Gilbert Keith Chesterton*. New York: Sheed and Ward, 1943.
Whiteside, Thomas, "No Lobster Men from Neptune," *The New Yorker*, March 1, 1952.
Yaszek, Lisa. "Adapting Print Science Fiction for Television." In *The Essential Science Fiction Reader*, edited by J. P. Telotte, 55–68. Lexington: University Press of Kentucky, 2008.
Yeoman, Ann. *Now or Neverland: Peter Pan and the Myth of Eternal Youth*. Toronto: Inner City Books, 1998.

CHAPTER 3

Boy's Wonder: Male Teenage Assistants in 1950s Science Fiction Serials and Cold War Masculinity

Robert Jacobs

When the rocketmen of the 1950s took to the air(waves), they sought to bring as many young male audience members onboard as they could recruit. Boys were not the sole audience for the series—which, like the pulp magazines and movie serials of the 1930s and '40s had attracted girls and adults, as well—but they remained its most numerous and most dedicated fans. Science fiction, in print or on television, was still perceived as a form of "boys' adventure," and to succeed the series' producers had to win the hearts and minds of preteen boys. Where the rocketmen went, so—nearly always—went their young male sidekicks. Flash Gordon had no protégé to follow him into battle against Emperor Ming, and Tom Corbett had to seek adult guidance by radio, but Captain Video had Video Ranger, Captain Z-Ro had Jet, and Rocky Jones had both teenaged Winky and preteen "junior lieutenant" Bobby to follow them on their adventures in time and space.[1] These cadets and junior space men were part of a tradition of boy-heroes begun by Mark Twain's Tom Sawyer and Robert Louis Stevenson's Jim Hawkins in the nineteenth century and commodified in the Tom Swift, Hardy Boys, and Air Scouts series in the early twentieth. More specifically, they were a made-for-television version of the teen sidekicks in the comic books and movie serials of the 1940s. Like Robin the Boy Wonder or Captain America's young friend Bucky Barnes, they provided a character for young viewers to identify with—someone more human-scaled than the seemingly flawless hero. They also created a space in the narrative where viewers could insert themselves into the adventure.

The cadets, rangers, and junior space men of the rocketman series appeared in a variety of roles: some as fully formed younger versions of the heroes; others as heroes-in-training, slowly being groomed for leadership in various space organizations; still others too young and boyish to do more than dream of exploring the universe on their own. Regardless of their roles in the fictional narratives, however, all played a similar educational role. The young sidekicks, reaching toward adulthood in their fictional futures, acted as models of adult masculinity for the boys watching the shows. At the same time, their relationships with the adult rocketmen functioned as a form of male mentorship, and led young fans along the road toward the idealized masculinity their superiors embodied.

While the series typically featured simple morality tales that functioned as a means of passing on Cold War values and ethics in a futuristic framework, the masculinity modeled by their characters was complex. Drawing on a range of distinctly *American* male archetypes, these role models conveyed values—and sometimes, conflicting—traits of conformity and independence, stability and risk-taking, intellect and instinct. Rocketmen such as Captain Video, Rocky Jones, Tom Corbett, and others embodied patriotism, virtue, and order—father figures, political-military leaders, and Scout leaders, all rolled into one—and served as the ultimate Cold War heroes. Their crews, however, typically made up of adolescent males, while destined to become leaders themselves, "tried on" various strategies for success—innovating, trusting instincts and emotions over orders and protocol, and questioning authority—allowing audience members to experience the consequences and rewards, in the security of their own living rooms. Together, rocketmen and their sidekicks tutored their audiences in what it meant to be an American male, whether military officer, frontier innovator, intellectual gatekeeper, or corporate leader.

In this chapter, I examine the ways in which rocketmen and their adolescent protégés not only served to model valued archetypes of masculinity and guide their young male audience members along the path to adulthood, but also functioned to facilitate the introduction of a new model of male heroism—the disciplined, corporate Cold War hero—as he rose to prominence over earlier exemplars of heroism: the rugged and independent Western pioneer and the daring World War II fighting ace.

Masculinity on the Frontier:
Individualism and Ingenuity

These archetypes of masculinity and heroism are deeply rooted in American culture, and one of their most colorful and enduring contexts was the American West. From the early days of westward expansion through the Golden Age of the Cowboy, the frontier provided challenges that helped shape notions of rugged American individualism and ingenuity.

Initially, it was tales of heroic "pioneers"—men who expanded the borders of the new nation ever westward and engaged in a constant struggle with "savages" to establish order in the wilderness—that set the stage for sagas of moral triumph. "As every child learned in school, our history was an inclusive saga of expanding liberties and rights that started in a vast, fertile, nearly empty land," writes Tom Engelhardt.[2] Those sagas of expansion nearly always included "sanguinary tale[s] of warfare against savage, lesser peoples" in order to expand "the boundaries of that space within which freedom might 'ring.'"[3] This was the model of American expansion and triumphalism that was, in a sense, assumed to be the birthright of all American children, and the archetype of masculinity it conveyed was one of a capable and fair pioneer who innovated and conquered in order to establish civilization and cultivate prosperity.

As engagement with the West expanded and deepened, so too, did tales of its heroic figures: in the form of cowboys, rough riders, cavalrymen, and lawmen. The classic Western emphasized the establishment of law and order, and presented an essential and ritualistic conflict between civilization and savagery. The boundaries that existed between the two were clearly marked off for all to see, and displayed in characters' dress, speech, and morals. Heroic figures of the classic Western frequently found themselves balancing their allegiance to the spirit of the West (as M. Elise Marubbio points out), and their moral commitment to promote "civilization," maintaining a "tenuous existence on the edge of both."[4] Half wild themselves, masculine heroes of the West were nonetheless charged with taming the wilderness, so that it might be drawn into the civilized scope. Ultimately though, these champions of national fairy tales were just and fair men, pushing back against the tide of disorder to unfurl clean and prosperous towns, as if unrolling a carpet of progress across the chaotic forests and teepees that retreated before them.[5]

The independent spirit of the pioneer could still be found among the rocketmen, despite the strong pull of the Cold War military-industrial organization. Here, however, the qualities of the Western hero were most frequently found in the rocketmen's teenage sidekicks, who, armed with the natural inquisitiveness of healthy young American boys, skirted regulations, bent rules, innovated, and sometimes, defied orders, to save the day and carve out a place for themselves in the adult world.

One such hero-in-the-making is Bobby (Robert Lyden), the eager young rocketman-in-training featured in *Rocky Jones, Space Ranger* (1954). A "junior lieutenant," Bobby is clearly destined to become a great leader like his hero Rocky (Richard Crane), but unlike his highly disciplined mentor, Bobby often strays from the straight and narrow in the name of initiative. In the episode "Silver Needle in the Sky," Rocky and his crew are held captive by his nemesis, the evil femme fatale Cleolanta (Patsy Parsons), leader of the planet Ophiuchus.[6] When their air supply is cut off, Bobby climbs through the ventilation system in order to save his crewmates. Unable to open the hatch that leads to the controls, Bobby takes literally the crew's advice to "use his head." In a moment of inspiration, his eyes light up and he begins to bang his head on the door, eventually opening it. He proceeds to pick the lock of the cell door to free his companions and save the mission. Upon the crew's return to Earth, a grateful commander presents "special citations for the crew of the *Orbit Jet*, and that includes Bobby!" While protocols and procedures are highly valued in the military world, the young cadet's pioneering spirit and natural adolescent impulsiveness proved to be his path to success as a rocketman.

Image 3.1   Bobby (Robert Lyden) rescues his crew mates and saves the day in *Rocky Jones, Space Ranger*.

Similarly, in *Captain Z-Ro* (1954–1960), Jet (Bruce Haynes), the young assistant to the title character (Roy Steffens), often follows his instincts, rather than his orders. Within a framework for adulthood where compliance is coded as "maturity," Jet's character is also "young," both chronologically and socially. Not only does he lack the scientific and historical knowledge that the Captain's missions are intended to impart, he also lacks the conformity and discipline to keep himself out of trouble. His adolescent curiosity and empathy often complicate the Captain's missions as they visit historical moments and characters, but also guide the junior rocketman to important lessons about history, humanity, and "growing up"—and as with his counterpart, Bobby, they sometimes save the day. In the episode "Leonardo daVinci," for example, the Captain's time-traveling rocket ship, the ZX-99, visits daVinci's (Sydney Walker) studio, to teach Jet and the viewers at home about the origins of human flight. When Jet sneaks off to fulfill his ambition to be the first man to fly using daVinci's ornithopter, his youthful curiosity puts his life in jeopardy, but his empathy for the despondent daVinci (who believes that *all* his inventions are failures and his life's work has all been for naught) leads to the artist/inventor's renewed inspiration.

As with Bobby, Jet's abilities to function as a rocketman are continually put to the test. The degree to which either can be entrusted with adult duties in his respective crew is often a source of tension. Bobby must repeatedly claim and earn his place on Rocky's ship, while Jet often lapses into the role of passive apprentice. Nonetheless, it is their curiosity, innovation, and disobedience that help to establish their roles in these tales of time and space. Their success as a junior rocketmen does not derive from ready obedience and submission to superior males, but from their shared ingenuity and impulse to explore – to stray outside of traditional boundaries and occasionally break rules—that is their contribution and path to heroism. Just as in tales of the Old West, however, that success is only affirmed through their ultimate willingness to conform.

WORLD WAR II MASCULINITY: HEROES OF THE WORKING CLASS

The lone cowboy persisted as a symbol of American masculinity into the 1940s and beyond, but World War II, the event that defined the men of what came to be known as the "Greatest Generation," was not a loner's war. The cowboy ethos of independence and improvisation flourished among fighter pilots and submariners, and among the agents of "Wild Bill" Donovan's covert Office of Strategic Services, but in the rank and file of the wartime armed forces a new, group-centered model of masculinity emerged. Particularly in the infantry units that bore the brunt of the fighting, the wartime army was composed largely of men in their teens and early twenties who—volunteer and draftee alike—were new to soldiering, much less to combat. Units raised by an identifiable individual, or drawn from a particular city or state, were a thing of the past by 1941. The scope of the conflict was too vast, and its demand for manpower too great. Virtually every unit was a mélange of soldiers from different states, different ethnic backgrounds, and different peacetime occupations, led by senior officers the men rarely saw and barely knew.[7] Cast into a sea of strangers, GIs reached out to those closest to them for support and reassurance: men of the same barracks, or the same squad. The career soldiers who supervised their training encouraged such bonds, knowing that—in combat—men fought and died not for their country or the ideals it represented but for the buddies on either side of them.

Wartime culture, and Hollywood in particular, celebrated these bonds and the tightly knit small units they produced. The welding of a disparate collection of individuals—rich and poor, white and colored, native and immigrant, urban and rural—into a tough, effective combat unit is, as Jeanine Basinger has argued, the *ur*-narrative of the American World War II combat film.[8] Films made during the war, like the archetypal *Bataan!* and *Air Force* (both 1943), typically took the bonding process for granted or attributed it to the inclusive, democratic spirit that naturally motivated all Americans. Beginning in the last year of hostilities, however, memoirs like Bill Mauldin's *Up Front* (1945), novels such as Norman Mailer's *The Naked and the Dead* (1948), and "realistic" combat films like *Battleground* (1949) began to reveal—for those who had not experienced it firsthand—the dynamics of the bonding process and the nature of wartime masculinity.

Bonds among the members of a small military unit were, such works revealed, sustained by unspoken memories of shared experiences (Mauldin referred to "The Benevolent and Protective Brotherhood of Them What Has Been Shot At"), mutual kidding, and endless discussions of shared interests (sex, sports, home) and shared grievances (wet clothes, bad food, incompetent officers).[9] Eloquent griping about "chickenshit"—petty annoyances created by the army's obsession with form over function—and wistful discussions of women filled the long, boring hours between actions.[10] When action came, however, their place was taken by a different form of bond: a fierce, almost obsessive desire *not* to fail in one's job—not to prove incompetent or, worse, cowardly—and thus let the unit, and one's buddies, down.[11] Willie and Joe, the infantry privates who served as everyman figures in Mauldin's wartime cartoons (collected in *Up Front*), exemplified the distinctive blend of qualities. They wielded their rifles and grenades against the hated enemy, and their deadpan, cynical wit against the detached leadership of their own ranks. "Able Fox Five to Able Fox," Willie radios to an artillery battery in one panel, crouching beside Joe in a foxhole over which an immense German tank has just parked, "I got a target for ya, but ya gotta be patient."[12]

This hardscrabble working-class archetype of American manhood also blasted off to explore space in the 1950s. Viewers needed only look as far as the crew of the *Orbit Jet* in *Rocky Jones, Space Ranger* (1954) to find classic World War II masculinity flexing its muscles. Despite his narrative status as a Cold War space hero, Jones was a feisty reminder of wartime heroes of an earlier age. Although his dialogue throughout the series' episodes carries mandates for peace, tolerance, and free will, his instincts are those of a fighter, rather than a diplomat. In chapter 1 of "Beyond the Curtain of Space," the *Orbit Jet* is assigned a new crewmember—its first *female* crewmember—Vena Ray (Sally Mansfield). The presence of a woman on board troubles Jones, in much the same way the presence of women in the military was problematic in the audiences' real world. He resists her attempts to prove her worth as a navigator, suggesting instead that she knit him a sweater, and asking if her sightings are confirmed or "women's intuition." He confides in his first officer, Winky (Scotty Beckett): "You know, I've never questioned an order from Drake before, but I just can't see where it helps having a girl aboard on a dangerous mission like this." When Winky reminds him that Vena speaks the Ophiuchian's language, a skill necessary to the success of their mission, Jones retorts, "I'd rather have an extra pair of fists. Anybody understands *that* language." Later, when a mysterious vessel menaces the *Orbit Jet* in the midst of a rescue mission, Jones again demonstrates his willingness to scuffle; he deviates from his assignment to meet the challenge, proclaiming to Winky, "All right—we'll make a fight of it!"[13]

Wry and cynical, navigator Winky is even more reminiscent of Mauldin's wartime working stiffs, and his role as the series' "comic relief" makes him unique among rocketmen. An able first officer, Winky is, nonetheless, as ready with a wisecrack as his captain is with his fists. His capabilities are often masked by his carefree attitude: He is the first to lobby for vacation, indulging in fantasies of beaches and beautiful women, and generally responds to orders with a wry aside. He boldly offers his opinion to subordinates and superiors alike, in dialogue full of color and slang, more closely resembling a hip teen than a disciplined space ranger. He is a foot soldier, not a leader, but he is also a mentor. While rocketman Jones inspires their young protégé Bobby's sense of duty and ability, it is Winky who serves as the inspiration for the boy's confident ingenuity, modeling adaptation and independence, even as he embodies steadfast devotion to Jones, the *Orbit Jet*, the Space Rangers, and an Earth only subtly coded as postwar America.

COLD WAR HEROES: ORDER AND DISCIPLINE

Little more than half a century after the symbolic 1893 "closing" of the Western frontier, and less than half a decade after its triumph in World War II, the United States found itself at the very center of world affairs. Managing a burgeoning nuclear-arms race with the Soviet Union, carrying on a global ideological struggle, and maintaining a global military empire required different skills than those necessary to conquer a frontier or win a shooting war. Stern-faced managers replaced wildcatting innovators, and centrally planned strategies pushed aside sparks of ingenuity. The Cold War was to be won by the disciplined actions of tightly integrated hierarchies in which every member played his assigned part, did his job as directed, and unquestioningly accepted the wisdom of those in authority over him. The job was too big, and the stakes too high, to allow individuals to improvise.

Cold War masculinity thus departed from that exemplified by the pioneer and the World War II soldier. The title figures in Sloan Wilson's novel *The Man in the Gray Flannel Suit* (1955) and William Whyte's sociological treatise *The Organization Man* (1956) are rewarded for projecting the values and ideals of their companies rather than any distinctive personality of their own. Conversely, in Herman Wouk's bestselling novel *The Caine Mutiny* (1952), the naval-officer "heroes" are savagely denounced by their own attorney for failing to "support" an incompetent, mentally unstable captain whose actions endanger their ship. Hollywood's best-known films of the period—from *On the Waterfront* (1954) and *From Here to Eternity* (1953) to *High Noon* (1952) and *The Thing from Another World* (1951)—dramatize the need for collective solidarity and the dangers of straying from the group.[14]

Simply immersing oneself in *a* group was not sufficient, however. Being an American man of the Cold War meant pledging allegiance to groups that promoted American ideals, and outright rejection of those who neglected or undermined them. New patriotic organizations, such as the National Conference on Citizenship and the All-American Conference to Combat Communism, proliferated, drawing their members from those eager to establish, and be *seen* establishing, their credentials as right-thinking Americans. The newly formed groups joined with existing ones such as the American Legion and the Daughters of the American Revolution to model right-thinking thought and behavior through pageants and speeches, and educational programs.[15]

The boy heroes of the rocketman series served, for young fans, as models of the new Cold War masculinity. Winky, Jet, and the rest follow orders far more often than they break them, and rarely think beyond the orders they are given. They are invariably respectful of their rocketman mentors—that is, their superior officers—and to the more senior officers who assign them to their missions. They also express complete, unquestioning acceptance of the values embodied and promoted by the organizations they serve. Their role in the narrative is to learn how to become men by internalizing the values of the group, rather than thinking for themselves about whether those values are legitimate or worth defending.

This modeling was particularly striking in the case of Captain Video (Al Hodge), whose battles against interplanetary villains were also aided by a teenaged assistant

Image 3.2   Video Ranger (Don Hastings), as usual, takes a back seat to Captain Video (Al Hodge).

(Don Hastings), known only as Video Ranger. Members of the Captain's secret organization, whose ranks young viewers were invited to join, were also known as Video Rangers, and the young aide thus stood for all of them. His lack of a distinct personality and his use of a title in lieu of a name made it easy for viewers to project themselves into his place and so into the story. It also, however, made him an idealized vision of Cold War masculinity: defined—even in name—by the organization he serves and inseparable from it. Video Ranger himself exhibits very little individuality, never questions orders or thinks for himself, and unlike Jet in *Captain Z-Ro*, does not even play a role in advancing the narrative. He is simply one more worker bee for democracy, piloting the rocket ship and ferrying people around as the plot demands, while Captain Video fights a series of interplanetary villains. Viewers who wished to join the Video Rangers could bind themselves to the organization by purchasing Captain Video merchandise, or signing pledges that declared their support for its aims.

Those aims, expressed in brief "Video Ranger Messages" in which the Captain addressed the audience directly, mirrored those of Cold War America. Young viewers were encouraged to practice racial tolerance, to be wary of "those who would destroy our American heritage of freedom of thought and action, who would tear down our ideals, trample underfoot our flag," and (mirroring a phrase in constant use in civil-defense literature at the time) to "be alert and know that freedom is our job, Video Rangers."[16] Another message urged Video Rangers watching at home to sign the "Freedom Scroll," and so declare their belief "in the sacredness and dignity of the individual," their willingness to "resist aggression and tyranny wherever they appear on Earth," and their support for "the millions of people around the world who hold the cause of freedom sacred."[17] The Freedom Scroll itself—not just the ideas it contained—belonged to the real world of the viewers, not the fictional world of Captain Video. It was an actual political totem of the early Cold War, part of a "Crusade for Freedom" spearheaded by retired generals Mark Clark and Dwight Eisenhower, and designed to express American solidarity with the peoples of Soviet-controlled Eastern Europe.[18]

The fictional villains Captain Video battled on screen likewise blurred the line between fantasy and reality. They dressed as ethnic enemies of America or as mythological figures, and despised the values of freedom, self-determination, and democracy that the Captain (and all the Video Rangers, on screen and at home) had sworn to uphold. The goals of Captain Video's enemies were those of Cold War America's enemies: to rule despotically, oppress their people, and exploit the labor of the masses for personal power and wealth. Enlisting in the struggle against such evildoers, the Captain reassured viewers, was as easy as it was vital. The would-be Video Ranger needed only to acquire the organization's symbol—the Captain Video Picture Ring, worn "to show that you're fighting alongside Captain Video in his battle as guardian of the safety of the world"—adopt its creed, and, like Video Ranger himself, look to its leaders for guidance and orders.

BECOMING COLD WAR HEROES

These space rangers, waiting patiently for orders from a distant superior to flash across the airwaves, are light years removed from the frontiersman who rode out alone into the West, confident of his ability to improvise a solution to any challenge he met. Both, however, are emblematic of their times: the pioneers of the mid-nineteenth century moved westward in order to spread American values and ideals across what they saw as a savage, empty continent; the GIs of the mid-twentieth century shipped out for the jungles of the South Pacific and the beaches of Normandy to bring them to a world in the grip of tyranny; and the Americans of the emerging Space Age stood ready, by the mid-1950s, to extend those same values and ideals to the Moon, Mars, and the universe beyond. As the country's ambitions to expand its influence extended farther and farther from home, the demands placed on American men—and so, the idealized image of American masculinity—adapted and changed with them.

The actual traits most highly prized in American men—bravery, loyalty, integrity, resourcefulness—changed little across those eras, but their close entanglement with constructions of national identity and political economy led to ongoing shifts in the ways in which they were expressed, emphasized, and encouraged. Celebration of the individual, and of the uniqueness and rugged independence they marshaled in the face of adversity, gradually gave way to valorization of the "company man" whose skills and talents seamlessly meshed with the functioning of an organization, and supported a mission far greater than the sum of its parts. Risk-taking and ingenuity began to fade from glory, appearing careless and immature when compared to efforts carried out with precision and discipline. The blue-collar, roll-up-your-sleeves, feisty laborer who took pride in a nation built with his sweat was displaced in the public eye by the educated executive who manipulated numbers and ideas, and the spit-and-string endeavors that were once the hallmark of American innovation were threatened with extinction in the face of complex, multilayered project funding.

The displacement of the blue-collar maker of things by the white-collar shaper of ideas extended even to the battlefield. American men still made war on the enemies of freedom—and were glorified for doing so—but the terms of the conflict were changing. The enemy grew more distant, and the battle less personal. Frontier heroes like Kit Carson and Wyatt Earp had looked their opponents in the eye as they fought, and subdued the wilderness with bare hands and simple tools. The fighting men of World War II, even when they rode to battle in B-17 bombers or Sherman tanks, still placed their bodies in harm's way and pitted their physical skills—strength, quickness, and endurance—against those of the enemy. World War II was ended, however, by men who fought with their minds rather than their muscles, and who slew the enemy with cool dispassion rather than hot-blooded fury. America's triumph in the "long, twilight struggle" of the Cold War depended on scientists like Edward Teller and engineers like Wernher von Braun, strategists like Herman Kahn and spymasters like Allen Dulles: a new breed of "warriors" wielding balance sheets and slide rules, capable of outthinking the most devious of opponents.

So, we have the rocketmen—Captain Video, Tom Corbett, Buzz Corry, Captain Z-Ro, and Rocky Jones—and their crews of cadets, rangers, and junior space men, blazing trails across time and space, and paving the way for Cold War masculinity to join models of American manhood already embraced by their audiences. They were, man and boy alike, embodiments of Americans' idealized visions of themselves: strong, smart, and noble, brave in the face of danger, stalwart in the face of the enemy, and resourceful in the face of unexpected challenges. They enjoyed near-total freedom of movement and action, yet they wore the uniform, embraced the principles, and did the bidding of vast, hierarchical organizations. They spoke for all of Earth, the "Solar Guard" or the "United Planets," but they did so in a distinctive American voice, and swore to uphold recognizably American values. Their presence in space, and on distant worlds, assured viewers that the 20th would be far from the last American Century.

The rocketmen and their followers were—in their intense identification with and commitment to the organizations they served—exemplars of the new masculinity of the Cold War era. The unquestioning loyalty and infinite willingness to take direction exhibited by Captain Video's nameless sidekick, Video Ranger, would have served him well as a junior executive or newly minted second

Image 3.3 Captain Z-Ro (Roy Steffens), master of advanced technology, educates his assistant, Jet (Bruce Haynes), about a new invention.

lieutenant. Captain Z-Ro—scientist, inventor, expert on history and politics— would have fit in easily with Teller at Los Alamos, von Braun at the Redstone Arsenal, or Kahn at the Rand Corporation. On the shows, as in the real world, however, older models of masculinity also persisted, slightly deprecated by their association with less-mature sidekick characters, but still revered and acknowledged as valuable. Rocky Jones could have stepped off the bridge of a World War II destroyer, or led one of George Patton's tank battalions across France, and his navigator Winky mingled the cool competence of a Cold Warrior with the cocky self-assurance of a fighter pilot. Even the frontier spirit of independence and improvisation had its moment in the sun, albeit represented by the youngest and flightiest of the sidekicks: Jet of *Captain Z-Ro* and "junior lieutenant" Bobby of *Rocky Jones: Space Ranger*.

This diversity of role models assured viewers that, in the face of rapid social change, familiar characters and ways of being would not simply be discarded. Although ideas about masculinity were undergoing a significant sea change, rocketmen and their crews demonstrated that all could exist simultaneously in a new Atomic Age America. In fact, the Cold War hero could not succeed without the heroic archetypes of earlier eras—the risk-takers, the rule-breakers, the feisty warriors who talk with their fists—as counterparts that freed him to keep pace with social change. Thus, the universe of the rocketmen included and celebrated a range of masculinities—from adventurer to wildcat, and foot soldier to intellectual— confirming all as valuable and necessary, even as they reinforced the notion that the new Cold War hero was first among equals.

Notes

1. All quotes are from the DVD version of the series. *Classic Sci-Fi TV* (Golden Valley, MN: Mill Creek Entertainment, 2009).
2. Tom Engelhardt, *The End of Victory Culture: Cold War America and the Disillusioning of a Generation* (New York: Basic Books, 1995): 4.
3. Ibid.
4. M. Elise Marrubio, *Killing the Indian Maiden: Images of Native American Women on Film* (Lexington: University Press of Kentucky, 2006), 113.
5. Richard Slotkin, *Gunfighter Nation: The Myth of the Frontier in Twentieth-Century America* (1992. Norman: University of Oklahoma Press, 1998), 10–13.
6. *Rocky Jones, Space Ranger*, "Silver Needle in the Sky."
7. Stephen C. Ambrose, *Citizen Soldiers: The U. S. Army from the Normandy Beaches to the Bulge to the Surrender of Germany* (New York: Simon and Schuster, 1997), 273–277.
8. Jeanine C. Basinger *The World War II Combat Film: Anatomy of a Genre* (Middletown, CT: Wesleyan University Press, 2003), 46–58.
9. Bill Mauldin, *Up Front* (New York: Henry Holt, 1945), 55–63, 100 [quotation].
10. Paul Fussell, *Wartime: Understanding and Behavior in the Second World War* (New York: Oxford University Press, 1989), 79–115.
11. On the psychology of infantry combat, see S. L. A. Marshall, *Men against Fire: The Problem of Battle Command* (1947. Norman: University of Oklahoma Press, 2000). Notable first-person narratives include: William Manchester, *Goodbye Darkness: A Memoir of the Pacific War* (Boston: Little, Brown, 1980); E. B. Sledge, *With the Old Breed at Peleliu and Okinawa* (Novato, CA: Presidio Press, 1981; and Paul Fussell, *The Boys' Crusade: The American Infantry in Northwest Europe, 1944–1945* (New York: Modern Library, 2003).
12. Mauldin, 10.
13. *Classic Sci-Fi TV*, DVD collection, Mill Creek Entertainment, 2009. Unless otherwise noted, all television programs referred to are from this collection.
14. Peter Biskind, *Seeing Is Believing: How Hollywood Taught Us to Stop Worrying and Love the Fifties* (New York: Pantheon, 1983).
15. Richard Fried, *The Russians Are Coming! The Russians Are Coming!: Pageantry and Patriotism in Cold-War America* (New York: Oxford University Press, 1998), 11–28.
16. *Captain Video and His Video Rangers*, "Captain Video Prepares to Visit Regus," originally aired 1949 (specific date unknown).
17. *Captain Video and His Video Rangers*, "Code of Honor," originally aired June 1950. For the text of the pledge taken by viewers of *Tom Corbett, Space Cadet* and the Junior Rocket Rangers, see J. Fred McDonald, *Television and the Red Menace: The Video Road to Vietnam* (New York: Praeger, 1985), 124–125.
18. Jonathan Herzog, *The Spiritual-Industrial Complex: America's Religious Battle Against Communism in the Early Cold War* (New York: Oxford University Press, 2011), 153–154.

Bibliography

Ambrose, Stephen C. *Citizen Soldiers: The U. S. Army from the Normandy Beaches to the Bulge to the Surrender of Germany*. New York: Simon and Schuster, 1997.

Basinger, Jeanine C. *The World War II Combat Film: Anatomy of a Genre*. Middletown, CT: Wesleyan University Press, 2003.

Biskind, Peter. *Seeing is Believing: How Hollywood Taught Us to Stop Worrying and Love the Fifties.* New York: Pantheon, 1983.
Classic Sci-Fi TV. Golden Valley, MN: Mill Creek Entertainment, 2009.
Engelhardt, Tom. *The End of Victory Culture: Cold War America and the Disillusioning of a Generation.* New York: Basic Books, 1995.
Fried, Richard. *The Russians Are Coming! The Russians Are Coming!: Pageantry and Patriotism in Cold-War America.* New York: Oxford University Press, 1998.
Fussell, Paul. *The Boys' Crusade: The American Infantry in Northwest Europe, 1944–1945.* New York: Modern Library, 2003.
———. *Wartime: Understanding and Behavior in the Second World War.* New York: Oxford University Press, 1989.
Herzog, Jonathan. *The Spiritual-Industrial Complex: America's Religious Battle against Communism in the Early Cold War.* New York: Oxford University Press, 2011.
Manchester, William. *Goodbye Darkness: A Memoir of the Pacific War.* Boston: Little, Brown, 1980.
Marrubio, M. Elise. *Killing the Indian Maiden: Images of Native American Women on Film.* Lexington: University Press of Kentucky, 2006.
Marshall, S. L. A. *Men Against Fire: The Problem of Battle Command.* 1947. Norman: University of Oklahoma Press, 2000.
Mauldin, Bill. *Up Front.* New York: Henry Holt, 1945.
McDonald, J. Fred. *Television and the Red Menace: The Video Road to Vietnam.* New York: Praeger, 1985.
Sledge, E. B. *With the Old Breed at Peleliu and Okinawa.* Novato, CA: Presidio Press, 1981.
Slotkin, Richard. *Gunfighter Nation: The Myth of the Frontier in Twentieth-Century America.* 1992. Norman: University of Oklahoma Press, 1998.

CHAPTER 4

GIRLS AND "SPACE FEVER"
AMY FOSTER

According to historian Brian Horrigan, as televisions were entering the American (white, middle-class) home in the 1950s, popular media began to portray the race for space as the "Promethean struggle for survival."[1] With the appearance of science fiction television series, young American boys embraced the vision of a future in space. Since the 1930s, when science fiction movie serials such as *Flash Gordon* (1936, 1938, 1940) and *Buck Rogers* (1939) were springing up and growing in popularity, boys served as the primary audience for juvenile science fiction. But what about young American *girls*?

Girls were also reading and watching science fiction, including such television shows as *Commando Cody* and *Rocky Jones, Space Ranger*. What influence did these television shows from the Golden Age of Science Fiction have on the young female audience? Despite a growing body of literature on the relationship between sex, gender, and science fiction books and magazines, this chapter breaks from that scholarship to examine the specific relationship between gender and the science fiction shows on television in the 1950s and early 1960s. These shows helped to challenge the prevailing social attitudes about women, their place in space, and their role in fighting the Cold War.

By looking at how women are represented (as females, as scientists, and as partners), in science fiction television of the 1950s and early 1960s, and specifically in shows made for children, this chapter explores how these shows used Cold War rhetoric to encourage patriotism in its young viewers. By placing the series in the larger historical context of national trends in education, it also argues that these shows served as a conduit for shaping American girls' attitudes about their place in society and their potential careers in science and engineering, particularly in the post-Sputnik era when Americans reevaluated their strength as a global power in science and technology.

THE POWER OF WOMEN "IN SPACE"

Science fiction serials had their heyday in the 1950s, with a number of them targeting juvenile audiences. *Tom Corbett, Space Cadet* premiered in 1950, followed by *Flash Gordon* and *Rocky Jones, Space Ranger* (1954), *Commando Cody* (1955), *Clutch*

Cargo (1959), and *Space Angel* (1962). These serials follow a similar storyline to the one we see in the juvenile science fiction novels and comic strips, such as *Buck Rogers in the 25*th *Century*, which had its own television incarnation between April 1950 and January 1951. The protagonist is always male, and any female roles are supporting cast. Tom Corbett (Frankie Thomas) is a young man training with his team at Space Academy USA. As a team, they often travel in their ship, *Polaris*, to far-off places, such as Alpha Centauri. Commando Cody (Judd Holdren), who first appeared in the serial *Radar Men from the Moon* in 1951, is a scientist and "military man" tasked with traveling to the Moon in a new rocket to end the mysterious attacks on oil fields. Rocky Jones (Richard Crane) fights for the United Worlds of the Solar System and has sworn to protect the planet. Clutch Cargo, a character in one of the few animated series, along with his prepubescent sidekick, Spinner, experience adventures around the world, including one episode in which they accept the challenge to fly the new American rocket to the Moon as part of a space race. Scott McCloud, the Space Angel, works for the Earth Bureau of Investigation and travels with his sidekicks Crystal Mace and Taurus, an out-of-shape, but rough-and-tumble engineer.[2] Flash Gordon (Steve Holland), one of the most well known of the Golden Age space heroes and who, like Buck Rogers, also made the transition from comic strip to TV, is an agent for the Galaxy Bureau of Investigation, who travels aboard the *Sky Flash* with his teammates, Dale Arden (Irene Champlin) and Dr. Zarkov (Joseph Nash), in protection of the Milky Way.

Even though all the leading characters were male, we consistently see female characters in these shows. Crystal Mace and Dale Arden serve alongside the Space Angel and Flash Gordon, respectively, as active and respected members of the team. Mace serves as the team's electronics and communications expert (perhaps an inspiration for *Star Trek*'s Lt. Uhura). Arden, although she is Flash's girlfriend, is often seen flying the *Sky Flash*, facing potential death bravely, and even getting into physical fights with the enemy, climbing on the back of one in episode 5, "Akim the Terrible," subduing him with a stun gun, then joining with Flash in breaking Akim's mind-control device.

Mace and Arden are particularly strong female characters, but often the female characters play roles consistent with 1950s' American ideals about the role of women in society. In *Radar Men from the Moon*, the television serial that introduced Commando Cody (George Wallace) to national audiences in 1952, Joan Gilbert (Aline Towne) joins Commando Cody, his lab partner, Ted Richards (William Bakewell), and his pilot, Hank (Wilson Wood), on their mission to the Moon to stop Retik (Roy Barcroft), the leader of an advanced lunar civilization, from invading the Earth. Before their departure, Cody laments, "I still think that this is no trip for a woman." Gilbert replies, "Now don't start that again. You'll be very glad to have someone along who can cook your meals."[3] In episode 3, "Bridge of Terror," Joan sits and drinks coffee with the men as they discuss what Cody and Ted had discovered about Retik's plan to attack Earth. Once the decision is made to return to Earth with their information, Joan stoically tidies up the dishes.[4]

Similarly, in the premiere episode of *Rocky Jones, Space Ranger*, Jones' future girlfriend Vena Ray (Sally Mansfield) joins Rocky and his navigator Winky (Scotty Beckett) under orders from Secretary Drake (Charles Meredith), the head of the Office of Space Affairs. Drake orders Jones' crew to the planet Ophecius to rescue scientist Professor Newton (Maurice Cass) and Newton's young ward, Bobby (Robert Lyden).

Vena, who originally traveled to Ophecius with Newton and Bobby, knows the language and is a qualified navigator, which is why Drake insists that she travel with Jones. Although his position on the matter does change over the course of the episode, initially Rocky is insistent that space is "no place for a girl." Rocky belittles her at every opportunity, calling her "our 'glamour girl' navigator."[5] In a later episode, Vena is traveling aboard a cargo ship hijacked by space pirates. When the pirates shut down all power to the vessel, leaving it stranded in perpetual orbit around a distant planet, Vena comments that they were stuck there "till our food gives out. Right now, I'm hungry. I'll get lunch."[6] In the second season of *Space Angel*, as the crew is preparing for an exploratory mission to observe solar eruptions, Crystal Mace asks Scott McCloud, "Did you bring the lipstick I wanted?"[7] Despite these stereotypically "female" behaviors, however, the female characters differed in important ways from those on popular series, such as *I Love Lucy* and *Father Knows Best*. When women in these more conventional 1950s programs attempted to move into the masculine world of work, their efforts to succeed and to fit in were depicted as comically inadequate, disruptive of their families' home lives, or both. Their efforts invariably ended in failure, and the stories concluded with their reconciliation to their "proper" roles as wives and

Image 4.1   Vena Ray, navigator and alien linguist, examines a piece of twenty-third-century high technology with her Orbit Jet crewmates in Rocky Jones, Space Ranger. [Credit: PhotoFest]

mothers.[8] The women of the rocketman series, on the other hand, showed themselves to be competent professionals and equal contributors to their crews, demonstrating to young female viewers—in a way that few other shows of the era did—that intellect, along with scientific and technological skill, were not the sole property of men.

The impact on girls of seeing female characters in nontraditional professional fields cannot be underestimated. First and foremost, all of these women—Mace, Arden, Gilbert, Ray—were flying in space! Until 1958, with the creation of the National Aeronautics and Space Administration (NASA), the idea of flying in space was still very much science fiction. Americans, led by Robert Goddard, began launching liquid-fueled rockets in the 1920s and expanded their rocket capacity following World War II with the help of dozens of German rocket engineers who emigrated after the war. But when these shows started appearing, the first human space flights were nearly a decade away.[9] Scientists and engineers openly admit that science fiction inspired them to dream about and create the technology of the future. That influence was present among Goddard and his colleagues in the 1930s, many of whom were inspired by the writings of Jules Verne and H. G. Wells, and it continues today, in television programs such as the History Channel's *Star Wars Tech* (2007), and the Discovery Channel's *How William Shatner Changed the World* (2005). At a commemoration of NASA's forty-fifth anniversary, Eileen Collins, the first woman to pilot and command the space shuttle, was introduced to the audience by two of the stars of the science fiction drama *Stargate SG-1*—actors Michael Shanks and Christopher Judge. She praised the pair—along with their colleagues—for the imagination they embodied as creators and portrayers of the world of science fiction, and for the inspiration they provided those who go on to create science *fact*. In the 1950s, the rocketman series did their part, too, fueling the imaginations of their young fans and instilling in them a sense of possibility. By depicting women in space, they offered girls a glimpse of a potential future in space—one that became reality in June 1963 with the launch of Soviet cosmonaut Valentina Tereshkova aboard *Vostok 6* and the selection of NASA's Group VIII astronauts in January 1978, which included America's first six women astronauts.[10]

When looking at the female characters on these shows, we have to take into account that their work and skills were atypical; these women worked as scientists or serve in technical fields. Crystal Mace was the navigator for the Space Angel's ship, *Starduster*. *Rocky Jones*' Vena Ray was also a skilled navigator. More than just navigators, we also see women scientists. In "Operation Moonbeam," Clutch Cargo and Spinner meet with Dr. Knockwurst (a rocket engineer with a thick German accent reminiscent of Wernher von Braun, the head of the German rocket team that emigrated to the United States after World War II). Knockwurst informs them about a space race to the Moon. He also introduces Clutch and Spinner to his new assistant, Dr. Mary Hoganweiler, an expert in "astro-spatial-temporal impermanent relationships." She trains Clutch and Spinner for their trip into space. In *Radar Men from the Moon*, despite Joan Gilbert's damsel-in-distress persona, she, too, works as a scientist, often seen in Commando Cody's lab wearing a white lab coat amidst the towers of beakers, chemicals, and Bunsen burners.

Having women on these shows in scientific and technical roles helped to shape public attitudes about women in those careers. Although there is a long history of women as scientists, positive role models of women in the sciences were scarce for girls growing up in the 1950s. None had the iconic status that Marie Curie held in the 1920s, or that Rachel Carson would enjoy in the 1960s, and in general, the numbers of women scientists in America were in sharp decline. In 1946–1947, after World War II had ended and employers thanked women for their contributions to the war effort and told them to return to their proper place in the home, only 12,460 women remained in science and engineering positions (down from 20,212 in the final months of World War II).[11] By 1954–1955 that number dropped further to 7,712. Not until 1966 did the number of women in science and technical professions return to wartime levels. The number reached 29,293 by 1970.[12]

Even representations of women scientists in films of the early 1950s created a complex dialectic about women's roles. As Bonnie Noonan wrote in her book, *Women Scientists in Fifties Science Fiction Films* (2005):

> The emergence of women into the public and professional sphere during World War II destabilized and threatened the existing family structure of male as provider and woman as mother and homemaker. Accordingly, the speculative films of the postwar era incorporated the percolating tensions between the role of woman as professional and her ability to fulfill the gender expectations that would relegate her to a private, domestic sphere.[13]

The image of the successful woman scientist was either that of a doggedly professional, asexual scientist—like Osa Massen's icy chemist in *Rocketship X-M* (1950) or Neva Patterson's prim computer expert in *The Desk Set* (1957)—or that of a woman whose sexuality overshadowed her professional skills, like the swimsuit-clad

Image 4.2 Dr. Lina Van Horn (Osa Massen) reads about rocketmen as she travels aboard Rocketship XM. [Credit Wade Williams Enterprises]

zoologist played by Julie Adams in *The Creature from the Black Lagoon* (1954). The challenge, as Noonan explained it, was to create a balanced view, one that showed women scientists as middle-of-the-road characters who were neither blinded to the world around them by their commitment to science nor overtly sexual to the point of vulgarity.

So what changed? Why did girls begin to think about science and engineering as possible career choices in the 1960s and 1970s? Sci-fi television (or novels or films for that matter) may not have been the most important factor in that transition. But historians can look at how attitudes changed and use those historical events to interpret the message being imparted by the sci-fi shows for children. The resulting analysis shows that sci-fi TV clearly was *a* factor, and likely a significant one.

That message about careers for girls in science, engineering, and technology was unambiguously positive. In some cases, the women on these shows served in important positions of influence. Dr. Joan Dale (Margaret Garland) was the one female character in *Tom Corbett, Space Cadet*. Despite infrequent appearances on the show, the character's role was influential. Corbett and his team of cadets were at Space Academy USA studying to join the space-based protection force dedicated to "safeguarding the cause of universal peace in the age of conquest."[14] Dr. Dale was the only professor seen in the classroom during the show's five-season run. Although strict, Dr. Dale was clearly respected by the space cadets for her brilliance as an astrophysicist and her technological innovations.

Further, when we look at these female characters in 1950s science fiction, we often see more than just a female scientist. Instead, we see women who were scientists or engineers as well as active members of a team; they were partners in saving the Earth, and they had normal emotional relationships with men. Consider Crystal Mace, Dale Arden, and Vena Ray in particular. All three could be seen either piloting or navigating their spacecraft. In addition, Arden proved a valuable asset in a fist fight, and Ray possessed an extraordinary skill with languages ("I can say what I think about you in thirty-seven different languages!")[15] These were not women who were simply valued for their skills in the kitchen.

In some cases, these female characters were the love interests of the male protagonists. Despite an awkward working relationship in the premiere episode, Rocky Jones and Vena Ray quickly started dating, leaving Winky to search through his little black book for some female companionship of his own.[16] Dale Arden and Flash Gordon, as well, had an intimate relationship. Even Clutch Cargo seemed smitten with Dr. Hoganweiler. For the young female audience of these shows, having female characters as role models in science and engineering was important, but seeing them working as scientists, navigators, and engineers and still being able to maintain healthy relationships with men held greater significance.

Women who worked in the sciences and engineering during World War II returned home after the war ended partly because of a cultural expectation that they take up their patriotic duty as wives and mothers. Arguably, throughout history but still the case into the 1960s, women who pursued careers in science and engineering often understood that getting married and having children excluded them from full-time positions, important grants, and fellowship opportunities. They felt forced to choose a career or a family; having both was rarely a possibility.[17]

The women in these shows projected an image to girls watching them that they too could have it all.

These early sci-fi shows offered their audiences—both male and female—a complex view of women in space. First, we see men and women working side by side. Second, the women were performing as valued members of their crews. And third, these women were never asked or expected to sacrifice the gendered ideals of what it meant to be a woman in that era (all the women were fashionably dressed, they dated men, and Crystal Mace even got her lipstick!).

SCIENCE FICTION TELEVISION AND COLD WAR RHETORIC

In addition to how the writers chose to depict female characters, we can look at the stories themselves and how the creators of these shows used patriotic Cold War rhetoric as a powerful device in engaging and inspiring their young viewers of boys and girls. What made the rocketmen shows unique from other programs of the era and particularly powerful for girls was that they depicted women participating as equal partners in the fight to defend the Earth (or the United States), not as temporary replacements for male labor as they were during World War II and not as preservers of the home front as they appeared in *I Love Lucy* or *Father Knows Best*.

As the earliest of these children's programs began appearing on television, the United States was embroiled in the Korean War (1950–1953). Dwight Eisenhower, former commander-in-chief of the allied forces in Europe during World War II, was president. Ten years later, the first humans—both Soviet and American—flew in space for the first time, East Germans had erected the Berlin Wall, and the number of American troops in Vietnam tripled. American children spent some of their time in school practicing "duck-and-cover" drills in the event of a nuclear war with the Soviets. Science fiction television shows exploited those American fears, particularly among children, as a way to engage their audiences. Through the use of Cold War imagery and rhetoric, these sci-fi shows helped to shape patriotic values in children, which would ideally turn them into good citizens and Cold Warriors.

In each of their respective universes, rocketmen were at the forefront of the battle between good and evil. That alone made their series vehicles for Cold War ideology. The parallel between their imaginary worlds and the real world ran considerably deeper, however, with the rocketman series mirroring—in precise and concrete ways—the Cold War as it was in the 1950s. For American children—both boys *and* girls—of the 1950s, to whom the threat of global war remained palpable, the battle between good and evil that they saw on these shows undoubtedly resonated.

Each of these series—*Rocky Jones, Space Ranger, Tom Corbett, Space Cadet, Flash Gordon, Radar Men from the Moon,* and *Space Angel*—depicted a clear threat from a foreign invader. The enemy, though never specifically identified as the Soviet Union, China, or communists from Southeast Asia, invariably represented a threat to the Western way of life, and their goals of conquest and enslavement were familiar from Cold War headlines. For Commando Cody, the threat was an imminent attack from Retik and his race of people from the Moon. In the *Flash Gordon* episode

"Flash Gordon and the Planet of Death," invaders from the planet Eben staged an attack on Earth, only to be defeated by Flash and the rest of his team from the Galaxy Bureau of Investigation (GBI). Similarly, on *Space Angel*, Scott McCloud and his team repelled attempted invasions, as in episode 146, "Power Failure," when the people of planet Anthenia set out to "enslave the universe."[18]

Except for *Clutch Cargo*, all these shows were clearly set in the distant future, and portrayed the countries of Earth united as a global community.[19] Comparisons to the United Nations would likely have been clear even to young viewers. Rocky Jones, Tom Corbett, Flash Gordon, and Scott McCloud (*Space Angel*) and their crews all served either a global or interplanetary service committed to protecting the planet, the Solar System, or the universe. When those crews included female members, those young women were thus drawn into a vast interplanetary community. In the opening credits of *Tom Corbett*, the voice-over boomed, "Cadets train for duty on distant planets. In roaring rockets, they blast through the millions of miles from Earth to far-flung stars to brave the dangers of cosmic frontiers, protecting the liberties of the planets, safeguarding the cause of universal peace in the age of the conquest of space."[20]

The tension between these interplanetary alliances and villains bent on conquest was never-ending, and—like Cold War bomber and submarine crews—the heroes were obliged to remain ever-vigilant. On *Rocky Jones*, Cleolanta (Patsy Parsons), the tyrannical ruler of the planet Ophecius, regularly threatened Earth, but also persisted in a personal vendetta against Jones. In Flash Gordon's world, Earth's enemies changed from week to week, but the threat remained imminent. In the episode "Akim the Terrible," Akim, the ruler of the lawless planet Charon, intended to spread his "doctrine of evil," but knew he would fail as long as Flash and the GBI stood in his way.[21] Only dedicated men and women in uniform, the shows taught young fans, stood between such evil despots and the peaceful citizens of the future.

The imagery used to depict these threats was often as familiar as the threats themselves. In "Race Against Time," episode 19 of *Flash Gordon*, Flash and his team are forced to defuse a bomb with the potential to destroy the planet. In episode 35, "Deadline at Noon," Flash, Dale, and Dr. Zarkov[22] traveled back in time to 1950s Berlin to find a hidden nuclear bomb, similar to ones that had already vaporized five other planets in their own time. Shot in Europe on a miniscule budget, the series used actual footage of contemporary Berlin, still battle-scarred a decade after World War II. In *Space Angel*'s episode "Power Failure," the Anthenians paraded their weapons through the streets in scenes reminiscent of tanks and rockets rolling through Moscow's Red Square. These themes and images permeated American society through the news media and current-events lessons in schools. The images children watched on their favorite rocketmen series, as their heroes fought for the security and safety of the planet, were consistent with messages they received from parents and teachers about the threat from the Soviets, communists, and nuclear war.

In a March 1958 article published in the *American Journal of Sociology*, Walter Hirsch argued that science fiction served as a vehicle for both social criticism and the construction of possible futures.[23] The messages about vigilance against the

Image 4.3 Rocketman fantasies mirroring Cold War reality. (top) Rockets paraded through the city on the planet Anthenia in the episode "Power Failure" from the series Space Angel (1961); (bottom) CIA photograph of an R-12 rocket in Moscow's Red Square (1959–1962). [Credit: CIA]

enemy, fighting for peace (while ignoring the irony), and preserving what was clearly a Western—if not American—way of life that came across in these shows played directly on the concerns and fears that children in the Cold War era harbored about their own – very real—futures. For that reason, these shows sought to influence and inspire children of both sexes into similar pursuits, be it the military, the space program, or science and technology.

SCIENCE FICTION AND EDUCATION

The tone of juvenile science fiction shows of the 1950s reflected American attitudes and fears. Not only were they distinct products of the Cold War, but they also shaped and perpetuated the rhetoric. In each of the rocketmen series, we can see how new vehicles and gadgets as well as scientific and technological skill play a role in the success or failure of their heroes. When we examine federal responses to Cold War tensions and the potential of America's technological decline, we can see how these science fictions shows for children fit into the larger historical context of the era.

The Soviet Union tested its first atomic weapon in 1949. By 1955, it succeeded in creating the more powerful hydrogen bomb as well. Despite the Soviet Union's lag behind the United States in the development of both types of weapons (the United States first tested the atomic bomb in 1945 and the hydrogen bomb in 1952), as well as the growing fleet of jet bombers and medium-range ballistic missiles that gave the United States powerful nuclear strike capabilities, Americans obsessed over the possibility that the Soviets were taking the lead in science and technology. American anxieties over perceived Soviet technological superiority were rooted in fears of a "nuclear Pearl Harbor," but also in another kind of fear—the fear that the nation would be found lacking—as such scientific and technological prowess increasingly came to reflect national strength.

Television programs of the 1950s reflected similar convictions. Educational shows were getting air time thanks to the Ford Foundation, which created the Fund for Adult Education and the Fund for the Advancement of Education in 1951.[24] This new focus on educational broadcasting led to the creation of some of the first science shows, most notably *Mr. Wizard*, which ran from 1951 to 1966, and Walt Disney's own three-episode "Man in Space" series (1955–1957) for his *Disneyland* television show, which depicted how rocket engineers envisioned man's first voyages into space, the first missions to the Moon and to Mars.

As children watched these shows, they were increasingly captivated by science and technology. Students began participating in science clubs in the late 1920s. In 1950, the United States held its first National Science Fair in Philadelphia. As a way to encourage both boys and girls to engage in scientific research, the competition sponsored separate awards for the two in the biological and physical science categories, something that infuriated NASA astronaut (a member of the first class of astronauts to include women) and one-time National Science Fair participant Shannon Lucid. She admitted how angry she was to learn that her work would not be judged against that of boys. In her mind, her work was as good if not better than that of her male counterparts and deserved equal treatment.[25]

In spite of how girls such as Lucid felt about being singled out for their sex, these science clubs and science fairs provided a gateway into scientific, engineering, and medical research, something that most Americans at the time felt was desperately needed. Partnered with actual forays into science and engineering, the sci-fi television shows that these children were watching in the 1950s and 1960s fueled their imaginations about the future, just as astronaut Eileen Collins would acknowledge five decades later.

Image 4.4 Dr. Shannon Lucid, a biochemist, flew as a scientist-astronaut on four space shuttle missions, and spent 188 days in orbit aboard the Russian *Mir* space station. [Credit NASA/Kennedy Space Center]

Even when science fiction shows failed to present solid science "fact,"[26] they delivered messages about the significance of science and technology. The scientists portrayed—whether they were women or men—were morally "good" characters, firmly allied with the hero of the series or with a "Good Guy" organization, such as the Galaxy Bureau of Investigation (*Flash Gordon*) or Space Academy USA (*Tom Corbett, Space Cadet*), and dedicated to the public good rather than (like traditional "mad scientists") to selfish goals of their own. All of the protagonists in the series, whether scientists or not, possessed masterful scientific or technical skills of some kind. What was clear in each of these series was that the future world demanded proficiency in scientific and technological fields.

Walter Hirsch, reflecting in 1958 on positive images of scientists in science fiction, saw them as critical in light of America's growing shortage of scientists and engineers in the fight against the Soviet Union. The fear of such a shortage—already intense at mid-decade—was compounded in October 1957 by the launch of *Sputnik* I, the world's first artificial satellite. Americans responded on both local and federal levels. The late 1950s witnessed the birth and growth of the backyard bomb shelter, an effort by individuals and families to prepare for the potential attacks that might come if the Soviet Union's technological edge became great enough.[27] In 1958, the federal government announced its own responses to Sputnik. In addition to the creation of NASA, Congress also passed the *National Defense Education Act* (NDEA).

The new public law stated that: "the security of the Nation requires the fullest development of the mental resources and technical skills of its young men *and women* [author's emphasis].... The defense of this Nation depends upon the mastery of modern techniques developed from complex scientific principles." It noted further that the program would "correct as rapidly as possible the existing imbalances in our educational programs which have led to an insufficient proportion of our population educated in science, mathematics, and modern foreign languages and trained in technology."[28] Even as it clearly identified science and technology among the greatest weaknesses in the American education system, the Act acknowledged that women were capable of contributing to advancements in science and technology and so, to the American cause.

CONCLUSION

The rocketmen shows of the 1950s survived largely on limited budgets, cheap sets and models, and low-paid (and some may say equally talented) actors. The final products reflected those realities. These shows are far from riveting, Emmy Award-winning entertainment. But that takes nothing away from the mark they left on American culture and American youth, particularly its girls.

All the shows discussed in this chapter appeared before Betty Friedan published *The Feminine Mystique* in 1963, which gave women permission to say out loud that being a wife and mother was not necessarily enough to find fulfillment. Yet, these shows were full of examples of women who got to fly in space, work in scientific and technical fields, were considered valued members of a team, and still found time and opportunities to fall in love. For a young female audience, the message these shows sent was that you could be smart, pretty, have everything you want and a life of adventure. Coeditor of the *Encyclopedia of Science Fiction* Peter Nicholls may have been right in his interpretation of television sci-fi as "a cultural scandal" and the worst kind of science fiction, but the influence these female television characters had on girls watching these shows should count for something in our examination of their historical significance.[29]

What Nicholls failed to consider more generally is the power of television. In print, the author possessed the ability to downplay a female character through his or her description, leading the reader to draw the desired interpretation of her—that she is inferior, a spinster, or unattractive. Television, being a visual medium, quietly but persistently pushes the images of competent, skillful, yet conventionally feminine, women in high-tech settings into the audience's consciousness.

Scriptwriters have less control over an audience's interpretation. Consider the well-documented case surrounding *Star Trek*, which aired from 1966 to 1969. This author has argued elsewhere that the role of Lt. Uhura, played by Nichelle Nichols, problematized American attitudes about women in space. Despite being a member of the senior staff, which should give have given Uhura some influence

Image 4.5 Dr. Mae Jemison, physician and NASA astronaut, carries out experiments aboard the space shuttle *Endeavour* on mission STS-47 in September 1994. [Credit NASA/need to check the specific branch]

over the decisions that affected the entire starship's crew, her entire job as communications officer aboard *Enterprise* was to answer the phone.[30] Although the characterization of Lt. Uhura lacked a strong message about what jobs women were capable of performing beyond the "pink-collar" jobs of the 1960s, what is more important is that she was there. Female fans of the show identified Nichols as one of their role models. The first female African American astronaut, Mae Jemison, noted that seeing Lt. Uhura on television inspired her to dream big and believe that a career in space was possible.[31] More than a decade before Uhura's presence in space inspired Jemison and other female viewers, however, Crystal Mace, Dale Arden, and Vena Ray had inspired the young girls of their own era—transported into living rooms across America via the then-futuristic technology of television.

Girls watched, and read, and dreamed. For some, like Jemison, those dreams were very big, indeed; for others, the dreams were a bit more "earthbound," and they became scientists, engineers, astronomers, scholars, and writers.[32] Rocketmen series encouraged girls to look at the emerging Space Age and seem themselves as a part of it because, on their TV screens, they already *had* seen girls and women as a part of it. The female navigators, electronics experts, and scientists aboard interstellar rockets paved the way for girls' dreams and wonder. The female characters in these shows, while staying within the confines of 1950s/1960s gender identities, challenged conventional thinking about women's roles even before *The Feminine Mystique* encouraged open discussion about women's contributions to American society. They simultaneously modeled admiration for heroic rocketmen and resistance to stereotyping as helpless females; concern for their appearances, and concern for their careers; a sense of propriety and a sense of adventure. The presence of these female characters, and the dynamics of their relationships with other crewmembers, broadened the range of possibilities for the young girls in their audiences, even if they never dreamed of space. Whether aiming for the stars or more "down to earth" in their ambitions, female cadets, rangers, and junior space men gleaned more than simply "space man's luck" from their favorite rocketman series. They came away from each episode with new ideas about the future of women in America—and in space.

NOTES

1. Brian Horrigan, "Popular Culture and Visions of the Future in Space, 1901–2001," in *New Perspectives on Technology and American Culture*, ed. Bruce Sinclair (Philadelphia: American Philosophical Society, 1986), 59.
2. Speculation that Taurus, with his vague Scottish brogue, may have been the inspiration for the characterization of *Star Trek*'s (1966–1969) Montgomery "Scotty" Scott litters the Internet. See Gord Wilson's review of the *Space Angel* collection on Amazon.com; "Scottius Maxiumus: Commentary on Culture, Christianity and the Cardinals" blog, http://scottiusmaximus.blogspot.com/2005/02/scott-mccloud-space-angel.html; Anime Archive, http://8store.8thman.com/spaceangel.htm.
3. Unless otherwise noted, all quoted dialogue in is taken from episodes contained in:*Classic Sci-Fi TV*, DVD collection, Mill Creek Entertainment, 2009.
4. Similar characterizations appear in some of the sci-fi films of the era, particularly *Rocketship X-M*, in which Lisa Van Horne, a "Doctor of Chemistry," also finds herself performing kitchen duties. See www.archive.org/details/RocketshipXM.
5. *Rocky Jones, Space Ranger*, "Beyond the Curtain of Space: Chapter 1."
6. *Rocky Jones, Space Ranger*, "Pirates of Prah: Chapter 1."
7. *Space Angel*, "Scratch One Chimp."
8. Susan J. Douglas, *Where the Girls Are: Growing Up Female with the Mass Media* (New York: Times Books, 1994), 36–38.
9. Soviet cosmonaut Yuri Gagarin became the first human to orbit the Earth on April 12, 1961, followed shortly after by Alan Shepard, the first American in space, who launched aboard *Freedom* 7 on May 5, 1961.
10. The six women selected as mission specialists as part of NASA's Group VIII astronauts were Anna Fisher, Shannon Lucid, Judith Resnik, Sally Ride, Margaret Rhea Seddon, and Kathryn Sullivan. This class of astronauts was also the first to include African American men (Guion Bluford, Frederick Gregory, and Ronald McNair) and an Asian American man (Ellison Onizuka). One reporter referred to this class as "a NASA affirmative-action poster." See Amy E. Foster, *Integrating Women into the Astronaut Corps: Politics and Logistics at NASA, 1972–2004* (Baltimore: Johns Hopkins University Press, 2011), 87.
11. Margaret Rossiter, *Women Scientists in America: Before Affirmative Action, 1940–1972* (Baltimore: Johns Hopkins University Press, 1995), 28–29.
12. Rossiter, 98.
13. Bonnie Noonan, *Women Scientists in Fifties Science Fiction Films* (Jefferson, NC: McFarland, 2005), 48–49.
14. *Tom Corbett, Space Cadet*, "Season 4: Episode 11: Assignment Mercury," DVD, PRS Studio, 2009.

15. *Rocky Jones, Space Ranger,* "Beyond the Curtain of Space: Chapter 1."
16. See *Rocky Jones, Space Ranger,* "Pirates of Prah: Chapter 1."
17. See Rossiter, *Women Scientists in America: Struggles and Strategies to 1940,* 139–142; Rossiter, *Women Scientists in America: Struggles and Strategies to 1940,* 149–164; Julie Des Jardine, *The Madame Curie Complex: The Hidden History of Women in Science* (New York: The Feminist Press, 2010), 88–116.
18. *Space Angel,* "Power Failure."
19. As late as 1955, the majority of Americans (62 percent) still did not believe that man would walk on the moon within fifty years. What changed was a concerted effort by scientists and popular writers, such as Wernher von Braun, Willy Ley, Walt Disney, and Arthur C. Clarke, to explain the facts behind space flight. The launch of *Sputnik* in 1957 solidified those ideas for Americans, at which point 41 percent of Americans believed we would get to the Moon within 25 years. See Howard McCurdy, *Spaceflight and the American Imagination* (Washington, DC: Smithsonian Institution Press, 1997), 29–41, 47.
20. *Tom Corbett, Space Cadet,* DVD, PRS Studio, 2009.
21. *Flash Gordon,* "Flash Gordon and the Planet of Death"; "Akim the Terrible."
22. Although he had a Russian name, Zarkov spoke with an American accent
23. Walter Hirsch, "The Image of the Scientist in Science Fiction: A Content Analysis," *Journal of American Sociology,* 63, no. 5 (March 1958), 506.
24. Robert A. Levin and Laurie Moses, "Television, Fred Rogers, and the History of Education," *History of Education Quarterly,* 43, no. 2 (Summer 2003), 264.
25. Shannon Lucid, interview with author, June 29, 2004.
26. One glaring example is that these shows never integrated any discussion of the experience of microgravity on living and working in space
27. Despite the talk and genuine fear in this period, historian Kenneth Rose found that relatively few families actually invested in backyard bomb shelters. See Kenneth Rose, *One Nation Underground: The Fallout Shelter in American Culture* (New York: New York University Press, 2001), 204.
28. Full text of the *National Defense Education Act* of 1958 (P.L. 85–864) is available at the Federal Education Policy History website, http://federaleducationpolicy.wordpress.com/2011/06/03/national-defense-education-act-of-1958-2/.
29. Quoted in Thomas M. Disch, *The Dreams Our Stuff Is Made Of: How Science Fiction Conquered the World* (New York: Touchstone, 1998), 97.
30. Foster, *Integrating Women into the Astronaut Corps,* 38.
31. "Transition," *NASA Magazine* (Spring 1993), 6, Impact: Star Trek (Movie/Trek) file, NASA Headquarters.
32. See Janice M. Bogstad, "Editor's Introduction I: Girls and Science Fiction," *The Lion and the Unicorn* 28 (2004), vi; Justine Larbalestier, *Feminist Science Fiction in the Twentieth Century* (Middletown, CT: Wesleyan University Press, 2006), xi.

BIBLIOGRAPHY

Bogstad, Janice M. "Editor's Introduction I: Girls and Science Fiction" *The Lion and the Unicorn* 28 (2004), v-viii.

Classic Sci-Fi TV. Golden Valley, MN: Mill Creek Entertainment, 2009.

Des Jardins, Julie. *The Madame Curie Complex: The Hidden History of Women in Science.* New York: The Feminist Press, 2010.

Disch, Thomas M. *The Dreams Our Stuff Is Made Of: How Science Fiction Conquered the World.* New York: Touchstone, 1998.

Foster, Amy E. *Integrating Women into the Astronaut Corps: Politics and Logistics at NASA, 1972–2004*. Baltimore: Johns Hopkins University Press, 2011.

Hirsch, Walter. "The Image of the Scientist in Science Fiction: A Content Analysis" *Journal of American Sociology*, 63, no. 5 (March 1958): 506–512.

Horrigan, Brian. "Popular Culture and Visions of the Future in Space, 1901–2001." In *New Perspectives on Technology and American Culture*, edited by Bruce Sinclair, 49–67. Philadelphia: American Philosophical Society, 1986..

Larbalestier, Justine. *Feminist Science Fiction in the Twentieth Century*. Middletown, CT: Wesleyan University Press, 2006.

Levin, Robert A. and Laurie Moses. "Television, Fred Rogers, and the History of Education" *History of Education Quarterly*, 43, no. 2 (Summer 2003): 262–275.

McCurdy, Howard. *Spaceflight and the American Imagination*. Washington, DC: Smithsonian Institution Press, 1997.

Nichols, Nichelle. *Beyond Uhura: Star Trek and Other Memories*. New York: G. P. Putnam, 1994.

Noonan, Bonnie. *Women Scientists in Fifties Science Fiction Films*. Jefferson, NC: McFarland, 2005.

Rose, Kenneth D. *One Nation Underground: The Fallout Shelter in American Culture*. New York: New York University Press, 2001.

Rossiter, Margaret. *Women Scientists in America: Strategies and Struggles to 1940*. Baltimore: Johns Hopkins University Press, 1982.

———. *Women Scientists in America: Before Affirmative Action, 1940–1972*. Baltimore: Johns Hopkins University Press, 1995.

Tom Corbett, Space Cadet. Los Angeles: PRS Studio, 2009.

PART II

REACHING FOR TOMORROW

CHAPTER 5

SPACE FEVER: FROM FANTASY TO REALITY

HOWARD E. MCCURDY

Imagine a world in which no one has seen the home planet from space. (Satellites did not capture the first high-quality, full-color photograph of the whole Earth in sunlight until 1967.)

Imagine a world in which no one has seen the detailed face of the nearest inhabitable planet. (The *Mariner 4* spacecraft returned the first close-up images of Mars in 1965.)

Imagine a world in which no one has viewed the surface of the brightest sister planet in the night sky, hidden as it is under a thick mantle of clouds. (A Soviet spacecraft, *Venera 9*, returned the first photographs of the rocky surface of Venus in 1975.)

Imagine a world with no communication satellites, weather satellites, GPS, or NASA. No astronauts, no space stations, no space shuttles, no robots on Mars, and no automated spacecraft traveling to the edge of the planetary system and beyond.

THE EARTH, AT THE MIDPOINT OF THE TWENTIETH CENTURY, was such a world. Space travel had not yet begun, and imaginations were free to soar, unencumbered by reality. It was also a time when many families in the United States were purchasing their first television sets. These sets, and the programming they delivered, played a key role in allowing humans to imagine space and its exploration. Together with magazines, movies, novels, and short stories, television created a great deal of interest in space and what lay ahead.

Much of what appeared on television, however, was fantasy—space cadet programs designed to fascinate adolescent males. The programs excited interest, but also encouraged disbelief. Space exploration was "that Buck Rogers stuff," entertaining but not real. Advocates of space exploration in the United States thus faced a serious challenge. They needed the audience that science fiction stories had assembled, but in order to encourage public support for investments in space travel, they needed to transmit a new message; they needed that audience to hear a different tale.

A Base in Fantasy

Space travel, as fantasy, was informed by the larger American tradition of Western and adventure stories as popular entertainment. Early Westerns began to appear around the mid-1800s in mass-market publications, known as dime novels, that sensationalized the lives and deeds of real and fictional characters on the American frontier. Adventure stories set in foreign lands helped to boost newspaper and magazine sales. In 1869, editors at the *New York Herald* dispatched the journalist Henry Morton Stanley to lead and report on an expedition into the heart of Africa to find missionary David Livingston, who did not know that he was lost. Public interest in such stories spawned the so-called pulp magazines, named after the cheap paper on which they appeared. In 1896, Frank Munsey transformed *Argosy* magazine into an all-fiction publication featuring adventure stories set in foreign lands (including the first appearance of Edgar Rice Burroughs' *Tarzan of the Apes*), sea sagas, Western tales, and science fiction. Inspired by its commercial success, other, increasingly specialized pulp magazines followed—including, by the mid-1920s, ones devoted solely to science fiction.

Hugo Gernsback premiered the first of these, *Amazing Stories*, in 1926. The inaugural issue featured reprinted stories by Edgar Allan Poe and H. G. Wells, and the opening installment of a two-part serialization of Jules Verne's 1877 novel *Off on a Comet*. The cover artwork, rendered in the pulps' brightly colored, eye-catching style, depicted the explorers in Verne's story ice-skating on the comet's surface as the planet Saturn passed by. Other science fiction pulps with similarly fantastic offerings and equally spectacular covers followed. *Astounding Stories* (later *Astounding Science Fiction*) began publication in 1930, *Thrilling Wonder Stories* in 1936, *Startling Stories* and *Planet Stories* in 1939—more than a dozen in all by the time the United States entered the Second World War.

The pulps certainly enlarged the audience of people interested in space travel. But like the adventure stories and Western tales that accompanied them, the science-focused writings exaggerated possibilities and stretched credulity. Given a choice between entertaining an audience with fantastic tales and realistically depicting the challenges of cosmic flight, science fiction writers commonly sought to entertain. The pulps were successful because they presented fascinating stories in a form that was cheaply priced. Realism was an occasional byproduct, but not a primary goal.

Writers of science fiction typically avoided the challenges that real rocket scientists struggled to overcome. In his pre-pulp description of a flight to the Moon, Verne solved the propulsion problem by dispatching his travelers using the power of a giant cannon. Serious readers noted that the force necessary to expel a space capsule from a cannon at escape velocity would reduce the travelers to thin smears on the cabin floor, but that technical error did not affect sales.

Even more extreme, when Burroughs began serializing a set of Mars stories in *All-Story* magazine (later merged with *Argosy*) in 1912, he avoided technical details altogether, and relied upon a form of astral projection to transport his hero, John

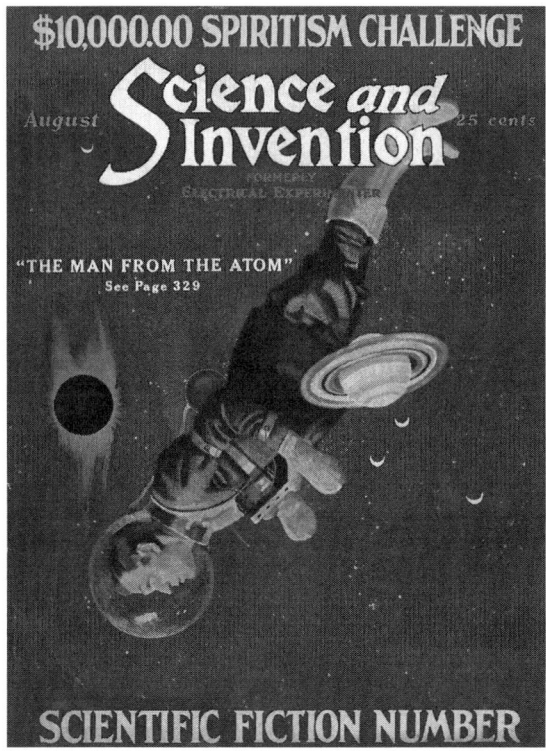

Image 5.1 Pulp science fiction stories, like those in this 1923 issue, often featured the heroic exploits of lone space explorers.

Carter, to Mars. Carter falls asleep in an Arizona cave and wakes up on Mars, where he encounters various tribes and a beautiful princess. The stories attracted legions of followers ostensibly interested in science fiction, even though the plots more resembled the sword-and-sorcery tales of medieval adventure stories than treatises on science.

Amazing Stories began its serialization of E. E. Smith's *Skylark of Space* in 1928, introducing a new narrative model to space-adventure stories. The complex tale established the formula for the so-called "space opera," adventures modeled after well-known Western "horse operas," in which characters resolve their melodramatic conflicts in a galactic setting. The main character in *Skylark*, scientist-adventurer Dr. Richard Seaton, discovers an element "X" that permits the construction of an extremely powerful space drive. In the real world, the Wright brothers' first flight was not yet a quarter century old, but this fantastic craft their work inspired easily crossed 237 light-years of space in just 24 hours.

While literature took ample liberties with the fantasy-reality divide, filmmakers took steps to negotiate its resolution. Hermann Oberth, president of the *Verein für Raumschiffahrt* (*VfR*; roughly, Society for Spaceflight) and Germany's leading rocket theorist, acted as a technical advisor to German filmmaker Fritz Lang when

Lang began work on a silent film depicting an expedition to the Moon. Released in 1929, *Frau im Mond* (US title: *By Rocket to the Moon*) opens with a realistic sequence showing a large multistage rocket emerging from an equally sizeable vehicle-assembly building. Yet once on the Moon, realism disappears. The first explorer lights a match, discovers that the lunar atmosphere contains enough oxygen to sustain life, and removes his protective gear.

In many of science fiction's best-loved tales, this retreat from realism continued for decades. When Isaac Asimov published his first robot story in a 1940 issue of *Super Science Stories*, a pulp magazine, he gave his robots "positronic" brains, a term he characterized as "gobbledygook."[1] Needing a device to provide his robots with intelligence, Asimov invented a word instead of an actual apparatus. Only much later did he realize that he had accidentally forecast the creation of the personal computer.

Several years later, in the summer of 1946, Ray Bradbury began publishing the short stories that would form *The Martian Chronicles*. He refused even to characterize the stories as science fiction, because fictional forecasts of the future of technology could too easily be rendered inaccurate, even absurd, by developments in the real world. Rather, Bradbury sought to write stories rooted in fantasy because, as he said: "Fantasy is a depiction of the unreal.... That's the reason it's going to be around a long time—because it's a Greek myth, and myths have staying power."[2]

This was a lesson hard learned by entertainment mogul Walt Disney. Disney opened his Disneyland theme park in 1955 with a "Rocket to the Moon" attraction, but park managers had to replace the attraction with "Mission to Mars" after humans landed on the lunar surface. The new attraction lasted scarcely one year before the first *Viking* spacecraft revealed that the planet was a frigid and lifeless place. In frustration, Disney officials replaced "Mission to Mars" with "Alien Encounter," a complete fantasy. "One way for an attraction to remain timeless is for it to be based in fantasy, rather than reality," park planners confessed.[3] Similarly, producers of the 1955 film *Conquest of Space* realistically depicted the challenges presented by a multiyear voyage to the surface of Mars. The film flopped so badly at the box office that movie titans refused to finance any similar efforts for 12 years. Like Disney, the producers learned the pitfalls of attempting to accurately portray science. In most such tales, science forms a backdrop to the main story. Like the scenery in a play, the science presents an interesting setting or locale, but remains ancillary to the central narrative.

The commercial appeal of the fantastic encouraged writers of science fiction to experiment with ideas that reached far beyond contemporary science, and even to delve into the supernatural. Advances in science permitted the presentation of rockets and space travel; advances in imagination allowed the contemplation of time travel, mental telepathy, miracles, and the possibility of biological creatures moving into spiritual realms. A persistent theme, present in the works of writers like Bradbury and Arthur C. Clarke, advanced the idea that a sufficiently advanced species could move out of its corporeal form and into a higher realm. No longer dependent upon organic chemistry for its existence, the species could live or travel anywhere. Clarke defended the plausibility of fantastic ideas such as these with the third of his Three Laws. "Any sufficiently advanced technology," he observed, "is indistinguishable from magic."[4]

COMMUNICATING SCIENCE

The fantasy in science fiction created a special opportunity, one not present to the same degree in adventure stories and Western tales. Set in an as-yet-unknown future, science tales held out the promise that humans could actually develop some of the outlandish technologies described. Sword and six-gun stories promised entertainment and a bit of romanticized history; audiences for science fiction received a glimpse of the future.

The bad science in science fiction frustrated serious rocketeers. Fantasy attracted a large following, but led to serious mis-expectations. Robert Goddard—soon to become one of the world's leading experts in liquid-fueled rockets—scribbled corrections in the margins of Verne's *From the Earth to the Moon*. Science fiction inspired Goddard, but so did the impulse to correct its errors.

Willy Ley, a German rocketeer who emigrated to the United States in 1935, agreed, complaining that no one in the United States had any interest in the subject of space travel except writers of science fiction.[5] In Germany, Ley had helped

Image 5.2   Workers ready the projectile that will carry Verne's hearty adventurers into space.

organize the VfR, which conducted a series of successful rocket tests on the outskirts of Berlin. Eighteen-year-old Wernher von Braun, a fellow member, sought his assistance in 1930 on making a career of rocketry. Some of Ley's colleagues, including von Braun, went on to join the German government's rocket-development program at Peenemünde, where they built the big missiles that rained terror on London and Antwerp during the Second World War. Ley fled to America, where he struggled to survive by writing popular-science books such as *The Lungfish and the Unicorn, Bombs and Bombing,* and, in 1944, *Rockets: The Future of Travel Beyond the Stratosphere.*

The US counterpart of the *VfR* was the American Interplanetary Society (later the American Rocket Society), whose members met in the Manhattan apartment of G. Edward Pendray. A reporter for the *New York Herald Tribune,* Pendray wrote science fiction stories under the pseudonym of Gawain Edwards. David Lasser, who organized the gathering, managed one of the pulp magazines in which the members' stories appeared. The group launched a few small rockets and enthusiastically embraced the idea of actual space travel. Yet most of their work emerged in fictional form. Even von Braun, who escaped to the United States with the nucleus of his German rocket team at the end of World War II, sought to promote public interest in space travel in the United States through fiction. While stationed at isolated Fort Bliss, Texas, in 1948–1949, helping the US Army build rockets, he penned a novel—*The Mars Project*—describing an imaginary but realistic expedition to Mars. The novel itself, featuring a preface describing a global nuclear war and a climactic encounter with intelligent Martians, was so awful that it could not find a publisher, but the lengthy technical appendix, in which von Braun displayed the engineering calculations behind the fictional expedition, did excite interest. Published in German in 1952 and English in 1953, it was the first serious feasibility study of a human flight to Mars.[6]

In presenting this possibility, exploration enthusiasts adopted the narrative form found in science fiction. Writers of popular science informed the public by telling stories. Rather than present a dry treatise on the technical specifications of cosmic stations and rockets capable of reaching space, their tales described actual voyages from liftoff through landing. David Lasser, cofounder of the American Interplanetary Society, used it in his 1931 book *The Conquest of Space.* Ley used it in his first volume on rockets in 1944, and again five years later in *The Conquest of Space.* Von Braun did it with his 1949 Mars novel, and in a series of later projects based on similar calculations: a classic 1952 *Collier's* magazine article on the assembly of an Earth-orbiting space station, titled "Crossing the Last Frontier"; articles on expeditions to the Moon and Mars; contributions to Walt Disney's television episodes on space exploration; and participation in a string of popular-science books published by Viking Press, including *Across the Space Frontier* (1952) and *The Conquest of the Moon* (1953).

Their fact-based stories, moreover, often appeared alongside works of outright fiction. When Ley sought an outlet for an early article on the use of rockets for space travel, he turned to *Astounding Stories,* and his article, titled "Dawn of the Conquest of Space: An Authoritative Article on Rockets," appeared in its March 1937 issue. Arthur C. Clarke regularly interspersed his production of science fiction stories like "The Sentinel" with serious works on communication satellites and the exploration of space, creating a single audience for both.

Space art followed a similar path. Pulp publishers commissioned dramatic covers for their magazines. Some were fantastic, depicting heroes and heroines battling variously constructed aliens. One particularly impressive cover for the January 1951 issue of *Amazing Stories* showed a pair of scantily clad heroines riding on top of flying-saucer-shaped transport devices that looked like cosmic surfboards. Other covers were realistic, presenting spindle-shaped spacecraft visiting foreign bodies whose landscapes artists anticipated based on the latest astronomical findings.

The most influential artist to combine realism and imagination was Chesley Bonestell. An architect and Hollywood special effects artist, Bonestell had a lifelong interest in astronomy. In 1944, the editors at *Life* magazine presented a series of Bonestell landscapes showing how the planet Saturn might appear if viewed from the surface of its moons. The stunning landscapes also invited readers to imagine how the moons themselves might actually look if travelers ventured there. Bonestell relied upon real science to prepare miniature models for his art. He knew, for example, that Saturn's moon Titan had an atmosphere, and used that knowledge to prepare one of his most famous renderings. Only later did astronomers discover that the atmosphere was likely opaque, spoiling Bonestell's clear-sky view.

Bonestell collaborated with Willy Ley, in 1949, to present the influential book *The Conquest of Space*, which combined technically sound narrative by Ley with realistic art by Bonestell. The cover showed a tall winged rocket resting on the surface of a weathered Moon, a painting that foreshadowed Bonestell's scene paintings for the realistic but fictional 1950 film *Destination Moon*. Concurrently, the book contained wholly fantastic landscapes, including a painting of the surface of Jupiter in which a waterfall of lava spills over a dramatic cliff.

Fact and fantasy seemed indistinguishable as television and movie producers began to present science fiction. Ley, now well established as a popular-science writer, worked as a technical adviser for the producers of the television program *Tom Corbett, Space Cadet*. Science fiction author Robert Heinlein provided scientific advice to the producers of *Destination Moon*, a movie based on his 1947 novel *Rocket Ship Galileo*.

However, as the midpoint of the twentieth century approached, fantasy still prevailed. In 1949, the George Gallup organization polled Americans on possible developments in science and technology over the ensuing 50 years. Eighty-eight percent of the respondents agreed that scientists would find a cure for cancer before the twenty-first century. Sixty-three percent believed that engineers would build atom-powered airplanes and trains. Yet when asked whether humans would land on the Moon by 2000, only 15 percent replied in the affirmative. A large proportion of the American public had been exposed to stories about space travel, but few believed that it would happen soon. Advocates of space exploration sought to change that perception.

Fantasy Becomes Real

During the first half of the twentieth century, depictions of fantastic science moved from print to film, radio, and eventually, television. Buck Rogers, for example, began in the pulps, transitioning first to the comic pages of daily newspapers in 1929, then, to a radio serial in 1932. The hero's exploits were adapted for a movie serial in

1939, and finally, for a weekly television series in 1950. Flash Gordon debuted on the comic pages in 1934, in an undisguised effort to tap into the audience already assembled by Buck Rogers, then followed the same path to the airwaves and the screen. Tom Corbett (Frankie Thomas), Buzz Corry (Ed Kemmer), Rocky Jones (Richard Crane), and the other rocketmen who joined Buck and Flash on the television screens of the early 1950s were only a small part of a vast outpouring of science fiction that emphasized fantastic adventure over scientific accuracy. Magazines, novels, movie serials, motion pictures, radio, and increasingly television had created a significant audience for such science tales, but as of the midpoint of the twentieth century, the tales—and the audiences—favored fantasy over realism.

Attempts to portray rocketry and space travel seriously lagged behind these more fanciful representations. David Lasser's book on the possibility of space travel did not appear until five years after *Amazing Stories*, the first science fiction pulp, arrived at the sales counter. Hollywood's first realistic portrayal of space travel, *Destination Moon*, appeared in 1950—more than a decade after the release of the first Buck Rogers and Flash Gordon movie serials.

Advocates of space travel rushed to catch up. Following the release of *Destination Moon*, officials at the New York Museum of Natural History's Hayden Planetarium assembled a group of exploration advocates to discuss the future of space travel. The considerable audience generated by science fiction in conjunction with current

Image 5.3   *Destination Moon* (1950), the first science fiction film to strive for accuracy, featured background paintings by Chesley Bonestell.

advances in rocket technology provided organizers with a special opportunity. "The time is now ripe to make the public realize that the problem of space travel is to be regarded as a serious branch of science and technology," Willy Ley announced in his invitation to speakers.[7] Planetarium officials used the symposium as a vehicle for publicizing their new exhibit on space travel, which included an imaginary trip to Mars.

Following the first Hayden Planetarium symposium and a subsequent meeting on space medicine in New Mexico, editors at *Collier's* magazine decided to present an eight-part series on the exploration of space, beginning on March 22, 1952. For the cover, Chesley Bonestell painted a winged space shuttle dropping its second stage as it ascended toward Earth orbit. Inside, readers encountered a two-page panorama—also painted by Bonestell—depicting the shuttle, space taxis, an orbiting telescope, and a large rotating space station, along with articles by Ley, von Braun, and other rocketry experts describing the venture. "Man Will Conquer Space Soon," the cover announced, "Top Scientists Tell How in 15 Startling Pages."[8]

The *Collier's* series offered a striking counterpoint to the proliferation of science fiction series on television. In the spring of 1952, when the issue appeared, readers could tune their television sets to a collection of offerings portraying space travel in a more fanciful way. ABC offered *Tom Corbett, Space Cadet* (1950–1955). *Captain Video and His Video Rangers* (1949–1955) appeared live five to six days a week. Saturdays featured Buzz Corry and his United Planets Space Patrol (1950–1955). Viewers in the San Francisco Bay area could watch *Captain Z-Ro* (1954–1960), which would receive national syndication two years later. Buck Rogers had materialized in 1950, but gone off the air in 1951. Although they attracted large audiences, the scientific quality of these science fiction shows was not high. The limitations imposed by the primitive nature of the medium, the need for frequent production (often in a live format), and the lack of funds conspired, in such series, to produce costumes and special effects that were more comical than realistic. Workers on the *Captain Video* set spent $25 weekly for devices such as the Opticon Scillometer and the Cosmic Ray Vibrator.[9]

By contrast, the illustrations prepared for the eight-part *Collier's* series were stunning. Bonestell, Rolf Klep, and Fred Freeman contributed paintings of spaceships, passenger vehicles, lunar bases, Martian landings, and cosmic landscapes. The technical quality of the illustrations was much higher than the images presented on TV. Magazine editors continued the tradition of presenting technical information in a narrative form, but did so in a manner and with images designed to inspire commitment to the idea as well as attention.

The audience for television viewing expanded rapidly. Between 1949 and 1955, the proportion of households with television sets in America increased from less than 10 percent to more than 60 percent. Beginning in the fall of 1954, Walt Disney offered those eager new viewers a weekly television program titled *Disneyland*, designed to promote and help fund his soon-to-be opened theme park in Anaheim, California. One of the animators responsible for producing the weekly show, Ward Kimball, had been following the *Collier's* series and thought space travel would provide a good theme for the segment of the program dealing with the future. Park designers placed a simulated rocket ride to the Moon at the center of the Tomorrowland section of the park, along with a one-third scale rocket that Ley and von Braun helped to

Image 5.4   Wernher von Braun (R) and Walt Disney (L) inspect a spaceship model used in the "Man in Space" episode of Disneyland. [Credit: NASA/Marshall Spaceflight Center]

design. Kimball produced a televised series of three episodes tied to Tomorrowland that dealt with space travel, and invited Ley and von Braun to help develop and appear in the show.

The programs were the first on television to depict space travel as it might actually occur. "Until recently," Disney explained in his introduction to the first—*Man in Space*, aired in March 1955—"one of man's oldest dreams has …seemed to be an impossibility." Disney assured viewers that the situation was about to change. "Great new discoveries have brought us to the threshold of a new frontier—the frontier of interplanetary space."[10]

Disney animators presented cartoon figures who explain the history of rocketry and the dangers of cosmic rays, interspersed with onscreen lectures by Ley, von Braun, and other real-world rocketeers. They used a mixture of voiceover narration and animation techniques—reminiscent of the *Collier's* articles and Bonestell's artwork—to depict the launch of a giant rocket ship from a small Pacific atoll and its return from space. The result was a legendary piece of speculative science.

The second program in the space series—*Man and the Moon*, shown in late 1955—discussed what scientists knew about the Moon, and dramatized a flight around it by a spaceship and its four-person crew. The simulated mission contained a sequence in which the captain drops a flare while passing over the far side of the Moon, which in 1955 had not yet been visited or seen by human explorers. Kimball adapted the sequence, including a brief glimpse of ruins suggesting previous visitation, from the simulated "Rocket to the Moon" attraction that served as the centerpiece of Tomorrowland. It was the Disney space programs' closest approach to the science fantasy of the rocketmen series, made possible by the fact that no one knew what awaited human explorers on other worlds.

Fantasy and realism combined, in the early 1950s, to set the stage for space exploration. As the public's interest grew, serious discussions of space travel became more commonplace and elaborate. Rocket experiments became more ambitious, and the balance in the conversation shifted away from fantasy and toward realism. The Disney space programs were hallmarks of that shift, and as the first two aired, in 1955, the rocketman television shows began to disappear. *Space Patrol*, and its hero, Buzz Corry, left the airwaves in February 1955, the month before *Man in Space* aired. *Rocky Jones* had ended production the previous November. *Captain Video, Tom Corbett, Rocky Jones*, and *Flash Gordon* all ended their initial runs in the four months following *Man in Space*. *Captain Z-Ro* ran its course in early 1960. These early shows were replaced by more adult fare like *Science Fiction Theater* (1957–1959), a forerunner of the more popular *Twilight Zone* (1959–1964), and by widespread coverage of the actual expeditions into space.

In October 1957, less than two years after airing of the second Disney space program and exactly two months before the third, *Mars and Beyond*, the Soviet Union launched the first Earth-orbiting satellite; *Sputnik I*. The United States responded with *Explorer I*—built by a team that included Wernher von Braun—in January 1958, and the Space Race was on. If anything of value could be gained by placing humans and their machines in space, public officials in the United States wanted to make sure that the US got there first. Shows such as *Man and the Challenge* and *Men into Space* (both 1959–1960) dramatized the race, but the exploits of their fictional heroes were soon supplanted, on television and in Americans' thoughts, by those of real astronauts like Alan Shepard and John Glenn.

The space fever excited by television, film, theme parks, novels, and pulp magazines created a market for adventure stories laced with science and set in space. With that audience in place, advocates of space exploration appealed for actual exploration. Science fiction created the fever, advocates seized the opportunity, and the launch of the first Earth-orbiting space satellite by the Soviet Union cemented the deal. By late 1957, following the launch of *Sputnik 1*, the number of Americans who anticipated a lunar landing before the next century had increased from 15 percent to 41 percent. Eleven years later, in December 1968, the three-man crew of *Apollo 8* achieved a critical milestone on the road to that landing, becoming the first humans to fly around the Moon. Their mission paralleled the one imagined in Disney's 1955 *Man and the Moon*, but the astronauts' pictures of Earth rising over the lunar horizon thrilled far more than the imagined glimpse of mysterious ruins on the lunar far side. Real space travel had, at last, surpassed science fiction writers' fantasies.

NOTES

1. Isaac Asimov, *Robot Visions* (New York: ROC New American Library, 1990), 7.
2. Devin D. O'Leary, "Grandfather Time: An Interview with Ray Bradbury," Weeklywire.com, September 27, 1999, http://weeklywire.com/ww/09–27–99/alibi_feat1.html.
3. Ryan A. Harmon, "Predicting the Future," *Disney News*, Fall 1991, 35.
4. Arthur C. Clarke, *Profiles of the Future* (New York: Harper & Row, 1973), 21.
5. Quoted in *Current Biography, 1953*, s.v. "Willy Ley."
6. Wernher von Braun, *The Mars Project* (Urbana: University of Illinois Press, 1953).
7. Willy Ley, letter of invitation, First Annual Symposium on Space Travel, 1951, American Museum of Natural History, Hayden Planetarium Library, New York, NY.
8. "Man Will Conquer Space Soon," *Collier's*, March 22, 1952 [cover].
9. Gary Grossman, *Saturday Morning TV* (New York: Dell Publishing, 1981), 138.
10. *Man in Space*, directed by Ward Kimball (Walt Disney Studios, 1955).

BIBLIOGRAPHY

Asimov, Isaac. *Robot Visions*. New York: ROC New American Library, 1990.
Clarke, Arthur C. *Profiles of the Future*. New York: Harper & Row, 1973.
Grossman, Gary. *Saturday Morning TV*. New York: Dell Publishing, 1981.
Harmon, Ryan A. "Predicting the Future." *Disney News*, Fall 1991, 35.
"Man Will Conquer Space Soon," *Collier's*, March 22, 1952 [cover].
O'Leary, Devin D. "Grandfather Time: An Interview with Ray Bradbury." Weeklywire.com, September 27, 1999. http://weeklywire.com/ww/09–27–99/alibi_feat1.html.
Von Braun, Wernher. *The Mars Project*. Urbana: University of Illinois Press, 1953.

CHAPTER 6

SHOOTING FOR THE STARS: CAPTAIN VIDEO, THE ROCKET RANGERS, AND AMERICA'S CONQUEST OF SPACE

PATRICK LUCANIO AND GARY COVILLE

> The child is father of the man.
> —William Wordsworth, "My Heart Leaps Up" (1802)

IN 1899, A BOY NAMED ROBERT GODDARD CLIMBED TO the furthest reaches of a cherry tree, gazed at the limitless sky, and allowed his sense of wonder to contemplate just what was out there. Just the year before, he had been awestruck by H. G. Wells' imaginative *War of the Worlds* (1898) in which Martians in fantastic machines descended upon mankind with a vengeance, and now, Goddard imagined how such applied science would be necessary to turn that fiction into fact and allow humankind to rise up and touch the surface of Mars. Thus the young Goddard, who would become the father of American rocketry, received his inspiration and his epiphany. His great achievements would be felt most keenly as the 1950s got underway. It was the era of televised rocketman series, when youngsters spent their nights not only looking at the stars and wondering about them, but like Goddard, contemplated the very means and methods by which to reach and conquer them. Science fiction writer Ray Bradbury echoed these imaginings in his introduction to the 1962 edition of *R is for Rocket*, recalling that, as a boy in the Midwest, he would go out and look at the stars at night and wonder about them, and guessing that every boy of his era had done likewise.

For the child of the 1950s, that inspiration had been advanced by a pervasive popular culture that was itself steeped in wonder. Prodded by great advancements in science, of which the atom served as both protector and destroyer, the literature promised a new century free of the tumults of war and economic hardship that had marred the previous decades. Perhaps historian Frederick Lewis Allen, in *The Big Change*, best summarized the advancements when he wrote that the most significant concept of the age was "the idea that man could produce materials to order...superior to what nature could produce."[1]

These materials made possible advanced technology like the rockets and missiles, inspired by Goddard's work, whose launches were now omnipresent in newsreels and the ubiquitous science fiction films of the age like *Destination Moon* (1950), *Rocketship X-M* (1950), *Riders to the Stars* (1954), and *The Conquest of Space* (1955). These superior technological marvels offered the means by which humans could reach the stars and the means by which to make all that "Buck Rogers stuff" of previous decades reality. At first, rocket experimentation was top secret and rumored, but by the middle of the decade, as one movie title so aptly put it, American rocket experimentation had placed man "on the threshold of space." Far-off locations with names like Cape Canaveral, Edwards Air Force Base, and White Sands Proving Ground were suddenly part of the public vernacular as America prepared for the conquest of space, and in 1955, the Eisenhower administration committed the United States to launching an artificial satellite.[2]

America's fascination with reaching the stars was reinforced by fears that *others from the stars* might be visiting Earth. White Sands—where the US Army conducted its first postwar rocket tests—was also newsworthy because, according to naval commander Robert B. McLaughlin in a 1950 *True* magazine article, the site had been buzzed in 1947 by unidentified flying objects (UFOs).[3] A private pilot also reported seeing UFOs in 1947, near Mount Rainier in Washington State.[4] A superfluity of bizarre stories followed, of things seen in the sky, namely flying saucers and the odd but ubiquitous "cigar-shaped" objects, and soon, tales of both benevolent and malevolent encounters with aliens were commonplace. One of the more bizarre accounts was related by White Sands worker Daniel Fry, who claimed in *The White Sands Incident* (1954) that a flying saucer had given him a ride from White Sands to New York and back. Fry's story was only the beginning, as titles such as *Inside the Space Ships,* by George Adamski, and Orfeo Angelucci's *Secrets of the Saucers* made their way to bookstores in the following year.

As bizarre as these accounts were—Angelucci claimed to have met Jesus Christ on one of his encounters—they shared a single dynamic: visitors came to Earth in *machines*. Aliens were no longer ethereal forces or ectoplasmic apparitions, as were their predecessors in popular culture, like ghosts and vampires. They were, to 1950s kids, what Wells' Martians were to Goddard—beings with superior intellects, capable of producing materials far superior to those found in nature and technologies far more advanced than any on Earth. To some, the aliens with their machines were, as Sergeant Rinaldi explains in William Cameron Menzies' film *Invaders from Mars* (1954), "Mankind developed to its ultimate intelligence," and thus a glimpse into the possible evolutionary future of the human race.

The confluence of fanciful alien encounters and futuristic technology in popular culture helped to define the 1950s, and those themes were quickly and readily appropriated and dramatized for children. Long before launch pads were constructed at White Sands and Cape Canaveral, there was a launch pad at Ninth and Broadway

Image 6.1 Watching rocketmen on television and participating in fan clubs created a generation of children who dreamed of space travel. [Credit: Tom Noel]

in Manhattan. From an upper floor of Wanamaker's Department Store, in a rented studio, *Captain Video and His Video Rangers* first rocketed into public awareness on June 27, 1949. That event caused many youngsters—and adults—to train their eyes on the stars with a new sense of wonder and a view toward exploration and discovery, triggering a cultural chain reaction that would materially influence America's attitude toward space flight in the years to come.

What emerged is what we call "The Rocket Ranger Movement," which was a loose-knit—indeed, most of the members did not know each other—interest group whose focus was part fantasy, part social networking, part spiritual quest, and part science. This movement evolved from a childhood diversion to a cultural and political force that lent credence and enthusiasm to America's fledgling space program. Although a juvenile-focused phenomenon, the pervasive influence of the Rocket Ranger Movement virtually assured the conquest of space.

I

The Rocket Ranger Movement began on the DuMont Television Network, with the premiere of *Captain Video and His Video Rangers* (1949–1955), a program conceived to capitalize on the nation's fascination with technology, particularly television itself. It is, perhaps, no coincidence that DuMont's hero was christened "Video," since the network's founder, Allen DuMont, was a leading innovator in electronics and seller of television sets. The series, as developed by James Caddigan and Maurice Brock, would be a continuation of the kinds of adventures seen in comic books, comic strips, and motion-picture serials exemplified by *Flash Gordon* (1936, 1938, 1940) and *Buck Rogers* (1939), but with a difference: Captain Video would be a space hero, but more importantly, he would be, as the opening narration eventually stated, a "hero of science" in an epoch where science reigned.

As the format played out in two incarnations of the series, Captain Video (Richard Coogan, later Al Hodge) was a private citizen who used his vast knowledge of electronics and technology to police the universe. The setting was Captain Video's secret mountain-top electronics laboratory in the twenty-first century where he and his assistant, a youth known only as the Video Ranger (Don Hastings), used superior technology to keep the world safe from the treachery of various villains. The most dangerous of these was Dr. Pauli (Hal Conklin), who possessed a scientific mind as keen as that of Captain Video. The implications of their antagonism did not go unnoticed by Richard Schwartz in *Cold War Culture*, when he described it as representing "the evolving Cold War belief that scientific and technological superiority would determine the fate of the world."[5] Added to this mix was a network of video rangers composed of young people like those watching at home whose scientific knowledge, technical skill, and moral resolve would aid the Captain and the Ranger in their battle "against the forces of evil everywhere."

Initially Captain Video was earthbound, primarily because the budget was limited—just $25 per week in the initial stages of the series.[6] It was simply cheaper to keep the Captain's feet on the ground than to incur the added expense of other worlds, since exotic worlds would involve more sets and more special effects. For almost a year, DuMont resisted sending Captain Video into space, despite the urgings of viewers and the series star, Richard Coogan. In a 1950 interview with Val Adams, Coogan voiced his displeasure with his character's inability to zoom into outer space. Adams wrote, "As a self-appointed protector of all things noble, he [Video] is itching to throw off his earthly yoke and take up messenger work in the planets beyond." Adams quotes Coogan as declaring that, "It's about time we get into the interplanetary stuff."[7]

But what Captain Video lacked in space-flight technology he made up for in electronic gadgetry. Indeed, he was rivaled only by Tom Swift in his ownership of futuristic gadgets and widgets. His arsenal of weapons was fanciful to the extreme—beyond even the wishful thinking of the child viewer—but nonetheless believable in the language of scientism. The Captain's gadgets sounded authentic, and their designations jibed with the exotic-sounding instruments described by science writers in papers, magazines, and newsreels. Advertisements in mass-market periodicals for Grumman Aircraft, Sperry Corporation, and Packard Bell Electronics, respectively, explained the prowess of the Reeves Electronic Analog Computer, or REAC; the Sperry Gyropilot Flight Control Electronic Brain; and the "Digitizer." Such jargon was similar-sounding to Captain Video's own Cosmic Ray Vibrator, Atomic Disintegrator Rifle, Opticon Scillometer, Solenoid Assentuator, and an Electronic Strait Jacket among a host of other devices. some of which had been suggested by young viewers.[8] Indeed, Captain Video's gadgets were legion. In 1951, a DuMont spokesman estimated that the number of such devices was upwards of 50, all supposedly concocted from the genius of Captain Video himself, whom the spokesman described as "Einstein, Edison and Jules Verne rolled into one and carried to the Nth power."[9]

DuMont finally yielded to pressure and sanctioned Captain Video's flight plan to new worlds, in a tacit admission that matters had been taken out of the network's hands, as it were. DuMont may have created *Captain Video,* but the network held no monopoly on the creative concept of an intergalactic superhero. As noted, *Flash Gordon* and *Buck Rogers* in addition to *Brick Bradford* were already staples of the comics and now *Buck Rogers* (1950–1951) was being touted as a new ABC series and thus competitor to *Captain Video.* Adding to DuMont's discomfiture was that headlines were increasingly referencing real issues surrounding man's pending travels beyond Earth's gravity.

Scripts now called for exploits in the far reaches of space, and Captain Video entered his second incarnation. It did so, however, without Coogan, who had publicly derided *Captain Video* for all the "corny lines,"[10] and regularly used interview and personal appearances to promote himself rather than *Captain Video,* even distancing himself at times from the role.[11] Coogan's lack of belief and dedication to the role would eventually have been apparent to viewers, and the show would have been irreversibly devalued. So in 1950, with sponsorship from Post Cereals, *Captain Video and His Video Rangers* became a space opera complete with a rocket ship called the *Galaxy* and a new Captain Video in the person of Al Hodge, a radio actor who had been the voice of the Green Hornet. The new Captain Video was properly introduced as the "master of space" as well as the "hero of science."

Although the budget was increased, the production remained constrained, and, as in its previous incarnation, relied more on talk than anything else, but with a difference. What mattered now was that the talk was presented with conviction; the so-called corny lines despised by Coogan were now presented with confidence by Hodge, who stated publicly that he always attempted to insert "moral value" into the program. In 1954, while testifying before a Senate subcommittee investigating the supposed connection between television violence and juvenile delinquency, Hodge stated that *Captain Video* had a responsibility to represent science in a positive light and to use that science in a moral and ethical fashion. He asserted that the weapons in the Captain's arsenal were all designed to subdue, never to kill.[12] The imposing Cosmic Vibrator, for example, was actually an instrument that shook the weapons out of the opponents' hands.

Moreover, Hodge, a Sunday school teacher and a man of faith, had scripted a short *Captain Video* adventure for the inspirational *Guideposts* magazine. In this clever story, the Earth was being bombarded by a hate ray from somewhere on the Moon. The hate ray, which was the diabolical invention of Count Callisto, was being aimed at the churches. Captain Video explained Callisto's plan to the Video Ranger: "They're [the churches] our greatest strength, Ranger. Callisto knows it. First he destroys the churches. Then it'll be race against race, planet against planet. It'll mean *fear* in the universe again. Greed. Selfishness. War. That's how he can run things."[13] After a brief battle on the Moon, Callisto and his men were all *captured* and placed in Space Penitentiary, and the blueprints for the hate ray were located and destroyed.

Critics may have scoffed at such simple narratives, along with the pseudoscience and scientific mumbo-jumbo, but the Captain's ethical use of science was never in question. Science existed for the advancement of civilization, and the weapons and other inventions derived from it were designed to defeat evil without killing, to subdue tyranny without turning tyrant in the process. As Hodge told the Senate committee, "We don't even use the word 'kill'... [and we] don't use capital punishment... [but] confine our criminals to rehabilitation centers on the planet Ganymede."[14]

The series' low production values are well worth noting. The inexpensive nature of *Captain Video* was actually one of its strengths, despite the common verdict of most media critics that the series suffered from lack of resources. Perhaps the program lacked in sophistication, but it certainly did not lack in popularity, as evidenced by its eight-year run. The program remained a long-term favorite of children as far away as Great Britain.[15] *Captain Video and His Video Rangers* succeeded as a cultural phenomenon because of, not in spite of, the many budgetary contradictions for an obvious reason: the program fit the existing templates of children's fantasy role-play of the backyard and the schoolyard. Just as, in the imaginative world of the show's juvenile audiences, a large cardboard box would suffice for a spaceship and a stick for a ray gun, in the fantasy world of Captain Video, Wannamaker's toy and hardware departments would suffice for a prop department. One script, for example, called for a stethoscope and a doctor's bag, according to Donald Glut and Jim Harmon in *The Great Television Heroes*.[16] With production about to begin, a harried prop man produced a full-size suitcase and a *child's* stethoscope—just the sort of thing a child could find at home.

For decades, youngsters had been putting on cowboy hats and strapping on six-guns and replaying the settling of the American frontier. Suddenly, with the coming of *Captain Video*, children were donning space helmets and ray guns and projecting the settlement of an entirely new frontier. To them, one frontier was just as real as the other, and in this regard, nothing presented on *Captain Video and His Video Rangers*, nor any of the similar shows that followed, seemed to stretch credulity; secondary considerations did not get in the way of what was being said on the screen, and thus the message was transcendent. The young Rocket Rangers were most willing to consider the future without prejudice or closed minds, and thereby gave authority to theologian Martin Buber's observation that, "Play is the exultation of the possible."

The Rocket Ranger Movement pushed back the boundaries of the playground to encompass much more than the usual grass- and sawdust-covered schoolyards, backyards, and parks of America. Captain Video and his sidekick, the Video Ranger, became regular figures at grand openings, parades, fairs, and sundry special events all across the country. In the process, they were greeted by tens of thousands of Rocket Rangers and their parents. Even Ed Sullivan welcomed Captain Video and the Ranger to *Toast of the Town* on the December 24, 1950, broadcast. *Woman's Day* magazine featured a series of patterns for colorful homemade space helmets in its August 1953 issue. On all fronts, it seemed, a child's vision of the coming frontier was playing out to an ever-widening audience.

Without fully realizing what they had done, the DuMont executives had ignited a trend that developed throughout the network's existence and then faded with the network's own final fade-out in 1956, a year before the launching of the world's first artificial satellite. Captain Video may have kicked off the procession of fellow space heroes, but he could not have expected to maintain his singular status for long. Soon, national and local networks entered their own rocketmen into the space race. *Tom Corbett, Space Cadet* (1950–1955); *Space Patrol* (1950–1955); *Rod Brown of the Rocket Rangers* (1953–1954); Johnny Jupiter (1953–1954); *Flash Gordon* (1954–1955); *Rocky Jones, Space Ranger* (1954); *Commando Cody, Sky Marshal of the Universe* (1955); *Captain Z-Ro* (1954–1960) and others joined the ranks of space explorers who championed American ideals. These television series, along with concomitant radio versions of *Tom Corbett* and *Space Patrol* and several Saturday matinee theatrical serials (including an adaptation of *Captain Video* in 1951), formed a cadre of childhood heroes of the Space Age.

II

Just as Captain Video had his group of Video Rangers at home watching his exploits, virtually every other space hero had his own organized brigade of members sworn to the ideals of their leaders. This camaraderie came about according to an informal social compact between young viewers and television unfamiliar to today's audiences. During the 1950s, television provided role models, respect for viewers, and a sense of inclusion in return for the enthusiasm, loyalty, and attentiveness of the audience. To make this reciprocal loyalty official, as it were, the programs offered membership cards, pledges, oaths of allegiance, and contest participation to grateful audiences. Often, all it took was a box top from a cereal carton or a wrapper from

Image 6.2   Premiums like this Rocky Jones Space Ranger Calculator created a sense of shared identity among young fans of a particular program. [Credit: Tom Noel]

a candy bar, courtesy of the sponsors of the programs, to *belong* to an organization dedicated to high moral principles. With these proofs of purchase, and perhaps, a dime or a quarter, membership kits, rings, comic books, official photographs, plastic figurines, ray guns, badges, and walkie-talkies were routinely available for young rangers. The viewer was not only linked with other viewers in the group but also with the space hero himself, as if child and hero were best friends. Members shared a feeling of kinship with fellow fans across the country whom they might never meet in person—a rudimentary form of social inclusion among strangers, synthesized long before the Internet and social networking.

A ranger setting out to explore distant planets in his playground or backyard could find just the equipment needed at his closest department store. The merchandising of space, as it were, naturally followed the popularity of the numerous rocket-men series, and everything from space helmets to ray guns to space suits were made available to eager space cadets and rangers. One of the more interesting pieces of merchandising seemed to define the age of the Rocket Ranger: the rocket ship. And, indeed, models of rocket ships abounded on toy shelves and as premium offers on television. Backyards all across America were filled with the carcasses of homemade spaceships, supplanting the usual tree house and army fort. Emblematic of this backyard building boom was a book by the beloved children's author Evelyn Sibley Lampman, who had a unique talent for understanding what moved and motivated her young readers. Published by Doubleday in 1957, *Rusty's Space Ship* took spaceship construction one step further. The book's promotional material set the stage, reading in part: "Can you imagine building a space ship out of a box and a few tin cans in your garage and then having it take off into outer space? That's exactly what happened to Rusty and Susan and Cookie, Rusty's dog..."

Any number of girls and boys were likely harboring just such secret thoughts, and youngsters for whom construction of a spaceship was not a reasonable option had a unique opportunity to win a ship of their own. In 1953, Ralston Purina, sponsor of *Space Patrol*, one of the most successful of the space-minded shows then on the air, moved beyond the usual plastic figurines and paper items, offering a premium of unusual magnitude, even for the 1950s: a specially commissioned $30,000, 35-foot replica of Commander Buzz Corry's *Terra IV* spaceship clubhouse. The Ralston Rocket—and a $1,500 cash prize—would be delivered by truck trailer to the lucky contestant who provided the winning name for the mysterious Planet X, which was then an important part of the show's story line. The replica was fully equipped with bunks, electric lights, stove, utensils, and camping equipment. A national tour was arranged, and the *Terra IV* made appearances in supermarket parking lots and schoolyards all across the country with a box top from any Ralston cereal as the price of admission.[17] Space Patroller Ricky Walker of Washington, Illinois, won the *Terra IV* in early 1954 by christening Planet X "Cesaria."[18]

Philip Hamburger, a columnist for *The New Yorker*, described this playground experience as manifested in the actions and attitudes of his own four-year-old son, whom he continually alluded to as "The Boarder." Hamburger recorded the evening that the boy announced that he was through with the usual bedtime stories, insisting that he wanted Captain Video. The youngster proceeded to turn down all parental entreaties to resume his previous infatuation with Peter Rabbit, Mickey

Mouse, and toy trucks. Hamburger noted that earlier that day his son had spent time at a local park playing with several friends who had apparently introduced him to the extraordinary exploits and prowess of Captain Video. When the boy returned home apparently nothing would do for him but to inspect *Captain Video and His Video Rangers* for himself.[19]

Hamburger's frustration with childhood fads clouds the otherwise constructive aspects of the space fellowships; indeed, at the time few complained about the messages being conveyed by the space heroes. For instance, a pledge endorsed by youngsters when signing up for a tour of duty with Rocky Jones' Space Rangers is typical of the code of ethics that would have made any parent exultant: the Space Ranger at home pledged "to obey my parents at all times; to be kind and courteous to all; to be brave in the course of freedom; to help the weak; to obey the law at all times; and to grow up clean in mind and strong in body."[20] Moreover, each member of Rod Brown's Rocket Rangers affirmed among other things that he or she would "never cross orbits with the Rights and Beliefs of others" and "keep my scanner tuned to Learning and remain coupled to my Studies."[21] Captain Video's own oath, shorter than many, was nonetheless all encompassing. Video Rangers solemnly pledged: "We, as Official Video Rangers, hereby promise to abide by the Ranger Code and to support forever the cause of Freedom, Truth, and Justice throughout the universe."[22]

Such codes were also being promoted, and thus reinforced, closer to home, as well, as the Rocket Ranger phenomenon was being appropriated by scores of locally produced children's programs. In the age of *Captain Video*, children could come

Image 6.3 Advertisement for the radio serial "Chris Conway, Rocket Ranger," one of numerous imitators of the nationally televised rocketmen series. [Credit: Author's collection]

home from school and tune into programs whose hosts—many of them rocketmen with names like Space Commander 8, Captain Galaxy, Major Astro, and The Man From Planet X—mixed cartoons with live-action performances and entertainment with education.[23] On the West Coast, for instance, KOIN television in Portland, Oregon, aired *Mr. Moon*, hosted by a rather grotesque figure in space suit, flowing cape, and head in the shape of the moon itself. In the personage of Ed Leahy, Mr. Moon, accompanied by a host of hand puppets, reached an audience of a hundred thousand. The friendly visitor from Luna was welcomed by parents, since Mr. Moon routinely instructed his youthful audience on the importance of good manners, personal hygiene, respect, keeping their rooms in order, bicycle safety, and a multitude of other essential life lessons.[24] Likewise, in Buffalo, New York, Dave Thomas commanded *Rocketship 7*, a program that WKBW executives promised "would have an academic focus with a foundation deeply rooted in scientific facts rather than fanciful fiction."[25]

Moral codes and scientific edification, however simple, carried heavy responsibilities for youth, but rocketmen role models, who illustrated these teachings through feats of derring-do, eased the burden. In turn, it was hoped, the rocketmen's moral codes would be played out in home, at school, and on the playground by the rangers.

Even without these high expectations, the imaginative play of the Rocket Rangers was serious business. Parents who, like Hamburger, indulged their children's enthusiasm for space and exotic gadgets but dismissed it as "kid stuff" were, like Hamburger, missing the point. The new medium of television was suddenly being integrated into playground interactions and, through the fan clubs, into an early form of social networking. More importantly, the Rocket Rangers' enthusiasm for all things space-related connected them to the future that was, even then, being built and tested at White Sands, Cape Canaveral, and, it became clear in October 1957, the Soviet Union as well. The fact that Russians—not, despite the Eisenhower administration's promise, Americans—had launched the world's first artificial satellite, and so conquered space, turned rockets and space travel from the silly stuff of science fiction and children's games to matters of national security. The launch of *Sputnik I* was a technological marvel, but also cause for deep concern. The Cold War enemy had scored what physicist and H-bomb designer Edward Teller called "a technological Pearl Harbor."

Suddenly, an *I-told-you-so* attitude gripped the nation, and the task of besting the Russians fell upon a small cadre of visionaries and scientists—the heirs to Robert Goddard, scientists like Willy Ley and Wernher von Braun—who, along with storytellers like Arthur C. Clarke, had been passionately advocating for the idea of exploring space. They were convinced the scientific underpinnings were in place to make space exploration entirely feasible, but the general population at that time remained skeptical and unmoved. So, in the 1950s, as Howard McCurdy writes, these visionaries "undertook a deliberate public relations campaign to convince Americans that space flight was real."[26]

This proselytizing on behalf of space exploration took place on many fronts. Lectures at planetariums and science museums—notably a 1951 "space symposium" at New York's Hayden Planetarium—reached out to those already interested in scientific and technical matters, while articles in general circulation magazines like *Life* and *Collier's* courted a broader audience. Large-format books like *Across the Space Frontier* (1952) and *The Conquest of the Moon* (1953), which combined authoritative text with spectacular artists' renderings of space hardware, appealed to both. Most importantly, however, rocket experts utilized the persuasive power of television. Ley served as technical adviser for *Tom Corbett, Space Cadet*, his highly touted presence assuring viewers that the science and technology discussed in the series were accurate. Together with von Braun, he appeared on numerous programs including *Johns Hopkins Science Review, Camel News Caravan*, and *Today*, and collaborated with Walt Disney on three hour-long documentaries about space travel that aired, between 1954 and 1957, on the weekly television series *Disneyland*. The rocket experts acted as technical advisers for the animated sequences, and appeared as on-screen experts who explained rocket propulsion, orbits, and weightlessness to the immense viewing audiences that the Disney name guaranteed. They revealed the science and technology behind the imaginary world in which the Rocket Rangers played, and reinforced—in children and parents alike—the idea that such play reached toward a very real (and very near) future.

Von Braun's and Ley's best efforts, however, did little to reach the group they most wanted to influence: the political and military leaders who had the power to make space travel a reality. To most in Washington, space travel remained "kid stuff" until October 1957, when *Sputnik* made it a stark matter of national prestige and, indeed, national survival. Confronted by evidence of superior technology in the hands not of imaginary aliens but of real Soviet enemies, American politicians scrambled to find both a solution and a scapegoat. The Eisenhower administration, in an ironic coda to a decade of government indifference to such "fantasy," arranged for the *Disneyland* space episodes to be screened at the Pentagon as a primer on the emergent Space Age.

Politicians, meanwhile, turned their ire on the American educational system, which had already been under assault for its perceived malfeasance. Critics from both the right and the left deemed John Dewey's progressive education a failure, and several books at the time had criticized progressive education's emphasis on educating the whole child at the expense of academic subjects.[27] The turning point came with a five-part series in *Life* magazine one year after the launch of *Sputnik*. Titled "The Crisis in Education," the series boldly concluded that "the schools are in terrible shape."[28] *Life* had done what the scholarly essays and books had not; *Life* had reached the masses and the result was swift: the nation had to do something to gain scientific superiority, and the only way to achieve that goal was by producing scientists. So, in September 1958, Congress passed the National Defense Education Act, which sent billions to schools for the advancement of science and math.

Suddenly, science was de rigueur. It was, in the vernacular of the time, "cool," and for young people being a scientist was being a hero just as Captain Video had been the "hero of science." Toy stores that had been supplying the paraphernalia of fictional space men were now supplying toys of real-world science that transformed Erector Sets and chemistry sets into complete home-scientific laboratories. "Educational hobby sets" like Electricity and Solar Power Labs, Weather Stations, Communications Labs, and Electric Sets in which the youthful scientist could experiment with light and electromagnetism, not to mention toy Geiger counters, were filling the pages of Christmas catalogs. Indeed, with the "Digicomp I," which was a "real operating digital computer in plastic," a child could add, subtract, shift, memorize, solve problems, and learn *new math*.[29]

If parents were panicked, the Rocket Rangers were not. What seemed so new and crucial to adults at this point was not so new or so consequential to the youngsters. Scientific technology was a consistent thread in their popular-culture worlds: they had already been exposed to science, or at least to scientific principles, in *Captain Video* and other rocketman shows, and since the early 1950s, they had been educated in science proper by a friendly tutor known as Mr. Wizard, in the appropriately named *Watch Mr. Wizard* (1951–1972) television series. By drawing science into the domestic sphere, Mr. Wizard, in the personage of the show's creator, Don Herbert, made experimentation and inquiry safe, familiar-seeming, and fun. Boys and girls simply "dropped by" to learn exciting new scientific knowledge, imparted by an easygoing neighbor who casually encouraged their questions and active participation.

Mr. Wizard's actual science was no different in appearance and effect from the fanciful science offered by the "electronic *wizard*" Captain Video, and the other adventurers, in that it simply asked that children open their minds and imaginations to the "what if"s of science and technology. While Mr. Wizard relied on the notion of "what if" in order to complete his homegrown experiments, Captain Video and his rocketmen colleagues relied their own "what if"s—on fantastic inventions designed and created by "heroes of science"—in order to subdue threats to the universe.

Image 6.4 Mr. Wizard introduces one of his young guests to the wonders of real-world science. [Credit: Author's collection]

The learned elders of the space community, along with parents like Philip Hamburger, looked upon the likes of Captain Video, Tom Corbett, and their brethren with a mixture of condescension, disdain, and perplexity. In the eyes of most adults, it was all nonsense, but in the eyes of their offspring, something much more basic was in play. Reason and imagination were coalescing in such television offerings as *Watch Mr. Wizard* and the *Bell System Science Series*, hosted by the avuncular Dr. Frank Baxter, but the young Rocket Rangers were also taking away from their fanciful television friends a sense of wonder and an enthusiasm for space science, something that the adult population prior to Eisenhower's America would never have been able to comprehend.

By 1956, however, the various space-adventure programs that had anchored the Rocket Ranger Movement had ceased production, and the DuMont network itself ceased broadcasting. There is no valid connection between the two other than coincidence, but with the demise of *Captain Video* and DuMont space fantasy gave way to more scientifically predicated series, as science itself was taking a prominent position in society. Flying-saucer sightings had escalated throughout the 1950s, reaching decade highs in 1952 and 1957.[30] The exploits of real-world "rocketmen" were becoming as well known as those of Captain Video and his cohort: test pilots Chuck Yeager and Scott Crossfield competed for the title of "fastest man alive" as they pushed the air speed record past Mach 2; Bill Bridgeman broke world altitude records, flying to nearly eighty thousand feet, and wrote about it in his successful memoir *The Lonely Sky* (1955); and US Air Force flight surgeon Lt. Col. John Paul Stapp was dubbed "the fastest man on Earth" for testing the limits of human endurance by strapping himself to a 450-mph rocket sled.[31] The line between "real" science and imaginary science became increasingly blurred as reality, science, and science fiction merged in the rapidly advancing space program. Popular television series like *Science Fiction Theatre* (1957–1959), *Man and the Challenge* (1959–1960), and *Men into Space* (1959–1960) were now capturing the ongoing interest of viewers with science that was more like *Mr. Wizard* than *Captain Video*.

But if *Captain Video* faded away, the Rocket Ranger Movement did not; it merely matured. The ten-year-olds who started out with *Captain Video and His Video Rangers* were of college age as the 1950s drew to a close. These former Rocket Rangers had witnessed the fantastic, almost surrealistic space adventures of 1949 slowly become reality before their eyes, with the launch of the *Sputnik* and *Explorer* satellites and the subsequent flights of Yuri Gagarin and Alan Shepard. And in a contest reminiscent of the Ralston Rocket challenge, Kraft Foods launched a new spaceship giveaway in 1959. While Ralston's 1954 *Space Patrol* promotion had featured the mockup of what amounted to an impressionistic space vehicle, Kraft went to great lengths to offer a replica of an authentic training ship. Built by Aerojet-General Corporation, a producer of equipment for NASA, as well as the US Army, Navy, and Air Force, the Kraft ship screamed authenticity. "Actually moves—simulates climb, glide, roll! Holds crew of four," the Kraft publicity department assured contestants. The Kraft simulator came complete with space suits and helmets based on authentic equipment. Kraft was clearly going for serious-minded Rocket Rangers. Lesser prizes also reflected a serious space approach: 50 Jupiter Astronomical Telescopes,

500 "realistic" missiles and launchers, 300 spaceship model kits and 5,000 giant full-color Hammond space maps.[32]

Nowhere, however, is this sea change better illustrated than in a true Rocket Ranger's memoir appropriately called *Rocket Boys* (1998). The launch of *Sputnik* in 1957 had a mesmerizing influence on Homer Hickam Jr., of Coalwood, West Virginia, a 14-year-old boy whose reading habits included Verne, Clarke, Bradbury, Robert Heinlein, and Isaac Asimov, and whose childhood consisted, in part, of "playing cowboys or spacemen or pirates."[33] Hickam was so caught up in satellites that he extended his Rocket Ranger fellowship, as it were, to like-minded friends and together they formed The Big Creek Missile Agency (BCMA). The fantasy of the missile, the rocket, and the spaceship of his Rocket Ranger days now turned to actually building and firing off model missiles that would lead Hickman to NASA as an engineer. His childhood fantasies and dreams had become reality.

Even though few Rocket Rangers went on to careers in space, many carried away a full-fledged appreciation for the wonder of space and what it meant to extend one's reach beyond the observable horizon. Prior to *Sputnik*, when the rocket experts themselves were courting a mostly disinterested adult population, the Rocket Rangers were becoming consumed by the idea of investigating space, and they became true advocates for America's space program. Rising in the wee morning hours to view a scheduled space launch became as routine for many of them as standing and saluting the flag in school later that same day. It was this new generation that would someday fill the ranks of the astronaut corps and pay the taxes used to buttress space

Image 6.5   Many of the Rocket Rangers of the 1950s went on to become passionate followers of NASA's real space program in the 1960s. [Credit: Wade Williams Enterprises]

research as well as provide the political support and popular enthusiasm necessary to sustain the space program.

There is a suggestion today that children are no longer allowed to be children, that virtually from the age of awareness they are robbed of their rightful playtime and instead are all too often forced to confront adult issues if only because slighted adults themselves lost their childhood in the ensuing age of drugs, homelessness, divorce, gang violence, and predatory adults. To whatever extent this may be so, we all lose when childhood dreams turn dark and foreboding. But we profit mightily when childhood insights are allowed the opportunity to stand or fall on their own merits.

Captain Video and his space brethren befriended children as children through shared imagination, and by so doing they armed the Rocket Rangers with the most powerful weapon of all: knowledge.

NOTES

1. Frederick Lewis Allen, *The Big Change: America Transforms Itself* (New York: Harper and Brothers, 1952), 120.
2. During the International Geophysical Year in 1957–1958
3. Robert B. McLaughlin, "How Scientists Tracked a Flying Saucer," *True*, March 1950.
4. Curtis L. Peebles, *Watch the Skies! A Chronicle of the Flying Saucer Myth* (Washington, DC: Smithsonian, 1994).
5. Richard A. Schwartz, *Cold War Culture: Media and the Arts 1945–1990* (New York: Checkmark Books, 2000), 52
6. George W. Woolery, *Children's Television: The First Thirty-Five Years, 1946–1981* (Metuchen NJ: Scarecrow Press 1985), vol. 2, 107–108.
7. Val Adams, "'Space Opera' Hero," *New York Times;* March 26, 1950, B11.
8. Woolery, 109, 41.
9. Harriet Van Horne, "Space Rocket Kick," *Theatre Arts*, December 1951, 41.
10. Adams, B11.
11. David Weinstein, *The Forgotten Network: DuMont and the Birth of American Television* (Philadelphia: Temple University Press, 2004), 78.
12. "Captain to the Rescue." *Newsweek*, November 1, 1954, 20.
13. Al Hodge, "Captain Video's Toughest Mission," in *Faith Made Them Champions*, ed. Norman Vincent Peale (Carmel, NY: Guideposts Associates, 1954), 165.
14. "Captain," 20.
15. David Kyle, *A Pictorial History of Science Fiction* (New York: Hamlyn, 1976), 128.
16. Donald F. Glut and Jim Harmon, *The Great Television Heroes* (Garden City, NY: Doubleday, 1975), 6–7.
17. "Look...Girls!—Boys!" *The Evening Observer* [Dunkirk], September 28, 1953, A9.
18. Gary H. Grossman, *Saturday Morning TV* (New York: Dell, 1981), 235.
19. Philip Hamburger, "Now I Lay Me Down to Sleep," *The New Yorker*, December 22, 1951, 57.
20. Ted Hake, *Hake's Price Guide To Character Toys*, 3rd ed. (Timonium, MD: Gemstone Publishing, 2000), 360.
21. Glut and Harmon, 86.
22. J. Fred MacDonald, *Television and the Red Menace: The Video Road to Vietnam* (New York: Praeger, 1985), 124.

23. Tim F. Hollis, *Hi There, Boys and Girls* (Jackson, MS: University Press of Mississippi, 2001), *passim*.
24. "Local Creative Talent, Ingenuity Goes into Production of Mr. Moon," *The Oregonian* [Portland], September 29, 1957, C8.
25. Rocketship7.com. September 12, 2011.
26. Howard E. McCurdy. *Space and the American Imagination*, (Washington, DC: Smithsonian Institution Press, 1997), 39.
27. Lawrence A. Cremin, *The Transformation of the School: Progressivism in American Education 1876–1957* (New York: Alfred Knopf, 1961).
28. "The Crisis in Education," *Life*, March 24, 1958, 25.
29. Thomas W. Holland, *Boys' Toys of the Fifties and Sixties: Memorable Pages from the Legendary Sears Christmas Wishbooks 1950–1969* (Sherman Oaks, CA: Windmill Press, 1997), 245.
30. David Michael Jacobs. *The UFO Controversy in America* (Bloomington: Indiana University Press, 1975), 304.
31. Richard P. Hallion, *Supersonic Flight: Breaking the Sound Barrier and Beyond* (Washington, DC: Brassey's, 1997); Nick T. Spark, *A History of Murphy's Law* (Hove, UK: Periscope Films, 2006).
32. "Boys! Girls! Enter Kraft's Naming Contest!" *Salt Lake Tribune*, August 23, 1959, A75.
33. Homer H. Hickam Jr. *Rocket Boys*. (Logan, IA: Perfection Learning, 1999), 11, 21.

BIBLIOGRAPHY

Adams, Val. "'Space Opera' Hero." *New York Times*, March 26, 1950, B11.
Adamski, George. *Inside the Space Ships*. New York: Abelard Schuman, 1955.
Allen, Frederick Lewis. *The Big Change: America Transforms Itself*. New York: Harper and Brothers, 1952.
Angelucci, Orfeo. *Secrets of the Saucers*. Amherst, WI: Amherst Press, 1955.
"Boys! Girls! Enter Kraft's Naming Contest!" *Salt Lake Tribune*, August 23, 1959, A75.
"Captain to the Rescue." *Newsweek*, November 1, 1954.
Cremin, Lawrence A. *The Transformation of the School: Progressivism in American Education 1876–1957*. New York: Alfred Knopf, 1961.
"The Crisis in Education." *Life*, March 24, 1958.
Fry, Daniel. *The White Sands Incident*. 1954. Madison, WI: Horus House Publishers, 1992.
Glut, Donald F., and Jim Harmon. *The Great Television Heroes*. Garden City, NY: Doubleday, 1975.
Grossman, Gary H. *Saturday Morning TV*. New York: Dell, 1981.
Hake, Ted. *Hake's Price Guide To Character Toys*. 3rd ed. Timonium, MD: Gemstone Publishing, 2000.
Hallion, Richard P. *Supersonic Flight: Breaking the Sound Barrier and Beyond*. Washington, DC: Brassey's, 1997.
Hamburger, Philip. "Now I Lay Me Down To Sleep." *The New Yorker*, December 22, 1951.
Hickam, Homer H. Jr. *Rocket Boys*. Logan, IA: Perfection Learning, 1999.
Hodge, Al. "Captain Video's Toughest Mission," 1954. In *Faith Made Them Champions*, ed. Norman Vincent Peale, 164–167. Carmel, NY: Guideposts Associates 1954.
Holland, Thomas W., ed. *Boys' Toys of the Fifties and Sixties: Memorable Pages from the Legendary Sears Christmas Wishbooks 1950–1969*. Sherman Oaks, CA: Windmill Press, 1997.

Hollis, Tim F. *Hi There, Boys and Girls*. Jackson, MS: University Press of Mississippi, 2001.

Jacobs, David Michael. *The UFO Controversy in America*. Bloomington: Indiana University Press, 1975.

Kyle, David. *A Pictorial History of Science Fiction*. New York: The Hamlyn Publishing Group, 1976.

"Local Creative Talent, Ingenuity Goes into Production of Mr. Moon." *The Oregonian* [Portland], September 29, 1957, C8.

"Look...Girls!—Boys!" *The Evening Observer* [Dunkirk], September 28, 1953, A9.

Lucanio, Patrick, and Gary Coville. *Smokin' Rockets: The Romance of Technology in American Film, Radio and Television, 1945–1962*. Jefferson NC: McFarland, 2002.

MacDonald, J. Fred. *Television and the Red Menace: The Video Road to Vietnam*. New York: Praeger, 1985.

McCurdy, Howard E. *Space and the American Imagination*. Washington, DC: Smithsonian Institution Press 1997.

McLaughlin, Robert B. "How Scientists Tracked a Flying Saucer." *True*, March 1950, 24–27.

Peebles, Curtis L. *Watch the Skies! A Chronicle of the Flying Saucer Myth*. Washington, DC: Smithsonian, 2004.

Schwartz, Richard A. *Cold War Culture: Media and the Arts 1945–1990*. New York: Checkmark Books, 2000.

Spark, Nick T. *A History of Murphy's Law*. Hove, UK: Periscope Films, 2006.

Strong, Jean. "All Aboard for the Moon—!" *The Cedar Rapids Gazette*, January 3, 1954, A10.

Van Horne, Harriet. "Space Rocket Kick." *Theatre Arts*, December 1951.

Weinstein, David. *The Forgotten Network: DuMont and the Birth of American Television*. Philadelphia: Temple University Press, 2004.

Woolery, George W. *Children's Television: The First Thirty-Five Years, 1946–1981*, vol. 2. Metuchen, NJ: Scarecrow Press, 1985.

CHAPTER 7

SPACE OPERA TV: SEEING THE WORLD OF TOMORROW

J. P. TELOTTE

VIEWED TODAY, AN EARLY TELEVISION SPACE OPERA LIKE *CAPTAIN Video* seems far more than quaint. There is almost a surreal dimension to it—or what some might describe as a postmodern tone. For regularly in the midst of an episode involving heroic adventures in space or on other planets, the Captain, his companion Video Ranger, or another Ranger assistant will suddenly turn on a video monitor, the Captain's "Special Remote Carrier Beam," as it is termed, so that audiences can watch the exploits of some of the Captain's "special agents"—actually scenes from a B-western or serial from the 1930s or 1940s.[1] More than just a sop to youngsters who, as one contemporaneous commentator suggested, "might otherwise pine for TV cowboys,"[2] that strange interruption/eruption (of both another genre and another medium) brought with it a certain self-referential baggage, as if this serial narrative seemingly intended for children had suddenly taken stock of itself and was reflecting on its potentially pervasive and transportive power—offering a kind of lesson in watching. Yet *Captain Video* (1949–1955) was hardly unique in this reflexive regard, for its many imitators, the pervasive space operas that colonized American television screens between 1949 and 1956 (and then suddenly disappeared from those screens as real-life science overtook science fiction), all seem in their own ways quite conscious of the new medium and their place in it. And that reflexive character, I would suggest, can help us to better understand the attraction of these series, as well as the role they played in constructing an audience for early television.

What did it mean to be a television viewer in the late 1940s and early 1950s, to be involved with this new technology that was suddenly linking our homes to another sort of "outer space," to the larger world "out there" somewhere? How were we supposed to respond to this new space that was suddenly just a window away yet beckoning to us, especially with its pitchmen who regularly "beamed in" to us, directly addressing us in our homes? Francesco Casetti has argued that film fashioned its powerful attraction by developing a "gaze" that "taught us not only to take a second look at the world, but to look in a different way."[3] Television, I would suggest, followed suit, suggesting its own, rather different manner of looking for its fledgling audience in this early period.

While still relatively new to American audiences, television—and by extension the televisual experience—was something that, for many years, had been presented as a futuristic device, in fact, as science fictional. As I have shown elsewhere, popular science fiction films of the 1920s through the 1940s repeatedly presented television as part of their speculative regimes, as one more technological development that, when it finally arrived, might in various fantastic ways change our lives.[4] It was a component in a system of instantaneous communication and observation in the German *Metropolis* (1927), part of an all-seeing panopticon arrangement in the serial *The Phantom Empire* (1935), a device that could bring a dangerous "death ray" into the home in *Death by Television* (1935), a means of time travel by capturing and broadcasting images from the past in *The Invisible Ray* (1936), even a method for duping and panicking a naive public in *S.O.S.—Tidal Wave* (1939). Consequently, it had already become—long before the 1950s when television finally made its presence felt in everyday American life—a familiar icon of science fiction, much like such other popular icons of the genre in those days: rocket ships, ray guns, hand-held communicators. As such, television was, in the late 1940s and early 1950s, more than just another domestic appliance, and more than, as Cecelia Tichi once styled it, a kind of "electronic hearth." It was a link to the fantastic—to utopian concepts, to far-off places, to danger—and ultimately to the changing nature of our world and our place in that world.

Even as it became more familiar—or domesticated—in this early television era, the medium was unable to shake off elements of that earlier character. As William Boddy reminds us, a variety of "anxieties and conflicts" had "accompanied the post-war launch of commercial television in the United States," and those attitudes still show traces of that science fictional character. Thus he suggests that those attitudes "reveal a profound cultural ambivalence about the television set as an object, television viewing as an activity, and about television's relation to the ideals of post-war domesticity."[5] That broad ambivalence would make it essential that television find ways of modeling and inculcating a proper audience attitude, of suggesting how both television and its viewers might function. And as John Ellis has shown, television generally followed this imperative rather quickly, developing "distinctive aesthetic forms to suit the circumstances" of broadcast presentation, with an emphasis on short, discrete narrative segments, a greater reliance upon dialogue than we find in the cinema, and a kind of dislocated viewer gaze, or what he terms—with an eye to the many other distractions to be found in a domestic rather than theatrical setting—a "glance." And with science fiction, a form that was fundamentally invested in issues of visual spectacle and already tied in viewers' minds to the post-war prominence of science and technology, the new medium also located a narrative model that could support a proper sort of viewership, one that could help counter or properly frame those free-floating cultural "anxieties and conflicts" by letting us see them "in a different way."[6]

In his discussion of American science fiction television, Lincoln Geraghty adds an important cultural dimension to this effect. For he suggests that while the early space operas, works like *Captain Video, Tom Corbett, Space Cadet* (1950–1955), *Space Patrol* (1950–1955), *Rod Brown of the Rocket Rangers* (1953–1954), *Rocky Jones, Space Ranger* (1954), and others "may have relied overly on archetypal characters, tired generic tropes and the same plot structures...they also offer an insight into how television was reflecting back and responding to the Cold War psyche."[7] Specifically, he suggests that the technological developments depicted in these shows were but markers in a larger cultural conflict, that "the aesthetics of technological innovation and visualizations of the future" they offered audiences were emblematic of "American domination in science and technology" during the Cold War, convincing signs of Western culture's advantages over the communist societies with which we increasingly found ourselves in conflict.[8] And indeed, the space operas of the 1950s regularly played out those Cold War tensions, often using planetary stand-ins for East and West. But in consort with this ideological work, these technological marvels, I would suggest, also played an important subjective role, helping to turn audiences into proper viewers, right-*seeing*, as well as right-*thinking*, members of modern American society.

Of course, constructing the spectacle of technology—much less conveying that spectacle—was no simple task for shows that found much of their narrative inspiration in the cheaply made serials of previous decades and that suffered under the notoriously minimalist budgets of early juvenile television. *Captain Video*, as has often been noted, accomplished its futuristic vision with just a $25 per-episode effects budget.[9] In fact, in surveying the many toys and kids' products created to promote and profit from the series, one discussion of this preeminent space opera archly suggests that the products "inadvertently recreated some of the cardboard feel of the sets for the program."[10] And another critique noted that "sponsors and licensees could credibly claim that the guns, rings, and uniforms for sale at the local store were the same ones that were used on the set."[11] Working in a similar mold, most of the other series relied heavily on a narrative pattern of cheapness, intercutting small, crudely crafted rocket miniatures with interior dialogue scenes. And while it was one of the more visually ambitious of the space operas, *Tom Corbett, Space Cadet* found another sort of economy by modeling its rockets in the shape of the German V-2 of World War II. With that likeness, historical footage of that rocket in flight could be inserted to depict the takeoff of Tom's craft, the *Polaris*, at the start of each episode, as well as at other key points in each story, as the series co-opted a filmic spectacle for the new televisual context.

Moreover, even while most of the space operas were set far in the future—*Captain Video* in the twenty-second century, *Tom Corbett* in the twenty-fourth century, and *Space Patrol* in the thirtieth century—very little effort was actually made to *depict* that future. For doing so would have required far more than the few miniatures of rockets and spaceports that these series, as well as such similar efforts as *Buck Rogers* (1950–1951), *Rocky Jones, Space Ranger*, and *Rod Brown of the Rocket*

Rangers largely used to denote their future eras. Instead, these series typically relied on limited, broadly suggestive sets, with most of the action limited to interiors. Thus Patrick Lucanio and Gary Coville note that the most iconic of these series, *Captain Video*, "was earthbound" for many months in its early run, with "most of the action" taking place at Video Ranger Headquarters where audience point of view could be carefully framed and constructed, directed toward effects like the Special Remote Carrier.[12] The rather more thoughtful *Tom Corbett, Space Cadet*, with its primary emphasis on character relationships, would use its central characters to *suggest* futuristic spectacle—a technique remarked upon in a review of the very first episode that describes "a rocket crash sequence, in which light flickered on the faces of the watching cadets to give the *impression* of the ship in flames."[13] While the far more expensively produced *Space Patrol* typically promised at the start of each episode "high adventure in the wild vast reaches of space," the interior of Commander Buzz Corry's rocket ship *Terra IV* or, later, *Terra V*, was usually the location of much of that action with Buzz (Ed Kemmer), Cadet Happy (Lyn Osborn), and others reacting to events, looking out through the eye-like windows of the ship, or *monitoring* them on television-like screens. When land-based action did occur, it was most often keyed by painted backdrops, such as that of the flat-looking castle on a hill within which most of the "Secrets of Eternal Youth" (1953) episode occurs. And the very *lack* of a concerted focus on the usual fascination of media science fiction, that is, on the spectacle of wonder, is itself telling, reminding us that, as Ellis suggests, a televisual "glance" was enough to limn those future realms.

Besides emphasizing the *seeing* of and *reaction* to spectacle rather than spectacle itself, all of these series did offer another sort of wonder, as they richly larded their

Image 7.1 Captain Video tunes in his "Remote Carrier" TV screen. [Credit: DuMont Television Network]

narratives with various futuristic gadgets, used not only to defend the solar system, galaxy, and/or universe, but also to connect to that largely *suggested* or crudely depicted universe out there. Certainly, *Captain Video* was the template in this regard, since the Captain in each episode used a variety of such devices, all with highly scientific-sounding names, such as: the Opticon Scillometer that allowed him to see through solid objects, the Mango-Radar for eavesdropping on conversations anywhere on the planet, the Ultraplanetary Transmitter, a galactic communication device, and the Discatron, a portable video screen and intercom. These devices—and many others—not only attested to the Captain's status as, the show's narrator often intoned, "Master of Science," but they also modeled a properly futuristic way of interacting with the world. In fact, a contemporary commentator argued that the show "derives its appeal" precisely from its constant use of such "fancy gadgetry."[14] And that argument is not far off the mark, since those strangely named props suggested that, in the future, we would interact with our world largely *through* technology—technology that would allow us to see, hear, and even control the world in ways that had never before been possible. They hinted, in effect, at the very power of new technologies of surveillance and control such as television itself.

And when, in each episode, the Captain or a Ranger would turn to the Special Remote Carrier, the video screen that was centrally placed in a wall of the Video Ranger Headquarters, always looking back at us, that reflexive connection, as well as the true import of the Captain's name, became most explicit. The camera would typically dolly in to the screen while Ranger Rogers or another of the Captain's helpers directed our attention with a phrase like, "What do you say we beam in Captain Video's Western agents?" It is an invitation that effectively frames another sort of adventure (in this case, the Western) within the following short, discrete narrative segment, that establishes our role as passive viewers—and consumers—of the ensuing narrative, and that prepares us for other sorts of direct address that would ensue, easily interrupting our "glance" relationship to the screen to afford other, equally appealing relationships.

The key other relationship to which I refer is seen in those instances when Captain Video's own adventures would often and rather suddenly be framed on that same video screen by one of the Rangers, who would then segue into a commercial for one of the sponsoring products, such as Post's Sugar Crisp cereal or PowerHouse candy bars. The resulting *mise en abyme* created by this sort of narrative shift, a typical camera track back, and transitional comments such as, "Suppose the Ranger and the Captain don't come through all right?" or "Things couldn't be worse for Captain Video and the Ranger," situated viewers not in the sort of narrative immersion common with classical Hollywood storytelling of the period, nor even quite in the cliffhanger circumstance common to the series' close cinematic cousin, the adventure serial. Rather, they construct a realm of discrete narrative segments, such as Ellis describes, that easily shift from one level of narrative to another, and from narrative to commercial, in fact, that blur the lines between the show's various "levels," while also both underscoring and suspending our relationship to the narrative—a double move that would prove essential to the further development of commercial broadcast television with its constant negotiation between the imperatives of story and of advertisement.

With *Captain Video*'s primary space opera imitators, many of these audience characteristics would find further development. However, in few cases were there the sort of enforced narrative breaks associated with watching the Captain's "Western agents," since that show had so quickly and effectively demonstrated the primary appeal of the space opera itself, and especially of its stalwart futuristic heroes who were clearly attractive in their own right and, as Lucanio and Coville note, were even invested with "enough mythic quality to compel a considerable number of adults to take notice."[15] A series like *Johnny Jupiter* (1953–1954) did feature a young inventor, Ernest P. Duckweather (Wright King), who, we are told at the beginning of each episode, "invented a television set unlike any ever known before, for on this set he was able to tune in the planet Jupiter." With it he would converse with two of that planet's inhabitants, Johnny Jupiter and his robot companion B-12 (both hand puppets), who could see Ernest even without a camera. Thus at various points in each episode the action would break as Ernest contacted his planetary neighbors for advice or help on his latest Earth-bound dilemma. And as with *Captain Video*, these television-breaks-on-television would also provide the opportunity for another reframing—or remonitoring—as the show would pull further away from the action to directly address the audience, urging them to buy the sponsor's product, M&M candies. That link between the television as a source of advice and power and as product appeal, though, only makes more explicit the connection that *Captain Video* had already firmly established and formularized.

The more famous and longer-lived space operas, particularly those that derive most clearly from the *Captain Video* mold, such as *Tom Corbett, Space Cadet* and

Image 7.2 Hawking a toy version of Commander Buzz Corry's ray gun on *Space Patrol*. Credit: American Broadcasting Company.

Space Patrol, suffered few such shifts of narrative level, reserving their self-referential breaks solely for the commercials, typically featuring Tom or other space cadets in the former and, in the latter, frequently Commander Buzz Corry himself (originally Kit Corry), the leader of the Space Patrol that policed the galaxy, keeping peace in the name of The United Planets. In both cases, the principles would directly address the "boys and girls of the audience," looking directly into the camera as they urged them to "wear Red Goose shoes" (*Tom Corbett*)—which came with a free "space cadet identification bracelet"—or to hear a "special message" from Commander Corry, one that urged the junior members of the Patrol to "get supercharged like I do" by eating the various Ralston Purina cereals, such as Rice Chex and Wheat Chex, or to enjoy Nestlé's chocolate candies (*Space Patrol*) so they would be properly "fueled" for their own adventures.

That easy shift of the central characters from their narrative immersion to the hawking of sponsors' products and back again is consistent both with Jeffrey Sconce's description of early television's "uncanny electronic space capable of collapsing, compromising, and even displacing the real world," and with the still-new medium's "greater reliance on sound" that Ellis notes.[16] And in fact, it might underscore the extent to which, for all of their supposed fantastic action, these shows, but especially *Tom Corbett*, were typically much more invested at every level in talk—especially talk as a kind of narration—and in character reactions than in the frenetic activity associated with their serial forebears. As an example, we might consider an episode like "The Runaway Rocket" (1954) in which Tom Corbett (Frankie Thomas) and his fellow cadets on board the *Polaris* are tasked with tracking a new test rocket on its speed trials during a run to Mars. Their task is largely that of visual and telemetric observation, as Tom and fellow cadet Astro (Al Markim) spend much of the episode simply looking out through the viewport and toward the audience, describing their tasks, while their usual companion, Roger Manning (Jan Merlin), watches on a telescopic device and later on the ship's long-range scanner. Consequently, most of the show's action is measured out through their visual and verbal reactions as they watch—electronically—the test ship malfunction, veer off course and out of control, and head toward the sun. Even their ensuing rescue of the "Runaway" is played as a series of crosscut scenes between the cockpits of the two rockets, during which the *Polaris*, as we learn solely from their *dialogue*—since there are no visuals of the action—pulls alongside the other ship and nudges it away from danger, while the crews of each rocket observe from their seats. Here and elsewhere, space—both *outer* space and the physical space in which action typically occurs—has indeed been collapsed into dialogue and framed by the act of looking, as the on-screen characters in their watching and talking effectively construct the typical science fiction spectacle.

This construction offers a good deal of narrative economy, and does, as we have noted, serve the series' primary focus on character, as we can observe in a remarkably similar episode, the following season's "The Pursuit of the Deep Space Projectile" (1955). In this show much of the plot derives from the introduction of cadet Monroe, a specialist who helped design a rocket sent to collect information on the planet Sirius. Monroe quickly comes into conflict with the usual *Polaris* crew, Tom, Astro, and T. J. Thistle (the final season's replacement for Manning), as he questions their

Image 7.3 T.J., Tom Corbett, and Astro survey the world of outer space through their rocket's window. NBC. [Credit: Wade Williams Enterprises]

navigation and flying ability, as if they were not able to "see" properly—either electronically or physically. Tensions rise when they are unable to locate the "deep space projectile," and the resulting disagreements play out once more against a background of anxiously looking into scanners, watching radar screens, and inspecting a large, wall-mounted plotter. In fact, one extended scene emphasizes the tension that has built up around their search by superimposing a radar screen over close-ups of the various characters. When the rocket is eventually located, all must work together to retrieve it before it can fall into Sirius' sun. In this episode, models of the *Polaris* and the smaller projectile briefly serve to depict their docking, but again Tom largely describes that activity as he watches, as Astro attends to a bank of various monitors, and as Monroe, now, because of the emergency, fully integrated into the crew, assists by plotting the proper course. And with the rocket successfully retrieved, the show ends with the crew once again seated and happily looking out toward space, in effect, looking toward their next adventure together. Like the larger narrative, the ending is a fairly commonplace one, but it also underscores how much of the series is spent not *in action*, but in *inaction*, with the cadets, like a proper television audience, *watching* events, talking about them, effectively seated before a spectacle that unfolds on their screens, scanners, or other technological tools. And its satisfying resolution, one marked by unity and good fellowship, suggests the sort of benefits that this unmistakably *televisual* situation might produce.

While running in approximately the same six-year period as *Tom Corbett*, *Space Patrol* would gradually differentiate itself from that show, as well as from *Captain Video*, by placing more emphasis on production values, such as the use of models, matte paintings, and complicated exterior sets. In fact, we might see a telling measure of its reputation for placing more emphasis on such visual spectacle in a singular event: the show's participation in a first—and abortive—demonstration of 3-D television broadcasting during the height of the cinematic 3-D craze of 1953. Reviewing this landmark event, *Variety* termed the selection of *Space Patrol* as a demonstration vehicle a "wise choice of space and dimension as a rocket ship goes forth in quest of the 'fourth dimension.' Some of the shots actually conveyed depth."[17] But more than that, its appearance here, even in what was generally regarded as a *failed* demonstration,[18] suggests the extent to which *Space Patrol* benefited from a quickly developing sense of the televisual. For while its earlier episodes were also dialogue heavy and prone to demonstrating how the television audience should see this future world—in reclining seats, watching it on monitors, and as part of a nearly "domestic" group (modeled in this case by Buzz Corry, his young cadet Happy, the Commander's love interest Carol Carlisle, and the male and female supporting figures of Tonga and Robbie Robertson)—*Space Patrol*, later in its run, became far more action driven with its characters always involved in events that threatened to upset that almost familial grouping.

Yet even fairly late in this series we can still see traces of that ongoing space opera project of properly constructing and situating the television viewer. As a primary example, we might consider an episode from approximately the same period as that 3-D experiment, "The Laughing Alien" (March 28, 1953). While it begins with fairly elaborate establishing model work that shows the *Terra V* voyaging in space, dramatic music keys a cut to the rocket's interior where Commander Corry looks out and, as he announces, begins seeing strange images, first of Cadet Happy, bound and in pain, and then of an unfamiliar "laughing alien," both of which we subsequently see in subjective shots, as figures superimposed on the dark spacescape. However, only the Commander can see them, and he admits to Major Robertson how strange this sort of vision is—"I know it sounds like I'm space happy"—and that feeling is only underscored when, back at the base, Buzz once again begins "seeing images." But in an elaborately furnished medical lab—the sort of set that is simply absent from shows like *Captain Video* and *Tom Corbett*—and using a Brain-O-Graph machine, Buzz effectively broadcasts the images he is seeing to a monitor and even produces a copy of the alien's face. We eventually learn that the alien, evocatively named Muzak, is a telepath, able to project images and thereby dominate "weak-minded" races, but the Commander's own unsuspected telepathic abilities—developed in a prior confrontation with such types—eventually overcomes Muzak and saves Cadet Happy.

While visually quite rich, thanks to its extensive model work (of the *Terra V*, the space base, and various celestial bodies), its varied sets (including several rocket interiors, the Space Patrol headquarters, and the laboratory), and technology like the Brain-O-Graph, "The Laughing Alien" episode also repeatedly reminds us of that ongoing concern with audience construction we have seen in the other space operas of this period. There is, throughout the episode, much sitting and looking into space, talking about what is being seen (or not seen), and monitoring or looking at things through electronic technologies. Moreover, the show effectively thematizes the televisual experience, presenting Buzz Corry, Major Roberston (Ken Mayer), and Cadet Happy all initially as passive consumers of broadcast (telepathically) images who are challenged to resist their controlling power. And in his ability to turn the tables on the alien who wields this power, Commander Corry demonstrates for his audience their own proper relationship to such projective technology; he reassures them—in a way that might have made sponsors uneasy—that they had little to fear from those broadcast images which, as Boddy noted, might still have evoked some lingering "anxieties and conflicts," that the viewers were in control.

Yet we can still see such traces in one of the last of the space operas: *Rocky Jones, Space Ranger*, a series even more elaborately produced than *Space Patrol*. Coming near the end of the space opera cycle in 1954–1955, *Rocky Jones* draws together most of the characteristics associated with the form in this period. Like the far more successful *Captain Video* and *Space Patrol*, it draws heavily on the template provided by the motion-picture serial, with its continuing narrative arcs, emphasis on physical action, and sometimes even cliff-hanger endings. And also in keeping with that narrative type, it is highly formulaic, both in terms of its adventure-story action and its

Image 7.4 Rocky and Space Ranger Winky tune in across the galaxy in *Rocky Jones, Space Ranger*. [Credit: Roland Reed Productions]

cast makeup that includes the hero (Rocky), comic sidekick (Winky), female love interest (Vena Ray), older scientist (Professor Newton), and a child protégé (Bobby). The show is also clearly driven by the cultural fascination with science and technology of the period, especially rocketry, and that fascination is, again, mirrored in a specific sort of language that recalls *Captain Video*'s constant introduction of technological gadgets with mystifying names, like Trisonic Compensator, Opticon Scillometer, and Cosmic Vibrator. Yet as Lucanio and Coville offer, *Rocky Jones* was visually quite different; it "had the look of a Hollywood film" rather than an early television-era series, since it was shot on film rather than done live, employed veteran Hollywood cinematographers, used much location photography (frequently employing the Griffith Park Observatory), and seemingly was intended for subsequent theatrical release.[19] Perhaps that very double identity, as both television series and erstwhile theatrical release, helps to explain why, even at this relatively late date for space operas, it also constantly evoked—and addressed—those "anxieties and conflicts" bound up in the early televisual experience.

Thus while *Rocky Jones* offered rather sophisticated model work for such series, including repeated scenes of Rocky's ship, the *Orbit Jet*, docking with a space station, many of those scenes are framed and viewed on video screens. And the repeated fistfights wherein Rocky (Richard Crane) and Winky (Scotty Beckett) physically best alien figures—fights that immediately evoke the show's movie-serial ancestry—are always balanced by extended versions of what I have termed "televisual scenes," those in which characters sit and watch events on monitors or, rather more ominously, use monitoring devices, such as the Vizeograph, for spying or even as a weapon. More than just, as Lucanio and Coville offer, "adventurous themes played out before a *milieu* of scientific gadgetry,"[20] then, *Rocky Jones* presents a late glimpse of the lingering tension between the televisual and the more common matter of the space opera, one hinting that even by the mid-1950s the television and the television-viewing experience retained an aura of the new and the strange, and the space opera series continued to provide models for our relationship to the still relatively new technology of television.

While most of the *Rocky Jones* episodes currently available are fairly similar, we might consider the very first three-part story arc, "Beyond the Curtain of Space," to illustrate this characterization. Fittingly, given our concerns, the first line of the series' first chapter is "Let's take a look," as Rocky directs his copilot Winky's attention—and by extension the attention of the audience—to a central video screen, dials in the Office of Space Affairs, and through this televisual link arranges to land on Earth. Back at Earth headquarters, Rocky and Winky join Secretary Drake (Charles Meredith), Vena Ray (Sally Mansfield), and the Secretary's assistant Griff to watch a video of Earth's most famous scientist, Professor Newton (Maurice Cass), mysteriously declaring his new allegiance to the rogue planet of Ophicius. When Rocky subsequently takes off for Ophicius to investigate, Griff, who is a spy for that world, monitors his flight on another video screen that recalls 1930s' predictions of television as a device capable of gathering images from anywhere without the aid of a camera. A subsequent fight with an Ophician rocket is largely viewed through the monitor on the *Orbit Jet*, as is the landing on Ophicius that begins the second chapter and that Rocky again introduces with the tag line, "Well, let's take a look." On that planet we quickly see that television is the chief way Cleolanta (Patsy Parsons), the Ophician leader, communicates with her officers, as well as a mysterious means of monitoring deep-space events, as she demonstrates when watching the progress of the escaping *Orbit Jet*, now bearing Professor Newton and Bobby. Back on Earth the traitor Griff uses the Space Ranger Vizeograph to contact his fellow agents and plan to sabotage the Space Ranger base. However, that device also proves his undoing, since thanks to its panoptic capabilities, Rocky manages to detect his escape and, with a simple push of a button, almost magically destroy his car.

Besides establishing a continuing set of character and plot relationships that would be explored in subsequent story arcs and suggesting the broad (galactic) scope of *Rocky Jones*' action, this initial three-episode story demonstrates a kind of centrality for the televisual that pointedly resonates with *Captain Video*'s reflexive elements.[21] Here, it seems, video screens, monitors, television relays, even video weapons like the Vizeograph figure into every element of the extended narrative; they effectively tell the story by suggesting a future world in which the televisual experience is not just commonplace but even crucial for human—and alien—interaction. Moreover, that repeated invitation to "take a look," with its echoes of *Captain Video*'s daily efforts to "beam in" actions on the Special Remote Carrier, links the audience's own position to this elaborately screened world, as it draws us into this realm of distant viewing, constant surveillance, and even visual defense, showing just how important proper viewing—and screening—will be in the future.

Of course, in the postwar period of the early space opera's popularity, we were already entering into a new regime of vision. We were beginning to craft new sorts of "sight machines," as Paul Virilio has termed them, that would ultimately insist on a new relationship to our world.[22] Television was only one of these emerging and decidedly science fictional technologies—"machines" like the communications satellite, the spy satellite, the jet or rocket-propelled reconnaissance vehicle, all of which would subtly forecast the work of *Rocky Jones*' Vizeograph, permitting, as Virilio prophesied, "eyeshot" to "finally get the better of gunshot."[23] And those machines were entering the home, insinuating themselves as a part of the postwar domestic regime, even a key part given their kinship to the modern technological culture that was taking hold and the commonplace distance and detachment that were an inevitable part of the emerging suburban realm.

In these efforts of the space operas of the 1950s—and their early depictions of television and the televisual experience—we begin to sense how important it was for these cultural developments to inculcate a proper televisual attitude, to frame our relationship to the new visual environment, in effect, to teach us how to see. Casetti, as we earlier noted, has suggested that in the first half of the twentieth century, film "gave form to the modes of vision of its time, negotiating ongoing cultural processes;"[24] and, I would argue, in the second half of the century, television managed a similar feat. Before we could move culturally into the New Frontier of science and technology, before we could begin "to scrutinize outer space as an attainable technological possibility,"[25] and before science entertainment could be placed in the expert hands of Walt Disney's *Man in Space* shows (1955, 1957) and Frank Capra's *Bell System Science* series (1956–1964) with their rather different emphasis on "edutainment," we first had to master a fundamental technology; we had to learn how to be good television viewers.[26] The space operas of the 1950s, with their repeated invitations to "beam in" and "take a look," with their demonstrations of domestic-like group watching, with their emphases on the power and even necessity of broadcast images and visual surveillance, taught that lesson well and in the process helped us to prepare for the world of tomorrow.

NOTES

1. Lucanio and Coville in their *American Science Fiction Television Series of the 1950s* explain that the parent DuMont network had purchased a package of old Westerns with the original intention of using the Captain Video character as a host who would introduce the films. Despite the change in format to a science fiction adventure, the network decided to go ahead with the generic combination, since "DuMont wasn't about to waste the broadcast rights to all of those old Western movies" (99).
2. Murray Robinson, "Planet Parenthood." *Collier's*, January 5, 1952, 63.
3. Francesco Casetti, *Eye of the Century: Film, Experience, Modernity*, trans. Erin Larkin and Jennifer Pranolo (New York: Columbia University Press, 2008), 7.
4. For a detailed discussion of television's cinematic presentation as a science fiction icon, see J. P. Telotte, "Lost in Space: Television as Science Fiction Icon," in *The Essential Science Fiction Television Reader*, ed. J. P. Telotte (Lexington: University Press of Kentucky, 2008), 37–53.
5. William Boddy, *New Media and Popular Imagination: Launching Radio, Television, and Digital Media in the United States* (Oxford: Oxford University Press, 2004), 45.
6. John Ellis, *Visible Fictions*, rev. ed. (London: Routledge, 1992), 111–112
7. Lincoln Geraghty, *American Science Fiction Film and Television* (New York: Berg, 2009), 28.
8. Geraghty, 27.
9. While sets were notorious for being low cost, the actors in many of the space operas fared little better. Ed Kemmer of *Space Patrol*, for example, recalls that he received only $8 per episode at the start of that series' run.
10. Joseph J. Corn and Brian Horrigan, *Yesterday's Tomorrow's: Past Visions of the American Future* (Baltimore: Johns Hopkins University Press, 1984), 26.
11. David Weinstein, "*Captain Video*: Television's First Fantastic Voyage," *Journal of Popular Film and Television* 30.3 (2002), 149.
12. Patrick Lucanio and Gary Coville, *American Science Fiction Television Series of the 1950s* (Jefferson, NC: McFarland, 1998), 96.
13. *Variety*, October 4, 1950. Author's emphasis.
14. Jack Gould, "Television in Review," *The New York Times*, November 20, 1949, 9.
15. Lucanio and Coville, *Science Fiction*, 9.
16. Jeffrey Sconce, *Haunted Media: Electronic Presence from Telegraphy to Television* (Durham, NC: Duke University Press, 2000), 18; John Ellis, *Visible Fictions*, rev. ed. (London: Routledge, 1992), 129.
17. *Variety*, April 30, 1953.
18. Unfortunately, this test presentation was almost comically unsuccessful. A polarized light system was used and polarized glasses issued to viewers, but only some time into

the broadcast was it discovered that the "polarization had been reversed" on the broadcast, which required the viewers to then "turn their glasses upside down" in order to see the space images in their intended depth. See the *Variety* review of April 30, 1953.
19. The series was divided into three-episode narrative arcs, each with an overarching title. Lucanio and Coville suggest that, given their narrative unity and subsequent availability as unified narrative, these various three-part installments were "part of the intention of Roland Reed Productions" [the company that created the series] (Lucanio and Coville, *Science Fiction,* 161).
20. Patrick Lucanio and Gary Coville, *Smokin' Rockets: The Romance of Technology in American Film, Radio and Television, 1945–1962* (Jefferson, NC: McFarland, 2002), 116.
21. It is worth noting that a number of the other story arcs begin with much the same emphasis on the televisual as the key mode of interaction with both this world and the space beyond. The first chapter of the "Rocky's Odyssey" arc also opens with Rocky, Winky, and Professor Newton viewing a planet on the *Orbit Jet*'s video screen and speculating on its atmospheric conditions. And one of the more spectacular story arcs, "Menace from Outer Space," which focuses on efforts to ward off interplanetary warfare, begins with Professor Newton looking through his telescope, resulting in a framed image of a rocket hurtling toward the Earth—an observation he immediately reports to Secretary Drake via the Vizeograph and which he then follows up with similar video contact from his car.
22. Paul Virilio, *War and Cinema: A Logistics of Perception*, trans. Patrick Camiller (London: Verso, 1989), 2.
23. Ibid.
24. Casetti, 5.
25. Lucanio and Coville, *Science Fiction*, 116.
26. "Edutainment" is a term frequently used in discussion of the Disney space shows, thanks to their effective combination of the principles of popular entertainment, including the use of animation, caricature, and exaggeration, in effective combination with the programs' educational purpose.

BIBLIOGRAPHY

Boddy, William. *New Media and Popular Imagination: Launching Radio, Television, and Digital Media in the United States.* Oxford: Oxford University Press, 2004.

Casetti, Francesco. *Eye of the Century: Film, Experience, Modernity.* Trans. Erin Larkin and Jennifer Pranolo. New York: Columbia University Press, 2008.

Corn, Joseph J., and Brian Horrigan. *Yesterday's Tomorrows: Past Visions of the American Future.* Baltimore: Johns Hopkins University Press, 1984.

Ellis, John. *Visible Fictions.* Rev. ed. London: Routledge, 1992.

Geraghty, Lincoln. *American Science Fiction Film and Television.* New York: Berg, 2009.

Gould, Jack. "Television in Review," *The New York Times*, November 20, 1949, 9.

Lucanio, Patrick, and Gary Coville. *American Science Fiction Television Series of the1950s.* Jefferson, NC: McFarland, 1998.

———. *Smokin' Rockets: The Romance of Technology in American Film, Radio and Television, 1945–1962.* Jefferson, NC: McFarland, 2002.

Robinson, Murray. "Planet Parenthood," *Collier's*, January 5, 1952, 31, 63–64.

Sconce, Jeffrey. *Haunted Media: Electronic Presence from Telegraphy to Television.* Durham, NC: Duke University Press, 2000.

Telotte, J. P. "Lost in Space: Television as Science Fiction Icon." In *The Essential Science Fiction Television Reader*, edited by J. P. Telotte, 37–53. Lexington: University Press of Kentucky, 2008.

Variety Television Reviews, 1946–1956. vol. 1. London: Garland Science, 1990.

Virilio, Paul. *War and Cinema: A Logistics of Perception*. Trans. Patrick Camiller. London: Verso, 1989.

Weinstein, David. "*Captain Video*: Television's First Fantastic Voyage." *Journal of Popular Film and Television* 30, no. 3 (2002): 148–57.

Part III

As Seen on TV

CHAPTER 8

The Sky Is the Limit: Advertising and Consumer Culture in "Rocketman" Television Series of the 1950s

Lawrence R. Samuel

> They're the favorite cereals of the whole world, the whole universe!
> —1950s Kellogg's commercial on *Tom Corbett, Space Cadet*

How could the makers of a seemingly ordinary breakfast food make such an astounding (and impossible to prove) claim? When spoken by characters like Tom Corbett, Buzz Corry, or Captain Midnight, virtually any product pitch, no matter how farfetched, retained a strong semblance of truth. This chapter examines advertising embedded in "rocketman" television series of the early 1950s and discusses their social impact. These promotional messages, which were integrated into the shows themselves, as was typical of the time (especially for kids' programs), were instrumental in establishing an ethos of consumerism among the generation that would one day be known as baby boomers. Consumption was a means to demonstrate one was a valued member of society, these commercials clearly showed, the pursuit of the good things in life that money could buy an essential part of one's civic responsibility. Wrapping up this ideology in the emerging "space culture" was an especially powerful device, linking the ideas of progress, achievement, success, competitiveness, and leadership to consumerism. Although boomers would soon rebel against this ideology as they explored the possibility of an alternative American way of life, they would come to fully embrace it when they reached positions of power and influence. Finally, I argue that "rocketman" advertising helped to plant the seed of limitless possibilities among Americans, espousing the compelling idea that "the sky is the limit."

The rocketman television series, as well as television itself, served as an ideal platform by which to promote such aspirational values. With Cold War fear and paranoia raging, series like *Tom Corbett, Space Cadet* (1950–1955), *Space Patrol* (1950–1955), *Captain Midnight* (1954–1956), and a handful of others made it abundantly clear that the world (and universe!) was a dangerous place. Although shows were typically set in the future and often on planets other than Earth, even ten-year-olds likely knew that these grainy images flickering on their Zenith or RCA boxes related somehow to events in play in postwar America. Just as in *The Lone Ranger* (1949–1957), a sister ABC show promoted on *Space Patrol*, much of life appeared to revolve around some kind of Darwinian struggle for survival and power (and often financial and material gain), making it the sacred duty of the good and righteous to defeat the morally corrupt. Nations with foreign-sounding names served as televisual surrogates for the Soviet Union, that real-life evil empire also on a desperate pursuit for global domination and preeminence. (The "bad guys" unfailingly talked with concocted Russian or German accents and were unattractive, while the "good guys" spoke with American accents and seemed to hail from Santa Monica or Brooklyn, reinforcing superpower stereotypes.) Foreshadowing the likes of *Star Trek* and *Star Wars* (and anticipating some *Jetsons*-esque futurism), rocketman series of the 1950s offered both children and adult viewers an easily understood narrative that in many ways paralleled the anxiety-filled cultural climate of the Atomic Age. "Despite their veneer of innocent entertainment, early science fiction television series...tapped into America's fear of ... the power of the atomic bomb, as well as the rapid technological developments ongoing in other fields," observed Wheeler Winston Dixon, a distinctly dark current running through these seemingly silly shows.[1]

Geared around the promise (and, in the wrong hands, perils) of science and technology, rocketman television series also mirrored the postwar era's fascination with air and space travel. "It is during this era that the new wonders of science inspired a grandiose sense of wonder that was manifested in a belief that man could finally reach the stars," wrote Patrick Lucanio and Gary Coville in their *Smokin' Rockets*, no destination too far when a ship was equipped with a jet or rocket engine.[2] Flight, especially that taking place out of Earth's orbit, was a prime symbol of the miracles of science and technology, literally pointing the way to tomorrow. Machines with wings led directly to excitement and adventure, everyone knew, the mystery of faraway lands just waiting to be discovered. And if a Pan Am or TWA jetcould take one to exotic places like Europe or Asia, a rocket ship could take one to the outer limits of the galaxy, about as thrilling an idea as could be imagined in the space-crazy 1950s.

Not everyone knew how to fly a commercial jet, however, and even fewer people knew how to fly something that went exponentially faster. Training in the art of aviation was necessary, as was some kind of regulation by a governmental agency or paramilitary organization. The institutional authority embedded in rocketman series was a key element of children's television programming of the 1950s, serving as a foundation to instill principles of good citizenship and consensus thinking in general. (With juvenile delinquency a major concern, presenting law-enforcement officials as quasi-superheroes was clever thinking.) Like Superman who fought for "truth, justice, and the American way" (the television show *Adventures of Superman*

Image 8.1   Captain Midnight's rocket-powered Silver Dart, from the cover of the booklet sent to 1957 Secret Squadron members. [Credit: Roger A. Freedman]

ran from 1952 to 1958), rocketmen like Tom Corbett, Buzz Corry, Captain Midnight, Captain Video, Flash Gordon, Buck Rogers, Rod Brown, Commando Cody, and Rocky Jones (along with a sidekick or team) were presented as being on missions of the utmost importance. The American Way of Life itself was at stake in this do-or-die battle between good and evil, virtually every episode of these series intimated, our nation's best interests requiring we all pull together for the common good. "The message in all these series was often the same: the universe was in peril, and only the forces of the United States could put matters right," wrote Dixon, these "space rangers" and "sky marshals" taking some of the wildness out of the intergalactic Wild West.[3]

It was within this framework that leading marketers of the day pitched their products to children and their mothers. With the sponsorship system of television in its heyday, companies and brands were indelibly connected to the respective television (and radio) shows they produced and aired. Much more so than today (although a sponsorship-style system has made somewhat of a comeback in recent years), a company or brand became heavily identified with the show it funded. A typical television show of the 1950s was thus an integrated package of entertainment and salesmanship, as I explained in my book *Brought to You By: Postwar Television and the American Dream*, an almost seamless blend of popular and consumer culture.[4] Others have taken note of the singular voice of early television series. "Sponsors of television programs during the fifties swiftly began to exercise an increasing amount of control over not merely the kind of program they made possible, but its content as well as its manner of presentation," Michael Kammen observed in his *American Culture, American Tastes*, an extension of the power they wielded during radio's heyday a generation earlier.[5] Along with this power and control would come, sponsors believed, a greater facility to sell products to consumers. Television was viewed as a surrogate salesman invited into viewer's living rooms, an electronic display room filled with the cornucopia of the good life. "Never before had so many people heard so often that happiness and security rested in ceaseless acquisition," observed Douglas T. Miller and Marion Nowak in their book *The Fifties: The Way We Really Were*, the populist, egalitarian nature of television one of its most appealing elements.[6]

The rocketman series were no exception to this standard paradigm of 1950s television. *Tom Corbett, Space Cadet* (1950–1955), *Space Patrol* (1950–1955), *Captain Midnight* (1954–1958), *Captain Video and His Video Rangers* (1949–1955), *Flash Gordon* (1954–1955), *Buck Rogers* (1950–1951), *Red Brown of the Rocket Rangers* (1953–1954), *Commando Cody: Sky Marshall of the Universe* (1955), and *Rocky Jones, Space Ranger* (1954) were all "brought to you by" marketers delighted to know that once the coaxial cable became "coast to coast" in 1951, they could show their products to 15 to 25 million Americans at once. (While some shows were broadcast on one of the four networks, others were syndicated and aired by affiliates or local stations.) The first era of American television advertising also happened to coincide with the presence of more children in any one time or place in history, a demographic windfall for marketers of products like breakfast cereals and snacks. Research showed that kids as young as three were drawn to television advertising, with commercials acting as an incentive for them to persuade their moms to buy a certain brand. Advertisers thus not surprisingly pounced on these seventy-six million miniconsumers, realizing they controlled much of the spending power of American households.[7] Television advertising to kids was often the driving force of huge national marketing campaigns aimed to sell licensed merchandise or cross-promote other media

Image 8.2 Rocky Jones' picture: An incentive for 1950s mothers to buy Silver Cup bread for their junior space rangers. [Credit Tom Noel]

products, even more reason for Corporate America to invest in this new, powerful medium.[8] The lead characters from rocketman series typically delivered pitches in costume on shows' sets and used its props, an intentional attempt to blur the lines between entertainment and advertising. The underlying message was that characters from the show were consumers, a tacit endorsement for a consumption-based way of life. (Why people million of miles away made the effort to tell children of Earth about the merits of a particular product was not explained, nor was how they could communicate from the future to the present.)

Show-related merchandise was an essential element of sponsorships, used to raise brand awareness and, more importantly, as a sales incentive. A package box top or wrapper plus ten or twenty-five cents could reap any number of space-themed premiums, an almost sure way to keep young viewers tuned in and to make sure mom bought the right product at the grocery store. "*Captain Video* gave space-age pizzazz to the prosaic snack foods and cereals promoted by national sponsors," wrote David Weinstein in his *The Forgotten Network: DuMont and the Birth of American Television*, that show, like other rocketman series, offered an array of trinkets and gadgets to boost ratings and move product.[9] In 1949, for example, sponsor PowerHouse candy bars offered a Captain Video secret identifying ring free with a purchase of the product and a dime for postage and handling, precisely the kind of "space-age pizzazz" that added value to ordinary consumer products. With a picture of Captain Video on it, the ring was "proof you're a qualified video agent," a commercial during the show assured children, should "anyone question your identity." Owners of the totemic ring were "on the side of Captain Video fighting to defend law and order," viewers learned, thus the instruction to "wear it at all times."[10]

Image 8.3 The mark of a Video Ranger: A Captain Video picture ring.

Combining heroic deeds with the less-than-heroic consumption of familiar brands served as an especially effective selling technique. While up to any challenge or threat, rocketmen (and the occasional sidekick rocketwoman) enjoyed Kraft caramels and Nestlé's cocoa just like us, these series demonstrated. These shows were a mash-up of the extraordinary with the ordinary, making rather pedestrian consumer products somewhat special. Rocket ship pantries were stocked with these brands, after all, a clear sign that they were superior in some way to other Earth-bound, twentieth-century products. As respected role models with uncommon abilities, rocketmen served as ideal brand spokespeople, more so in fact than contemporary Earthlings perhaps presumed to work for the company or to be getting paid to say nice things about the product. On a deeper level, rocketmen advertising represented a vote of approval for the American Way of Life based in domestic consumption. When not working hard to defend freedom and democracy from dictators or petty criminals, rocketmen enjoyed their leisure time, reaping the rewards of consumer capitalism. Eating nutritious (but good tasting) meals and snacks comprised a big part of their off-the-job time, not all that different from the lives of the average American family. Such a lifestyle stood in stark contrast to nonconsumptive communism, it was implied but never said, these shows thus functioning as a propaganda weapon in the Cold War.

It is rather surprising that within the relatively small body of literature dedicated to series featuring rocketmen, there has been little attention paid to the advertising embedded in the shows. Selling products was the *raison d'être* for rocketman (and all commercial television) shows, of course, the only reason the programs were produced and broadcast. The particular thematic elements of the series make it all the more important to examine the genre within a commercial context. Story lines lauding the values of freedom and democracy reinforced the ethos of consumerism, I believe, each program steeped in the ideals of the "American way." The freedoms to be found in a laissez-faire economy and the democracy of the marketplace were what rocketmen were really fighting for, part of the larger social forces that equated citizenship with consumerism. Defeating despots who ruled their nations by fear and intimidation, and eating a delicious and nutritious bowl of (American-made) cereal were each political, patriotic acts that demonstrated the liberating capacity of free will and free choice. (Many shows featured brainwashing as a plot device, an extreme example of the restrictions and controls believed to exist within communism.) If rocketmen's bravery illustrated democracy in action, then product pitches made real the "pursuit of happiness," the two elements of shows complementary and synergistic in effect. And by traveling across the universe, rocketmen disseminated or exported this ideology throughout the "colonies," making them missionaries with an imperialist, procapitalist agenda. It was "the age of the conquest of space," as the introduction to *Tom Corbett, Space Cadet* told viewers, this idea of victory and defeat resonating back on Earth in mid-twentieth-century America.

Airing live on all four major networks and juggling three different sponsors over the course of its five-year run, *Tom Corbett, Space Cadet* was a prime example of the rocketmen genre and its advertising. In the series, Corbett (Frankie Thomas) and fellow cadets Astro (Al Markim) and Roger Manning (Jan Merlin) vie to become members of the elite Solar Guard in the mid-twenty-fourth century, occasionally leaving the Space Academy to go on training missions aboard their rocket ship *Polaris*. Perhaps more so than any other rocketmen series, advertising was intricately woven into the scripts of *Tom Corbett, Space Cadet*, ensuring sponsors got the biggest bang for their buck. In an early episode of the series, for example, a package of Kellogg's Corn Flakes becomes an instrumental, rather than incidental part of a scene. Discovered as a stowaway at the Space Academy, Rocky Corbett, Tom's kid brother, is in trouble when he has to meet with the commander. It happens to be breakfast time, however, and Rocky happens to be holding a minibox of the cereal. Rocky informs the commander that Corn Flakes are "packed with super-jet-powered breakfast food," winning over the gruff officer who understands his cadets need lots of energy to do their difficult jobs.[11]

In the postmodern universe of rocketmen series, it did not matter that people like Tom Corbett lived in the twenty-fourth century yet were somehow able to speak to viewers in the twentieth. What did matter was that sponsors' brands like Kellogg's Corn Flakes appeared to transcend space and time, their attributes beneficial to anyone wanting to excel and outperform others. Characters in rocketman series like *Tom Corbett, Space Cadet* unapologetically appealed directly (and didactically) to consumers in the advertising segments of shows, as enthusiastic in pitching the sponsor's product as when performing in their heroic roles. Besides being visibly happy to have a starring role in this new medium, actors appeared to be excited to be contributing to the postwar economic boom. Marketers were proud to display their products in the pro-business climate of the 1950s, and audiences were happy to take part in the consumer paradise that emerged after the war. After the scarcities of the Depression and war years, the abundance and prosperity of the 1950s was a welcome relief, even if one had to endure the occasional annoying commercial (like Anacin's "Drumbeat" spot). Advertisers took full advantage of these consumerism-friendly times, presenting their brands in a manner that would today be deemed considerably over the top. In another part of this same episode, for example, Tom Corbett appears in full space regalia and gulps down a bowl of cereal as a jingle plays:

> Who do you know that doesn't like Kellogg's Corn Flakes?
> When you rocket by the man in the moon,
> You can hear him singing this Corn Flakes tune
> Who do you know, who do you know, who do you know?
> Not a planetary soul doesn't like Kellogg's Corn Flakes.[12]

Kellogg's used its CBS sponsorship of *Tom Corbett, Space Cadet* to promote two other cereal brands, Raisin Bran and Pep (as well as a "Variety-Pak"). Show-related merchandise was an essential component of the advertising for these brands, with premiums inserted into packages or available by mail. A model of the latest jet fighter could be found in packages of Raisin Bran, Tom Corbett let viewers know in one episode, an "exact replica" of real ones being flown by test pilots. There were ten different models, in fact, all of them made from heavy cardboard that kids could easily punch out and assemble.[13] Knowing that there was a whole set of toys available made children that much eager to collect all of them, a psychological impulse marketers interested in multiple sales knew very well. For its Pep brand, Kellogg's

Image 8.4   Tom Corbett (Frankie Thomas) enjoys a bowl of Pep, "The Solar Cereal." [Credit Wade Williams Enterprises]

offered no less than 16 different picture rings, all of them free in boxes of what the company called "the build-up cereal" (and sometimes "the Solar Cereal"). Reaching one's hand into a package of the wheat flakes cereal would reward kids with a finger ring stamped with an image of a movie star, sports hero, cowboy, Indian, jet, or airplane, Kellogg's perhaps borrowing a page from the Cracker Jack school of prize-based marketing.[14]

If there was one word that described Pep advertising, it was "aspirational." Although the brand (which was introduced in 1923 and for decades gave Wheaties a good run for its money) eventually ran out of pep, Kellogg's sensibly tied the desirable attributes of strength and energy to the cereal, a positioning platform that ideally dovetailed with its sponsorship of *Tom Corbett, Space Cadet*. (Pep was also a major sponsor of the *Adventures of Superman* radio and television series, another show that allowed Kellogg's to creatively illustrate the benefits of good nutrition.) In one spot, "Grippo the Great," a circus strongman, lifts a five-hundred-pound barbell, his source of amazing strength the vitamins and minerals found in Pep. A young boy is envious of the powerful man's muscles, a variation of the "before-and-after" style of advertising popular in the day.[15] (Another variation was the "bully-kicking-sand-in-the-face-of-the-weakling" found in "Bazooka Joe" comics and

"Popeye" cartoons.) As in all Pep commercials, an arm with a bulging muscle served as a visual mnemonic, a device that writers cleverly translated into a constellation in the introduction to *Tom Corbett, Space Cadet*.

Kellogg's found many ways to express its marketing hook of aspiration—a powerful concept in the postwar years—in commercials for Pep. As "the prettiest girl in school and the liveliest cheerleader of them all," as a spot in an episode of *Tom Corbett, Space Cadet* went, Ann serves as a role model for Pat, her little sister. Naturally, Pat seeks to be just like her popular sibling, whose breakfast includes Pep. (Somewhat disturbingly, the cereal promises not just strength and energy but "steady nerves.")[16] In another spot, we find sons Tommy and Bob in the kitchen with Dad (Mom is nowhere to be found, it being "Mother's Day off"). The boys want to grow up to be as strong as their dad and other "menfolk," the answer regular helpings of Pep.[17] Finally, we have Jack, a high school student, football player, in a locker room after a victory. Younger boy Ray's varsity uniform is just eight years away, the announcer says, reason enough for him to start eating Pep as Jack does.[18] Such scenarios based in relationships involving superiority (and inferiority) meshed with the aspirational nature of rocketmen series like *Tom Corbett, Space Cadet*, in which viewers wanted to be a lot like their always-confident and victorious heroes.

Other brands populated Tom Corbett's universe as the series hopped from network to network. Red Goose Shoes sponsored the series' brief visit on DuMont from October 1953—May 1954, until Kraft took over lead sponsorship in December 1954 on NBC. Like Thom McAn, Red Goose was both a brand and retail chain specializing in children's shoes. While there was a certain kind of logic to the dynamic between rocketmen and breakfast cereals and snacks (even space heroes had to eat), children's shoes were a bad fit, so to speak, for the genre. One sympathizes with Frankie Thomas, the man behind Corbett, as he urges kids in a 1954 episode, "Runaway Rocket," to ask their moms or dads to buy them a pair of Red Goose (or John C. Roberts, a sister brand targeting teens) shoes. Like his rocket, Red Goose were "perfectly designed for the job," Corbett explains, a tough sell given that the brown oxfords displayed do not match in any way the twenty-fourth-century space suit he is wearing. (That Corbett was an adult and the shoes were for children, some of them girls, was a whole other problem.) The Space Cadet identification bracelet that came free with a purchase of the "smart-looking" shoes might have persuaded boys to ask for a pair of Red Gooses, but the sponsorship proved that not all brands should be pitched by a futuristic rocketman.[19]

The relationship between Ralston Purina and *Space Patrol* was a much happier one than Red Goose and *Tom Corbett, Space Cadet*. In the show, which ran live in Los Angeles and on kinescope in syndication on local ABC stations, Buzz Corry (Ed Kemmer), Commander in Chief of the United States Space Patrol, and Cadet Happy (Lyn Osbron), his oddly older-looking companion, scamper across the universe in the thirtieth century to keep order. The two principal brands advertised on the show were Chex, which had been introduced in 1937, and Instant Ralston, a hot cereal. Ralston Purina aggressively promoted its brands on the show, a masterful cross-pollination of entertainment and advertising that helped define the genre. Premiums were often used as props in the show, increasing their desirability considerably. The next best thing was to advertise a space-related premium that was free with a product purchase, just as Kellogg's did on *Tom Corbett, Space Cadet*. In "Baccarratti and Black Magic," an episode from 1954, for example, Chex cereals used a character-driven commercial to support its on-package promotion of a "Magic Space Picture." Kids would have "fun power" with their Magic Space Picture, the same attribute that allowed the two space cops to keep the universe safe from bad guys like Prince Baccarratti.[20]

Sending away for an advertised premium or snatching one out of a box was great, but seeing Buzz or Happy use one in an actual episode was even better. Once informed what Ralston's premium of the month would be, scriptwriters scrambled to somehow incorporate them into the action of the upcoming show. A "Cosmic Smoke Gun" was employed in one episode, the "real hard plastic" weapon available to viewers (along with a bag of "reloading powder") with the standard box top and quarter. (Parents were told the powder was "guaranteed harmless," but this assurance probably did little to lessen the havoc the toy must have caused in many an American household.)[21] "Space Binoculars" were featured in a number of episodes, with viewers happy to learn they were "just like the ones Buzz Corry used." (A scene of him using the binoculars in a show was shown, in case there was any doubt.) With its "pure Lucite lens," the red binoculars (viewers had to be told their color, of course, it being black-and-white television) were capable of making things and people "blocks away" seem closer.[22] In one show, viewers were initially shown a "mystery box" with a question mark on it, but not informed what was inside. Only by watching the whole episode could one learn the identity of the "latest thing in *Space Patrol* equipment," Buzz Corry teased, hinting that it would be "used in today's program."[23] Secrets like this were not only a good way to keep viewers from turning the channel, but lent a sense of intrigue and feeling that one possessed a kind of "insider information."

Ralston Purina understood the value of extending its costly partnership with *Space Patrol* to other media and promotional opportunities. In 1953, for example, the company did a cross-promotion with *Woman's Day*, a smart way to appeal directly to those carrying the purse strings. Instructions for how to make a *Space Patrol* Guard Helmet were placed in the August issue of the magazine, Buzz Corry and helmet-clad "Danny" told kids and moms watching the show, the good news being that materials likely found around the house (like a clothesline) were all that were needed to put it together.[24] Like Kellogg's, which offered *Tom Corbett, Space Cadet*-themed toys that children (or their parents) could construct themselves, Ralston advertised self-assembly premiums inspired by *Space Patrol*. A 1952 promotion, a "Man from Mars" mask with "magic forehead vision," for instance, capitalized on the 1950s obsession with hobbies and crafts. Kids could not only wear the rather frightening "spook from outer space" mask (it had a face on both the front and back), but, with four or five of them, erect a stackable totem pole. Building such a thing (which oddly mixed an alien theme with Native American culture) was "fantastic fun," a good example of the kind of creative, do-it-yourself activities that children were encouraged to pursue.[25]

In another well-thought-out tie-in, Ralston Purina used its *Space Patrol* sponsorship to tell consumers about its support of the 1953 March of Dimes campaign. "Help a crippled child get well again," Buzz Corry appealed to viewers, urging them to give a dime to fight infantile paralysis.[26] In addition to cross-promotion, Ralston Purina occasionally traveled through time to bring the show to life. In fact, perhaps the most exciting news Ralston Purina ever delivered on *Space Patrol* was when kids and adults were informed that the Ralston Rocket was currently making its way across the country. Even if was not real, this was quite a thrill in these early days of the Space Age, a rare opportunity to see what one of those spaceships looked like. Residents of Altoona and Johnstown, Pennsylvania, and Albany, New York, would be lucky enough to see "Buzz Corry's own space battle cruiser" next week, an announcer stated in a 1953 show, a clever way to publicize *Space Patrol* and to spark local sales of Ralston brands.[27]

Ralston Purina also used real, twentieth-century aviators like Tony Lavier, a Lockheed test pilot, to advertise Chex on *Space Patrol*. As an actual flyboy, Lavier (who "started flying at age fifteen," viewers were told) helped connect the imaginary world of *Space Patrol* to reality, thus adding more credibility to the sales pitch. (With "astronauts" still a few years away, test pilots were the closest thing on Earth to the futuristic space patrollers.) Besides tasting "swell," Chex cereals "keep you ready for real action," Lavier explained, a tempting proposition given his status as a kind of living, breathing Buzz Corry.[28] In a similar spot, Bob Love is the test pilot, flying his Northrop Scorpion at lightning-fast speeds. Sleeping well and eating well is the key to having the energy to handle the jet, he explains, with Chex cereals just the thing to remain in top condition.[29] Ralston Purina's scrambling of time and space and of fiction with nonfiction through the use of test pilots in advertising on *Space Patrol* was a powerful communications strategy, especially when directed to children whose ability to distinguish between such realms had yet to fully develop.

Ralston Purina did not limit itself to space-themed or flight-related advertising and promotions on *Space Patrol*, however. In one commercial for Instant Ralston, for example, the company introduced viewers to "Professor Checkerboard," a bespectacled man wearing a checkered top hat and vest. (The company's logo was and is a checkerboard.) "Hello children," the human checkerboard says, asking them to send in a picture of themselves along with a letter describing their own "Ralston invention," that is, how they prepared the cereal. Professor Checkerboard would show winners' photographs and read their letters on their air, he explained, a tempting proposition that foreshadowed today's all the rage "relationship marketing" predicated on consumer involvement. "Wonderful things happen when you eat hot Ralston," the peculiar character says, welcome news for those kids suffering from space overload.[30]

Although the "Big 3" breakfast cereal partnerships (Kellogg's and *Tom Corbett, Space Cadet*, Ralston Purina and *Space Patrol*, and General Foods/Post and *Captain Video*) were solid and mutually successful, the one between Ovaltine (made by The Wander Company) and *Captain Midnight* became, to use that overused word, "iconic." No sponsor was or is more associated with a rocketman series than Ovaltine, the instant, chocolaty food or dietary supplement that began its association with *Captain Midnight* during radio days. If seamlessness was (after sales and ratings) the principal goal of marketers, producers, and broadcasters, which I believe it was, Ovaltine, Screen Gems, and CBS achieved it best. In the show, ace aviator Captain Midnight (a code name) leads a (private) paramilitary organization fighting crime, espionage, and sabotage on Earth in the present day. Of rocketman series, Captain Midnight's appeals to viewers seemed the most earnest and believable, in part because the series was not set in the future or a faraway galaxy. Membership in Ovaltine's Secret Squadron also felt more "urgent" than in Corbett's Space Cadets, Corry's Space Patrol, or Captain Video's Video Rangers, this another factor for the show and its advertising becoming part of Americans' cultural vocabulary. From September 1954 to January 1956 (39 episodes, before being renamed and going into syndication), steel-jawed Richard Webb as Captain Midnight, speaking from the library in his mountain headquarters, effectively enlisted American children in the cause of defeating evildoers by drinking as much Ovaltine as possible.

One of the primary reasons why the *Captain Midnight*/Ovaltine package worked so well was that both the entertainment and advertising portions of the series were grounded in the values of achievement, competition, and success. Such values resonated deeply among both children and adults in the postwar years, the basis for Henry Luce's American Century or, if you prefer, the American Dream. Captain Midnight and his team had their important job to do and young people had theirs, each episode made clear. Through hard work (and good nutrition) would come results, the series convincingly suggested, although both the characters in the show and viewers at home had to be prepared to take on tough challenges. Captain Midnight and to a somewhat lesser extent other rocketman series made it vividly clear that not everyone had the same abilities or could achieve the same level of success. There were leaders and winners, and there were followers and losers in any kind of group, these series sermonized, and it was incumbent for all Americans—parents, students, friends, athletes, or space cadets—to try to be the former. Rocketman series thus helped instill a competitive streak among the baby-boom generation in the already intense peer-oriented atmosphere of the 1950s. Its primary benefit being "energy," Ovaltine was ideally suited to echo this message.

A typical episode of the series from 1951 illustrated the Darwinian nature of both the universe and Anytown, USA. Wearing his uniform, naturally, including helmet, Captain Midnight demonstrates how to make Ovaltine, a bit domestic perhaps but certainly not unmanly. Standing in front of a map of the (forty-eight) United States and near a globe on his desk, the Secret Squadron officer explains how easy the drink is to prepare. We are transported to a scene of a girl with her mom at the kitchen table. "Sulky Sue" appears sloth-like, making it not surprising to learn that she is getting poor grades and does not feel like exercising. Concerned, the girl's teacher recommends Ovaltine to her mom, and presto!—Sulky Sue has the energy to be all she can be. Now an ace student and able to skip rope "like a kangaroo" (with the help of sped-up film), Ovaltine has turned a loser into a winner.[31]

Famous athletes drank Ovaltine, some episodes of *Captain Midnight* revealed, living proof of the product's efficacy. In one commercial, the captain and a little boy named Jimmy stride through the Secret Squadron Hall of Fame, a room filled with pictures and trophies belonging to sports stars, including professional football player "Crazy Legs" Hirsch, Brooklyn Dodger Duke Snider, and English Channel swimmer Florence Chadwick.[32] In separate spots, the pair meets with the three respective athletes (wearing their uniforms or outfits), who praise the benefits of the food supplement.[33] One did not have to be a top athlete to belong to the Secret Squadron, however. A myriad of premiums emblazoned with the exclusive club's emblem were available to young viewers, free in fact with a purchase of a jar of Ovaltine. "Be the first in your neighborhood" to have a Secret Squadron patch, Captain Midnight urges, with wearing the insignia very important should an "emergency" arise or "in case I need your help." Trying to fight off competitive flavored drinks (without the nutritional benefits of Ovaltine, advertising for the brand made clear), The Wander Company used *Captain Midnight* promotions like the emblem, an official drinking mug, and a shaker as vehicles of repeat sales and brand loyalty. "Never be without one," Captain Midnight instructs fellow members of the Secret Squadron, the insignia shorthand that its wearer belonged to a special fraternity.[34]

Patches, mugs, shakers, and such were all very nice, but it was owning and using the Secret Squadron decoder that left no doubt that one was on the same side as Captain Midnight. Each week, for much of the series run, Captain Midnight or another member of the crew posted a series of letters and numbers on the screen as a clue to solving next week's adventure. The string of symbols could be figured out only with a decoder "ring," again free with a purchase of Ovaltine. Using audience involvement, continuity (linking one week's show to the next), and a cryptic puzzle solvable only with a product premium were all brilliant devices that set *Captain Midnight* off from other television shows and Ovaltine from other beverages. Like Ralphie in the film *A Christmas Story* (1983), boys and girls scurried to solve each week's cipher with their decoder rings, the world's safety hanging in the balance. (The scene was a fictional account in which Ralphie was a regular listener of the Ovaltine-sponsored *Little Orphan Annie* radio show.) Real-life children were certainly more satisfied with the results than was Ralphie (whose secret message simply read, "Be sure to drink your Ovaltine").

Not belonging to the *Captain Midnight* Secret Squadron carried a high price, viewers were told in the series. As on other rocketman series, the sponsor's product was positioned on *Captain Midnight* as an opportunity to get a competitive edge

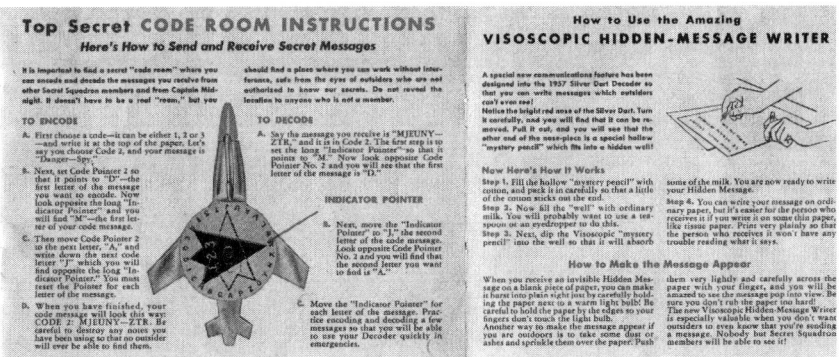

Image 8.5   The secret decoder ring: Essential equipment for members of Captain Midnight's Secret Squadron. [Credit Roger A. Freedman]

in life. Ovaltine delivered "rocket power," enabled "thrust," and kept one "revved up," space-themed assets displayed by Captain Midnight and his fellow aviators. Kids who "live[d] up to the [Secret Squadron] pledge" would be the beneficiaries of such quasi-superhuman abilities, while those who did not would find themselves runners-up in their own battles.[35] In one show, for example, Johnny Jones and a friend, Wilbur, engage in a foot race. Not a member of the Secret Squadron (i.e., Ovaltine-challenged), Wilbur quickly runs out of gas and loses the race to Johnny.[36] In another show, Joe scurries up a rope in a gym but Sam cannot, the choice in beverages the critical difference. Only Ovaltine, the official drink of the Secret Squadron, gives you the "rocket power you need to be a leader in your gang," we learn, a considerable dose of shame attached to not being the best at something within one's peer group.[37] The first wave of boomers-to-be took this message – evident to some extent in all rocketman series – seriously, adopting a me-versus-you attitude that carried over to their professional and personal lives for decades to come.

Finally, the trope of science, this too common to all rocketman series, added to the assumed veracity of Ovaltine advertising on *Captain Midnight*. An older, eccentric scientist was a staple of the genre, the Einstein-esque characters lending an aura of expertise (and a dash of humor) to the shows. In *Captain Midnight*, there was Dr. Aristotle "Tut" Jones (Olan Soule), who mixed Ovaltine concoctions ("Tut specials") in his lab as edible, delicious experiments. Such scenes demonstrated the science that went into the product, specifically the 27 vitamins, minerals, and "other important food elements."[38] Setting itself apart from other flavored (and arguably better-tasting) drinks was key to Ovaltine's success, making Dr. Jones an important character in the show. Science and technology were enabling America and Americans to assume their rightful role as leaders of the free world (and universe), rocketman series demonstrated, the sky the limit as the nation looked forward to the bright and shiny future.

Notes

1. Wheeler Winston Dixon, "The Space Opera and Early Science Fiction Television," in *The Essential Science Fiction Television Reader*, ed. J. P. Telotte (Lexington: University Press of Kentucky, 2008), 93.
2. Patrick Lucanio and Gary Coville, *Smokin' Rockets: The Romance of Technology in American Film, Radio and Television, 1945–1962* (Jefferson, NC: McFarland, 2002), 1.
3. Dixon, 93.
4. Lawrence R. Samuel, *Brought to You By: Postwar Television and the American Dream* (Austin: University of Texas Press, 2001).
5. Michael Kammen, *American Culture, American Tastes: Social Change and the 20th Century* (New York: Alfred A. Knopf, 1999), 59.
6. Douglas T. Miller, and Marion Nowak, *The Fifties: The Way We Really Were* (Garden City, NY: Doubleday, 1977), 346–352.
7. Samuel, xv-xvi.
8. Kammen, 166.
9. David Weinstein, *The Forgotten Network: DuMont and the Birth of American Television* (Philadelphia: Temple University Press 2004), 70.

10. Youtube.com; One of these rings recently sold for $188.48 in an online auction, a nice return on the ten-cent investment even with 60-plus years of inflation.
11. *Tom Corbett, Space Cadet* corn flakes advertisements, http://www.youtube.com/watch?v=l8DzoUJLEIE.
12. Ibid.
13. Joe Sarno, "Tom Corbett Summer Reruns," *Solar Guard* website, http://www.solarguard.com/tctv1.htm.
14. Kellog's Pep "Free Picture Ring" advertisement, http://www.youtube.com/watch?v=yZ2EQQQWhkg.
15. Kellog's Pep "Grippo the Great" advertisement, http://www.youtube.com/watch?v=k5UpMmv-Ln8.
16. Kellog's Pep "Anne & Pat" advertisement, http://www.youtube.com/watch?v=tvNB27zz6MU.
17. Kellog's Pep "Mother's Day Off" advertisement, http://www.youtube.com/watch?v=YSn6Bc7FQQA.
18. Kellog's Pep "Jack & Ray" advertisement http://www.youtube.com/watch?v=8oySEV-eM0E.
19. "The Runaway Rocket," *Tom Corbett, Space Cadet* (1954), http://www.youtube.com/watch?v=YrTUvgKpwmA&NR=1.
20. The Paley Center for Media, T78:0531.
21. *Space Patrol* "Cosmic Smoke Gun" promotion, http://www.youtube.com/watch?v=DuTuHrUrZVw.
22. *Space Patrol* "Space Binoculars" promotion, 1953. http://www.youtu.be/watch?v=EBxyxZ2VQFg.
23. Ibid.
24. http://www.youtube.com/watch?v=YRKRhYoRcZ.
25. *Space Patrol* "Totem Head from Mars" promotion, 1952. http://www.youtube.com/watch?v=V5whc8b1Dtw.
26. *Space Patrol* "Space Binoculars" promotion, 1953.
27. *Space Patrol* "*Women's Day* Magazine" advertisement, 1953, http://www.youtube.com/watch?v=1GfMEDS9XN4.
28. Ralston Wheat and Rice Chex "Tony Lavier, Test Pilot" advertisement, http://www.youtube.com/watch?v=l85Z2sJV9Tk.
29. Ralston Wheat and Rice Chex "Bob Love, Test Pilot" advertisement http://www.youtube.com/watch?v=tGESdwbuP7M.
30. Hot Ralston "Professor Checkerboard" advertisement, http://www.youtube.com/watch?v=UpmyM8dF_1Y.
31. Ovaltine "Captain Midnight" advertisement, http://www.youtube.com/watch?v=X5ZAISx-jdw.
32. Ovaltine "Secret Squadron Hall of Fame" advertisement. http://www.youtube.com/watch?v=rlQy_xtfqsU.
33. Ibid.
34. Ibid.
35. Ovaltine "Join the Secret Squadron" advertisement http://www.youtube.com/watch?v=Ttj60ytNr4s.
36. Ovaltine "Rocket Power" advertisement, http://www.youtube.com/watch?v=rXnw8hSX3cg.
37. Ovaltine "Secret Squadron Hall of Fame" advertisement, http://www.youtube.com/watch?v=rlQy_xtfqsU.
38. Ibid.

BIBLIOGRAPHY

Dixon, Wheeler Winston. "The Space Opera and Early Science Fiction Television." In *The Essential Science Fiction Television Reader*, edited by J. P. Telotte, 93–110. Lexington: University Press of Kentucky, 2008.

Kammen, Michael. *American Culture, American Tastes: Social Change and the 20th Century.* New York: Alfred A. Knopf, 1999.

Luciano, Patrick, and Gary Coville, *Smokin' Rockets: The Romance of Technology in American Film, Radio and Television, 1945–1962.* Jefferson, NC: McFarland & Company, 2002.

Miller, Douglas T., and Marion Nowak. *The Fifties: The Way We Really Were.* Garden City, NY: Doubleday, 1977.

Samuel, Lawrence R. *Brought to You By: Postwar Television and the American Dream.* Austin: University of Texas Press, 2001.

Weinstein, David. *The Forgotten Network: DuMont and the Birth of American Television.* Philadelphia: Temple University Press, 2004.

CHAPTER 9

CREATING A SENSE OF WONDER: THE GLORIOUS LEGACY OF SPACE OPERA TOYS OF THE 1950S

S. MARK YOUNG[1]

> **Lone Starr (Bill Pullman)**: "But, Yogurt, what is this place? What is it that you do here?"
> **Yogurt (Mel Brooks)**: "Merchandising."
> **Barf (John Candy)**: "Merchandising, what's that?"
> **Yogurt**: "Merchandising, come, I'll show you.... We put the picture's name on everything. Merchandising, merchandising, where the real money from the movie is made. *Spaceballs*-the-T-Shirt, *Spaceballs*-the-Coloring-Book, *Spaceballs*-the-Lunchbox, *Spaceballs*-the-Breakfast-Cereal, *Spaceballs*-the-Flamethrower."
> —*Spaceballs*, Metro-Goldwyn-Mayer (1987)

THE MERCHANDISING MANIA SURROUNDING *STAR WARS* THAT MEL BROOKS is referring to in *Spaceballs* actually has its roots in the space operas of the 1950s. Sandwiched between Buck Rogers and Flash Gordon in the 1930s, and *Star Trek* and *Star Wars* in the 1960s and 1970s, *Tom Corbett, Space Patrol,* and *Captain Video*[2] generated an impressive array of toys and other merchandise that have long outlasted many people's memories of the actual shows.[3] That these toys are still highly sought after is testimony to their intergenerational appeal. In this chapter, I suggest that the enormous success of merchandising efforts was due to the legacy of Buck Rogers, the convergence of technological advances in science and scientific speculation, and the deep penetration of television into American homes, which popularized the shows and promoted merchandising. Companies created some of the most memorable toys of any era, and promoted the fantasy of extraterrestrials and outer space to a new generation eager to move beyond the dark shadow of World War II.

Buck Rogers and a New Form of Play

Buck Rogers' influence on science fiction and popular culture is universal. Beginning in 1934 with Daisy Manufacturing's XZ-31 Rocket Pistol, Buck Rogers toys created a new form of play. While dolls, games, blocks, puzzles, and trains were toy standards, space toys opened up a fantasy world and sense of wonder that was entirely the domain of Depression-era children. These playthings also fascinated dad and mom, but since they had not grown up with them, their role in guiding play was minimal.[4] What did provide a roadmap for kids were the actual Buck Rogers comic strips. With their surprising success, an opportunistic marketing executive at Daisy convinced Philip Nolan (the creator) and Dick Calkins (the artist) to redesign the guns and helmets they used in the comic strip to mimic Daisy's new line of Buck Rogers toys.[5] These early toy creations have served as inspiration for innumerable outer-space-themed television shows and motion pictures.

German Technology and Flying Disks

Buck Rogers set the stage for the wide embrace that the American public gave the space operas and their associated toys, but new technology and media fueled the postwar hope for the future. While Buck appealed to pure fantasy, technological developments in rocketry during World War II suggested that space travel and extraterrestrial adventures could become a reality. Beginning in the late 1920s, German scientists developed rockets that would lay the groundwork for space exploration.[6] With the onset of World War II, top scientists led by Wernher von Braun were forced to turn their attention to designing rockets for military purposes, notably the A-4 long-range ballistic missile, which Adolf Hitler renamed the V-2—"V" being short for *Vergeltungswaffen*, or weapons of retaliation. The development of the V-2 rocket is considered one of the greatest technological advances of the period, second only to the atomic bomb. The power and sleek design of the V-2 captivated the world's imagination and, as the war ended, interest in adapting rocket technology to the service of space travel soared. A few years later, Tom Corbett's elegant rocket, the *Polaris*, was modeled after the V-2.

In mid-1947, another peculiar event made headlines and created a keener curiosity about space. On June 24, businessman and part-time aviator Kenneth Arnold was flying over the Cascade Mountains in Washington State where he claimed to have seen "saucer-like discs" in the sky that "flipped and flashed in the sun."[7] The press quickly labeled Arnold's sighting as "flying saucers" and UFO mania was born. Hollywood wasted no time in capitalizing on the public's interest, and almost two years to the day (June 27, 1949) of Arnold's report, the DuMont television network launched *Captain Video*, the first space opera hero. ABC followed with *Space Patrol* in March 1950, and CBS began broadcasting *Tom Corbett, Space Cadet* beginning in October 1950. Early feature films such as *Destination Moon* (1950), *The Day the Earth Stood Still* (1951), *The Thing from Another World* (1951), and *When Worlds Collide* (1951) all contained extraordinary images of rockets, aliens, and other worlds that encouraged the public's desire to believe that alternative life forms and living in space could be real possibilities. These films have shaped our global preconceptions of outer space.

Advertising, Merchandising, and the Business of Television

Unlike the motion picture and music industries, the television business is built around advertising. The general business model has not changed significantly since the Bulova Watch Company paid $9 to air the first 20-second spot on a televised baseball game in 1941. Advertisers gauge the potential success of a show based on ratings and market share, and make decisions about which shows to sponsor. As ratings rise and fall, so does interest by advertisers, who ultimately determine the fate of a show. The shows that have the broadest appeal influence companies in auxiliary markets (toys, games, fashion) to obtain licenses to produce show-related merchandise.[8] Television, the main technological innovation that brought the space operas into living rooms, began to penetrate American households at an exponential rate. Between April 1949 and June 1951, the number of television sets jumped from two million to thirteen million.[9] During Buck Rogers' heyday in the 1930s, radio and newspapers were the only viable mass media outlets that existed.[10] Television created and amplified the imagery that would collectivize the American imagination and ultimately galvanize public support for the imminent space program.

As noted earlier, the space operas of the 1950s owe their popularity and longevity, in large part, to the promotional campaigns and merchandising efforts of many major sponsors of the day. While the earlier Buck Rogers craze led to the production of a wide variety of toys, the level of output and the sheer beauty (and in some cases campiness) of the toys increased significantly once the space operas gained popularity. Many children of the Buck era, now young parents themselves, reveled in the memory of their childhood play with ray guns and rocket ships and encouraged their kids to live the fantasy.

The Power of a Quarter

Growing up in the early 1950s, the average child received an allowance of 25 cents. During that era, a kid could purchase a comic book for a dime, attend a movie for a quarter, or buy a Premier or Archer space man for 15 cents. The best deal for kids were the premiums. For 25 to 50 cents plus postage and a box top or two, a child could get just about any premium. Premiums could not be purchased at stores like the toys of the major manufacturers could, but rather had to be acquired through the mail. Premiums were a very clever way of sucking kids into the vortex of their favorite shows and engendering their sense of identification and allegiance. As they did for Buck Rogers, the cereal companies played a huge role in promoting the space opera heroes. Some of the most popular premiums were the membership kits that Kellogg's and Ralston offered. For a quarter and a box top, a budding space cadet could send away for a membership kit filled with neat atomic age stuff. Kellogg's Tom Corbett kit consisted of a cast photo that was inscribed, "Spaceman's Luck—Tom Corbett Space Cadet," a pinback badge, an embroidered arm patch, and membership card with decoder, all in a brown manila envelope adorned with space graphics.

Not to be outdone, Ralston launched the Space Patrol Membership Kit, a mammoth set that today is very highly prized. A child had to send a box top from either Rice Chex or Wheat Chex with 25 cents in order to get the kit. To a child's delight, the kit contained:

- Space Patrol Badge with pinback
- Buzz Corry signed photograph
- Space Patrol Handbook—15-page booklet
- Chart of the Universe
- Space Patrol Membership card
- Signed photograph of the Space Patrol crew
- "Dear Cadet" letter from the Ralston Purina Company
- A mailing envelope with space graphics, customized to the address of the child's choosing

Some insightful kids opted for a "two-for-one" offer that combined the Membership Kit with a red cosmic-glow rocket ring. This ring is exceedingly rare in today's market.

A Space Cadet pledged to "uphold and support the articles of government of the United Planets, and that I will defend the rights of free men against all enemies; that I will bear true faith and allegiance to the principles of right, goodness, and justice." *Captain Video* did not have a full membership kit like the ones for *Tom Corbett* or *Space Patrol*, but viewers could get a signed photo of the Captain and a Video Ranger Membership Card. Children who became Video Rangers had to adhere to the following pledge: "We, as Official Video Rangers, here-by promise to abide by the Ranger Code and to support forever the cause of Freedom, Truth, and Justice throughout the universe." Similarly, *Rocky Jones* had a Space Ranger Code card that laid out five principles that a good space ranger should follow.

Complete kits are still some of the most sought-after collectibles. They helped create a sense of belonging to something larger than oneself, and kids would proudly wear their pinbacks to school to demonstrate their loyalty.[11] The impact of this allegiance to the space heroes is still evident. Ed Pippin's Solar Guard Academy continues the legacy with a wonderful homage to all the shows of the era.[12] The Solar Guard Academy is the most comprehensive website of its kind, and Academy members still convene with surviving stars of the actual shows in Williamsburg, Virginia, on a semiregular basis.

THE TOYS

Merchandisers of the 1950s also benefited from the development and application of polyethylene, vinyl, and polystyrene plastic to produce toys in mediums other than metal. Plastics opened up completely new options for a wider variety of toys that could be produced much less expensively than their pressed-metal progenitors. While the three major shows were associated with similar toys, unique items were created for each.

CAPTAIN VIDEO

Captain Video (1949–1955) was the first space opera, but generated the least amount of merchandise compared to subsequent shows. Nevertheless, a number of premiums were available, including, secret rings, pins, walkie-talkies, and comics. Sponsors of the show included Post cereals and PowerHouse candy bars. Futuristic devices like the Opticon Scillometer and the Radio Scillograph are still favorites (See Image 9.1 and Table 9.1).[13]

Table 9.1 Examples of Captain Video Toys and Merchandise*

Captain Video Toys	Manufacturer
Superior Space Port	T. Cohn (Superior)
Secret Seal Ring	PowerHouse Candy Bars
Flying Saucer Ring Set	Post Toasties
Comic Books	Fawcett Publications
Radio Scillograph Set	Premium (TV)
Secret Ray Gun	PowerHouse Candy Bars
Collectible Cereal Boxes	Kellogg's Pep
Space Men (cereal)	Post Raisin Bran
Electric Video Goggles with Envelope	PowerHouse Candy Bars
2-Way Telephone	Air Champ Mfg. Co., Inc.
Captain Video Board Game	Milton Bradley

*Many of the manufacturers of the premiums are not known. In most cases, a company like Ralston would outsource production, and no manufacturer's name would appear on a toy. In those instances where we know that there is some tie to a premium, I have listed the name of the sponsor, but in those where we do not, I have simply used the designation "Premium."

Image 9.1 Mysto-Coder Brass Decoder, Purity Bread Pin, a photo of Al Hodge, the Secret Seal brass ring. Second row, left to right: Flying Saucer Ring, Photo Ring. Third row, left to right: Video Ranger membership card, Rite-O-Lite Gun kit. [Credit: Courtesy of Dark Horse Entertainment]

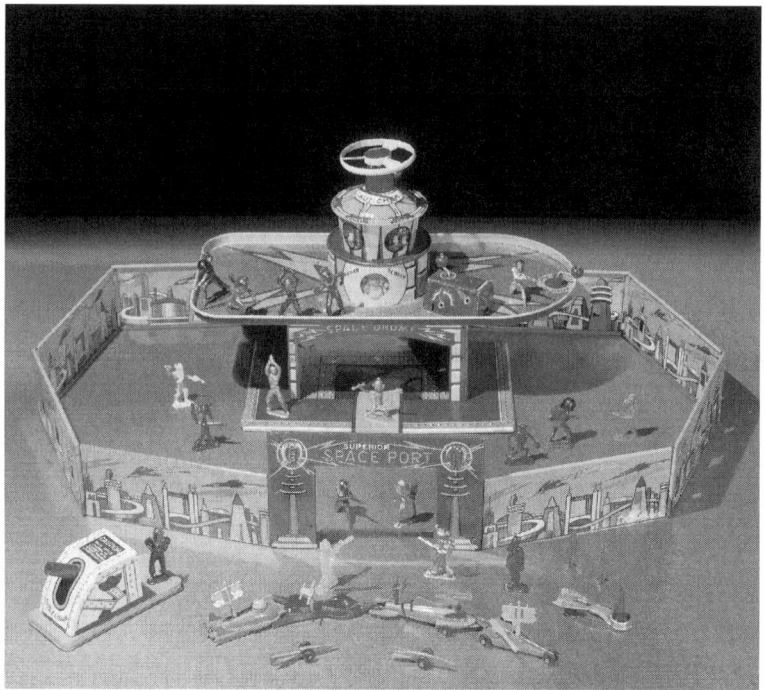

Image 9.2 The marvelous Streamline Moderne, Superior (*Captain Video*) Spaceport. [Credit: Courtesy of Dark Horse Entertainment]

The jewel in the *Captain Video* crown was the Superior Space Port created by T. Cohn (also known as Superior). The spaceport was a highly creative structure that had a strong Streamline Moderne feel to it. When assembled, this playset is one of the most delightful and inspired toys of the 1950s.[14] The top of the bi-level port was used as a landing strip for plastic spaceships adorned with atomic cannons and radar dishes. At its peak was a flying saucer launcher that could actually fire a disc. A windup siren warned everyone when aliens were about to attack. Nine spectacularly lithographed tin walls, depicting a futuristic city, surrounded the central spaceport. Also included in the playset were some of the campiest polystyrene aliens (or interplanetary space men) ever produced.[15] Defending against them were space soldiers with removable helmets. The space men, aliens, and space vehicles were made by Lido, a leading plastic toy maker that specialized in very inexpensive toy soldiers and cowboys and Indians. Alliances of this kind were common among toy companies of the period.

Space Patrol

Of the three main shows, *Space Patrol* (1950–1955) toys were by far the most numerous. Similar to *Captain Video*, there were comics, ray guns, rings, pinbacks, walkie-talkies, binoculars, trading cards, flashlights, and even a periscope (see Images 9.3 and 9.4). *Space Patrol* was also the most aggressive at promoting their sponsor's monthly premiums on every episode—a very early example of blatant product placement.

Image 9.3 Top row, left to right: Space-O-Phone instructions, mailer, and phone; space microscope; space binoculars; and Space-A-Phones. Middle row: Cosmic smoke gun, long barrel; Terra V Project-O-Scope with film; and plastic membership badge. Bottom row: Cosmic smoke gun, short barrel; metal buckle on "Jet Glow" belt; Hydrogen Ray gun ring; and Cosmic Glow rocket ring. [Credit: Courtesy of Dark Horse Entertainment]

Image 9.4 Ray-O-Vac produced this incredible flashlight. When found, it is often missing the rocket tip and/or fins. [Credit: Courtesy of Dark Horse Entertainment]

Table 9.2 Examples of Space Patrol Toys and Merchandise

Space Patrol Toys	Manufacturer
Lunar Fleet Base (premium)	Premium
Membership Kit	Premium
Trading Cards (set of 40)	Ralston Premium
Space Patrol Playset	Louis Marx
Auto Sonic Rifle	Unknown Mfg.
Man From Mars Totem Head	Premium
Space Patrol Jigsaw Puzzle	Milton Bradley
Rocket Ship Cockpit	Premium
Monorail and City of Terra	Premium
Official Wrist Watch	U. S. Time
Space Patrol Atomic Pistol Flashlite	Louis Marx
Space Patrol Official Rocket Lite	Ray-O-Vac
Space Patrol Comics (2 Issues)	Ziff-Davis Publishing

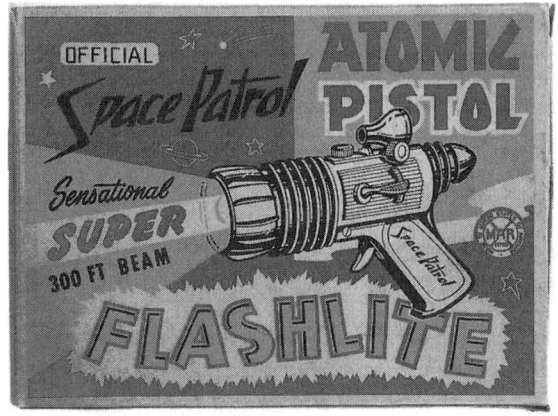

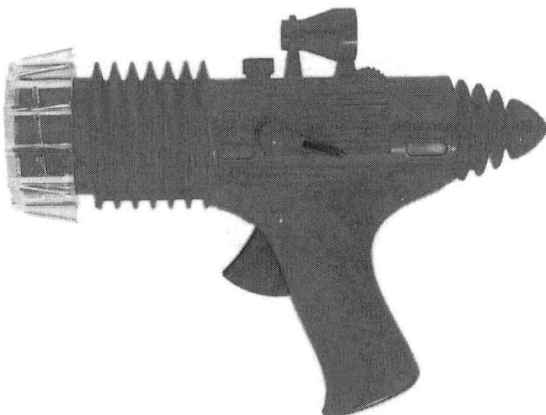

Image 9.5 What kid didn't want this beautifully styled ray gun? [Credit: Courtesy of Dark Horse Entertainment]

One of the most imaginative toys was Ralston's Lunar Fleet Base premium that contained a cardboard building and space people that could all be punched out and assembled. Today, a mint-in-box Lunar Fleet Base in the original mailer will sell for several thousand dollars.

Space opera toys are some of the most beautifully designed toys. In particular, the ray guns and space rifles took full advantage of the plastic from which they were made. Most of the guns have the kind of rounded edges and long lines of the Streamline Moderne Movement that must have made Raymond Loewy proud. Two of the best guns are the Space Patrol Atomic Flashlite (by Marx) and the Autosonic Rifle, a true gem of the period with its elegant design and two-tone red and yellow plastic (see Figure 5).

Without a doubt, the most impressive "toy" of the 1950s was actually a giveaway. Weatherbird Shoes and Ralston sponsored a contest in which a child had to suggest a name for a newly discovered fictitious planet. The prize was a 35-foot, 10,000-pound *Terra IV* Rocket Club House often called the Ralston Rocket. The intriguing story of the child who won the contest and subsequent history is recounted well by Jean-Noel Bassior in her definitive book on *Space Patrol*.[16]

TOM CORBETT AND LOUIS MARX

Tom Corbett, Space Cadet (1950–1955) toys were also plentiful. Favorites included a series of 12 plastic rings with inserted pictures by Kellogg's, beautifully illustrated bread labels from Butter-Nutt and Pennington Breads, cereal boxes depicting Tom and the gang on the front and back, viewmasters, caps, and of course, ray guns and space helmets (see Table 3). The best-known Corbett toy was the Tom Corbett Space Academy, manufactured by Louis Marx.

Toy collectors use the term "play value" when evaluating a toy. Simply put, play value increases the longer a child's interest is held, and correlates with the level of enjoyment the toy brings. While Daisy and Cocomalt reigned supreme in Buck Roger's time, it was the rise of one of the world's great toy impresarios—Louis Marx—that truly made a difference to manufacturing and creativity during the era

Table 9.3 Examples of Tom Corbett Toys and Merchandise

Tom Corbett Toys	Manufacturer
Playset	Marx, 1952
Polaris Rocket	Marx, 1952
Official Cadet Outfit	Yankiboy Play Clothes
Bread End Labels	Pennington's Bread
Kellogg's Pep Cutouts (on back of box)	Kelloggs
Pinback	Premium
Model Craft Set (casting set)	Model Craft
2-Way Phone	J. V. Zimmerman Company
Interplanetary Rings (9 different)	Premium
Coloring Book	Saalfield Publishing
Compass, Badge, and Insignia (in a set)	Jewelry Manufacturing Company

of the space operas. While Marx produced many of the most beloved and enduring toys of the period, including tin rocket ships and plastic ray guns, it is widely acknowledged that his greatest toy contribution was his playsets.[17]

Playsets were built around historical periods and consisted of toy soldiers, cowboys and Indians, dinosaurs, service stations, and many, many other themes. The toy figures could be set up in unlimited ways given the large number of accessories ranging from trees, fences, rock formations, tools, toy tin lithographed buildings, and anything else that was pertinent to each particular playset theme. Marx began to produce playsets around 1950, and in 1951 launched a series of Western themed sets including the Western Ranch and *Roy Rogers* Western Town sets. For collectors, however, the crowning achievement in playsets was the Marx space-themed sets.

While the vast majority of space opera toys were premiums, Marx created an entire miniature world that mimicked what a child saw on the television shows. The *Tom Corbett* set featured unmarked likenesses of Tom and Dr. Joan Dale, Tom's trusted scientist. Similar to the Superior Spaceport, the set contained a central metal space academy surrounded by nine walls and a front gate that bore the Space Academy name. The Academy housed a small army of cadets in three different colors. Space cadets had removable bubble helmets (Marx, of course, created a life-size Tom Corbett helmet for kids to purchase) and came in many poses. Some were depicted as students, and a classroom could be set up with plastic chairs, desks, and easels. Others brandished huge ray guns and protected the base. A space car, V-2-like rockets ready to be launched, a flying-saucer launcher, radar dishes and telescopes, and a series of bizarre aliens completed the set. Kids were enthralled with the Tom Corbett Academy (see Figure 6).

Marx was a master of marketing, and a significant part of his production and cost-conscious business style was to take existing playset pieces and repurpose them. The space sets were no exception. Marx took the main pieces from the Tom Corbett set, including buildings, space cars, and building accessories, produced them in different colors, and created a new set. As an example, the most sought-after Marx space playset today is the one for *Space Patrol*.[18] The *Space Patrol* set has the same components as the Corbett set except that the box art says "Space Patrol," the building is blue (instead of silver), the gate says "Space Patrol Academy," and the figures are slightly different colors. Sharp-eyed parents probably noticed that there were few differences between this set and the Corbett sets, and as a result, the set was not as successful as expected. In today's market, it is considered a rare find and can command a price as much as five times that of a Tom Corbett set.[19]

Marx also created two fictional characters: Rex Mars[20] and Captain Space. Based on these characters, and with no backstory, Marx produced "new" space sets, again with almost identical contents to the Corbett and Space Patrol sets. Some have speculated that once the licensing period was over, the frugal Marx decided to create new characters and repurpose all existing pieces, rather than continue to pay for the use of the Corbett and Space Patrol names. Over a two-year period, Marx produced 13 different playsets related to the space operas (see Table 4).

Creating a Sense of Wonder

Image 9.6   Kids spent many hours playing with this toy. Marx made 13 variations of this playset using four different names, Tom Corbett, *Space Patrol*, Rex Mars, and Captain Space, but the contents were the same, with minor variations. [Credit: Courtesy of Dark Horse Entertainment]

Table 9.4   The Marx Space Playsets

Marx Playset Set Number	Year of Issue
Tom Corbett Space Academy #7009	1952
Tom Corbett Space Academy #7010	1952
Tom Corbett Space Academy #7012	1953
Space Patrol Academy #7019	1952
Space Patrol Rocket Port Set, Official #7020	1952
Rex Mars Space Drome #7015	1954
Rex Mars Space Drome #7016	1954
Rex Mars Space Port #7004	1955
Planet Patrol Space Drome (Rex Mars) #7040	1952
Rex Mars Spaceport #7024	1953
Rex Mars Planet Patrol #7014	1953
Captain Space Solar Academy #7026	1953
Captain Space Solar Port #7018	1954

Epilogue

The space toys and memorabilia associated with the space operas of the 1950s are some of the most beautiful toys ever produced. Many, such as the Tom Corbett and Superior playsets are still highly sought after. They represent the fantasy era of space toys that ignited the imagination—and the desire to become collectors—in many kids. The same kids who could not afford the $6.98 price tag for such a playset in 1952 can now afford the $700-plus that many of these sets command today.

With the launch of *Sputnik* in October 1957, and John Glenn's three orbits of the Earth in February 1962, space travel became a reality, and the era of campy space toys drew to a close. In April 1962, *Life* magazine depicted NASA's newly designed space suit, and shortly thereafter, Mattel launched a new space hero: Major Matt Mason. Matt Mason heralded an era of more realism by donning NASA's newly designed space suit. This modern period would bring us toys made out of a new material, polyvinyl chloride (PVC), and space men and aliens became poseable with fully articulated joints.

Even though modern science has brought us images of the Moon and Mars, those who created the early images of space have instilled a fantastic impression of outer space that lingers in our collective imagination. With actual space exploration being only 50 years old, we are still many years away from discovering what might truly exist out there. What keeps bringing new generations of people back to these marvelous toys is that nothing we have discovered about other planets or solar systems has dispelled our preconceived notions of what other forms of life must look like. Even if we are successful in finding clear evidence of alien life, the space opera toys of the 1950s will forever amuse and inspire us, allowing us to continue to project our fantasies about the unknown onto miniature worlds inhabited by legendary heroes.

Notes

1. See S. Mark Young, Steve Duin, and Mike Richardson, *Blast Off! Rockets, Robots, Ray Guns and Rarities from the Golden Age of Space Toys* (Milwaukie, OR: Dark Horse Books, 2001) for many more images of, and stories about, space-opera toys. I thank Jill Stern for her astute comments on this chapter, and Dark Horse Entertainment for permission to use images from *Blast Off!*
2. While there were other shows during the period, such as *Rocky Jones*, they generated few toys compared to the top three shows.
3. I mean this with no disrespect to the shows. Copies of the original shows exist, but they are much harder to come by compared to the toys, and thus memories are harder to evoke.
4. Gary Cross, *Kids' Stuff—Toys and the Changing World of American Childhood* (Cambridge, MA: Harvard University Press, 1997).
5. Buck Rogers has resurfaced numerous times in popular culture, and with every incarnation, a new generation of toys was produced. The last heyday of Buck toys appeared once more in the late 1970s when *Buck Rogers in the 25th Century* regained popularity with a new television show starring Gil Gerard and Erin Gray. The toys related to this show, however, do not have the same charm as their predecessors.
6. The origins of modern rocketry go back to antiquity, and the development of gunpowder by the Chinese. Since the late nineteenth century there has been significant interplay between science fiction writing about rockets, beginning with Jules Verne and H. G. Wells and scientists such as Konstantin Tsiolkovsky and Robert Goddard in the early twentieth century.

7. Kenneth Arnold, "I Did See the Flying Disks," *Fate Magazine* 1, no. 1 (Spring 1948), 4–11.
8. It is often surprising which shows are successful, and sometimes even more surprising when associated merchandise is produced. For instance, who would have thought that the four main characters on the History Channel's *Pawn Stars* would get their own bobble-head dolls?
9. http://www.tvhistory.tv/index.html.
10. Market penetration of new technology has always been a leading indicator of the speed with which innovation can occur. This is true for television, VHS recorders, broadband, Blu-Ray players, and HD televisions.
11. Some scholars believe that the space operas were blatantly pushing anti-imperialist thinking by having space rangers and cadets fighting to keep America safe, while others take a more benign view. I leave it to others to engage the debate.
12. See *The Tom Corbett Website*, http://www.Solarguard.com.
13. Show sponsors outsourced production of the premiums, which explains why so few have any manufacturer's name associated with them.
14. I was very fortunate to acquire a mint-in-box Superior Spaceport 20 years ago. The set had been opened but never played with. The box that houses this set is the only real disappointment for collectors, as it does not contain any lithography. On some boxes, there is a pasted photograph of the spaceport set up. Most other major space playsets of the period were much more heavily illustrated (such as Archer's Outer Space Set), so this may have reduced Superior's sales of the set. Perhaps this is why mint-in-boxes still can be found (typically with old store stock).
15. Many will remember that the Interplanetary Space Men could also be found in brown soft plastic in boxes of Post Raisin Bran. Each figure was sealed in a glassine envelope.
16. See Jean-Noel Bassior, *Space Patrol: Missions of Daring in the Name of Early Television* (Jefferson, NC: McFarland, 2005).
17. Other manufacturers of the period such as Multiple Products Corporation, T. Cohn, and the Ideal Toy Company produced playsets, but none had the depth and breadth of Louis Marx's lineup.
18. Several years ago, a boxed Space Patrol Playset, produced by Louis Marx and Company in 1952 and originally priced at $5.98, sold at auction for $3,500. Consisting of a tin building and plastic parts and pieces, the set, produced 60 years ago, is one of the most sought-after toys related to the space operas of the 1950s.
19. One collector whom I interviewed who owns every variation of the Marx space sets told me that, growing up, he and his friends did not really care that the Tom Corbett figure had suddenly morphed into Buzz Corry in the Space Patrol set. They all loved the series so much that having the figure in a different color was all that mattered.
20. I have always thought that Rex Mars meant "King Marx," as Louis was known for his king-size ego.

Bibliography

Arnold, Kenneth. "I Did See the Flying Disks," *Fate Magazine* 1, no. 1 (Spring 1948), 4–11.

Bassior, Jean-Noel. *Space Patrol, Missions of Daring in the Name of Early Television*. Jefferson, NC: McFarland, 2005.

Cross, Gary. *Kids' Stuff—Toys and the Changing World of American Childhood*. Cambridge, MA: Harvard University Press, 1997.

Curran, Douglas. *In Advance of Landing: Folk Concepts of Outer Space*, 2nd ed. New York: Abbeville Press, 2001.

Hake's *Price Guide to Character Toys*, 4th ed. Timonium, MD: Gemstone Publishing, 2002.

Kern, Russel S. *Marx Toy Kings, Volume 1: The Marx Men, 1919–1954*. Old Colorado City, CO: Atomic Enterprises, 2010.

———. *Marx Toy Kings, Volume 2: The Playset Era, 1955–1982*. Old Colorado City, CO: Atomic Enterprises, 2010.

Lesser, Robert *A Celebration of Comic Art and Memorabilia*. New York: Hawthorn Books, 1975.

Levinthal, David. *Small Wonder: Worlds in a Box*. Manchester, UK: Cornerhouse Publications, 1994.

Lucanio, Patrick, and Gary Coville, *American Science Fiction Television Series of the 1950s*. Jefferson, NC: McFarland, 1998.

———. *Smokin' Rockets—The Romance of Technology in American Film, Radio and Television, 1945–1962*. Jefferson, NC: McFarland, 2002.

Pippin, E. http://www.solarguard.com.

Young, S. Mark, Steve Duin, and Mike Richardson, *Blast Off! Rockets, Robots, Ray Guns and Rarities from the Golden Age of Space Toys*. Milwaukie, OR: Dark Horse Books, 2001.

CHAPTER 10

SPACE PATROL: MISSIONS OF DARING IN THE NAME OF EARLY TELEVISION

JEAN-NOEL BASSIOR

THE VOICE WAS URGENT: "Go inside and ask about *Space Patrol*."

I was standing alone—except for the eerie feeling that Someone or Something was at my side—in front of the new nostalgia store in Guerneville, California, a resort town on the banks of the Russian River. It was a crisp, spring morning. A block away, a few "river rats," as the year-round residents call themselves, ambled by King's Fish and Tackle on Main Street. Then, impatient, the voice spoke again: "Go inside and ask about *Space Patrol*."

I had not thought about *Space Patrol* in twenty-five years.

Inside, the store was dimly lit and crammed with memorabilia—comic books, vintage toys, and movie posters right out of the 1940s and '50s. The dusty-gold light brought a postwar childhood into soft focus, stirring memories of cap guns, hop-scotch, skate keys, war movies on TV, and long summers of street baseball and hide-and-go-seek. I ran fast for a girl—faster than any boy on the block—and played hard at handball and dodgeball until 6:40 p.m., when I beelined for home. Rush through the unlocked back door, race to the living room, plop down in front of the Hoffman console TV...

"This is the ABC Television Network," the announcer's voice booms... And then it happens...

> SPAAAAAAACE PATROL!! *High adventure in the wild, vast reaches of space! Missions of daring in the name of interplanetary justice! Travel into the future with Buzz Corry, Commander-in-Chief of the* ....

"*Space Patrol* memorabilia?" the bearded guy behind the counter smiles. "That show was my favorite!" His name is David, and we talk about ray guns like two members of the NRA. "Tell you what," he says finally, "I've got a *Space Patrol* tape and a video recorder at home. Can you come back tomorrow?" This is cool. It's 1984, and nobody I know actually *owns* a video recorder. It'll be fun to see the show after so many years.

* * *

The sun has burned off the mist rolling in from the river the following morning as I enter the pale golden gloom of David's store. True to his word, he's setting up the recorder. Then, saying he has errands to do in town, he leaves me alone in the dark with a huge, raw chunk of my childhood. I steel myself for disappointment: *Space Patrol* was a kid's show; viewing it as an adult is bound to shatter sacred childhood memories.

I press "play," and suddenly I'm watching Commander Buzz Corry, Cadet Happy, Major Robertson, and Carol Carlisle menaced by arch villain Agent X, but this is not kiddie fare. The script is not childish and everyone—actors, writer, director—seems to be taking it seriously. As the evil 'X' holds the comrades hostage, I'm concerned, and so are they. And there's something else...something I'm struggling to remember....

You see, as kids, my friends and I assumed we'd grow up to become like our heroes—that someday, we'd do great things and make a difference in the nonsensical world that belonged to adults. Now, watching the *Space Patrol* crew resist Agent X, the kid who dreamed of living heroically snaps out of a long, deep sleep. It's like awakening in the middle of the night—or in mid-life—remembering something you forgot to do. Something very important.

When David returns, I leave in a half-dream. I'm back from the outer galaxies, back on Main Street, but shaken by the magic I've revisited on that black-and-white screen. The haunting "*Spaaaaaace Patrol*" intro has stirred echoes of childhood, when life stretched ahead as an endless adventure. For in the timeless twilight between school and supper, and on Saturday morning, we kids rode horses and spaceships alongside our TV heroes. We patrolled a dimension that stretched from the lawless west to the uncharted outer galaxies, and we helped a lot of people who were victims of foul play. It was an eerie, black-and-white world, where outlaws could ambush you in a canyon, and aliens could trap you in time. But just when you reached the limit of your courage and endurance, your hero-companion—whether Buzz Corry or the Lone Ranger—would come up with a brilliant escape plan, and together you'd fight your way out, and justice would prevail. Then you were safe—until the next show; same time, same station.

If you've studied Earth's history, you know that from 1950 to 1955, three major shows—*Space Patrol, Captain Video,* and *Tom Corbett, Space Cadet*—plus a slew of also-rans, held kids and their parents spellbound as a new kind of galactic hero challenged the unknown. Department stores stocked space gear and weapons, and kids baffled their elders with phrases like "Blast me for a Martian mouse!" Concerned parents sought advice on how to deal with the juvenile space craze. "If your child has bad dreams about being lost in space," counseled one expert, "a doctor should be consulted."[1]

For weeks after I saw that *Space Patrol* episode, I thought I needed a shrink myself. That pesky Voice that had led me to David's store was now urging me to track down the show's cast and crew and tell their story. At the time, I was a musician, not a journalist, but over the next twenty years, I sought out everyone who'd worked on *Space Patrol*, recording his or her memories of what it felt like to pioneer live TV. Then I searched for ex-kids like myself who remembered the show. By then, it was the late 1990s, and fans of many old shows were connecting via the Web. I put out an all-galaxy bulletin, and they contacted me with their stories. Thus the *Space Patrol* saga emerged.

* * *

Space Patrol debuted on March 9, 1950, as a 15-minute daily show on ABC's Los Angeles affiliate, KECA. Nine months later, it went network as a half-hour, weekly broadcast and captured the dawning space-age fantasies of the nation. A sponsor-conducted survey revealed that adults were hooked along with their kids. In 1952, *Life* magazine reported that a convention of top stellar scientists opened with the chairman joking that he disagreed with Commander Corry's description of the moon. The article estimated the show's viewership at seven million.[2]

If you were looking for plenty of action, believable heroes, and steadfast camaraderie in the face of death, *Space Patrol* was your show. While fellowship was a key

Image 10.1   The Space Patrol crew blasts off for thrilling adventures in the wild, vast reaches of space. From left: Lyn Osborn (Cadet Happy), Ken Mayer (Major Robertson), Virginia Hewitt (Carol Carlisle), Ed Kemmer (Commander Buzz Corry), Nina Bara (Tonga). [Credit: Author's collection]

element in other space operas of the day, nothing came close to the loyalty and trust expressed by *Space Patrol*'s Commander Buzz Corry, Cadet Happy, Major Robbie Robertson, Carol Carlisle, and Tonga for one another. ABC crew members watched in awe as the cast merged with their characters, both on- and off-screen. "They would forget who they really were," says script girl Marg Clifton. Audio man Chuck Lewis recalls being swept up by an eerie feeling that what was taking place on the set was real. "The actors made *me* believe it," he marvels, "and I'm a guy who had been through a war."

It helped, of course, that the show's creator, director, and leading actor were all real-life World War II pilots, no strangers to panic and danger miles above the Earth. Creator William "Mike" Moser first conceived of an interplanetary police force fending off cosmic marauders as he flew missions for the navy over the South Pacific. Moser got to wondering about the universe, he told *Time* magazine, and his brain birthed the United Planets, a solar confederation devoted to peace, but willing to fight when menaced by villains whose morals had not caught up with their technology.[3] Moser created the characters and wrote the first scripts before bringing actor-writer Norman Jolley aboard. As *Space Patrol* soared to success, Jolley was churning out eight shows a week—six for TV and two for radio—delivering some scripts just moments before air time. "We got them hot from the typewriter," recalls Ed Kemmer, who starred as Commander Corry.

If, as a kid, you couldn't wait to take off on the next daring adventure with the *Space Patrol* gang; if you worried that the bad guys would do something awful to Corry and Hap and that the Commander wouldn't find a way out in time; if you laughed at Hap's jokes and identified with his vulnerability or Corry's strength; if you wanted to grow up to fight for truth and justice—you can thank Norm Jolley and radio writer Lou Huston. Those plots and characters came from their brains. "Actors love to say, 'When I created that character,' Jolley once joked to me, "but unless it's an improv, they *interpreted* that character. That character was created by some jerk sitting at a typewriter in a room all alone."

Character believability weaves back and forth through many memories as the thread holding the show together when guest actors went blank and special effects went berserk. "We were a family group, fulfilling a need, as soap operas have done for years," says Kemmer. "If one member didn't get you, the other did." And Kemmer got to most people, with his leading-man looks, daring but thoughtful: the perfect hero. Though barely thirty, he was, in fact, a real-life hero. A fighter pilot in World War II, he was shot down by the Germans, wounded, and imprisoned in a prisoner-of-war camp where he risked a daring escape. Recaptured by the Nazis, he managed to survive brutal conditions until the end of the war.

Commander Corry's romantic interest was Carol Carlisle (Virginia Hewitt), daughter of the Secretary General of the United Planets. Carol radiated dazzling blonde looks, even through your black-and-white TV screen, plus, she was a brilliant scientist and could fly a spaceship. Frequently kidnapped, she was resistant yet composed until Buzz could rescue her.

Major "Robbie" Robertson (Ken Mayer) was always there when you needed him. Calm yet concerned, like a favorite uncle, if the villains captured Corry and his cadet, you knew that Robbie was on his way. Robbie's assistant was Tonga—a bizarre state of affairs, since she was a reformed criminal. However, that thirtieth-century medical marvel, the Brainograph, which cleansed thoughts as easily as they used to wash clothes back in the twentieth century, had rid her of evil intentions.

And then there was Hap.

Cadet Happy, portrayed by Lyn Osborn, was the indelible character of the show. As Corry's lighthearted sidekick, Hap deflected terror into comedy and asked questions that allowed the Commander to deliver answers essential to the show's plot. Osborn's irrepressible, child-like energy made us kids feel we could be just like him. "You felt," says memorabilia collector Jim Buchanan, "that if you got the *Space Patrol* membership kit, you'd be just like Lyn Osborn, working with the Commander, protecting the Universe."

* * *

You could cut the tension on the ABC sound stage with an atomo-torch as the familiar *SPAAAAAAACE PATROL!* intro bent the air waves, intoned by announcer Dick Tufeld. Director Dick Darley: "Everything was happening fast, the equipment was whirling around.... You just had to ignore all that and be where you were supposed to be and talk when you were supposed to talk."

But even if you were where you were supposed to be, maybe the camera wasn't. *Space Patrol* was a *live* show, and as viewers watched, they had no idea that dramatic as well as galactic peril was taking place on the set. Cameras tripped over cables and barely made it to the scene, key lights went out, guest actors forgot their lines, and special effects followed their own evil timetables. To the cast and crew of the first live shows, television was a beast they were nudging from one hoop to the next, a genie struggling out of the bottle. And because *Space Patrol* was just one of ABC's many live shows, rehearsals and production time were often reduced to a day and a half. "There was never enough time," says Darley flatly. "We always skidded onto the air."

That was nothing new to the cast and crew, many of whom, just a few years earlier, had been skidding planes onto makeshift runways and dodging bullets overseas. Risk-taking was all in a day's work for these vets, who brought a can-do spirit to early live TV. "A lot of them were gung-ho guys out of the war," says Tufeld, who was younger than the rest. The fact that the show often came in on a wing and a prayer was something its millions of viewers never knew.

And yet, the sheer energy generated from the close calls and near misses of live TV seemed to heighten the drama, imbuing the kinescopes with an eerie tension and excitement that glows off the screen today. "*Space Patrol* had what it had because it was live," says Darley. "If it had been pre-taped and canned, cleaned up and made perfect, it would have been different. If everything came off well, I had a euphoric situation."

Stir in one more hazardous element: live commercials, in which Kemmer and Osborn, in character, had to convince kids that the sponsors' cereal and hot cocoa would give them the "get-up-and-go" of their heroes. In those days, actors could shamelessly tout products, so "Buzz" and "Hap," looking calm and relaxed, were often forced to choke down cereal and sip hot chocolate during commercial breaks hard on the heels of an action scene. "We'd finish a fight scene," Kemmer recalls, "out of breath, dirty...You could be a little bloody from scratches, and sweaty as hell." For months, he begged sponsors to film the commercials. "*Finally*, I guess they saw one too many spots with a sweaty, dirty, bloody guy trying to talk through no breath, and they agreed to do a bunch on film."

* * *

Meanwhile, ahead in the thirtieth century, the animate space junk was getting a little out of hand. You had mild-mannered professors intent on ruling the universe, advanced civilizations gone power-mad, belligerent androids, underwater spaceship pirates, crazed scientists with Z-rays, space spiders and other lowlifes, and invisible beings up to no good in general—all clamoring for state-of-the-art special effects. But, in the lean days before the ABC network picked up the show, you had to make do with what was on hand. "All the spaceship controls came from old World War II bombers," says actor Ken Mayer appreciatively. "You couldn't buy a knob for the *Enterprise* with what our special effects guys did for five or ten dollars a show."

When the daily segment was dropped in 1953, the budget for the weekly network show soared to $25,000. Then you had a new problem: if it misfired, blew up, or fell off the string, it did so before seven million viewers. "We were learning," points out Kemmer. "Remember, nobody had ten years' experience in TV yet—it just wasn't there," Kemmer sighs. "If you can look at it today, *knowing* it was done thirty years ago, *knowing* it was done live, it'll still stand up. But compare it to a million-dollar production with all sorts of special effects that were unknown then, and by those standards we were very crude, very simple."

* * *

In early 1951, The Gardner Advertising Company, a powerful agency whose clients included John Deere and Anheuser-Busch, was searching desperately for an outlet to replace *Tom Mix*. The radio adventure series had been a gold mine for their client, Ralston Purina, whose cereal division had reaped hefty profits from the box-top toy premiums touted on the show. Now, after a 17-year run, *Mix* had finally bit the dust, but with the new genre of TV space operas bursting onto the scene, Gardner saw a chance to go back to the future and recreate its mail-in marketing success. So in May 1951, they picked up *Space Patrol* for Ralston Purina.[4]

Thanks to Gardner, one of the best things about *Space Patrol* was that you could look and act like your heroes – in fact, there was no limit to the imaginative adventures a kid could think up between breakfast and supper. The box-top premiums and store-bought gear fueled endless fantasies, so you bugged your parents for quarters to send in with Wheat Chex or Rice Chex box tops and lobbied for trips to the nearest department store, where you could get the uniforms, caps, and boots the

Image 10.2 The cast made countless personal appearances, signing autographs for space-happy kids. From left: Nina Bara, Virginia Hewitt, Ken Mayer (front), Lyn Osborn, Bela Kovacs (Prince Baccarratti), Ed Kemmer. [Credit: Author's collection]

gang wore, and the weapons and gadgetry that saved their lives. It was like "carrying an object out of a dream," says Elliott Swanson. "That you could buy and own the objects used by Corry and Happy created a powerful psychological link to that imaginary world."

A must-have premium for future nuclear physicist Rory Coker was *Space Patrol's* Hydrogen Ray Gun Ring, which contained an actual "radioactive particle," although it emitted fewer rads than some luminescent watch dials of the day. As a kid, Coker was fascinated by this slice of real science. "I would shut myself in the closet with the ring and see a magical sight: tiny, brilliant explosions of ghostly, blue-white light, like short-lived supernovae. It made your hair stand on end."

Such was the science-in-your-living-room innocence of the 1940s and '50s, when placing a "radioactive particle" in a toy was neither a risk to homeland security nor cause for a lawsuit. It was a halcyon time when "Be the first kid to blow up your block" was a joke, not a threat. It's doubtful, points out space opera fan Chuck Lassen, that toys like the Space Patrol Dart Gun could be sold today. "It packed quite a wallop, and no doubt young Space Patrollers broke more than a few windows," he notes, adding that when that did happen, it was usually accidental, not malicious. "Today, that gun would be considered a 'potential safety hazard,' but kids of the '50s were generally smart enough to handle it with respect."

The merchandise forged a strong bond between kids and the show, and the partnership between Gardner and *Space Patrol* seemed like a match made in heaven, recalls 95-year-old Ralph Hartnagel Sr., then vice president of Sales and Promotion. So in 1953, hopeful that *Space Patrol* could rocket Ralston cereal to the stars, Gardner launched the biggest TV promotion to ever hit the airwaves, the "Name the Planet Contest." All you had to do was name Planet X, the mysterious orb ruled by Commander Corry's nemesis, Prince Baccarratti, which had suddenly invaded the solar system. The grand prize was staggering: Buzz Corry's very own battle cruiser, the *Terra IV*, plus $1,500 dollars.

The contest was Hartnagel's brain child. Since *Space Patrol* was all about spaceships, he reasoned, why not have Standard Carriage Works (who built anything for anybody) in Los Angeles fashion a mammoth ship that would descend on fairgrounds and market parking lots from coast to coast? Kids and their parents would be allowed on board when they presented a box top from a package of Ralston cereal. It was a mind-boggling concept. "Never before had a manufacturer used store parking lots for promotional devices," notes Beatrice Adams in *Let's Not Mince Any Bones*, a history of The Gardner Advertising Company.[5] When the "Name the Planet Contest" was announced on September 19, 1953, kids and their parents were stunned. That night, children on Earth fell asleep dreaming they had slipped into the pilot's seat of the *Terra IV* to go where no kid had gone before.

Of course, if you won the Rocket, you might consider donating the $1,500 to your parents, so they could flee to the outer galaxies before the neighbors went ballistic over the 35-foot-long rocket obstructing their view. And it turned out that entering the contest was no spacewalk. The folks at the Gardner Agency had devised a diabolical scheme to force you to scarf down tons of "good, Hot Ralston cereal" in order to get the space coins buried at the bottom of the box, which you needed to enter the contest. That took a lot of eating, but fortunately, you could drag your parents to a Weatherbird shoe store and get space coins from a friendly shoe salesman.

Young Chuck Lassen reported for duty on the day of the big announcement. "I ate Hot Ralston until I choked to get enough space coins to enter," he recalls. To seven-year-old Jack McKirgan, the contest was "the first challenge I faced as a child." After all, he reasoned, how many kids could force down enough cereal to get the space coins *and* think of a good name for Planet X? But he had underestimated the competition. Thousands of entries poured into the contest command post in Chicago.

Fortunately, both Lassen's and McKirgan's parents were spared the fate of John and Evelyn Walker, whose ten-year-old son, Ricky, submitted the winning entry—Are you ready?—*Caesaria*. The media swarmed over the kid who'd won the Rocket, and his photo appeared in newspapers as far away as England. But winning the Rocket did not give Ricky a perfect life or even make him a better kid. He still got

Image 10.3 It's Ricky Walker Day in Washington, Illinois, January 12, 1954, as the town honors the kid who won the "Name the Planet" contest. [Credit: Author's collection]

chosen last for the baseball team, and he was still a Catholic (which some kids in town didn't like), and he admits to using his newfound celebrity to lord it over his pals. But after a few months, Ricky's friends tired of playing in the Rocket. "At that point," says Walker, 50 years later, "I drifted into obscurity."

Meanwhile, a second Ralston Rocket, also 35 feet long, continued to tour the country. When the Rocket landed in a market parking lot in his town, Eric Hogling was stunned. "I climbed aboard in absolute awe," he recalls, "and I WAS Buzz Corry." Twelve-year-old Judd Lawson's experience was not as good. By the time he'd figured out the Cleveland bus system and got to where the Rocket was parked, hundreds of kids were in line ahead of him. "It was finally my turn," recalls Lawson, "and I'm at the controls for ten seconds when this guy dressed like Buzz Corry says, 'OK!' And I said, 'Wait a minute—I haven't even killed a Martian yet.' But he gave me the boot."

Walker's folks sold the Rocket to an amusement park, who sold it to a Chevrolet dealer, who sold it to a couple who wanted to turn it into a space museum, but sold it instead to a vice president at USA Network, who sold it to a construction company in Ghent, New York. And there this hulk of a fantasy sat, neglected, gutted, and rusted, until, "for safety reasons," it was demolished for scrap metal. "After all these years, we lose a wonderful treasure," says Dale Ames, President of the Galaxy Patrol space opera fan club. Ames found the dying Rocket in time to snap the last photos before it was ripped apart. "It was hard to drive home and leave this treasure behind," he says sadly. "If only they had been aware of its history."6

But while the physical Rocket may be space dust, we ex-kids know better. In some dimension that adults can't find, where they can never, ever throw out your favorite toys and comic books, the Rocket still prowls the galaxy. Because for months, we ate and slept that Rocket, eating the cereal to get the space coins, falling asleep at night as we piloted it out to the stars.

* * *

By mid-1955, it was obvious that space opera was dead.

A week before Christmas, 1954, "Davy Crockett, Indian Fighter," the first of a three-part series, aired on the "Frontierland" segment of *Disneyland*, a popular ABC Wednesday night program hosted by Walt Disney himself. With Fess Parker in the title role, the series chronicled the adventures of Crockett, a real-life frontiersman who died heroically defending the Alamo, a Texas fortress, against Indian attack. The ratings shot through the roof, the catchy theme song, "The Ballad of Davy Crockett," raced to the top of the charts, and overnight millions of juves developed a bloodthirst for coonskin caps. It seemed as if the country was back in the saddle again.

When *Space Patrol* crashed and burned in February, 1955, its 60 percent-adult audience was upset, but we kids took it the hardest. "*Space Patrol* just disappeared," says Warren Chaney. "There was no farewell, no good-bye to our trusted friends and leaders." Chaney pauses. "I guess what I'm saying is that when the series was canceled, I couldn't get over it. I still haven't. If I'm candid with myself, I'm just a kid who grew taller."

* * *

"Heroes and sidekicks," begins a CBS special on famous film and TV comrades narrated by *Star Trek's* William Shatner. "What they endure on the set creates a bond that endures off-screen. It's 'till death do us part,' even more than marriage."7 The sensitive camaraderie between Buzz and Hap was a key element in *Space Patrol*, and it modeled a trust and loyalty that stayed with many kids for a lifetime. Even the bad guys picked up on it. In one episode, a nasty villain holding Buzz Corry's girlfriend, Carol, hostage tells her what the Commander's priorities will be when he learns that both she and Cadet Happy have been kidnapped: "Buzz Corry, ha! He'll spend a week looking for the daughter of the Secretary General and the rest of his life searching all space and time for his cadet!"

"They had an awful lot of affection and respect for each other," says actress Virginia Hewitt (Carol), confirming the real-life bond between Kemmer and Osborn. Like the rest of the cast, she still calls the others by their character names. "We'd go to the projection room and watch the shows, and I'd see Buzz look at his

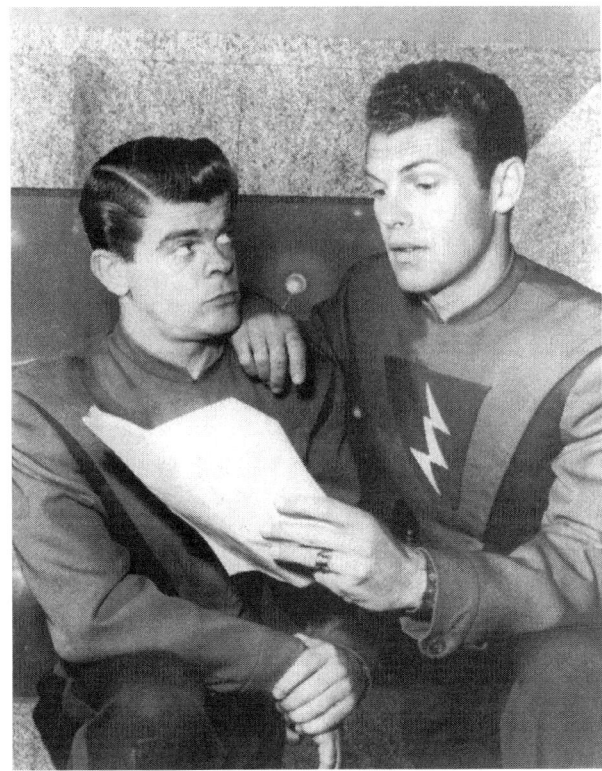

Image 10.4   Lyn Osborn and Ed Kemmer rehearse a scene. [Credit: Author's collection]

cadet and know that he was upset about something. And I'd see great compassion in his eyes, in his face. They were close."

"There was a magic between them," sums up Osborn's sister, Beth Flood.

* * *

The week Lyn Osborn checked into UCLA Medical Center in West Los Angeles, toward summer's end in August 1958, he received three offers: two movie roles and a show of his own. "My brother had it rough after *Space Patrol*," says Beth. "He got bit parts in movies and TV series, but if you didn't watch close, you didn't see him."

To casting directors, Osborn and Cadet Happy were synonymous forever. But beyond that, another problem was developing.

"He first started blacking out when he was doing a picture at MGM ," says Virginia Hewitt. "He was terrified. He didn't fall down, but there would be a few seconds when he couldn't talk." Osborn phoned his sister to tell her something was terribly wrong. "He finally saw a neurologist," Beth recalls, "and they found a brain tumor."

Kemmer summoned the *Space Patrol* cast. "He was going into the hospital the next day, so I invited the whole gang up to my house," Kemmer sighs. "Well, I'd just been through that with a director friend of mine who had a brain tumor. Five-day coma: dead. And, oh, I pushed that out of my mind, 'cause it was a very similar thing with Hap. But he went in with great hope." Osborn, 32, lingered in a coma for five days after surgery and never regained consciousness.

Cadet Happy could always make the best of a terrible situation. *Space Patrol* could get pretty dark, and when the villains were brutal, we kids counted on Hap for comic relief. At the end of each episode, Norm Jolley scripted a comedy routine for Hap that wrapped things up in a heartening package, proving that you could survive emotional and physical abuse unscathed. "Eventually," Osborn told *TV Guide* in 1954, "I want to be a comic. But I look around and see young guys like Sammy Davis Jr., and I figure I'd better get started."[8]

Kemmer made funeral arrangements. "Lyn's parents asked me to help," he says stoically. Though Kemmer held it together—even viewing Lyn's body first to make sure he looked OK—it was obvious he was hurting. "Ed Kemmer is not the type to tear his hair or break into uncontrollable sobbing," recalls actor John Buckley, "but he was visibly upset."

For many kids of the first, awestruck TV generation, Cadet Happy's death was scary and incomprehensible. Hap had come close to death many times on *Space Patrol*, but the Commander had always saved him. This time, something had gone horribly wrong, and for some kids, it took years to recover. "I had no experience with death in my family," recalls Jack McKirgan, then eleven. "Cadet Happy's passing was like losing my best friend, and I grieved for days."

* * *

On a visit with writer Jolley, six months before he died, I ask him about the subtleties of *Space Patrol*, the extraordinary caring between the characters, the strange power the show had to inspire that has lasted more than 50 years. I still want to know how he did it.

We're sitting outside his motor home, east of Palm Springs; a gentle breeze sweeps across the desert as daylight fades into dusk. "*Space Patrol* instilled a deep, unwavering belief in goodness, in heroic action to achieve the impossible, in good winning out in the end," I tell him. "As kids, we loved that stuff—the loyalty and trust between the characters, the self-sacrificing themes. It spoke to us because it was right. What *was* it that drove you to write it that way?"

Jolley falls silent, eyes half-shut. After a while he says softly, as if to himself. "It happened because...that's just the way it should go, is all. That's just the way it should go."

But that's not the way it goes today, says English professor Richard Felnagle. "*Space Patrol, Roy Rogers, Rin Tin Tin*—the shows I grew up on—taught us that we had moral duties and responsibilities, that by standing up, we could make things happen." But, he adds, other things happened, too. "It started with JFK and Martin Luther King—and we couldn't believe things like that could happen to people who were that good. And then we learned horrible things about them, and suddenly we couldn't believe in heroes anymore. What's worse, we began to believe that the bad guys can win, and it changed us." Felnagle pauses. "We've become cynical, blasé. We've lost the sense that we can change the universe by doing the right thing. The right thing doesn't count anymore. It'll get you killed."

Something else has changed, too, says Professor Rory Coker: the very concept of childhood. "In the 1950s, childhood was a sanctuary, protected by parents and society, and cherished by children. Kids, after school and through long summers, were left to their own ingenuity. They played self-invented games, rich in creative fantasy. If they wanted to turn a cardboard refrigerator box into the control deck of a spaceship, they just did it—with a minimum of parental supervision. The giant industries that exist today to exploit every stage of childhood were undreamed of. Drugs, alcohol, sex, gangs, delinquency—these things were encountered only at the movies. "There is more I could say," adds Coker, "but you guys who lived through it know it already."

* * *

On a clear, summer day, I visit the ABC studios in Hollywood where *Space Patrol* was shot. The catwalks where Corry swung from the rafters as he battled Prince Baccaratti have morphed into desk space where people now shuffle papers. Outside the newsroom, I encounter the *Eyewitness News* team. I start talking about the lot's rich history; they listen politely. I ask a vice president of Legal Affairs where the studio's archives are so that I can research *Space Patrol*. (In my mind's eye, I see a stately building labeled "ABC Archives" where historic scripts and kinescopes are carefully catalogued and preserved.) He looks at me strangely and says he'll get back to me.

The vice president doesn't call back, so I call him. He's apologetic. "Even *we* have trouble trying to research the early shows," he says vaguely. Now I get it: no archives exist. And while some of the old kinescope reels of the shows we grew up with survived and were dubbed onto video tape and DVDs, many are lost forever. "It seems funny, in retrospect," says memorabilia expert Joe Sarno, "that the common people—the guys in little houses with big mortgages—were able to save the old comic books and toys of the space opera era. But the big, multi-million-dollar networks could do nothing to save the films and kinescopes of the heroes they created."

The problem, says *Space* Patrol's technical director Bob Trachinger, is that the people who created our childhood memories were so busy doing it that there was no time to think about what it all meant. "Looking back, those were absolutely golden days when we unbelievably spun out those stories. A lot of us were World War II vets. We were like the early days of flying—we could crash at any time. And yet, if a piece of equipment went down or something went wrong, we knew what to do. We had a vision and we kept to it. We didn't reflect on it, we didn't deliberate about it. Hell, we just did it." Trachinger is a warm person who wears his heart on his sleeve, and right now he's going through some deep emotion. "The whole thing was like a dream," he says softly, "and I'm saddened by the fact that no one I knew kept a journal. We didn't know we were making history."

* * *

On a gray, winter day on the Oregon coast, Elliott Swanson relaxes in his office with a steaming cup of green tea ("which should be Nestlé's Quik," he explains, "but the ship's store was out") and stares at the brightly colored array of cardboard dials, gauges, and levers propped up on his desk. It's a perfect replica of *Space Patrol*'s "Rocket Cockpit" premium that Swanson—who has not managed to put childish things behind him, and is not sure he should—has expertly recreated. "It's more than a spaceship—it's a time ship," he explains.

Swanson twists the cardboard controls: "Port rocket tubes trimmed, course set on the directional indicator, thrust set on the anti-gravity rockets, starboard computer at 1955 on the Erg system scale. Pressure and vacuum readings within normal parameters. Cosmic and gamma protective shields active...."

"When the last of us who saw these programs in their original setting is gone, something will vanish from the collective unconscious," he says softly. "And while future generations may recreate the setting of the 1950s, complete with vintage black-and-white TV sets, they will never duplicate the feel of that time—a world where we didn't know if there were Martians. To us, the space opera ships were not models or sets of wood and cloth; they flew to the planets on the fuel of imagination and hope—planets inhabited by people like ourselves. And for those of us who were there—children captured by the wonder—a small place of belief somehow survives. We are supposed to give up childish things as adults, and probably to leave most of that in the past is for the best. But you give up all of it only at the peril of your soul."

Swanson leans back and takes a final sip of tea before blast off. "Headed for dreamtime... Let the rockets roar!"

Notes

1. Unless otherwise noted, all quotes are personal communication, drawn from the author's research interviews.
2. "Space Patrol Conquers Kids," *Life,* September 1, 1952, 79–83.
3. "Radio: Interplanetary Cop," *Time,* August 11, 1952.
4. It was not long before some *Tom Mix* premiums—toys, guns, rings, membership badges, and periscopes—showed up, redesigned and relabeled, as *Space Patrol* gear.
5. Beatrice Adams, *Let's Not Mince Any Bones* (Racine, WI: Western Publishing Company, 1972), courtesy Ralph Hartnagel III. Adams, Vice President of Ad Copy, worked for the Gardner agency for 30 years.
6. In the mid-'80s, Ames set up the Galaxy Patrol fan club to honor space opera and its heroes. Contact Dale Ames, 144 Russell Street, Worcester, MA 01609.
7. *Heroes and Sidekicks—Indiana Jones and the Temple of Doom.* CBS-TV, November 27, 1984.

8. Jean-Noel Bassior, *Space Patrol: Missions of Daring in the Name of Early Television* (Jefferson, NC: McFarland, 2005), 189.

BIBLIOGRAPHY

Adams, Beatrice. *Let's Not Mince Any Bones: An Admittedly Unorthodox History of Gardner Advertising's First Sixty-Five Years.* Racine, WI: Western Publishing Company, 1972.

Bassior, Jean-Noel. *Space Patrol: Missions of Daring in the Name of Early Television.* Jefferson, NC: McFarland.

Heroes and Sidekicks—Indiana Jones and the Temple of Doom. CBS-TV, November 27, 1984.

"Radio: Interplanetary Cop," *Time*, August 11, 1952.

"Space Patrol Conquers Kids," *Life*, September 1, 1952, 79–83.

PART IV

LOOKING AT THE EARTH

CHAPTER 11

MAKING THE UNIVERSE SAFE FOR DEMOCRACY: *ROCKY JONES, SPACE RANGER*[1]

WHEELER WINSTON DIXON

THE GALAXY THAT THE ROCKETMEN PATROLLED WAS A BATTLEGROUND where the forces of good and evil constantly competed—a clear reflection of the earthly Cold War—but reason, diplomacy, and the rule of law were presented as more effective solutions than blasters and missiles to the challenge of evil. *Rocky Jones, Space Ranger* was among the most beloved of these Cold War defenders. Along with the series' tales of interplanetary heroism, Rocky Jones presented his young fans with a consistently hopeful message about the world in which they were growing up, and the value—at home and abroad—of harmony, stability, and the postwar moral order.

Rocky Jones, Space Ranger (1954) has multiple distinctions as an early exemplar of 1950s television sci-fi. It was one of the few series of its type shot on film, rather than presented live, or via Kinescope (*Captain Midnight* being the other major series of its type also shot on film), but perhaps the most intriguing aspect of the series is its matter-of-fact acceptance of interplanetary space travel as something that would become commonplace in the near future. Though the costumes, sets, and special effects are resolutely rooted in the 1950s, along with the series' political and social philosophy, the solidity of the series' product design, coupled with above-average special effects for the period and the use of 35mm film, gave the world of *Rocky Jones* a credibility lacking in such competitors as the long-running *Captain Video* series, which was shot entirely on live video, and survives only in Kinescoped fragments.

The pilot for *Rocky Jones* was shot—quite meticulously—between January and April 1952, on film and with a then-generous $25,000 budget. It was ultimately deemed unsatisfactory, however, and went through substantial retooling, cast changes, and reediting before the series went on the air; portions of the pilot, which was never aired, were later used as part of one of the series' episodes. The approach was typical of producer Roland Reed, who cared—perhaps too much—about even the smallest detail, and would often order reshoots to improve production quality. Production of the series itself, under veteran television director Hollingsworth Morse, proceeded at a more rapid clip, with 26 half-hour episodes knocked out on three-day schedules (on average) between October 1953 and April 1954.[2] Despite the speed with which it was produced, however, *Rocky Jones* somehow never seems hasty in its execution, or cuts corners in matters of physical production. The sets are convincing and surprisingly high tech for the era, including doors that open and close automatically, realistically designed rocket ships, and the use of actual industrial locations as backdrops. All the actors play their parts seriously, without a hint of condescension, and subtle nuances of characterization permeated the series. The plots are, in retrospect, little more farfetched than those of the original *Star Trek* series more than a decade later.

Rocky Jones thus belongs to the past, present, and future of science fiction: created in the 1950s, the series nevertheless seems to inhabit a future time—perhaps 1970 or so—in which all that it presented would become an actuality. Photographed in crisp, metallic black and white, *Rocky Jones* still somehow seems modern, but its character and situations belong resolutely to the era that created it.

UPHOLDING THE MORAL ORDER

The series' premise was deceptively simple: in the near future, a group of Space Rangers, in the service of the United Worlds of the Solar System, patrolled the galaxy in a never-ending mission to preserve the peace, uphold democratic values, and overthrow totalitarian regimes. As Rocky, stalwart "B" actor Richard Crane—happy to get the work after several years of unemployment[3]—was solid and commanding in the title role, delivering his lines with authority and military precision, yet watchful for the slightest hint of a problem in his surroundings, as if anticipating his next ordeal.

Rocky's sidekick, Winky, was played by former *Our Gang* troupe member Scotty Beckett for the first 26 episodes of the series. A natural space mechanic and "can do" personality, Beckett's unfortunate off-screen troubles, which we will come to later, were in sharp contrast to his on-screen persona, which was actually slightly more multifaceted than that of Rocky's. Winky, in contrast to Rocky's rock-steady dependability, kept a "black book" of addresses of the attractive women he met throughout his interplanetary travels, and while serving as Rocky' lieutenant, Winky is very much his own person, thankfully devoid of the unquestioning hero worship, or blank agreeability, of many similar second-string "support" characters. Winky is confident, assured, and practical, but also likeably flawed, displaying a James Dean moodiness that makes him stand out as one-of-a-kind in '50s television sci-fi and sets him apart from Rocky, who is square-jawed '50s masculinity personified. When Beckett was fired from the series for his erratic behavior (including a failed motel robbery), veteran juvenile James "Jimmy" Lydon was drafted into Rocky's crew as Biffen "Biff" Cardoza. Lydon played the role with as much conviction as he could muster, but he simply lacked the heft and depth that Beckett had brought to the role, playing the part in a more awed, subservient manner.

Vena Ray (Sally Mansfield; birth name Marie Mahder) served as the series' female protagonist, and although she conformed to the gender stereotypes of the period, right down to her "short skirt and cape" uniform, and continual retouching of her makeup, functioned as the on-board navigator for Rocky and his crew, and was a full-fledged member of the team, rather than serving as mere decoration. Naturally, as was the case in so many essentially patriarchal 1950s teleseries, Vena often found herself in a perilous situation from which only Rocky and his colleagues could rescue her, but even then, she was never primarily a victim, a love interest, or merely a passenger; as with Winky, she was in many ways more two-dimensional than Rocky himself. Indeed, in the opening episodes of *Rocky Jones*, as we will see, Vena played an integral part in getting the series' basic premise off the ground, and she also was not afraid to confront authority when the situation demanded it.

Bobby (Robert Lyden) was the series' requisite "space cadet," a 12-year-old boy who dreams of joining the Space Rangers for real, and in the meantime tags along on Rocky's adventures, often on the flimsiest of pretexts. He was presented throughout the series as the "ward" of Professor Newton (Maurice Cass), though no mention was ever made of what became of his mother and/or father. Essentially a mascot for the crew, as well as a point of audience identification for younger viewers (who could "project" themselves into the series through Bobby's character), Bobby also served as a conduit for received wisdom and guidance, both

Image 11.1 Vena Ray is rescued from danger—again—by her male crewmates. [Credit: Author's collection]

from Rocky, as well as the series' resident sage, the much older Professor Newton. Bobby's commitment to their teachings is in evidence throughout the series' episodes, as he defends the honor and ideology of his home world. When enemies of the United Worlds attempt to lure him away, his response is as feisty and brave as any soldier whose passions strained against the confines of the Cold War: "I don't like what you teach, and if you think you'll ever lick Earth and the United Worlds of the Solar System, you've got another think coming!"[4] And yet, he was also a student of peace, as demonstrated in a scene from the second episode of "Bobby's Comet," when he explained to Zorovac (Walter Coy), the ruler of Fornax, one of Jupiter's moons, that he has been misled about Earth's goals to "deceive, colonize, and enslave" the galaxy:

> "The Space Rangers' job is to keep peace, Mr. Zorovac, don't you believe a word that Professor Kardoff's told you. We don't try to conquer anybody. The laws of the United Worlds of the Solar System give every planet and moon their independence, and the only fighting we do, Mr. Zorovac, is when someone gets out of line."

Bobby's mentor, Professor Newton, acted as the "chief science officer" of the series, in a manner of speaking, and was the designer, builder, and proprietor of the Newton Observatory (actually the Griffith Observatory in Griffith Park, Los Angeles), as well as being an adviser on all things scientific to Rocky and his crew. When Cass died in June 1954, British actor Reginald Sheffield was brought in as Professor Mayberry to fill the void, but—as with the replacement of Winky with Biff—the chemistry that had worked so well in the past seemed to be lacking. Newton, in particular, served as something of a philosophical lens for the series, ruminating on the continual conflict between good and evil that informed the main conflict of the series' overarching narrative, offering insight into the motives and machinations of Rocky's implacable enemies, in particular the devious Cleolanta (Patsy Parsons), ruler of the planet Ophiuchus, and her lieutenant Atlasande (Harry Lauter).

Cleolanta, the Suzerainne, or Queen of the planet Ophiuchus, Rocky's principal foe, was simultaneously attracted to, and repelled by the young space explorer, whose heteronormative unapproachability posed a perpetual threat to Cleolanta's despotic domain. Cleolanta seeks to destroy Rocky precisely because she cannot possess or control him; in much the same fashion, the matriarchy that Cleolanta maintains is seen in the series as aberrant, and a threat to the stability of the United Worlds, precisely because it is ruled by a capricious, unstable, and inherently unreliable woman. Cleolanta is presented as everything that Rocky is not: impetuous, vengeful, cruel, capricious, and obsessed with dreams of power and conquest. Rocky, on the other hand, presents a picture of placid stability, as does Juliandra (Ann Robinson, most famous for her leading role in the 1953 production of *War of the Worlds*), a later feminine addition to the series, who ruled the planet Herculon in a much more benevolent manner.

In contrast to Cleolanta, who rejects membership in the United Planets outright because she cannot dictate to it (the comparison to the Soviet Union, and the newly formed United Nations, is both inescapable and readily apparent), Juliandra welcomes cooperation with Rocky and his colleagues, ushering in a new note of interplanetary harmony as the series swept rapidly toward its penultimate conclusion.

Rounding out the cast was Secretary Drake (Charles Meredith), supreme commander of the Space Rangers, and in charge of the series' "Office of Space Affairs," who acted as an avuncular father figure for both Rocky and his crew. Tolerant, kind, wise, but capable of exerting his authority with a simple gesture, Secretary Drake was the absolute authority whose final decisions were faithfully executed with a fealty and devotion that approached blind and unquestioning obedience. In manner and appearance, he resembled no one so much as Dwight D. Eisenhower, then president of the United States.

ROCKY JONES AND THE COLD WAR WORLD

Asked by Tom Weaver if he thought about the children who were watching Rocky Jones, or their reaction to it, Lydon replied languidly, "Y' know, I never even thought about it. It wasn't my department."[5] Noting that he never watched an episode of the series when it was completed, he concluded his comments by adding that

> I don't mean to be cold and blasé about this business which I love dearly, but to us it was a job. Like you'd make a Ford Motor Company vehicle on a production line, that's the way we made film. Once we finished a thing, it was finished, it was over, and you go on to the next one, and the next one, and the next one, hopefully.[6]

I would argue that Lydon here is mostly speaking for himself. And despite Lydon's workaday attitude toward the series, there can be no question that the narrative of *Rocky Jones* carried considerable ideological freight.

The Cold War was a period of extended political and military contestation, in which the battle lines seemed clearly drawn between East and West. Without the instant access provided by the Internet, the Web, YouTube, Facebook, instant messaging, and other social networking technologies, it was relatively easy for a dictatorial personality to seize the reins of power and hold on indefinitely. Radio signals—as in Radio Free Europe—could be jammed, the simple act of owning a radio could be outlawed, and the press in Communist nations operated under severe conditions of constant government censorship. Rocky Jones reflected this in the story line of "Crash of Moons," in which Cleolanta is described as the despotic ruler of Ophiuchus, who "won't allow her people any information about life on other moons or planets—even the possession of an astrophone [read 'radio'] set is punishable by death."[7]

But even more disturbing was the territorially expansionist policy pursued after World War II by our one-time allies, Russia and China, who both underwent a complete shift in social policy, creating the Iron Curtain—as Winston Churchill noted in his famed speech at Westminster College in Fulton, Missouri, on March 5, 1946—thus betraying the cause of the Allies against the Axis Powers in World War II and creating a conflict that would dominate the world for nearly half a century. In the episode "Beyond the Curtain of Space," Secretary Drake makes a direct reference to Churchill's speech, telling Rocky that when he crosses into Ophiuchus' domain, there is "a curtain which separates our league of planets from the Ophiuchus group.

From that point on, they're able to jam our messages. After you've passed that point, you'll be without a communication link."[8]

In 1952, when the pilot for Rocky Jones was shot, Cold War tensions were at their height. The House Un-American Activities Committee was at its full power, and those who even dared to suggest that they deviated from the accepted social norms of the era were severely chastised—with loss of jobs, prestige, even imprisonment. Thus, a curious bifurcation emerged, with both sides, East and West, living in fear, with the threat of the nuclear bomb, and the principle of Mutual Assured Destruction—the so-called "MAD" principle, aptly named—creating a climate of distrust and fear that encircled the globe, reinforced on all sides by the media, which, even in Western countries, was very closely controlled (as it still is) by corporate and government interests. And yet, even in Rocky Jones, there emerged from this environment, a message of hope. In episode 2 of "Bobby's Comet," Zorovac resists the notion that tension, strife, and isolation are the only possibilities for interplanetary relationships. He argues with the evil Professor Cardos:

> "You've always taught me that we were surrounded by a galaxy of enemies—that there was no such thing as friendship in the universe. Now that I've seen these people from Earth, I'm beginning to question your teachings."

The social landscape of the period was thus both simple and complex; gender stereotypes were rigidly enforced for both women and men, racism (or fear of the "other") abounded, anything other than performative heterosexuality was absolutely

Image 11.2 The *Rocky Jones* "family" on the bridge of the *Orbit Jet*. L to R: Professor Newton, Rocky Jones, Cleolanta, Winky. [Credit: Author's collection]

proscribed, and behavior was thus on all levels severely regulated. *Rocky Jones'* cast, then, was presented as an extension of the 1950s nuclear (in every sense) family: the father figures (Rocky and Secretary Drake); the ingénue/mother (Vena); the son, or trusted lieutenant (Winky, and later "Biff" Cardoza); the grandfather (Professors Newton and Mayberry); and the young acolyte, Bobby. Family unity was a theme much stressed in the series, as were team loyalty, athletic fitness, and obedience to governing authorities. Indeed, one might argue that in the early 1950s, whether in the Soviet Bloc, or in America, *conformity* was the most sought after value. Stepping out of line made one a target; "fitting in" was the greatest compliment one could hope for. As with other children's space shows of the era, *Rocky Jones* had its own fan club, and a membership code to go with it. To become a member of the Space Rangers, a viewer had to promise to:

> obey my parents at all times
> be kind and courteous
> be brave in the cause of freedom
> help the weak
> obey the law at all times
> grow up clean in mind and strong in body
> —in short, to become a responsible,
> levelheaded member of 1950s
> Eisenhower America.[9]

Not surprisingly, the plots of the *Rocky Jones* episodes are, in essence, morality plays for the Cold War era, just as surely as if they had been presented on *Father Knows Best* or *Leave It to Beaver*. The family unit, initially at peace, is suddenly threatened by some malign, outside influence. Conflict ensues; instruction and discipline are administered; order is restored. Only in this case, it is the order of the universe, rather than just the domestic sphere, but then again, in the world of Rocky Jones, the domestic sphere *is* the universe. A brief sampling of some of the series' tripartite plot lines provides ample evidence of this.

The series' first three-part episode, "Beyond the Curtain of Space," also known as "Beyond the Moon," confronts the viewer with an interesting premise: Professor Newton, introduced here, as are all the other characters, is supposed to have sworn off any allegiance to the United Worlds of the Solar System, and decamped with his young ward, Bobby, to the planet Ophiuchus, where he is supposedly aiding those who seek to disrupt the peaceful coexistence of the various planets in the galaxy. Vena Ray storms into Commissioner Drake's office and convinces him that far from being a traitor, Professor Newton has been kidnapped, and urges the Commissioner to rescue him. Rocky, Winky, and Vena fly to Ophiuchus, and discover that the Professor is indeed being held against his will, and he is summarily rescued after the usual complications. Professor Newton's rescue sets up the basic premise for the series, as well as the central group of protagonists, both of which remained consistent for the first 26 episodes, and immediately established both Rocky and Vena as capable, idealistic, and dedicated to the ideals of the United Worlds, in an almost militaristic manner.

In "Rocky's Odyssey," also known as "Gypsy Moon," the three-episode plot arc follows Rocky as he discovers an isolated moon, Posito, ruled by the enigmatic Bovaro (John Banner, later Sergeant Schultz in *Hogan's Heroes*). Posito and a neighboring moon, Negato, are at war. Can Rocky bring peace to both planets? The names of the planets are obvious clues as to their constituency's attitudes: the inhabitants of Posito are generally upbeat and have an optimistic attitude on life, while those on Negato seem much more remote and unsociable. Trying to enact a peace treaty, Rocky falls under the spell of Negato Music, a weird, atonal wailing that the inhabitants use to ward off intruders. The music starts to drive Rocky insane until, taking a tip from the poet Homer—as suggested, surprisingly, by young Bobby—Rocky plugs his ears as Odysseus did, the better to resist the sirens' song. Eventually Rocky's intercession brings peace to the warring planets, and two very different cultures learn to coexist in peace. It does not take much to stretch this into another simplistic, yet effective Cold War analogy, with a certain wistfulness attached: if only the United States and Russia could get along, war might be averted, with a nod to the classics, in passing.

Similarly, "Silver Needle in the Sky," also known as "Duel in Space," concerns an interplanetary peace conference, disrupted by an angry Cleolanta, who is miffed that she has not been invited to attend. "Blast Off" (no alternate title given) follows Rocky and Bobby as they are forced to land on a desolate planet, populated by peaceful valley people and the warlike hill people. Again, Rocky is called upon to mediate between the two factions. Perhaps the most nihilistic scenario is offered by "Crash of Moons," also known as "Crash of the Moons," which depicts the destruction of the planets Posito and Ophiuchus, but not before a fleet of ships from the United Worlds of the Solar System has evacuated all the inhabitants. It is interesting to note here that although Rocky Jones is essentially presented as an action hero, his main skills seem to be in negotiation; more often than not, it is Rocky's powers of diplomacy and persuasion that bring about a satisfactory conclusion in which all parties feel enfranchised. Brute force is always used in *Rocky Jones* only as a last resort. This, of course, is in direct contrast to the much more direct approach of, for just one possible example, Flash Gordon, forever locked in violent, physical combat with the Emperor Ming and his minions.

There were also three "one-off" episodes: "Kip's Private War," "Vena and the Darnama," and "Escape Into Space." "Escape Into Space" dealt with an underworld figure escaping Earth with four suitcases full of cash to live a life of purloined luxury; Rocky is sent in hot pursuit. In "Kip's Private War," a young boy, whose father is a hoodlum, helps Rocky and his colleagues escape from the clutches of Pinto Vortando (Ted Hecht), and in the process comes to respect both Rocky and the dominant social order Rocky represents. The final episode of the series, "The Trial of Rocky Jones," also known as "Renegade Satellite," much like the "recap" chapter of a late 1940s Republic serial, finds Rocky on trial on the planet Ankapar for an infraction against the planet's code of laws. However, the episode is really an efficient manner of recycling footage from the previous episodes, depicting Rocky performing one service after another in defense of the united democracies of the universe. Done very quickly and cheaply, it is a rather melancholy conclusion to this otherwise lively series.

Image 11.3 Rocky, in his role as action hero, battles recurring villain Pinto Vortando. [Credit: Author's collection]

While the world of Rocky Jones was readily definable, the characters showed their mutability by changing their circumstances as the series progressed. When Ophiuchus, the planet she so despotically ruled, was destroyed in "Crash of the Moons," and her subjects rescued from destruction by the United Worlds forces, Cleolanta seemed to soften in her attitude toward Rocky, as if she were considering the possibility of life on the other side of the social spectrum and finding it more than a little attractive. Similarly, Cleolanta's henchman, Atlasande, also undergoes a change of heart in his dealings with the United Worlds, and is instrumental in bringing about Cleolanta's conversion to a more democratic vision of government. Thus, in contrast to many of the other children's sci-fi series of the era—especially the ultranihilist *Captain Midnight*, in which violence, death, and betrayal permeated every episode—a sense of hope ultimately pervades Rocky Jones, as well as character development. Rather than being static creations, the characters' loyalties and allegiances shift throughout the series, and as I have noted, Rocky Jones triumphs not just with force, but also with reason—in fact, more *often* with persuasion and argument than violence.

In short, *Rocky Jones, Space Ranger* inhabited a world that was at once hermetic and yet limitless, rigidly circumscribed and still elastic enough to contain a galaxy of eccentric characters and alien worlds. Though social conflict between competing planets was the main thrust of the series, *Rocky Jones* ultimately was less jingoistic in its approach to Cold War politics than many of its peers.

DEATH AND AFTERLIFE: PROPELLING DEMOCRACY INTO THE FUTURE

The quickness and cheapness of the final 12 episodes of *Rocky Jones*, a marked contrast with the perfectionism of the first 26, reflected a punishing production schedule that required director Morse required to shoot 13 to 15 pages of script a day. Jimmy Lydon, newly hired to play Biff Cardoza, recalled: "In certain master takes, we would run two minutes, sometimes two and a half minutes. Two or three pages of dialogue in one master take, and then they'd bounce in for a couple of close-ups here and there. If anybody made a mistake, we'd keep right on going until we got to the end of the scene, 'cause they could bounce in for a close-up where we made a mistake."[10] The schedule, in turn, reflected a financial crisis at Roland Reed productions. Reed relied on syndication for distributing his programs, and as a result *Rocky Jones* had neither a regular network time slot nor a continuing commercial sponsor, existing instead on a patchwork of advertisements cobbled together by syndicators and local stations. Profits were minimal, with licensing fees (sold on a station-by-station basis) ranging from $60 a week in the smallest market to $1,900 a week in the largest market (New York City), and Reed's distributor, Official Films, taking a 30-percent cut. Starved of money by Reed's insistence on quality and lack of business acumen, *Rocky Jones*—still in strong demand—ceased production in October 1954. Roland Reed Productions was out of business by November.[11]

Almost as soon as it ended its initial run, however, *Rocky Jones* proved a bonanza for more astute businessmen. MCA, the Music Corporation of America (which would soon become MCA/Universal), put its considerable marketing heft behind a syndication package containing all 38 episodes, intent on wringing every last dollar out of the series. Penetration went deep into all US and foreign markets, with the result that *Rocky Jones, Space Ranger* played to much wider audiences in its "second coming" than in its initial run. Data from the Arbitron Rating System, shows that *Rocky Jones* had a truly spectacular hold on the entire family audience during its first MCA-backed run in January-March 1955. Surprising even the hardened MCA executives, the series racked up a 24.8 rating in Providence, RI, or an 86% share of the *total audience for its time period* [emphasis added]; in St. Louis, a 24.5 rating, or 83% audience share; in Pittsburgh, a 26.1 rating, constituting an astounding *94% audience share* [emphasis added]; in Boston, a respectable 15.0 rating, or 60% of the total audience; and in Cleveland, a 15.6 rating, or a 62% audience share. In all these cities, Rocky Jones beat out all the televised competition, both network *and* syndicated. And this, mind you, is in *reruns*.[12]

Rocky Jones was also a marketing bonanza. There were Rocky Jones coloring books, lunch boxes, thermos bottles, tie-ins with Silvercup Bread, and record albums containing stories inspired by the series ("Shipwrecked on Planet X," "Rocky Jones and the Space Pirates"), as well as a series of Charlton comic books, Space Ranger pins (to be worn by loyal followers of the series), Rocky Jones boots and shoes for youngsters, and "playsuits, socks, shirts, pajamas, polo shirts, slippers, belts, suspenders, dungarees, jackets, ties, hats, and trousers."[13] Richard Crane, in his Rocky Jones uniform, spent six months in 1954 touring the country in support of the series to drum up additional business, appearing at supermarkets, Little League games, and other venues.

A cult audience grew around the series, as the episodes were usually run in the same sequence, both for overall story continuity, and also to preserve the 12 three-part story lines. Ten of the three-part story arcs were edited into feature films, which ran not only on television but also in theaters *after* their broadcast on television, both as first-run shows, and long after the series had been repackaged. Only Walt Disney pulled off a similar feat, with his Davy Crockett series of episodes on his weekly television show, which ran in five parts from December 15, 1954, through December 14, 1955, on television, and which were re-edited into several features, and enjoyed a prosperous theatrical run. So at least in one sense, with these "ready made" features, Roland Reed was ahead of his time.

On August 12, 1964, Official Films reported that the *Rocky Jones* features were still one of their top sellers. Fully a decade after the series wrapped, they were attracting a whole new generation of viewers, and at 78 minutes each, the features were ideal for a 90-minute time slot, with 12 minutes held out for commercials.[14] From here, *Rocky Jones* bounced from one library to the next, always profitable, endlessly cycling through the same adventures, but somehow managing to remain fresh, and timeless despite the show's Cold War origins. And, of course, it is still running today, on one video platform or another, a perfect testament to the series' lasting vitality and appeal. Almost 60 years ago, an unsigned review of the series' first broadcast recognized that appeal:

> What's going on behind the iron curtain is of small concern to the little shavers, who must stick their heads into the set when *Rocky Jones* "blasts off." Of greater immediate interest to them is what goes on beyond the curtain of space. For the young 'uns this is a dish to be devoured avidly and with childish imagination. They must have the vicarious thrill of riding the tail of the rocket ship high into the wild blue yonder.[15]

Variety declared the series "Every bit as good as the others"[16]—*Captain Video, Captain Midnight, Flash Gordon* and the rest—and yet, it very much possessed a slick, positive, and resonantly futuristic vision of its own. In that future, Rocky Jones and his crew faced challenges that reflected the world as it was, but their responses—rooted in idealism and the desire for words to triumph over weapons—reflected the world as Eisenhower-era Americans imagined it might be. The most hopeful dreams of Cold War America—democracy, peace, and cooperation among nations—were realized, while the worst of its nightmares—tyranny, espionage, and the constant threat of war—were banished to the far reaches of the galaxy.

Notes

1. The author wishes to sincerely thank Kristine Krueger, of the Margaret Herrick Library, Fairbanks Center for Motion Picture Study, at the Academy of Motion Picture Arts and Sciences, Los Angeles, for her remarkable research on this project; as well as Richard Graham, Research Librarian, at Love Library, University of Nebraska, Lincoln.

2. Allan Asherman. "Rocky Jones: Space Ranger Pt. II," *Filmfax*, May 1990, 83.
3. Sheilah Graham. "Just for Variety," *Variety*, April 11, 1952, 2.
4. *Classic Sci-Fi TV*, DVD collection, (Golden Valley, MN: Mill Creek Entertainment, 2009). Unless otherwise noted, all television programs referred to are from this collection.
5. Tom Weaver. "Jimmy Lydon: Rocky Jones: Space Ranger," *Films of the Golden Age*, Fall 2007, 61.
6. Weaver, 62.
7. Allan Asherman. "Rocky Jones: Space Ranger Pt. I," *Filmfax*, March 1990, 54.
8. Ibid.
9. Elaine Tyler May. *Coming Home: American Families in the Cold War Era* (1998; repr. New York: Basic Books, 2008), 25–30, 58–88.
10. Weaver, 61.
11. Asherman, Part II: 85.
12. MCA Pressbook
13. Asherman, Part II: 44.
14. "Sci Fi Rocky Jones Now Sold as Features," *Variety*, August 12, 1964, 30.
15. "New Telepix Shows: Rocky Jones, Space Ranger," *Variety*, January 20, 1954, 24.
16. Ibid.

Bibliography

Asherman, Allan. "Rocky Jones: Space Ranger, Pt. I." *Filmfax*, March 1990.

———. "Rocky Jones: Space Ranger, Pt. II." *Filmfax*, May 1990.

Classic Sci-Fi TV, DVD collection, Golden Valley, MN: Mill Creek Entertainment, 2009.Graham, Sheilah. "Just for Variety." *Variety*, April 11, 1952, 2.

May, Elaine Tyler. *Coming Home: American Families in the Cold War Era*. 1998. New York: Basic Books, 2008.

"New Telepix Shows: Rocky Jones, Space Ranger," *Variety*, January 20, 1954, 24.

"Sci Fi Rocky Jones Now Sold as Features," *Variety*, August 12, 1964, 30.

Weaver, Tom. "Jimmy Lydon: Rocky Jones: Space Ranger," *Films of the Golden Age*, Fall 2007, 61.

CHAPTER 12

"Justice through Strength and Courage": *Captain Midnight* and the Military-Industrial Complex

MICK BRODERICK

> On a mountaintop, high above a large city, stands the headquarters of a man devoted to the cause of freedom and justice...a war hero who has never stopped fighting against his country's enemies...a private citizen who is dedicating his life to the struggle against evil men everywhere....
>
> Captain Midnight!

FOR A GENERATION OF BABY BOOMERS THIS INTRODUCTORY ANNOUNCEMENT, with its high-pitched drawl elongating "Caaaapt'n Miiidnight," was instantly familiar. Accompanied by the staccato, punctuated beeps of radio telemetry, the rapid montage cut to a rocket-propelled jet fighter hurtling above an elevated runway. The roar of the engine quickly segued to a stirring patriotic theme with a correspondingly slow, inward zoom revealing a domed, high-tech laboratory. This powerful opening sequence was emblematic of the American Century, and it held sway over the imagination of millions of domestic and international television viewers throughout the 1950s and 1960s.[1]

This chapter examines the relationship between the US military and the *Captain Midnight* series producers. The program relied on official Pentagon cooperation and therefore explicit approval for several episodes featuring military stock footage. This was intercut throughout filmed sequences in order to provide an aura of authenticity and currency in scientific, military, and geopolitical affairs. At the end of each episode, viewers were reminded that use of the program's *Silver Dart* was courtesy of "Douglas Aircraft, US Navy." In concert with blurring the program's verisimilitude with inserted military film, interstitial advertising reinforced brand loyalty by foregrounding the association of privileged audience memberships, where the cast of Captain Midnight and/or children and sports heroes are shown consuming and promoting the sponsors' products (Ovaltine chocolate drink mix and Kix cereal).

Encouraged by offers from program sponsors, viewers could send in box tops, product seals, or labels to receive official *Captain Midnight* decoder rings, embroidered patches of the Secret Squadron—the official "covert" organization established by this fictional hero—and other membership privileges. As with the radio audiences from that medium's wartime programming, television viewers joined a nationwide club. Along with many related television series of the period these increasingly controversial premium merchandizing offers, inherited from prewar advertising, enabled "paid-up members of these semi-secret societies" to receive "cold war paraphernalia including Atomic Canons and Rocket Guns."[2]

Drawing from unclassified Pentagon Film and Television Branch files at Georgetown University, this chapter will show how *Captain Midnight* conformed to the then-secret US national security blueprints of postwar American policy to combat domestic subversion and international communism. The 1950s zeitgeist of counter-espionage, security paranoia, and threatened nuclear annihilation was counterbalanced by economic prosperity, ubiquitous consumer consumption, "atoms for peace," and Eisenhower's politics of national consensus.[3] This seemingly contradictory Orwellian doublethink is evident in concepts of both "containment" and "victory" cultures, documented by Alan Nadel and Tom Engelhardt respectively, and permeates the overall narrative of *Captain Midnight*.[4] The series established a veneer of techno-military credibility, aided by Pentagon and Atomic Energy Commission footage, where quasi-scientific partisan claims of nutritional benefit, or comparisons with inferior competitor products, held sway. Hence *Captain Midnight*, renamed *Jet Jackson, Flying Commando* for syndication and international distribution, provides a number of insights into Cold War America.

The mass-media genesis of this television series stems from a syndicated, prewar radio show (1938–1940) that was later franchised on the Mutual Radio Network and NBC with Ovaltine as sponsor (1940–1953). A tie-in comic book (Dell and then Fawcett, 1941–1948) was popular, and the character also ran in newspapers as a comic strip. A short-lived Columbia studio serial screened during 1942.[5] The television incarnation morphed the franchise World War I flying ace into a postwar, Cold Warrior.[6] *Captain Midnight* was adapted for television in the mid-1950s by Screen Gems and broadcast on CBS until syndication in 1958. However, the series was not without public controversy. During the 1954 US Senate subcommittee hearings into juvenile delinquency, for example, the President of the National Association for Better Radio and Television singled out *Captain Midnight* as "objectionable" due to its high degree of unsavory characters and violence.[7]

A key narrative conceit of the program was the foregrounding of Captain Midnight as a "private citizen" and "war hero" operating from a technologically advanced, secret base and utilizing a clandestine global network of confederates (the Secret Squadron) to aid and abet his missions. Borrowing its formal narrative design, quasi-governmental heroes, sidekicks, and Cold War adversaries from the existing children's television genre of the era (e.g., *Captain Video, Rocky Jones, Rod Brown, Tom Corbett*), Captain Midnight flew a state-of-the-art, rocket-and-jet-powered aircraft, the *Silver Dart*, modeled on the Douglas D-558 Phase II Skyrocket, which in 1953 became the first aircraft to travel twice the speed of sound.[8] Unlike the Columbia serial's cliffhanger structure, the television program foregrounded the participatory nature of the series by encouraging viewers to engage in fantasy activities (as members of the Secret Squadron) outside the regular flow of weekly broadcasts. By constantly addressing audiences during the episodes, either within advertising or via cross-promotional interstitials, announcers, the program characters and sporting stars provided an extended "family" for audiences to identify with. And that identification was chiefly with the series' eponymous hero, played by Richard Webb, a World War II veteran typecast from patriotic roles in *O.S.S.* (1946), *The Sands of Iwo Jima* (1949), *and I Was a Communist for the F.B.I.* (1951).

Critics have derisively described *Captain Midnight* (1954–1955) as a generic hybrid, merging two existing and highly popular serial forms (science fiction and the Western), and featuring a "contemporary Lone Ranger figure who jockeyed in a jet plane…instead of on a horse."[9] Network Westerns, espionage, and science fiction series of the era invited their juvenile audiences to memorize and/or chant patriotic pledges, codes, or oaths that formed part of the program's epistemology. In this regard *Captain Midnight* was hardly novel.[10] For Fred MacDonald, the persona of Captain Midnight typified "the perfect model for the United States at midcentury—an amalgam of technology, scientific investigation, and physical prowess…a patriot deeply involved on the American side of the cold war."[11]

While rhetorically championing fair play and decency, the series nevertheless exhibited troubling individual and collective examples of ideologically dubious behavior to justify actions that, ironically, would otherwise be considered antidemocratic, torturous, or treacherous. As MacDonald recognizes, the convergent historical trends of wartime propaganda and the alignment of industry with the military in further pursuing nuclear technologies led to television "becoming a willing conduit for imagery and rhetoric uncritically supportive of partisan Cold War politics".[12] In this way, *Captain Midnight* helped to inure a generation of children to the normative merging of capitalist ideology, the national security state, and electronic surveillance with nascent televisual forms.

THE MILITARY-INDUSTRIAL-SECURITY-ENTERTAINMENT COMPLEX

As several Cold War scholars have shown, President Eisenhower's 1960 farewell address to the nation identified the dangers, since the early 1950s, of the increasing surrender of civilian oversight and due diligence concerning the military and industrial synergies of maintaining a permanent (cold) war economy.[13] Eisenhower warned of the concentration of power and influence within the "military-industrial complex" and the abrogation of democratic rights of decision-making and review by an increasing uninformed American citizenry.[14]

Although implicit in the president's critique, the postwar rise of the national-security state during the Cold War was another major contributor to this "complex." The formation of the CIA in 1947 and the dominance of FBI counter-espionage powers domestically under J. Edgar Hoover and throughout the congressional House Un-American Activities Committees (1945–1975) coincided with two secret blueprints for reassessing America's role in the postwar environment. Less than a year after the Soviet Union detonated its own atomic device in 1949, ending the US monopoly on nuclear weapons, the National Security Council directive 68 (1950) dictated that any key area on the globe that America could not preserve under its sphere of influence would necessitate all-out nuclear war:

> The only deterrent we can present to the Kremlin is evidence we give that we make any of the critical points [in the world] which we cannot hold the occasion for a global war of annihilation.[15]

The second major policy shift came with the report of the Doolittle Committee, established by Eisenhower in 1954 to make recommendations concerning covert political action as an instrument of foreign policy:

> We are facing an implacable enemy whose avowed objective is world domination by whatever means and at whatever cost. There are no rules in such a game. Hitherto acceptable norms of human behavior do not apply. If the U.S. is to survive, longstanding concepts of "fair play" must be reconsidered.[16]

The report further stressed that "we must learn to subvert, sabotage and destroy our enemies by more clever, more sophisticated, and more effective methods than those used against us," adding that the American people be made familiar with "this fundamentally repugnant philosophy." As historian James A. Barry suggests, despite some of the report authors having unease at such a "repugnant philosophy," the threat of international communism became the de facto rationale for much covert action without need for specific justification:

> Thus the Cold War, and the perceived severity of the Soviet threat, made it possible for policymakers to ignore competing ethical considerations when they endorsed covert actions.[17]

Evidence of these policy shifts can be found in the cultural production of the time, and *Captain Midnight* provides an exemplar. The nexus between the entertainment industries, principally the American film and television industries is another unstated element of the Eisenhower "complex." For Gary H. Grossman, Hollywood B-features during the Cold War generally failed in selling their overt their anticommunist message, whereas "[t]elevision provided a much more successful channel for the cold war propagandists. And children received a full dose of the message on Saturday morning."[18] The new medium followed seamlessly from the propagandistic World War II broadcasting that reinforced American values such as "the sanctity of private property, the importance of individualism, the rectitude of the national cause, and the prevailing of justice."[19] Increasingly networks and stations offered "politicized programming in harmony with government policies," particularly those aimed at "thwarting the perceived threats from Communism."[20]

Christopher Anderson has argued convincingly that television's evolution outside of the Hollywood studio system enabled advertising, technology, and the electrical utilities industries to dominate programming agendas, such as Eisenhower's televised opening of the Atoms for Peace initiative and the push for domestic nuclear-power utilities to soften the apocalyptic visions of nuclear testing and war. For Anderson, "television offered the industry a chance to create its most sublime spectacle—the transformation of atomic energy into a beneficial source of power and profit."[21] Like Anderson, cultural critic Joyce Nelson found the medium (technology, apparatus, and its political economy) was inseparable from the message:

> In [the twentieth] century colonization is accomplished through the eye. At least that is its more subtle and "peaceful" form ....As a technological cataract, television has been at the forefront of disseminating an ideology of technological omnipotence, the sign of which is surely the bomb itself. By uniting North American society around television, the dominant military-industrial powers subtly united the populace around all technological advance, including the perfection of nuclear weapons."[22]

Despite landmark studies such as those by Lawrence H. Suid, much of the history of official military cooperation with independent producers and television program-makers remains unexplored.[23] Despite rigid military guidelines for full or limited assistance, entertainment producers could resort to personal relationships and intensive lobbying through back channels to occasionally succeed when requests were initially denied. Analysis of the files from the Pentagon's Motion Picture Branch reveals that the process of "official" cooperation was frequently and contradictorily fluid.

Two brief examples from Hollywood productions are indicative of contrary justifications for cooperation, or its rejection. When RKO and prominent producer Howard Hawks requested assistance to film *The Thing from Another World* (1951), Donald Baruch, chief of the Pentagon's Motion Picture Branch, was adamant that cooperation was to be refused since "the story revolves around flying saucers and their possible occupants," maintaining the air force's position "that there are no such things as flying saucers." He added that the service did not want to be associated with anything "that could be interpreted as perpetuating the myth of the flying saucer."[24] So perturbed by the possible association with UFOs and aliens, Baruch further warned the studio that "in the interest of maintaining mutual goodwill and relations, the Air Force wants no representation of personnel or equipment be included in the film."

In contrast to this unequivocal line, when a private citizen wrote to the Office of the Secretary of Defense complaining about inaccuracies and implausible facts in MGM's *Above and Beyond* (1953), the biopic of *Enola Gay* pilot Col. Paul Tibbets, the reply reveals the Pentagon's flexibility when adjudicating official cooperation, or its retrospective justification.[25] Harry Gildea of Trenton, New Jersey, found "there were many code words and 'Official' data given concerning the explosion of the

[atom] bomb which seemed contrary to general knowledge." Gildea proposed that the Department of Defense should "[g]uarantee the correctness" of the data, and questioned "whether the picture is largely fiction based on a few facts." The reply from Lt. Col. Claire Towne, Motion Picture Section, is both candid and revealing. It also demonstrates a pragmatic complicity between the studios and the military. Towne informed Gildea that "the primary purpose of a motion picture produced by the Hollywood industry for theatrical distribution is to entertain."[26]

> When writing a screenplay which is based on a true historical incident or an actual series of incidents, it is sometimes necessary to take a reasonable amount of poetic license in order to give the eventual film those human qualities which will make it acceptable to the people who have to pay their money to see it.

This frank concession seems to imply that the Hollywood's for-profit and entertainment agenda will necessarily override military authenticity. Towne readily affirmed the "excellent relations" between the Pentagon and the motion-picture industry, noting that the chief role of his office was to

> try to assure that every picture which possesses any degree of military significance at all is as accurate as possible; and whatever dramatic license is taken, that there is no violation of security, nor that any other aspect of the picture might be considered harmful to national defense or the public good.

This imprecise, subjective standard was similarly applied to emerging television industry producers and companies many of whom, like Screen Gems, were direct affiliates of Hollywood studios.[27]

The early years of television provided increased opportunity for the Pentagon to find entertainment partners to further the promotion of the military domestically and abroad. This was evident in the long-running, popular army series *The Big Picture* (ABC and syndication, 1951–1975), the navy's *Victory at Sea* (NBC 1952–1953, then syndicated) and the US Air Force's *Flight* (syndicated 1958–1959). The military's above-mentioned anathema shown to filmmakers with scenarios involving flying saucers in the early 1950s began to temper somewhat as more and more science fiction dramas found popularity in Hollywood and on the small screen. Regardless, official cooperation was never guaranteed, or taken for granted. Producers had to make a case for assistance on a per-episode basis, with preproduction script approval by the Pentagon.

THE PENTAGON AND *CAPTAIN MIDNIGHT*

In late February 1954, *Captain Midnight* producer George Bilson approached the army's Los Angeles Office of Information advising that he would be seeking stock footage for the new series, outlining the program philosophy:

> CAPTAIN MIDNIGHT is what is known in the trade as a "kid show." The stories are entirely fictional and depend for effect on strong plot, thrilling suspense and exciting

climaxes. It is important to point out that CAPTAIN MIDNIGHT is not a member of any branch of the armed forces. The uniform he wears is unlike anything official and each story identifies him as a private citizen devoted to the service of his country. The objectives of the CAPTAIN MIDNIGHT PROGRAM are to promote interest in children; make excitement wholesome, foster constructive social attitudes; develop a respect for good citizenship and fine personal qualities, develop self-reliance, and to promote interest in our current events.[28]

Bilson asked specifically for access to imagery of the army's new Nike guided-missile launching, adding somewhat sycophantically that the army's recent presentation of the Nike system on *The Big Picture* "was one of the most exciting and informative half hours to be presented on television."

Two weeks later, Colonel Patrick Welch, chief of the army's Public Information Division in Washington, recommended that "no cooperation be furnished on this film [sic] and that Screen Gems, Inc. be informed of this decision," adding:

> In looking at this project from an overall viewpoint, it appears that the Army, or any other government service, should not set a precedent by associating itself on a semi-official basis with any of the science fiction, "Buck Rogers," "Superman" or "Captain Midnight" types of filmed projects, in spite of the patriotic and good-American-youth development aspects which they may contain. Such cooperation would have a tendency to portray the Army in an unrealistic, push-button, outer-space role, and give the youth of America the wrong impression of the Army's role. Although the plan for this series specifically states that CAPTAIN MIDNIGHT is not a science fiction series, he still accomplishes incredible feats with ultra-modern equipment and methods.[29]

Welch further outlined objections addressing specific technical errors and fundamental problems with the script involving the rescue of a scientist kidnapped by foreign spies during a Nike missile test launch. While highlighting "the basic fact, of course, that the Army would not call on Captain Midnight to assist under these circumstances," Welch raised two major concerns. First, the premise of the episode gave "the erroneous impression that once the NIKE is launched it must strike its original target and cannot be diverted" and, second, the "obvious lack of military security measures...would normally prevent any unauthorized persons" from accessing the site.[30]

Filming was scheduled to commence on April 12, 1954, and Bilson was anxious to obtain official stock footage for this and a range of other episodes. On March 15, Baruch relayed the army's concerns to Raymond Bell, Columbia Pictures' military liaison point man, in New York. While Baruch reiterated the objections of Col. Welch, he nevertheless suggested a compromise: "Providing corrections could be made in accordance with the items listed under our comments, release of stock footage could be considered."[31] Hence, Baruch overrode Welch with the proviso of script revisions. Regardless, Baruch reinforced the Pentagon's policy for Bell:

> As you know, we do release footage on occasion for use in so-called fantasy motion pictures. However, these sequences which utilize our material are usually quite factual

and show the Services to advantage or the Service implication has been totally removed but the sequence remains plausible and the footage is made available because it is non obtainable from any commercial source. These circumstances are not applicable to the NIKE episode.[32]

After Bell passed on the Pentagon correspondence, Los Angeles producer Bilson assured Bell that he could "without hurting the dramatic effect of our story remove the Army's objections to various elements."[33] But Bilson would not acquiesce to some of the Pentagon's criticisms without challenge, especially the derisive "science fiction" appellation and the possibility of the program giving the wrong impression about the army's role:

> [Captain Midnight's] only digression from realism is his use of some scientific implement not yet available such as a jet passenger plane, a telephone-television combination, a short-wave person-to-person radio communicator, all of which are in the realm of immediate possibilities.... In fact, it is the opinion of the producers that the true representation and heroic deeds of the various branches of the Armed Services as presented in Captain Midnight will encourage enlistments, and it is hoped that Captain Midnight might, on occasion, explain the details of such weapons as Nike to let the public know the truth about America's leadership in modern weapons.[34]

These are significant concessions and revelations from an internal Columbia/Screen Gems memorandum. Bilson's missive was to brief the studio's military-liaison executive, and not primarily for the Pentagon's eyes. The series' creators clearly articulate in the memo that this "kid show" with a tacit propagandistic agenda was aimed at enhancing armed-forces recruitment. As Grossman points out, the Pentagon frequently cooperated with commercial broadcasters "to help producers achieve authenticity and to help shape the public's perception of the Armed Forces. But the Pentagon had another vested interest. In the 1950s and early 1960s the deluge of military stories help maintain recruitment levels."[35]

The series interstitial advertising reinforces this observation. During most episodes, Captain Midnight addresses viewers from his desk. We see Webb, stiff, starched-shirted, emotionless, and mannequin-like, holding a small radio transmitter while seated at his headquarters (HQ) desk.

> Captain Midnight from headquarters. Members of the Secret Squadron, this is important. Keep yourself in top condition. Remember to do your best you've got to be at your best. Because some day you may be called upon—to pilot a jet plane across the continent. Even to take the wheel and bring a great ship safely into port. To drive an ambulance into disaster areas. And when the time comes you've got to be ready for it. That's why I want all Secret Squadron members to drink Ovaltine every day as I do.[36]

So here we have a conflation of segments that are analogous to the Atomic Age. Each contributes a complementary narrative enhancing the program's overarching Cold War ideology. Specific episodes demonstrating American nuclear prowess

Image 12.1   Members of the Secret Squadron, fortified by Ovaltine, are ready to leap into action at a moment's notice.

threatened by foreign espionage sit alongside commercial sponsorship, emphasizing juvenile preparedness and strength. The fantasy vignettes of children behind the controls of the *Silver Dart*, steering ships while wearing the Secret Squadron insignia and driving ambulances, portray an imminent future where school-age viewers may be impelled to undertake such tasks.

The character of Captain Midnight, as outlined in the television series documents sent to the Pentagon, is described as

> a private citizen who enjoys semi-official status with various executive, military and law-enforcement branches of the government. He is a heroic figure who devotes his life to fighting the forces which menace our American way of life. He is explained as a former wartime flyer and qualified parachutist who is not now on active military duty, but who is frequently given governmental assignments "which an official governmental functionary could not perform."[37]

A letter from Bell less than a week later to Major Johanna Mueller, Pentagon film branch, suggested that the military's reservations had been overcome. Bell solicited additional stock footage for another episode, now noting that *Captain Midnight* "will be sponsored by Ovaltine and Kix cereal, both of whom are reputable business organizations."[38] Implicit in this note was the reinforcement by "reputable" commercial supporters providing an industry imprimatur to the series bona fides.

To further allay any lingering Pentagon concerns over the television character, Bell reiterated:

> Captain Midnite, [sic] under no circumstances, will be portrayed as some character from another world. He will bear no resemblance to Superman or others of this type to be found in the comic strips [ignoring the wartime radio and comic book popularization of the character]. Captain Midnite will not fly through space, he will not perform fantastic or unbelievable feats [such as surviving lethal irradiation by turning away his face?]. He will function as an agent of our government and will perform secret governmental service. Obviously we will take some license here and there to challenge and excite young minds, but there will be no hokum.[39]

But the military ambivalence only grew, generating some enmity around the series, and between the services and those responsible for overseeing cooperation policy. When Screen Gems requested use of the navy's new experimental jet fighter, the Douglas XF4D-1, to be identified as "the same plane which Capt. Midnight flies," a Pentagon memo described how the "Navy refused to mock up the [program] insignia" despite the service having "no objection to use of plane."[40] Yet the navy's film and broadcasting industry liaison, Lt. Commander Joe Wornom, later informed Columbia that "he didn't see why the Navy should cooperate in such a fantastic production." Unimpressed, Bell immediately contacted the Pentagon's Motion Picture Branch and accused Wornom of "showing partiality." The Branch formally sought the navy's objections in writing.

A day later, Bell wrote directly to Wornom, copying in Admiral Lewis Parks, the navy's Chief of Information, requesting that the refusal to film the XF4D1 be made in writing so that the studio could better understand "the basis for this decision." Bell added that the request was previously "discussed through channels and with other Naval personnel" while Wornom was on leave.[41] Columbia's representative made it clear that ongoing requests for navy cooperation would be made for the series, adding dryly: "Although the character of Captain Midnight may not appeal to you as an individual I think it is important to keep in mind that these pictures are intended primarily for a youthful audience." To further his case, Bell mentioned the endorsement of the "reputable business organizations" of Ovaltine and Kix as program sponsors. But Wornom would not be deterred. His reply reemphasized the original decision, noting that "the use of the F4D was not disapproved without careful consideration." The rationale for rejection was due primarily to the proposal breaching Department of Defense cooperation criteria.[42] Wornom detailed two other issues that specifically had an adverse impact on the decision. First, the "propriety of permitting fictional characters such as Captain Midnight the use of Navy planes…would likely start a chain reaction with similar requests from other fantasy type programs." Second, due to the high priority of production of the F4D aircraft, any cooperation rendered to *Captain Midnight* would create unacceptable delays. Perhaps disingenuously, Wornom concluded with:

> Actually I have nothing against Captain Midnight and I even enjoy a bowl of Kix occasionally. But current directives and the above reasons make it impracticable to cooperate with the series.[43]

With the commencement of production and location filming, Bell sent Baruch at the Pentagon a number of scripts with a shot-list for six additional *Captain Midnight* episodes, requesting further assistance in the form of stock footage.[44] The most comprehensive request was for stock sequences of Pacific nuclear testing to fill ten scenes for the episode "Isle of Mystery," including:

> Scene 135- Navy personnel helping natives load their belongings into shore boats (Eniwetok).
> Scene 136- Task force at anchor off a pacific island (atom bomb test).
> Scene 138- Group of officers & men watching for atomic explosion from deck of battleship (Atom bomb test).
> Scene 139- LS of target island before A-bomb blast (Atom bomb test).
> Scene 143- Nuclear mushroom cloud (Atom bomb test).
> Scene 149- A-bomb or H-bomb explosion on pacific island (Atom bomb test).

Script assessment approval for this particular footage was granted, while other stock film was either referred directly to the army, or refused, since the generic footage (aerial views over open, wooded, and jungle terrain, and an aerial shot over Washington DC) was readily available from commercial sources.[45]

Further stock-footage requests were regularly received throughout the *Captain Midnight* production schedule. By June, Baruch was directing the Navy department's

Image 12.2   Having helped evacuate the islanders to safety, Captain Midnight observes a nuclear test in "Isle of Mystery."

Lt. Commander Wornom to cooperate with Columbia representatives in order to "select unedited, unclassified stock footage" for two episodes, including the shot-list above.[46] Baruch conceded to Wornom that, "Although neither script is basically about the Navy, they are not detrimental and show the Navy in a favorable light." Aside from directing Wornom to cooperate with the producers, this softening of the Pentagon approach is interesting, especially given the colonial, nuclear geopolitics of "Isle of Mystery."

The episode in question features a South Pacific island queen at first agreeing to allow her atoll, Luana, to be destroyed in an H-bomb test by an American task force, only to rescind the offer while under the threatening influence of a criminal. When Captain Midnight intervenes, he manages to persuade the islanders to leave their homeland, and the nuclear tests summarily resume. At the beginning of the episode, when the series' resident scientist, Aristole "Tut" Jones (Olan Soule), dressed in his standard white lab coat, quizzes Captain Midnight about the necessity of the Pacific tests, he laments that "[i]t seems a pity to blow [the island] out of the sea." But Captain Midnight is adamant: "No. There are thousands like it, and it's going in the cause of peace." Nevertheless, Tut ponders any native concerns over "having their island used as a testing ground for the H-bomb." Again, Captain Midnight is reassuringly dismissive:

> When the State Department explained why we had to have it, and promised to move her people to a larger island that would better support them [she] was all for it.[47]

Perhaps not surprisingly, the Pentagon passed this script without revision for accuracy, agreeing to furnish the stock footage of "happy" Bikini islanders being removed from their atoll. In reality, atomic and thermonuclear testing devastated multiple Pacific territories, contaminating them for decades and some for centuries, and the Bikinians, like other indigenous Marshallese, were forcibly relocated to overcrowded and inappropriate islands offering far fewer resources. It is significant that the request for this footage came more than two months after the 15 megaton Bravo detonation at Bikini irradiated over 7,000 square miles with lethal levels of fallout, rendering a number of atolls uninhabitable and contaminating several island communities, despite the Atomic Energy Commission's initial denials and obfuscations.[48]

A fortnight after *Captain Midnight* premiered on network television in November 1954, Wornom was again questioning official assistance to the program via the ongoing supply of stock footage.[49] When Bell approached the Pentagon for film of a (navy or army) football game, ostensibly because Screen Gems could not access scenes in time for rights clearances, "Wornom thought we should draw the line some place on giving courtesy cooperation and didn't believe the 'gag' line about [Screen Gems] not being able to get the material commercially."[50] Due to conflicting interservice interests and the haste of the request, the desired footage was sent to the lab during these confused approval deliberations, and then simply sent on with instructions "not [to] say anything as long as Wornom wouldn't cooperate."

Surprisingly, it was not until the first season was produced and aired in its entirety that the Department of Defense sought an update of the program's status. It is remarkable that Baruch had to prompt Columbia's Bell for an update:

> We wonder if the films were ever produced and if the stock footage was utilized [as] we would like to review the pictures.[51]

Dutifully, the requested prints were dispatched a week later to Baruch at the Pentagon for viewing. A follow-up letter from Bell to series production executive Fred Briskin (copied to Major Mueller at the Motion Picture Branch), was ominous after the Department of Defense examined the episodes sent for scrutiny:

> It appears the the [sic] subject ELECTRONIC KILLER created a great deal of consternation because they say the sequence of the Nike used in this film was put together wrong and, among other things, violated security regulations. While I am sure that any heat this has generated can be cooled down, it is a serious matter which we must try and avoid. As you know, the Pentagon did not want to cooperate on the CAPTAIN MIDNIGHT series. But we have been getting footage regularly and are still obtaining a good quantity of material. Neither of us, I know, wishes to close down this important source of supply.[52]

Bell suggested all remaining episodes "involving military material" should be sent for review "before these subjects are televised," noting that a "courtesy screening for the branch of the service involved" is standard industry practice.[53]

Clearly this intervention worked, as a later letter from Bell to Mueller at the Pentagon attests. Any residual misgivings the army and Motion Picture Branch had over the Nike 'security regulations' had clearly been forgiven. Within a month Screen Gems was again, successfully, requesting a significant shot-list of stock footage from the 1951 US Air Force documentary *Target Nevada* for the *Captain Midnight* episode "The Frozen Man:"[54]

1. Atomic bomb explosion, ground level shots
2. All shots b-29 in air
3. LONG SHOT, Atomic bomb explosion
4. People watching atomic bomb explosion
5. Observers putting on dark glasses
6. Preparation for dropping of the bomb
   (interior shots of plane)
   (exterior shots of bombay [sic] doors opening)
7. Plane takeoff, vapor trail
8. Destruction reaped by Atom Bomb
9. DOWN SHOT, of Atomic Bomb exploding.[55]

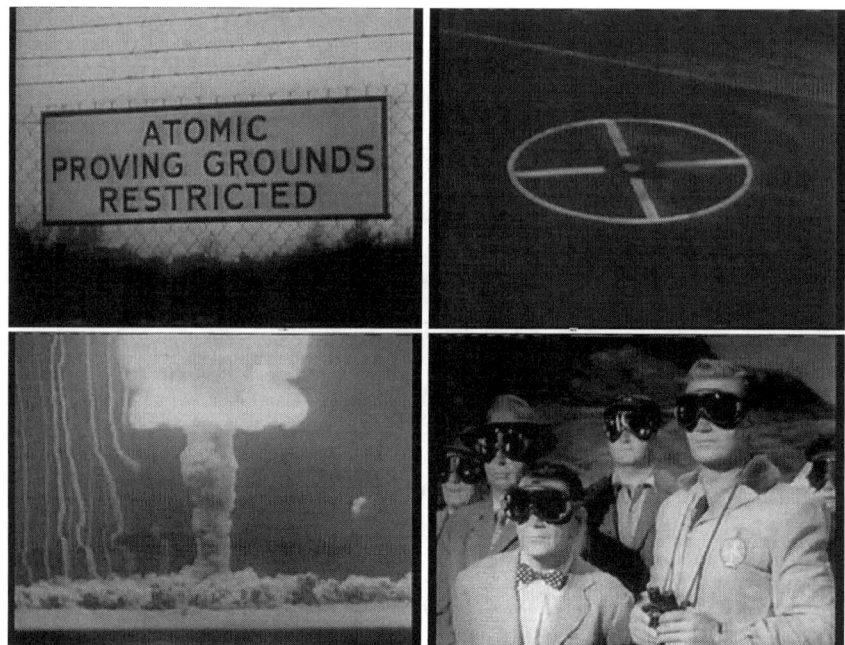

Image 12.3   Fact and fiction mingle as Captain Midnight stoically watches footage of a (real) atom bomb.

During this episode, a variation of the prior advertisement depicted the same children in different military and civil-defense guises, as Captain Midnight intoned commandingly:

> Your first duty is to keep yourself in top condition at all times, ready and able to do your best, to meet the test when your turn comes to undertake some vital mission. Because some day you may be the one called upon to parachute to a secret rendezvous. Or, to interpret radar warnings for Civilian Defense To cooperate with the Coast Guard and patrol the shores in time of danger. To bring much needed aid and comfort to disaster victims. When the time comes, when the test comes [almost pleading]. You've got to be ready for it with plenty of stamina in reserve. That's why I want all Secret Squadron members to drink Ovaltine every day, as I do.[56]

These direct appeals by Captain Midnight, intensely staring down the barrel of the camera lens, addressing the nation's youth, were a powerful plea to preserve the Eisenhower-era sense of national consensus and preparedness for nuclear war. At a time when children were being constantly drilled in the art of "survival," effectively as passive victims of geopolitical events beyond their control, joining *Captain Midnight*'s Secret Squadron and actively engaging in the fantasy of national "enlistment" and local surveillance, enabled this Duck and Cover generation to achieve a kind of personal agency outside the compliant passivity expected by their prewar elders.

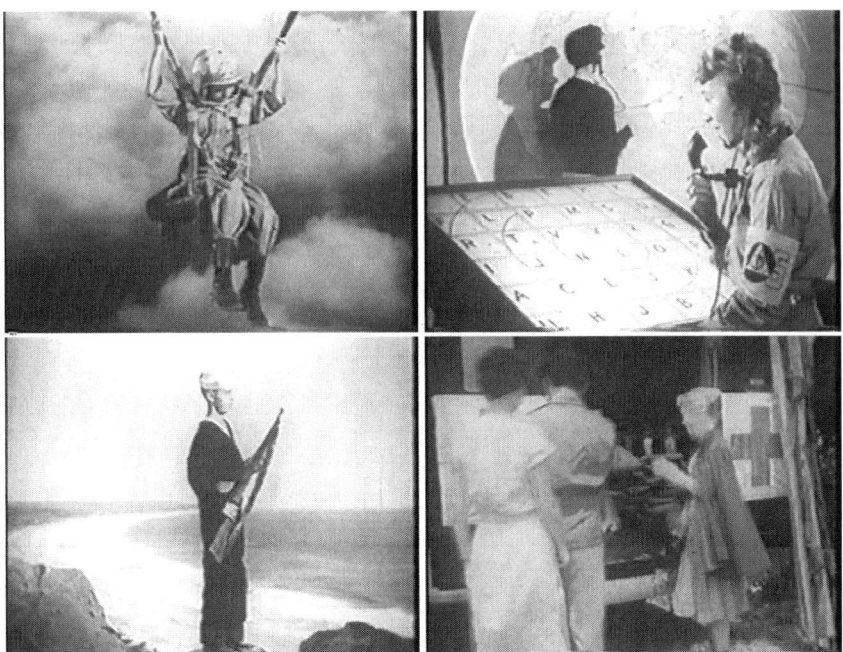

Image 12.4 Like civil defense films, *Captain Midnight* urged children to always be prepared for a national emergency.

With sustained, though occasionally contentious, Pentagon approval, *Captain Midnight* presented weekly scenarios of imminent national-security threats and superior American military-scientific technologies in danger of theft or sabotage. In times of crisis and emergency only the strong would be called upon and prevail. Given the inculcation of civil-defense preparedness, with regular elementary and high-school drills for atomic attack, *Captain Midnight* and its alternating commercial sponsorship may be usefully understood as metonymically presenting another mode of Cold War preparedness for survival in the nuclear era.

This is Captain Midnight signing off with the code of the Secret Squadron: "Justice through strength and courage." Out!

NOTES

1. For a discussion of hegemony and the American Century, see Michael J. Hogan, *The Ambiguous Legacy: U.S. Foreign Relations in the "American Century"* (Cambridge: Cambridge University Press, 1999).
2. Gary H. Grossman, *Saturday Morning TV* (New York: Random House, 1988), 333.
3. Christopher Anderson, *Hollywood TV: The Studio System in the Fifties* (Austin: University of Texas Press, 1994).
4. Alan Nadel, *Containment Culture: American Narratives, Postmodernism, and the Atomic Age* (Durham, NC: Duke University Press, 1995), and Tom Engelhardt,

The End of Victory Culture: Cold War America and the Disillusioning of a Generation (Amherst: University of Massachusetts Press, 2007).
5. See *The Classic Captain Midnight* at http://www.squidoo.com/classic-captain-midnight.
6. According to *The Classic Captain Midnight* website, two years before Ovaltine and Kix sponsored the Screen Gems/CBS TV series, in 1951 *Captain Midnight Adventure Theater* depicted screen announcer Vern Smith wearing flight suit and helmet based on the comic book/radio character:
   > Smith was featured in the opening, closing, and commercials wrapped around episodes of Republic serials which had been edited to 26 minutes, by, essentially, combining two chapters .... Ironically, the **Captain Midnight** serial from the 1940s was NOT shown on this tv show, because it was done by another movie studio and the show didn't have the rights to it!", at http://www.squidoo.com/classic-captain-midnight.
7. Grossman, 21.
8. See "D-558-II Fact Sheet," *Dryden Flight Research Center*, National Aeronautics and Space Administration, http://www.nasa.gov/centers/dryden/news/FactSheets/FS-035-DFRC.html and "Testing the First Supersonic Aircraft: Memoirs of NACA Pilot Bob Champine, *Langley Flight Research Center*, National Aeronautics and Space Administration, http://www.nasa.gov/centers/langley/news/factsheets/Supersonic.html
9. Grossman, 153.
10. Grossman, 332. On pledges, oaths, and codes, see J. Fred MacDonald, *Television and the Red Menace* (Westport, CT: Praeger, 1985), 134–137. The official Secret Squadron pledge is:
    > I will be faithful to my duty and obey the laws of my country, my state and my community. I will abide by the rules of my school. I will obey my parents. I will at all times be a loyal member of the Secret Squadron.
    >
    > I will tell the truth at all times because I know dishonesty is evil. I will be honest with my parents, my friends, my teachers and all others—for honesty is part of strength and courage.
    >
    > I will get plenty of sleep, fresh air and exercise. I will eat three good meals, daily. Then, with two glasses of Ovaltine each day, I will have the right combination of vitamins, minerals and other food elements which help give me "rocket power."
11. MacDonald, 122.
12. MacDonald, 3.
13. See, for example: Paul Koistinen, *The Military-Industrial Complex: A Historical Perspective* (Westport, CT: Praeger, 1980); Sidney Lens, *The Military-Industrial Complex* (Cleveland: Pilgrim Press, 1970); and Carroll Pursell, *The Military-Industrial Complex* (New York: Harper & Row, 1972).
14. "[The] conjunction of an immense military establishment and a large arms industry is new in the American experience. The total influence—economic, political, even spiritual—is felt in every city, every State house, every office of the Federal government. We recognize the imperative need for this development. Yet we must not fail to comprehend its grave implications. Our toil, resources and livelihood are all involved; so is the very structure of our society. In the councils of government, we must guard against the acquisition of unwarranted influence, whether sought or unsought, by the military-industrial complex. The potential for the disastrous rise of misplaced power exists and will persist. We must never let the weight of this

15. See Joel Kovel, *Against the State of Nuclear Terror* (London: Pan, 1983), 64.
16. Cited in James A. Barry, "Managing Covert Political Action," Central Intelligence Agency Library, at https://www.cia.gov/library/center-for-the-study-of-intelligence/kent-csi/vol36no3/html/v36i3a05p_0001.htm, accessed 20 October 2011.
17. Barry, ibid.
18. Grossman, 330.
19. MacDonald, 6.
20. MacDonald, 10. For a comprehensive chart of such programs, evident in even one genre (i.e., espionage), see MacDonald, 103.
21. Anderson, 73.
22. Joyce Nelson, *The Perfect Machine: TV in the Nuclear Age* (Toronto: Between the Lines, 1992), 25–26.
23. Lawrence H. Suid, *Guts and Glory: The Making of the American Military Image in Film* (Lexington: University Press of Kentucky, 1978). Lawrence H. Suid, *Sailing on the Silver Screen: Hollywood and the U.S. Navy* (Annapolis, MD: Naval Institute Press, 1996); Lawrence H. Suid and Dolores A. Haverstick, *Stars and Stripes on Screen: A Comprehensive Guide to Portrayals of American Military on Film*. (Metuchen, NJ: Scarecrow Press, 2005).
24. Letter from Donald E. Baruch, September 14, 1950. Department of Defense (DoD) collection, Box 16, Folder 12, Georgetown University.
25. Letter from Harry Gildea, February 15, 1953. DoD collection, Box 14, Folder 15, Georgetown University.
26. DoD collection, Box 14, Folder 15, Georgetown University.
27. Screen Gems was owned by Columbia Pictures.
28. Letter from George Bilson, February 25, 1954. September 14, 1950. DoD collection, Box 14, Folder 22, Georgetown University.
29. Memo from Col. Patrick Welch, March 9, 1954. DoD collection, Box 14, Folder 22, Georgetown University.
30. Welch, ibid.
31. Letter from Donald E. Baruch, March 15, 1954. DoD collection, Box 14, Folder 22, Georgetown University.
32. Baruch, ibid.
33. Memo from George Bilson, March 18, 1954. DoD collection, Box 14, Folder 22, Georgetown University.
34. Bilson, ibid.
35. Grossman, 331
36. *Captain Midnight*. Henderson, NV: A&A Media, nd. DVD.
37. Memo from Col. Patrick Welch, March 9, 1954. DoD collection, Box 14, Folder 22, Georgetown University.
38. Letter from J. Raymond Bell, April 2, 1954. DoD collection, Box 14, Folder 22, Georgetown University.
39. Bell letter, ibid.
40. Memo from Major Johanna Mueller, April 13, 1954. DoD collection, Box 14, Folder 22, Georgetown University. In fact, after cooperation was refused, the series' *Silver Dart* bore little resemblance to the XF4D1 (or F4D), and the model used against

rear-projection to simulate flying scenes was the earlier Douglas D-558-II Skyrocket. For comparisons, see http://www.vectorsite.net/avskyray.html and http://www.nasa.gov/centers/langley/news/factsheets/Supersonic.html.
41. Letter from J. Raymond Bell, April 14, 1954. DoD collection, Box 14, Folder 22, Georgetown University.
42. Letter from S. J. Wornom, April 20, 1954. DoD collection, Box 14, Folder 22, Georgetown University.
43. Letter from S. J. Wornom, ibid.
44. Letter from J. Raymond Bell, May 13, 1954. DoD collection, Box 14, Folder 22, Georgetown University.
45. Letter from J. Raymond Bell, ibid.
46. Memo from Donald E. Baruch, June 2, 1954. DoD collection, Box 14, Folder 22, Georgetown University.
47. "Isle of Mystery." *Captain Midnight*. Henderson, NV: A&A Media, nd. DVD.
48. Richard Rhodes, *Dark Sun: The making of the Hydrogen Bomb* (New York: Simon & Schuster, 1996).
49. Episode 1, "Murder by Radiation," was aired on CBS, November 4, 1954. The first season of *Captain Midnight*, totaling 26 weekly episodes, ran from September 4, 1954, to February 26, 1955, with the shorter second season (13 episodes) recommencing October 29, 1955, through to January 21, 1956.
50. Memo from Baruch and Mueller, September 17, 1954. DoD collection, Box 14, Folder 22, Georgetown University.
51. Letter from Donald E. Baruch, March 30, 1955. DoD collection, Box 14, Folder 22, Georgetown University.
52. Letter from J. Raymond Bell, April 22, 1955. DoD collection, Box 14, Folder 22, Georgetown University.
53. Bell, ibid.
54. For *Target Nevada*, see http://www.archive.org/details/TargetNevada. Described as "the story of United States Air Force support to the Atomic Energy Commission on continental atomic tests." Narrated by Carey Wilson, it uses footage shown also in "Operation Buster-Jangle" of 1951.
55. Letter from J. Raymond Bell, May 19, 1955. DoD collection, Box 14, Folder 22, Georgetown University.
56. *Captain Midnight*. Henderson, NV: A&A Media, nd. DVD.

Bibliography

Anderson, Christopher. *Hollywood TV: The Studio System in the Fifties*. Austin: University of Texas Press, 1994.
Barry, James. *Managing Covert Political Action*, CIA. Center for the Study of Intelligence, at https://www.cia.gov/library/center-for-the-study-of-intelligence/kent-csi/vol36no3/html/v36i3a05p_0001.htm.
Captain Midnight. Henderson, NV: A&A Media, nd. DVD.
Engelhardt, Tom. *The End of Victory Culture: Cold War America and the Disillusioning of a Generation*. Amherst: University of Massachusetts Press, 2007.
Grossman, Gary H. *Saturday Morning TV*. New York: Random House, 1988.
Hogan, Michael J. *The Ambiguous Legacy: U.S. Foreign Relations in the "American Century."* Cambridge: Cambridge University Press, 1999.
Koistinen, Paul. *The Military-Industrial Complex: A Historical Perspective*. Westport, CT: Praeger, 1980.

Kovel, Joel. *Against the State of Nuclear Terror.* London: Pan, 1983.
Lens, Sidney. *The Military-Industrial Complex.* Cleveland: Pilgrim Press, 1970.
MacDonald, J. Fred. *Television and the Red Menace: The Video Road to Vietnam.* Westport, CT: Praeger, 1985.
Nadel, Alan. *Containment Culture: American Narratives, Postmodernism, and the Atomic Age.* Durham, NC: Duke University Press, 1995.
Nelson, Joyce. *The Perfect Machine: TV in the Nuclear Age.* Toronto: Between the Lines, 1992.
Pursell, Carroll. *The Military-Industrial Complex.* New York: Harper & Row, 1972.
Rhodes, Richard. *Dark Sun: The Making of the Hydrogen Bomb.* New York: Simon & Schuster, 1996.
Suid, Lawrence H. *Guts and Glory: The Making of the American Military Image in Film.* Lexington: University Press of Kentucky, 1978.
———. *Sailing on the Silver Screen: Hollywood and the U.S. Navy.* Annapolis, MD: Naval Institute Press, 1996.
Suid, Lawrence H., and Dolores A. Haverstick. *Stars and Stripes on Screen: A Comprehensive Guide to Portrayals of American Military on Film.* Metuchen, NJ: Scarecrow Press, 2005.

CHAPTER 13

"To Learn from the Past...": Becoming Cold War Citizens with Captain Z-Ro

CYNTHIA J. MILLER AND
A. BOWDOIN VAN RIPER

"SOMEWHERE IN A REMOTE, UNCHARTED REGION OF THE PLANET Earth stands the laboratory of Captain Z-Ro...," a booming voice intoned, and the latest episode of the exploits of Captain Z-Ro, Research Explorer in Time and Space, began. His mission? Not to rid distant worlds of deadly foes, but "to learn from the past...to plan for the future."

He was a rocketman, like so many others, in an era of "space fever," but unlike his counterparts from other televised series of the 1950s—dashing figures like Tom Corbett, Captain Video, Rocky Jones, Buzz Corry—Captain Z-Ro was a hero of a different sort. Clad in a cape and elaborate helmet, sporting a Mephistophelean mustache and beard uncharacteristic of the more military-oriented champions, even his appearance was different. These features served to distinguish *Captain Z-Ro* in a field already crowded with uniformed space rangers. He was a researcher, a historian, and a scientist: the harbinger of a sea change in postwar American cultural history, and the forerunner of real-world space heroes to come. And while other rocketmen mentored their young charges—and their youthful audiences at home—in Cold War values and ideals such as bravery, loyalty, and national pride, Captain Z-Ro pursued another strategy for strengthening the characters of the country's postwar youth: he educated them.

Beginning in 1951, on San Francisco's KRON-TV, the series ran "live" for three years, before entering into national syndication (1954–1960). Each episode was a trip through space and time that tutored the Captain's young cadet, Jet, in the workings of technology, the workings-out of history, and the overall importance of knowledge to a Cold War future. With the help of the Captain's time machine—his own invention—and his rocket ship, the ZX99, the Captain, Jet, and the rest of his

Image 13.1 Captain Z-Ro (Roy Steffens) during the series' early years as a 15-minute live broadcast on KRON-TV. [Credit: Roy Trumbull]

crew ensured that history unfolded as it ought, intervening in mutinies, quelling uprisings, safeguarding innovations, and inspiring greatness among characters such as Leonardo da Vinci, Molly "Pitcher" Hayes, and Christopher Columbus.[1]

The series accomplished its goal so well that in 1955 it was cited by the Kefauver Committee on Juvenile Delinquency as "the best children's show on television." Senator Estes Kefauver, Chairman of the Senate committee bestowing the honor, enjoyed a nationwide reputation as an incorruptible defender of the public good, thanks to his chairmanship of an earlier Senate investigation of organized crime. He put that reputation to work as a fierce proponent of responsible children's programming, and of the role of the new medium in shaping the attitudes and characters of America's youth. The committee was not alone in its praise of the series, which was created by writer and star Roy Steffens.[2] The award-winning program was cited by Ohio State University's Institute for Education by Radio-Television, as well as by the Motion Picture and Television Council of the District of Columbia, for its excellence in educational programming. These awards were, for Captain Z-Ro and his crew, commendations for a mission well done. What follows is an exploration of that mission, and of how—in its quest to educate its fans, young and old, about science and history—*Captain Z-Ro* reflected the mind of a nation still coming to grips with its newfound role as a superpower.

THE ADVENTURE BEGINS

Unlike other rocketmen whose adventures lit up the small screens of postwar American living rooms, the character of Captain Z-Ro was not adapted from comic strips or movie-house serials. Instead, this champion of "knowledge as civic engagement" began as a sidekick to another sort of children's hero—Santa Claus.[3] Already a bold scientist experimenting with futuristic technology, as well as a close friend of the miraculous Claus, Captain Z-Ro had invented the Teletronic Tuner, a two-way television system that allowed Santa to see all the local children who were watching his show from their homes.[4] In 1951, the Captain was given his own show on KRON-TV, perhaps the earliest of television's spin-offs.

Captain Z-Ro was among the frontrunners in children's programming in the 1950s. It was an era of experimentation in the new medium, and shows targeting juvenile audiences exploded across the airwaves. In an effort to capture the attention and imaginations of their young viewers, these programs featured a range of endearing puppets, imaginative cartoons, and flamboyant hosts who portrayed characters from cowboys to ship captains to clowns. Some offered education, others simply entertainment. *Captain Z-Ro*, however, offered both. Situated at the intersection of early rocketmen serials,

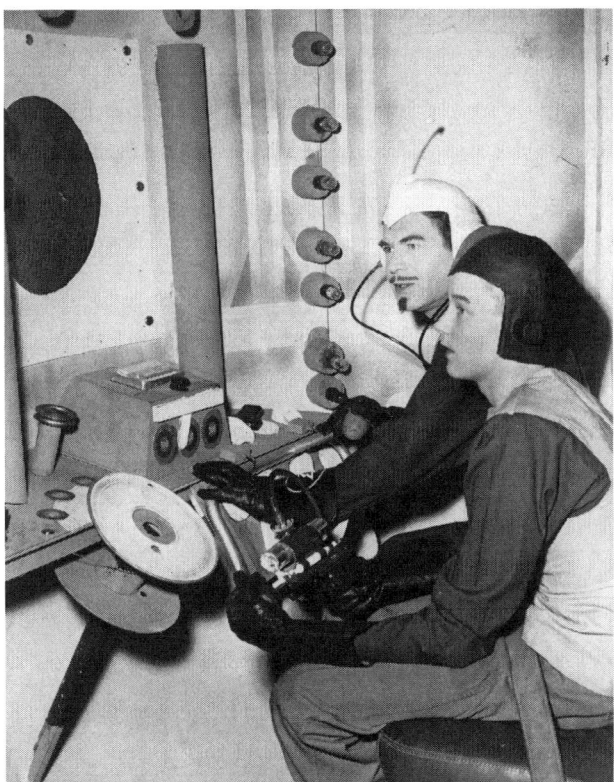

Image 13.2   Captain Z-Ro and Jet (Bobby Trumbull) blast off from the soundstage. [Credit: Roy Trumbull]

such as *Captain Video* (1949–1955) and *Tom Corbett: Space Cadet* (1950–1955), and more "terrestrial" children's shows, such as *Bozo the Clown* (1949–2001) and *Romper Room* (1953–1994), the Captain was far more than just another children's host—and far more than just another interplanetary peacekeeper, as well. He was an explorer, a teacher, a purveyor of fantastic science, and a space hero, all rolled into one.

Where did this space-age renaissance explorer come from? According to the programs' origin story, the Captain's exploits began in 1937:

> On the, night of August 7,1937, Captain Z-RO, his young ward Jet and fellow scientists blasted off the Earth on the first manned flight to the Moon. The early, pre-space age ship, the ZX-98, was cumber-some, balky, and overloaded with equipment, oxygen and supplies. Enthusiasm was high…the chance of survival low.[5]

Within 25 miles of the moon, the ZX-98 became unstable, and the crew was forced to return to Earth, crashing-landing in a remote and desolate site. From this secret location, the Captain and his crew built their research laboratory from the ship's wreckage and devoted their lives to "solving the mysteries of time and space."[6] Over time, Captain Z-Ro and his crew created not only an airstrip, a rocket platform, and his time machine craft, the ZX-99, but also developed such fantastic technologies as a Materialization Chamber, which allowed the Captain and Jet to transport themselves and others to and from the ZX-99; the Language Rectifier, an early version of what science fiction fans now know as the Universal Translator; and a Brain Wave Analyzer, which enabled the Captain to observe the inner workings of his subjects' minds. With these and other extraordinary devices created in the narrative world of the series, Captain Z-Ro explored other worlds, as well as his own. Series episodes covered a range of American history, including key people and events such as George Washington, Daniel Boone, the American Revolution, and the California Gold Rush, as well as the histories of Europe and Asia, including tales of the early great explorers Marco Polo and Christopher Columbus, freedom fighters such as William Tell, and dastardly pirates such as Blackbeard. With each foray into history, the Captain and his crew, armed with fantastic technology, assured that history unfolded properly, in spite of treachery, accidents, or faint hearts. His adventures occasionally took more fantastic form, as well, such as when Roger, a futuristic robot, ran amok in San Francisco, or when a shooting star threatened to destroy the ZX-99 and its crew, as they blasted into space to study celestial bodies.

The series united Steffens interests in education and adventure in a "live" 15-minute format, filmed with two cameras. One of the best-loved of San Francisco's local programs, *Captain Z-Ro* ran for three years, and a total of 150 episodes, before expanding to a longer, half-hour version for syndication that would bring the Captain's mission into homes nationwide, until his last appearance in 1960. Steffens also recreated the show for six months in Los Angeles, on KTTV, using a different cast.

Fittingly, it was a fan who propelled the show into its long, syndicated run. Like many of his fellow rocketmen and children's show hosts, the Captain not only brought the wonders of time and space into the lives of his audiences via television—he also brought them right into their neighborhoods, through personal appearances. Writer

Charles Ziarko relates the story of one such appearance, gleaned from an interview with Steffens, which resulted in the series' growth to national prominence:

> Grandly en route to a Southern California personal appearance Southern California—with a police escort!—"Captain Z-Ro" was spotted by Kathleen Rawlings and her son Stuart, both big fans of the San Francisco edition of the show. Mrs. Rawlings was greatly interested in children's programming, and when she returned home, she contacted Roy. They undertook the expansion of the show to thirty minutes, and twenty-six episodes were filmed by Palmer Productions for wider national syndication…[7]

It was this fan encounter that changed the course of history for Captain Z-Ro, dramatically expanding the rocketman's fan base and leading to national recognition and Kefauver praise.

Together with his youthful assistant, Jet (played, initially, by Bobby Trumbull, and later, by a much younger Bruce Haynes), Captain Z-Ro explored the worlds of time and space, simultaneously imparting knowledge about the past and the new Cold War ideology in which information, intellect, and global awareness were the keys to both individual and national success in the future. The most overtly didactic of all the rocketmen series, *Captain Z-Ro* tutored his young charges in physics, astronomy, and the history of the world, as well as in qualities essential to American

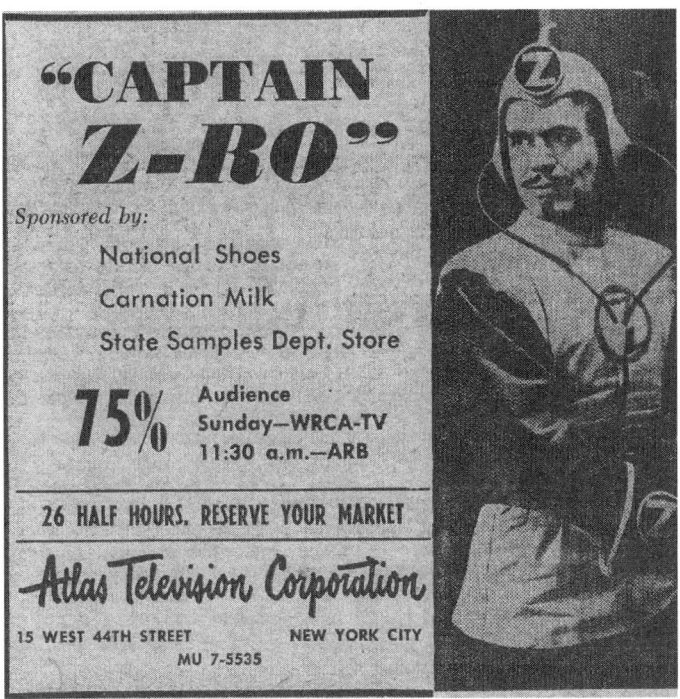

Image 13.3 The 26 half-hour episodes of *Captain Z-Ro* ran in syndication from 1954–1960, and remained on the air after other rocketmen series faded away. [Credit: Author's collection]

citizens of the future, such as the value of hard work, curiosity, and patience, the consequences of narrow-mindedness, and the rewards of imagination and forward-thinking.

WATCHING HISTORY BE MADE

Captain Z-Ro's trips through time gave Jet—and, by extension, young fans watching from their living rooms—a perspective on history that no classroom or textbook could match. The history taught in most American schools in the 1950s was grand and magisterial: a parade of towering individuals, world-changing events, and sweeping forces. It was a fully developed narrative, without missing pieces or unanswered questions, in which the events of the past led inexorably and inevitably toward the present. The tales told on *Captain Z-Ro* substituted intimacy for grandeur and contingency for inevitability. History is made not by impersonal forces or larger-than-life heroes, the series taught its fans, but by otherwise-ordinary men and women who do extraordinary things. Individual thoughts and actions are the pivots on which historical events turn, and the power to change history lies (potentially) within the grasp of anyone bold enough to try.

Exemplary figures are more prominent than notorious ones in the universe of *Captain Z-Ro*, and they fall into two broad types. The first group is driven by curiosity. Explorers like Columbus, Ferdinand Magellan, and Captain James Cook probe uncharted corners of the Earth—sailing off the edges of their maps and redrawing them to include the lands that lie beyond—while scientists like da Vinci and Jean de Champollion (translator of Egyptian hieroglyphics) redefine the limits of the possible. Marco Polo and Daniel Boone do both: traveling into uncharted, yet inhabited, lands and absorbing—with ever-open minds—the wisdom of those they meet there. The second group is driven by a thirst for justice. William Tell defies Switzerland's cruel Austrian overlords, Robin Hood undermines the greedy Sheriff of Nottingham, and Colonial housewife Molly Hayes defies the might of the British army at the Battle of Monmouth. Elsewhere in the series, Washington's army struggles to keep their hopes for American independence alive at Valley Forge, and English knights force the tyrannical King John to acknowledge their legal rights by signing the Magna Carta.

Both sets of historical figures pursue their goals with a single-minded boldness that, at times, borders on the reckless. Told by a fellow Swiss patriot that the occupying Austrian army outnumbers their small movement, William Tell scoffs: "Who ever heard about a good Swiss caring about the number of the enemy?" The following day, holding "the ancient rights and freedoms of the Swiss" more sacred than his own life, he defies an edict to bow before a symbol of the local Austrian governor in the public square. Hernando Cortez, whom Captain Z-Ro describes with obvious approval as "a man of action," burns his own ships in order to prevent his men from leaving Mexico for Spain after their hunger for gold is sated. Columbus and Magellan, though portrayed as explorers rather than conquerors, likewise defy their crews and risk mutiny by pushing their ships into unknown waters. Nine-year-old explorer-in-training Daniel Boone nods earnestly when his mother reminds him not to stray too far from their wilderness homestead, but curiosity soon draws him deep into Indian country. Captain Z-Ro himself is equally zealous in his own pursuit of knowledge and defense of freedom. He leaps into the midst of raging battles to ensure that the "right" side wins, and materializes aboard a sunken ship perched on the edge of a submarine canyon in order to retrieve a priceless treasure: not gold or jewels, but lost records and artifacts from the Aztec Empire overthrown by Cortez.

Whether in pursuit of new knowledge or in the defense of freedom, however, neither firm commitment nor bold action is sufficient (though both are necessary) to change history. Success, in the universe of *Captain Z-Ro,* often depends on chance, or on the actions of individuals whose names are lost to history. Attila the Hun loses the Battle of Chalons, which he should have won, when the disappearance of the fabled "Sword of Mars" from his tent the night before rattles his confidence. Da Vinci, despondent because he believes that his life's work has been of no value, returns to it when—in a vivid dream—he glimpses a future in which he is honored as an artistic genius, and inventions based on his ideas are part of everyday life. That all those "chance" moments were, in the context of the series, engineered by Captain Z-Ro and Jet does not diminish their significance. History as we know it and the world we take for granted are far from inevitable, and exist only because of the actions of people we know little about.

The idea that our knowledge of history is imperfect pervaded the series. Jet and the Captain travel to fourteenth-century Switzerland in order to find out whether the legend of William Tell shooting an apple from his son's head is true. The Captain uses the time viewer to study Attila's camp on the eve of the Battle of Chalons,

Image 13.4 Captain Z-Ro uses his time machine to show Leonardo da Vinci (Sydney Walker) the future and his lasting fame.

trying to understand the cause of the Huns' defeat. When Jet expresses a desire to travel to medieval England and meet Robin Hood, Captain Z-Ro reminds him that "we don't even know whether Robin Hood existed."

Where the show *does* grant its characters a clear understanding of the past, the picture that emerges is, itself, far from the triumphant narrative used to frame school textbooks of the era. Da Vinci is racked by depression and self-doubt; the lives of kings are defined by hard work and the fear of being overthrown; and Molly Hayes ends the battle of Battle of Monmouth weeping over the body of her dead husband. When early California landowner John Sutter is informed that gold has been discovered in the stream below his sawmill, he sees the sparkling nugget as a harbinger of "the ruin of everything I've built." News of the gold strike, he fears, will bring "people swarming in from everywhere, trampling down the land, ruining the crops, driving off the cattle. Our own workers will desert us. Nothing will be left—nothing!" Rather than mitigate Sutter's apocalyptic vision of the future, Captain Z-Ro affirms it. "I'll show you what Sutter meant," he tells Jet. "Move the time machine ahead one year, and watch!" Progress, the series suggests, does not come cheaply or easily.

Captain Z-Ro used deceptively simple stories to teach a complex lesson: that the outcomes of historical events are not inevitable, but contingent on the actions—good, bad, or unwitting—of countless individuals. The show's vision of history was thus both reassuring and unsettling: anyone can shape history, but history is too fluid and mutable for us to assume that it will simply "turn out right." Desirable outcomes, if they are to exist at all, must be actively created by the coordinated, thoughtful actions of knowledgeable and well-intentioned people.

THE FUTURE BELONGS TO THE KNOWLEDGEABLE

The popular fascination with history that drew adults and children alike to *Captain Z-Ro* was part of a wider cultural shift in postwar American culture that celebrated knowledge and valorized those who possessed it. America chose plainspoken "commoners" like Harry Truman and Dwight Eisenhower for the presidency, twice rejecting the conspicuously educated "egghead" Adlai Stevenson, but in the broader culture, formal education and the learnedness it conferred were treated with newfound respect, even reverence.[8] The future, Americans increasingly believed, belonged to the knowledgeable.

Americans' newfound reverence for knowledge was rooted in broad political and economic changes. Thriving in the emerging postwar economy required different skills than surviving the Great Depression or fighting World War Two: intellectual rather than practical, managerial rather than manual. Guiding the United States in its new role as the world's preeminent political and military power demanded a deep awareness of the historical roots and geopolitical context of world events. Events that took place in the wider world had the potential, as never before, to affect the everyday lives of ordinary Americans. Soldiers returned from overseas service newly aware of the cultural differences that could separate even societies such as Britain and America. Above all, still-vivid memories of World War II underscored the critical need not just to monitor but to thoroughly *understand* other countries, in order to never again be unaware of the threat posed by an emerging enemy.

Learning—broad, deep familiarity with entire fields of human activity—thus came to be seen as critical to both individual and national success in the postwar world. The GI Bill of Rights, which funded higher education for thousands of demobilized servicemen, reflected the new perception of colleges and universities as something to which all ambitious young men could and should aspire.[9] Americans already settled into career and families embraced the idea of continuing education as part of a larger commitment to purposeful recreation and self-improvement. Their children, at school, at home, and even in front of the television, felt the echoes.

Educational television flourished, reflecting and reinforcing the burgeoning interest in learning. On CBS, *You Are There,* adapted from a popular radio program and hosted by Walter Cronkite, featured members of the network's news department "reporting" on historical events as if they were breaking news and "interviewing" participants played by costumed actors. NBC's award-winning *Victory at Sea* used official documentary footage and voice-over narration to recount the history of the US Navy in World War II.[10] In its 1953–1954 season alone, the then-weekly anthology series *Hallmark Hall of Fame* presented hour-long dramas featuring Thomas Jefferson, John Marshall, Simón Bolivar, Clara Schumann, and James McNeill Whistler, as well as lesser-known figures like Henry Bergh, a nineteenth-century crusader against cruelty to animals and children. Elsewhere in the television landscape, viewers could explore science on *G. E. Science Theater,* current events on *Meet the Press* and its imitators, and subjects ranging from animal behavior to atomic energy on Walt Disney's weekly anthology series *Disneyland*.[11] More significant than all of them—in terms of viewing audience and cultural impact—were the ubiquitous quiz shows of the era, which allowed ordinary Americans to parlay knowledge into fortune and fame.[12]

Even with the television off, recreation and self-improvement routinely mingled in American homes at mid-decade. *Scrabble*, a crossword-style board game that rewarded players with expansive vocabularies, debuted in 1948, but became a nationwide craze in 1952. Elaborate military and political simulation games entered the market at mid-decade, allowing ordinary Americans to recreate Civil War battles (*Gettysburg*), turn-of-the-century European politics (*Diplomacy*), or campaigns for world conquest (*Risk*) on their dining-room tables. "Erector" building sets, home chemistry labs, and ant farms—designed to inspire, but also to help train budding scientists and engineers—appeared under thousands of 1950s Christmas trees. Sales of home encyclopedias flourished, and, even if they only left the shelves when children consulted them for school reports, the massive, uniformly bound, prominently displayed volumes conveyed the owner's respect for the idea of learning and for the value of knowledge.

The equation of knowledge and learning with success and fame was further reinforced by the cultural prominence of "public intellectuals." Some, like sex researcher Alfred Kinsey and philosopher George Santayana, were known primarily through their work, but others, such as economist John Kenneth Galbraith, linguist Noam Chomsky, and political commentator William F. Buckley, emerged as highly visible public figures, prominent in the political affairs of the day.[13] The most prominent of all was Albert Einstein, who in the postwar twilight of his life and career wrote frequently on faith, philosophy, and world affairs. The physicist became an improbable cultural icon: his name a synonym for genius, his grandfatherly face a symbol of gentle humanism.[14]

Younger scientists, still active in the laboratory, belonged, along with engineers and medical researchers, to another, even more revered, type of public intellectual. Their conceptual breakthroughs manifested themselves not simply as words on paper or equations on a chalkboard, but as new products, new processes, and new medicines: the building blocks of a better world. Jonas Salk's revolutionary vaccine vanquished the threat of polio; William Shockley and his team at Bell Labs turned electronics portable by inventing the transistor; Edward Teller and Freeman Dyson designed bombs that, they believed, would make war unthinkable, and dreamed of using nuclear explosions to excavate harbors and canals. Rocket engineers like Wernher von Braun sent satellites into orbit to gaze town at the Earth, then went home to write books about how larger versions of the same rockets could send men to the Moon and beyond.[15] When the newly formed National Aeronautics and Space Administration (NASA) chose its first astronauts in 1958, it insisted that they be superb pilots, but also university-trained engineers.[16] NASA, like a substantial portion of the American public, believed that the future belonged to the knowledgeable.

Planning for an American Future

Preparing America's youth for this new postwar world was Captain Z-Ro's mission as he propelled himself and his crew through time and space: "to learn from the past... to plan for the future." As a man of science, he was driven to explore and to use knowledge and the tools it created to advance the greater good. Each week, armed with the perspective of an educator and the bravery of a Cold War hero, he demonstrated the interdependence of past, present, and future—first, to California fans within the reach of his transmissions, and later, across the country—as he and his crew ensured that historical events achieved their proper outcome. In his role as "research explorer in time and space," he endowed the roles of "scientist" and "researcher" with the heroic cache of his military-modeled counterparts, and similarly, brought a more cerebral image to the existing pantheon of rocketmen.

Captain Z-Ro's approach to the world blended equal measures of action and thought. "Why risk going back in time over 1,500 years just to find out what you already know?" his assistant, Tetro, asks as he prepares to infiltrate the camp of Attila the Hun on the eve of a great battle. The swashbuckling scholar's response is simultaneously bold and matter-of-fact: "Because there's something I *don't* know!" Young Jet's musing over a failed attempt to assassinate the future William the Conqueror becomes another springboard for adventure. When he wonders aloud over what happened, his mentor responds: "You've got me, Jet—but there's one sure way to find out! Set the time machine..." Captain Z-Ro thus conveyed concrete knowledge but also, in both word and deed, the larger Atomic Age message that

Image 13.5 Equipped with the most advanced technology in the world, Captain Z-Ro and Jet prepare for another mission to defend Cold War American values.

knowledge was power, and that action, when knowledge was absent or incomplete, could cause disasters that would change the course of history.

In this, we find a complex new model of civic engagement, a particularly Cold War model, that marked a sea change in the relationship between the individual and larger historical processes.[17] The adventures of Captain Z-Ro and the crew of the ZX-99 demonstrated to postwar youth that history could no longer be profitably understood as a monolithic entity, detached from—or worse, victimizing—the lives of everyday people. "History," they illustrated, was constantly in the making, and its course was influenced by lives both great and small. Unlike the Great Man theory, which informed the narratives of most young viewers' textbooks, the series' adventures were infused with the notion that history is "personal," and that each individual possesses not only the ability to create or change it but also the *responsibility* to do so.[18] In a culture that was newly emphasizing the value of knowledge, beyond the practical, among the general population, Captain Z-Ro embodied these new civics of the era, as the knowledgeable, engaged citizen. With the Captain as mentor, Jet, and the viewers at home, learned the value of understanding the social, economic, and political processes that informed their adventures in history, as well as the ongoing need for carefully considered action and intervention to counteract wrongdoing and advance progress and justice.

The multiple messages inherent in that mentoring reflected, to a significant degree, the complexities that challenged Americans' understandings of their place in the world in the early years of the Cold War—and the newly-issued call for engagement with the global community and responsibility for the course of history proved to be a double-edged sword. On one hand, the series valorized broad-based knowledge and global awareness, and inculcated a sense of active participation in the advancement of the common good. Significantly, while that "common good" depicted in *Captain Z-Ro* was clearly informed by mainstream American postwar values, it did not always have an American face—it was British, European, Latin American, and Asian, as well. The real-world lesson derived from World War II, that the fates of Americans were inextricably intertwined with those of diverse peoples around the globe, was very much in evidence throughout the series, when considered as a whole.

On the other hand, a strong message that knowledge granted the right to intervention also united the series' episodes. Young viewers watched as Captain Z-Ro and Jet interceded, with the help of their futuristic superior technology, in the affairs of individuals and nations, defending and advancing values and ideals that were, in the context of the narrative, unquestionably "right" and universal. The heroes of history, regardless of their national origins, were cast as both valuing and embodying these notions, and so, were deemed worthy of the futuristic rocketman's aid. William Tell, fiercely defending "the ancient rights and freedoms of the Swiss," embodied the same spirit as a British colonist denouncing King George, or a Hungarian patriot defying Soviet tanks in the streets of Budapest. Seekers of justice were supported in their struggles against sheriffs and kings; the curious and inquisitive were aided in their quests for knowledge; the despondent were uplifted so that their efforts might continue. In narratives that followed the framework of other mid-twentieth-century juvenile fiction, tyranny, oppression, ignorance, and greed were simplistic wrongs, unfettered by deeper context, destined to be thwarted and overcome.

Written and aired long before the advent of "revisionist" and "subaltern" histories, the Captain's adventures were informed by then-mainstream Western understandings of the conflicts and challenges animating world history, but they also consistently recognized history's "supporting actors"—the lesser-known or seldom-recognized figures involved in the unfolding of historical events. Women typically invisible in the historical narratives of male characters are recognized for their influence: Sarah Morgan Boone (mother of frontiersman Daniel Boone) is portrayed as not only a strong pioneer who keeps the Boone homestead together, but also an herbalist and a tutor for her young son. Unsung heroes are given voice: William Tell is not alone in his fight for Swiss freedom; his fellow patriot, Walter Furst, quietly organizes the commoners while Tell is imprisoned for his open defiance of the Austrian authorities. And the vital role played by those in service is made apparent: when King Alfred loses hope that his tattered British forces will ever beat back the Danes, it is his loyal soldier Denewulf who reminds him of his duty to his people. In each of these episodes, Jet (and so, young viewers at home) is well positioned to observe that great men and women are only the beginning of history's story. "Golly," the awestruck cadet says at the end of one episode, "Robin Hood spent his whole life fighting for justice, didn't he?" The Captain, implicitly tying the medieval past to the Cold War present, confirms "he did, like many others. And the fight for justice still goes on."

CONCLUSION

The rocketmen television series of the 1950s were conceived and produced as space-age contributions to the venerable "boys' adventure" genre. They were fast-paced tales—filled with action, colorful characters, and exotic settings—designed to thrill and excite their audiences (not all of whom were male, and not all of whom were young). The series, however, were more than *just* entertainment. Between battles with interplanetary villains and near-collisions with meteors, they sought to impart serious messages about values and behavior. The rocketmen themselves, from the earliest *Captain Video* episode, forward, served as archetypes of bravery and heroism in a world now defined by the Cold War. Those with youthful crews and sidekicks had another task, as well, serving as mentors not only to their on-screen charges, but also to the thousands of fans who kept weekly rendezvous with them in their living rooms. They modeled ways of being, specifically *American* ways of being, for the new, uncertain, postwar world.

Each week, children's rocketmen heroes illustrated the perennial value of loyalty, honesty, ethics, obedience, and fairness during the course of their adventures to keep not just the world, but the universe, safe for democracy. Their youthful audiences learned not only by example, but also through the mandates of Ranger Messages and formalized Space Ranger Codes, which banished ambiguities about the meanings of good character and citizenship. For most rocketmen—from the ever-vigilant Captain Video to the feisty Rocky Jones—lessons about good Cold War citizenship typically ended there. Like the military heroes in whose footsteps they followed, their mission was to preserve and extend a way of life that Americans already knew, while ushering in the Cold War era.

Captain Z-Ro, however, blazed a different trail to the stars and to the future, one that emphasized the need for growth and change. Departing from the military model of rocketmen heroes, the "research explorer in time and space" continued to advance American values and ideals into the Cold War era, but rather than promoting them through pledges, codes, and other formal frameworks, he did so by showing the ways in which those values—or their absence—affected (and would continue to affect) the course of history. The Captain added a new ideal to the Cold War era: broad-based knowledge of science, geography, and history as vital to successful civic engagement by future Americans. Departing from a wartime worldview that emphasized practical know-how rooted in the present, Captain Z-Ro's missions, whether outward into space or backward into time, demonstrated to young fans that knowledge was a vital precursor to action. Intervention and expansion, designed to preserve and promote long-cherished American values, met with greatest success at the hands of those who understood and respected the lessons of the past.

The Captain served as an icon of this new citizen of the future for his young fans. Brave and daring—a man of action, like his fellow rocketmen—knowledge was always his most powerful weapon. He was as quick to grab a history book as his Para-Ray gun, and exercised patience and keen strategy more often than his fists. But this was no pale intellectual; the lesson he conveyed was "learn—plan—take action." Each week, the Captain and his fantastic inventions journeyed into time and space in defense of freedom and justice. As he boldly leaped to the aid of commoners and kings alike, he taught impressionable viewers that they could be both smart *and* heroic, adding a new facet to traditional masculine archetypes, rather than casting them aside. Intelligence and bravery *together*, he demonstrated, were the qualities that would give Americans of the future the power they needed to shape their individual destinies and, thus the course of history.

NOTES

Unless otherwise noted, all quoted dialogue in is taken from episodes contained in: *Classic Sci-Fi TV*, DVD collection, Mill Creek Entertainment, 2009.

1. The Captain's uncredited crew consisted of Tetro, Micro, and Arcro.
2. Originally, Steffens.
3. A heavily padded Steffens played the role of a televised Santa for seven years, according to interviewer Ziarko, including reprising the role on the ABC-TV national series *You Asked For It*.
4. Ziarko, "Captain Zero." http://www.classicimages.com/articles/2009/10/20/past_articles/captainzro.txt.
5. Berney, np.
6. www.captain-z-ro.com.
7. Charles Ziarko, np.
8. For a contrasting view of the decade, see Richard L. Hofstadter, *Anti-Intellectualism in American Life* (1964), which sees the 1950s as the high-water mark of the titular phenomenon.
9. Helen Lefkowitz Horowitz, *Campus Life: Undergraduate Cultures from the End of the Eighteenth Century to Today* (New York: Knopf, 1987), 184–187, 246; Michael J. Bennett, *When Dreams Came True: The GI Bill and the Making of Modern America* (Washington, DC: Brassey's, 1996), 237–276.
10. Peter C. Rollins, "*Victory at Sea:* Cold War Epic," *Journal of Popular Culture* 6, no. 3 (Spring 1973): 463–482; Philip D. Beidler, "Making a Production out of It: *Victory at Sea* and American Remembering," *Prospects* 22 (1997): 521–534.
11. A. Bowdoin Van Riper, ed., *Learning from Mickey, Donald, and Walt: Essays on Disney Edutainment Films* (Jefferson, NC: McFarland, 2011), esp. 84–102, 145–163, and 221–236.
12. Thomas A. DeLong, *Quiz Craze: America's Infatuation with Game Shows* (Westport, CT: Praeger, 1991).
13. Russell Jacoby, *The Last Intellectuals: American Culture in the Age of Academe* (New York: Basic Books, 1987), 8–25.
14. John D. Barrow, "Einstein as Icon," *Nature*, January 20, 2005, 218–219.
15. Carroll W. Pursell, *The Machine in America: A Social History of Technology*, 2nd ed. (Baltimore: Johns Hopkins University Press, 2007), 271–295.
16. Chuck Yeager, the first pilot to exceed the speed of sound in level flight, was famously barred from consideration as an astronaut because he lacked a degree. See Tom Wolfe, *The Right Stuff* (1979; New York: Picador, 2008), 57–59.
17. For more, see John L. Rudolph, *Scientists in the Classroom: The Cold War Reconstruction of American Science Education* (New York: Palgrave Macmillan, 2002), 9–32; Arthur E. Bestor, *Educational Wastelands: The Retreat from Learning in Our Public Schools*, 2nd ed. (Urbana: University of Illinois Press, 1985).
18. Scholarly literature on the role of Great Men and heroes in history abounds. For foundational work on the Great Men theory, see Thomas Carlyle's *On Heroes: Hero*

Worship and the Heroic in History (1888). One of the most significant counterarguments to Carlyle's theory is found in Sydney Hook's *The Hero in History: A Study in Limitation and Possibility* (1943), which argues that the social world creates both heroes and the contexts needed to evoke their heroism. For more recent considerations, see Charles W. Tait's "Great Men, Great Deeds," *OAH Magazine of History*, April 1985, 4–5.

BIBLIOGRAPHY

Barrow, John D. "Einstein as Icon," *Nature*, January 20, 2005, 218–219.

Beidler, Philip D. "Making a Production Out of It: *Victory at Sea* and American Remembering," *Prospects* 22 (1997): 521–534.

Bennett, Michael J. *When Dreams Came True: The GI Bill and the Making of Modern America*. Washington, DC: Brassey's, 1996.

Bestor, Arthur E. *Educational Wastelands: The Retreat from Learning in Our Public Schools*, 2nd ed. Urbana: University of Illinois Press, 1985.

Classic Sci-Fi TV. Golden Valley, MN: Mill Creek Entertainment, 2009.

DeLong, Thomas A. *Quiz Craze: America's Infatuation with Game Shows*. Westport, CT: Praeger, 1991.

Horowitz, Helen Lefkowitz. *Campus Life: Undergraduate Cultures from the End of the Eighteenth Century to Today*. New York: Knopf, 1987.

Jacoby, Russell. *The Last Intellectuals: American Culture in the Age of Academe*. New York: Basic Books, 1987.

Pursell, Carroll W. *The Machine in America: A Social History of Technology*, 2nd ed. Baltimore: Johns Hopkins University Press, 2007.

Rollins, Peter C. "*Victory at Sea:* Cold War Epic," *Journal of Popular Culture* 6, no. 3 (Spring 1973): 463–482.

Rudolph, John L. *Scientists in the Classroom: The Cold War Reconstruction of American Science Education*. New York: Palgrave Macmillan, 2002.

Tait, Charles W. "Great Men, Great Deeds," *OAH Magazine of History*, April 1985, 4–5.

Van Riper, A. Bowdoin, ed. *Learning from Mickey, Donald, and Walt: Essays on Disney Edutainment Films*. Jefferson, NC: McFarland, 2011.

Wolfe, Tom. *The Right Stuff.* 1979. New York: Picador, 2008.

Epilogue

The Twenty-First Century and Beyond

CHAPTER 14

Confessions of a *Commando Cody* Addict (or, How the Flying Suit Changed My Life)

Gary Hughes

As amateur psychiatrist Lucy once said to Charlie Brown, "Like they say on TV, the mere fact that you realize you have a problem means you are not too far gone." Time to fess up...

I am a serial junkie. I have been since I was six years old. From the first time I tuned in a small, snowy, black-and-white television and saw chapter one of *Radar Men from the Moon* (1952), I was hooked. Thus began a fondly remembered ritual, which kindled my long-standing love affair with cliffhangers and, in particular, one character: Commando Cody.

With a loud, whirring sound and cloud of dust, the Way-Back machine grinds to a halt in Sacramento, California, circa 1960. Arcade School is well within walking distance of home. I busy myself with the day's academic pursuits: arithmetic, reading, grammar, penmanship (which consisted of dragging a tree-trunk-sized, eraser-less pencil across blue lined pulp paper) and art class, with its dull, round-end scissors and mysteriously scented paste.

Mercifully, the clock finally crawls to 3:00 p.m. With the metallic jangling of the final bell, the classroom empties in a flash as 25 pent-up first graders charge toward their respective destinations. I am on a mission of the utmost importance; it's nearly time for Captain Sacto.

Hurrying along a winding street, I stop for just a moment to stuff a handful of grass through the fence toward a curious horse that eyes me watchfully. As I turn the corner onto Merrily Way (I'm serious), the tinkling jingle from a small, white ice-cream truck grows louder as it moves slowly toward me.

Image 14.1 My introduction to the world of rocketmen: Captain Sacto of KCRA-TV, Sacramento. [Credit: Tim Hollis]

At last, I reach the front door, unlocked as usual. I'm just in time. I switch on the TV set, and the large tuner dial makes a thick clunking sound as I turn it to number three. The steady hum of the transformer is gradually replaced by a tinny audio signal emanating from a single small speaker. The blank screen slowly dissolves into an image of the station's familiar call letters as a resonant voice proclaims, "K-C-R-A TV, Sacramento!"

Several scenes of a jet fighter in flight, backed by rousing fanfare, culminate with the sleek craft touching down on a runway and taxiing to a stop. The cockpit canopy slowly raises and Captain Sacto emerges, climbing down the fuselage ladder and trotting off camera. The premise here was a simple one: Captain Sacto (local television personality Harry Martin), who supposedly landed each weekday afternoon at a secret airfield just outside town, was a "Space Volunteer" who oversaw cartoon fun and scientific experiments, aided by the mysterious Dr. Zavier.

Young viewers were treated to all manner of classic cartoons, *The Three Stooges*, the aforementioned scientific experiments and, of course, numerous contests sponsored by area toy stores and other businesses. Long before the days of satellite and cable broadcasts, local programming like this ruled the afternoon airwaves. Let's face it, when you only had three or four channels to choose from, picking favorites was easy.

As much as I enjoyed the entire show, the best segment was the final one. It was here that the Captain introduced the latest chapter of something he called a serial. Each action-packed installment ran approximately 15 minutes and culminated with the hero and/or heroine being placed into yet another deadly situation from which there seemed no possible means of escape.

From fraying ropes to burning fuses, runaway stagecoaches to diving airplanes, deadly gun battles to breakneck car chases on winding, mountain roads, each serial chapter ended in high peril, and we were forced to wait until the following afternoon or, worse yet, the beginning of the next week, to learn the outcome.

My parents regaled me with tales of legendary Saturday Matinees, which were so popular during their childhoods. For a mere pittance, young theatergoers were treated to an entire afternoon's worth of B-Westerns or adventure films, cartoons, newsreels, various shorts, and a weekly serial chapter.

The backdrop for these adventures might be a steaming jungle, a western frontier, a great metropolitan city, or even another planet. Ruthless outlaws, saboteurs and power-mad scientists possessing fantastic weapons were pitted against straight-shooting cowboys, masked vigilantes and other assorted guardians of good. As with much of the juvenile programming of the day, science fiction-themed serials were numerous, dating back to the 1930s.

We were in the heart of both the Atomic Age as well as the Space Race, and science fiction was becoming more popular than ever. While people were building backyard bomb shelters and stockpiling canned food, kids everywhere traded in their cowboy hats and gun holsters for space helmets and ray guns. Popular toy companies promoted Robot Commando, Mr. Machine, and Great Garloo. I myself spent countless hours wearing my Ideal Colonel McCauley astronaut helmet while overseeing operations at the Marx Cape Canaveral playset.

Food companies were also flooding the weekday and Saturday-morning airwaves with products like Sugar-Frosted Jets cereal, Mars and Milky Way candy bars, Clanky Chocolate Flavor Syrup (packaged in a nifty, robot-shaped plastic

Image 14.2 (L-R) Brother Bill, Sister Karen, and I in the Willows Lamb Derby parade, November, 1966. [Author's collection]

dispenser), and a watery, foul-tasting citrus swill dubbed Tang, supposedly used by astronauts.

Thanks to syndication, we were also being exposed to many earlier space operas from the fifties, which helped fuel our interest in futuristic entertainment. Shows like *Captain Video, Rocky Jones: Space Ranger* (which also featured serialized episodes), *Space Patrol, Men into Space,* and later, the animated adventures of Scott McCloud, Space Angel.

For me, though, it was a serial character who captured my imagination, a character dating back to 1952, and one who used a very special device. His preferred mode of transportation was a rocket-powered flying suit. I got my first glimpse on that fateful afternoon when Captain Sacto announced the beginning of a new serial entitled, *Radar Men from the Moon,* which chronicled the adventures of Commando Cody, Sky Marshal of the Universe.

As explained in chapter 1, Commando Cody worked in a "special capacity" for the government, developing an experimental rocket capable of space travel. When a series of attacks on Earth's defense systems are believed to have originated on the Moon, Cody's finned airbus is put into action. For 12 chapters, he and his associates battled an impending global invasion both off world and on terra firma.

I had never seen anything quite like Cody's rocket suit. With an enclosed, bullet-shaped helmet, mid-length leather jacket, twin backpack-mounted rockets, heavy belt, and chest control panel it comprised a unique look: part jet pilot and part astronaut. This wondrous device was completely self-contained and allegedly ran on atomic power, thereby never in need of refueling. So, at least, ran serial logic. In a moment's notice, Cody could don the suit and soar into action. By adjusting the chest-panel knobs and launching himself "Superman-style," he took to the air in pursuit of invading Moon Men and their hired Earthling henchmen.

The retro sci-fi gadgetry from *Radar Men* was a contemporary glimpse into the future. Everything was big and clunky. The lumbering rocket ship that executed horizontal, "skid-style" take-offs and landings, a tripod-mounted ray cannon, and a clattering Moon tank were machines of tomorrow, which reflected current-day designs in the postwar automotive and aircraft industries. The abundance of cheap military surplus was evident throughout rocket interiors and laboratory sets, with the liberal use of large knobs and dials, knife switches, coils, and heavy wire. Cody's flying suit featured a modified safety belt buckle from a B-17 warbird. Even the classic bellows-jointed, fish-bowl-helmeted space suits were reminiscent of vintage navy Mark V deep-sea diving rigs.

No doubt, many of these design choices were influenced by cost-conscious producers endeavoring to give juvenile audiences as much space-age eye candy as possible within the confines of the miniscule budgets relegated to this type of Saturday Matinee fodder.

Despite all the recycled hardware and plywood facades, I was fascinated with *Radar Men from the Moon*. Never mind that Cody's rocket trips through space took place in broad daylight, or that wool slacks were the only protection from the searing exhaust of his rocket pack while in flight, he was a two-fisted, space-age hero. Equally appealing was that, while average people went about the business of their daily routines, Cody and his pals were rocketing through space, trading punches with bad guys or diving out of speeding cars seconds before they sailed off fast-approaching cliffs.

Before the onset of the digital age, with its multitude of video games, phone apps, and numerous interactive diversions, we relied on our imaginations for creative entertainment. A cardboard box with controls hastily scrawled in crayon became a futuristic rocket ship. Two empty paper-towel rolls magically transformed into an atomic-powered rocket pack, and the arm of the sofa was a perfect spot to simulate flying maneuvers. I would often act out the adventures of Commando Cody in this manner, sometimes enlisting the services of my younger brother, Bill, (much to his chagrin) to assume the roles of various bad guys. Little did I know that, nearly 40 years later, this afternoon role-playing ritual would evolve into an amateur film project years in the making.

As with many things in a child's early life, Commando Cody eventually faded away. Afternoon serial encounters were replaced with baseball or Cub Scouts. Its brief, local television run at an end, the rocket-powered adventures of Cody and his associates soon became fond memories.

Having relocated to the small Northern California farming community of Willows in 1964, my family and I were currently adjusting to new surroundings and people. Here, the pace of life was considerably slower, with everything a kid needed within walking or biking distance. We almost never locked our front door. Summers were occupied with Aqua Jets swim-team practice, Little League, or building plastic model kits. And, of course, there were our "make believe" adventures as cowboys or soldiers. We spent many fun-filled summer days decked out with either a set of gun holsters or plastic replicas of World War II headgear. We dug great holes in a nearby field and, once covered over with large pieces of scrap tin and dirt, these became secret headquarters or hideouts. In retrospect, it's a miracle we weren't all buried alive.

Acting out these improvised scenarios was something I thoroughly enjoyed. Depending upon how many participants showed up, one might be spontaneously called upon to play either hero or villain. Death was ever-present, and we all practiced diligently to polish our screams, falls, requisite facial expressions, and exaggerated body spasms. Since "extras" were in short supply, it was never necessary to remain out of the action for long. Each of us became adept (to our ears, at any rate) at imitating sounds for a wide variety of weapons, from six-shooter to carbine, from machine gun to the highly favored hand grenade.

Naturally, when our faux ammunition ran out, we were required to square off hand-to-hand with an opponent. Sometimes rubber or plastic knives were incorporated, but for the most part, these desperate confrontations involved spontaneous fight choreography. Again, sound was essential here, both with the delivery of near-miss punches, kicks, and interpretive karate chops, as well as the resulting impact of blows. No one ever really got hurt, with the possible exception of a skinned elbow or knee, and we could assemble any group of young, older, short, or tall kids and still pull it off. Sun-dried, powdery field soil provided the perfect arena. and by day's end, we were all happily sweat-streaked and covered with dirt.

Through it all, we never thought of ourselves as actors. We were merely creating scenarios as games. We were often inspired by television shows we liked or movies we'd just seen at the Tower Theater. Incredibly, we were able to entertain ourselves without expensive toys or any type of adult supervision. It was all about imagination.

Around this time, my brother Bill and I began to develop an affinity for another type of entertainment: monster movies. We began to read magazines like *Famous Monsters of Filmland*, *Eerie*, and *Creepy*. The walls of our room were adorned with posters of classic Universal monsters, magazine photos, and drawings of our favorite creatures. My model-building interest shifted from cars to Aurora monsters, and my headboard was soon lined with these classic plastic kits.

We had to thoroughly scan the week's issue of *TV Guide* to find anything worthy of our newfound interest. With only a handful of stations within the reach of rabbit-ear antennas, there were often long droughts between monster and science fiction movies. However, this situation was about to change, thanks to a new program. It was a weekly Saturday-night broadcast called *Creature Features*, hosted by an unknown named Bob Wilkins. More than anything we'd seen before, *Creature Features* most strongly influenced our interest in creating original films.

Saturday nights suddenly became a regular TV ritual. My mom, dad, brother Bill, sister Karen, and I would wade through the eleven o'clock news until, at last, the opening strains of Neal Hefti's, "Gotham City Municipal Swing Band" heralded another installment of *Creature Features*. Mild mannered, bespectacled, cigar-toting host Bob Wilkins, firmly ensconced in his trademark yellow rocking chair, introduced us to some of the best (and best of the worst) in science fiction and horror.

Running the gamut of classic Universal offerings like *Frankenstein, Dracula*, and *The Wolf Man*, we were also treated to all manner of gigantic Japanese monsters, Mexican vampires and masked wrestlers, Italian space operas, and fifties B-movie cult classics. Although I always kept my fingers crossed, I was never able to revisit here the beloved Commando Cody adventures I'd enjoyed years before. Not yet, at any rate.

Our family continued its nomadic ways, moving from Willows to East San Jose when my dad was called upon to open and serve as manager for one of the first Mervyn's department stores in 1967. We were suddenly immersed in the multicultural melting pot of a tough, South Bay city. Our former small-town lifestyle had been replaced by tense, sometimes dangerous surroundings as social and racial tensions of the late 60s were coming to a head. Here there were no unlocked front doors, and the walk home from school might be met with physical threats or occasional violence. Through it all, we continued our weekly Saturday nights with Bob Wilkins, whose quirky, off-the-cuff format had since gained widespread recognition among fans of the offbeat.

As the popularity of *Creature Features* grew, the format was expanded to include interviews with various actors, writers, and fans regionally involved in the horror and sci-fi genres. From time to time, Wilkins would even screen short films done by local amateur moviemakers. My brother and I were instantly drawn to these gems, so much so that we soon acquired a used Super 8 camera from a local pawnshop and began to experiment with our own original cinematic ideas.

With dreams of our masterpieces being shown on *Creature Features*, we embarked upon a series of short subjects dubbed "Shocking Tales," beginning in 1971. Working without the benefit of a tripod, lights, sets, and props, and with

Image 14.3 Back Row (L-R): Ruben Contreras, Ed Irvin, David Brunette (in robot costume), Daughter Nikki, and I. Front Row (L-R): Victor Contreras, my dad Vic, and TV Horror Host, Mr. Lobo. [Author's collection]

no real money to speak of, we tinkered together vignettes chronicling cardboard-fanged vampire encounters, a monster-making mad scientist, a private detective, and even a stop-motion animation featuring a runaway lawnmower. A standard 50-foot roll of Super 8 film afforded us approximately three minutes to get the proverbial point across, so necessity dictated keeping our themes brief. Most times, we preferred to improvise scenes and story lines as we filmed, utilizing whatever elements were available to us.

I became infatuated with makeup, having been influenced by monster creations (of widely varying quality), which I'd seen on *Creature Features*. We finally located a downtown theatrical supply shop and were able to procure the sum total of our "Shocking Tales" makeup assets: some crepe hair, a small bottle of spirit gum, plastic fangs, a tube of fake blood, and a rubber witch nose. My poor brother became the unwitting guinea pig, forced to inhale noxious fumes from the spirit gum as I struggled to fit him with an improvised moustache. My efforts were extremely primitive, as we were always more interested in filming than spending valuable time with elaborate disguises.

Some of our more memorable footage included test shots of a rocket ship crash landing we tried to simulate. Utilizing classic 50s technology, we fastened a sparkler onto the back of a model jet plane and pushed it down fishing line that ran diagonally from the top of our back fence to the ground. To recreate the interior "control panel" burning, I hit upon the bright idea of placing a smoke bomb in the ashtray of my Volkswagen, while Bill sat alongside filming from the passenger seat. To this day, I vividly remember the sharp sting of sparks hitting my face, and the thick, acrid smoke, which quickly filled the little car as I loudly implored my flabbergasted brother to, "Keep filming!"

As much as I would have loved to develop a Commando Cody short, I knew the prospect of replicating the famous rocket suit and figuring out how to create necessary flying effects was well beyond anything we were capable of. That artistic journey was destined to unfold many years later.

Although our goals often overstepped the reality of what we were actually able to capture on camera, our beloved "Shocking Tales" anthologies remained a perpetual source of teenage enjoyment. Fortunately, my brother had the foresight to preserve our original collection of Super 8 film reels, which still exist today and were eventually transferred onto VHS tape, as well as DVD, for posterity.

For the next few years, our future filmmaking efforts were put on hold. After completing high school, I embarked upon a short-lived community college stint in Roseburg, Oregon. A single semester monopolized by rather exuberant partying served as positive proof that my maturity was woefully inadequate. Needless to say, I returned home in desperate need of regrouping. After some much-needed soul-searching, I righted the proverbial ship and steered into the uncharted waters of my early twenties.

Yet another family move eventually returned us all to Sacramento, thanks to my father's promotion to store director of yet another new Mervyn's. We gradually settled in once again and busied ourselves with the business of life. It was here I met and married my wife of 30 years, Rae, whom I regard as the single most understanding soul on the face of the Earth. Not only did she support and encourage my assorted creative efforts, but literally became a participant. My brother had just procured a new camera, and once again the game was afoot.

Bill and I began to collaborate on a new film project entitled, *Blood Tong From Space*. Drawing from our love of low-budget 50s and 60s science fiction, we cobbled together a story of evil aliens bent on world conquest led by the Emperor Akio, a character based on my friend Alan Akio Ito, whom we hoped to cast in the role.

For the first time, some effort was made on preproduction. We visited a couple of surplus stores and grabbed anything we could afford that might lend itself to sci-fi apparel. I built and modified a large model of the space shuttle to serve as Akio's alien warship. We even scouted locations, finding a suitably isolated one on a sloping hillside adjacent to nearby Folsom Lake.

After some weeks of preparation, it was decided we would shoot test footage in order to check costuming, camera angles, and fight choreography. The date was set, and early one Sunday morning, we loaded our gear and headed to the remote spot. Upon arrival, we quickly set up and suited up. Before long, the camera was rolling.

In the test scene, my dad played the role of Akio's alien sentry on watch atop a large, granite boulder. Rae and I secretly made our way through the surrounding bushes until I slipped up behind the guard, quickly dispatching him with a karate chop. Suddenly, another guard (my brother Bill) sprang at me, setting off a rolling, tumbling life-and-death struggle. On cue, Rae attempted to make her escape by running off down the nearby hill. Near the bottom of said hill, my dad, partially swathed in alien tin-foil costume and wearing a bright orange military-surplus plastic hood respirator, was to leap out from behind a tree and grab Rae as she ran by.

On paper, it seemed like a sure thing. But, best-laid plans being what they are, we soon discovered that capturing the action would require much more work than originally anticipated. Timing leaps, punches, and reactions required several practice attempts. While rolling along the ground, Bill and I literally had to hold each other in place so as not to each go our separate ways. Throwing faux punches was tricky, time-consuming business as well. Too close and we might accidentally clip one another, too far away and the illusion was lost. After the third or fourth run-through, we were scraped, sore, and winded.

When we called action and sent Rae down the hillside for her first take, we marveled at the breakneck running speed and convincing arm flailing she was able to effect. Our appreciation quickly became concern when she roared right past the spot where Dad lunged out to grab her and continued on at full speed. When Rae returned, breathless, back to the top of the hill, we learned the secret of her realistic albeit modified performance: the hillside was so steep that, during the entire downhill run, she was propelled by momentum and completely out of control, narrowly avoiding both Dad and a nasty spill.

As we took a break from filming and reviewed the day's progress, two figures appeared in the distance, slowly working their way up the hillside from another direction. As they approached, I suddenly realized they were police officers. They arrived, surveyed the camera and our simple costumes, and asked what we were doing here. After a tense moment of silence, we explained the film project. Much to our collective relief, they both expressed interest in what we were doing and jokingly asked if there were parts for two cops, which elicited laughter all around. When I asked what two officers were doing out in the middle of nowhere, they informed us that an inmate had escaped from nearby Folsom State Prison and they were taking part in the search. At this point, it was mutually decided we had all the test footage required. Needless to say, we were packed and out of the area in record time.

We'd learned some valuable filmmaking lessons. What was anticipated to be a few hours of location work evolved into an entire day's worth of rehearsal, multiple takes, and experimentation. We discovered shooting almost never went exactly as planned and, above all, to expect the unexpected.

Bill and I later shot a couple of brief interior scenes and some footage of the miniature rocket ship, but nothing more. With lack of available time and funding, we eventually abandoned the project and sadly, *Blood Tong from Space* was never completed. When Bill left home a short while later to complete his master's degree, I began to wonder if this was, in fact, the final curtain descending upon our cinematic collaborations.

The birth of our daughter, Nikki, in 1981 heralded the beginning of a busy, wonderful time in our lives. The numerous responsibilities of raising a child took precedence over everything else. With the camera packed away and my brother abroad completing his studies, filmmaking was forgotten for a time. At this point, I began to embark on a long research project, which would eventually set the stage for a cinematic dream: the production of an original Commando Cody-based film.

The project's catalyst was the discovery of two books by Alan G. Barbour, *Cliffhanger* and *Saturday Afternoon at the Movies*, a compilation of three earlier works (*Days of Thrills and Adventure, A Thousand and One Delights*, and *The Thrill of It All*). Barbour, an authority on serials, chronicled information on the studios, actors, stunt performers, directors, technicians, and locations that played such key roles in the evolution of classic chapter plays. Best of all, each volume was chock-full of rare production stills and behind-the-scenes photos of these talented craftspeople at work.

Around this time, an afternoon visit to the local video-rental store led to an amazing discovery: several classic serial titles were now available on VHS, among them, my long-lost favorite, *Radar Men from the Moon*, which I hadn't seen in nearly 25 years. Once again, Commando Cody made a TV appearance, bringing with him a flood of happy childhood memories.

Of course, revisiting *Radar Men* as an adult was much different than my original experience. The corny dialogue, stock footage, marginal acting, and cut-and-run production values drove home the point that this was, without a doubt, juvenile-oriented material. That having been said, there was also a great deal of nostalgic charm, a handcrafted quality to which I was strongly attracted. The rousing musical cues, elaborate fight choreography, and realistic miniature-car crashes and effects still made for some great entertainment. I eagerly sought out as many serial titles as I could lay my hands on.

I was gradually piecing together a more complete picture of where Commando Cody came from. I learned that the "flying suit" made its first screen appearance in the Republic Pictures' serial *King of the Rocketmen* in 1949. Next up were *Radar Men from the Moon* in 1952, and later that year, *Zombies of the Stratosphere*, which feature 21- year-old Leonard Nimoy (Spock on the original *Star Trek* series) as a Martian malcontent. Finally, there was a short-lived theatrical series of 12 complete, half-hour episodes entitled *Commando Cody, Sky Marshal of the Universe*, which also made a brief run on television. However, it wasn't until entering the computer age that I really began to uncover information on the rocket-powered hero of my youth, as well as develop some lasting long-distance friendships.

By 1997, I'd begun to venture thorough cyberspace. After searching the Internet a short time, I was amazed to find a large contingent of fans on several serial-based websites. I immediately connected with a very talented artist named Chris Mason, who had done some amazing work colorizing serial production stills using Photoshop. Both Chris and his father, Tom, were well versed in serial lore and the retro sci-fi TV classic *Space Patrol*. When Chris learned of my interest in Commando Cody, he emailed a picture of someone wearing a full replica of the flying suit. He was a Burbank, California-based prop maker named Don Coleman, and with his help and guidance, along with numerous other sources, I embarked on the nearly four-year-long quest to create my own Cody rocket suit.

As I continued to research Commando Cody and gather together the components of my replica-flying suit, I had amassed enough information to launch my own fan-based website, dubbed The Rocketpage, in the spring of 2000. I was soon receiving emails from fans as far away as Rio de Janeiro and the United Kingdom who willingly shared their Cody photos, trivia, and personal reminisces. One individual in particular was in possession of something I was extremely interested in, the original leather stunt jacket and one of the "hero" helmets used during filming of the Rocket Man/Commando Cody serials, legendary prop collector and archivist, Bob Burns.

By 2003, The Rocketpage was gaining popularity, and I was finally close to completing the seemingly endless replica-flying suit project. By this time, I had also built a 1/6 scale custom figure of Commando Cody. Despite having attempted several times to connect with Bob Burns without success, I persevered and finally got the chance to meet America's favorite Monster Kid in person, as well as the actor who portrayed Cody in *Radar Men from the Moon*, George Wallace.

Months later, in early 2004, I had at last completed the replica-flying suit. The helmet (made from Don Coleman's fiberglass casting of an original) and rocket pack (from Don's own design), were rotocast by Acme Designs in Chicago, who provided both pieces in kit form, which I assembled and painted. San Leandro costumers, The Magic Wardrobe, designed the leather jacket based upon reference photos and information I provided. The trademark modified B-17 belt buckle and chest control-plate were made using Don's own research and fabrication techniques. The newly completed costume was a childhood dream realized, and I was anxious to share my work.

I emailed photos of the flying suit to Don, who informed me he was planning a tribute to original *Commando Cody* actor George Wallace, whom he'd befriended several years earlier. The event was to be held in December at the Hollywood Heritage Museum, which resided in the original barn used by Cecil B. DeMille.

Don asked if I'd like to attend and suggested I bring my new costume and Cody figure. He also mentioned that Bob Burns would be attending with some of his authentic Radar Men costume pieces. I was absolutely stunned by the news. After all the years of research, I finally had an opportunity to meet both my boyhood hero and Bob Burns...in the same evening.

Having completed his doctorate and secured a teaching position at Southern Oregon University in Ashland, my brother Bill was settled in once again. We gradually resumed our varied discussions of possible film projects, and I broached an idea I'd had for some time, a serial featuring my newly completed Commando Cody flying suit. After brainstorming the idea long distance, we decided on an original concept and characters. Our cliffhanger would be homage rather than a direct copy. It was also decided we would draw upon masked wrestlers and other elements to which we were exposed back in our days watching Bob Wilkins' *Creature Features*. While I set about the task of assembling props and costumes, Bill busied himself with a proposed four-chapter screenplay entitled *Thirty Second Doom*.

The basic premise revolved around a deranged scientist, Dr. Xavier, whose dangerous experiments are deemed too hazardous by his employer, GAS Laboratories. A sudden lab accident horribly disfigures Xavier, and he vows to seek vengeance against his associates and superiors. This threat coincides with the appearance of a mysterious masked figure calling himself Dr. X, who proceeds to wage a one-man war against everyone associated with GAS Laboratories. The intervention of another GAS researcher, Steve Bennett, and his associates sets the stage for gunfights, fisticuffs, and, of course, requisite cliffhangers. We were determined to capture the look and feel of the classic Commando Cody serial wherever possible.

After finding a suitable location with a large hill, the first order of business was to shoot some exterior flying scenes. Just as the Lydecker Brothers, special effects wizards for Republic Pictures, used a full-size dummy sliding down parallel wires to create the illusion of Rocket Man or Commando Cody in flight, we followed suit: in miniature. Using a hot-glue gun to fasten the joints of my 1/6 scale figure in horizontal flying position, we then attached short fishing lines to the wrists and ankles. A tall metal pull-up exercise stand was placed on top of the hill, with two parallel fishing lines strung downhill approximately 60 feet.

Making do with an ancient analog camcorder set up at various angles and distances, we slid the figure down the fishing lines and filmed the action. After some trial and error, we captured several convincing flights. To create the illusion of our figure descending, we slid him down headfirst. To replicate take-offs and ascending flight, we simply ran the figure down the lines backwards and then reversed the footage in postproduction.

Amateur filmmaking had progressed by leaps and bounds since we had last fired up our camera years ago on a Sunday afternoon near Folsom Lake. We were now in the midst of the digital age, where cameras captured action on miniDV tape, which was then transferred onto a computer via Firewire connection for editing. Needless to say, I knew absolutely nothing about this new technology and anxiously explored amateur film sites, trying frantically to get up to speed.

I researched and finally located a more modern and better-suited digital camcorder and recruited a handful of friends and family to participate in the project. After Bill and I reworked and fine-tuned the script, we set a Sunday in August as the beginning of our filming schedule for *Thirty Second Doom*, which was to be shot both inside and outside an office building to which we were permitted access. I spent the better part of Saturday night and Sunday morning frantically familiarizing myself with the new camera instructions, as Bill, still in Ashland, would not be on hand this time to assist with the filming duties. Armed with camera and sound gear, costumes, and an actual script, I met with cast and crew at our appointed location. After five hours work, we had successfully shot the first few scenes of *Doom*.

We all gathered three or four more times that summer and filmed everything needed to complete Chapter One Since our lack of budget prevented us from building and storing elaborate sets, we utilized a popular device for placing actors in any desired environment, the green screen. I set up a large screen, along with suitable lighting in my garage. This necessitated placing the camera tripod in the adjacent laundry room and crowding actors close together so the background area in frame was completely covered by the chroma key screen.

These were by far the most grueling filming sessions we had to endure. Keeping the garage "sound stage" quiet enough to record dialogue required closing the side door, and the bright lights quickly heated the stifling garage to almost unbearable levels. Nevertheless, despite the blazing summer heat, we persevered.

After much trial and error, I was able to assimilate enough basic understanding of our computer's video-editing software to complete a rough cut of Chapter One "Terminal Dive," shortly before the scheduled event at the Hollywood Heritage Museum. After adding sound effects and music from the original Republic chapter plays, we finally had at least part of our epic adventure burned to DVD for posterity. I sent copies out to several fans and posted clips on The Rocketpage, and the reaction was favorable. Despite technical and budgetary limitations, it seemed we had succeeded in capturing the flavor of a classic serial.

Before I knew it, December had arrived and plans were made for the trip south to the George Wallace tribute in Hollywood. My daughter Nikki, brother Bill, his son Miko, and I finally embarked on our great So-Cal adventure. Our hotel was within walking distance of the Hollywood Heritage Museum, and after checking in, we walked over to meet with event director Steve Saylor. It had been decided that, rather than simply show up in the suit that evening, I would secretly station myself just outside one of the infamous barn doors while George Wallace gave a brief talk about his career and answered audience questions. At the conclusion of the discussion, I was to be given a cue and begin pounding loudly on the door while my brother, standing just inside, would slide it open. I was to approach Wallace in full costume and implore Commando Cody himself to assist in thwarting an alien invasion just outside.

That night was magical. The small building gradually began to fill with fans, veteran participants in the film industry, and friends of Wallace. Bob Burns brought the original costume worn by Retik, Ruler of the Moon from the *Radar Men* serial, as well as one of the actual Commando Cody hero helmets. He also set up a display of original Rocket Man and Commando Cody movie posters. There was a display of some of the beautifully crafted helmet and ray cannon props created by Don Coleman. Amidst all this was my 1/6 scale Cody figure.

I turned just in time to see someone I immediately recognized as Bob Burns. After introducing myself, Bob proceeded to tell how much he'd enjoyed the first chapter of *Thirty Second Doom* and offered to play a bit part himself. He was also extremely complimentary regarding the miniature Cody figure and said he'd love to have one to display in his museum. Coming from someone who had befriended many noted actors, prop builders, and makeup artists in Hollywood, this was high praise indeed.

A short time later, the man himself entered. He was in his eighties now and moved rather slowly with his wife at his arm, but there was no mistaking the serial hero of my childhood, George Wallace. The building was jammed to standing room only capacity, fitting tribute for the actor, who received a spirited ovation when introduced.

I was soon signaled that it was time to head outside and man my post near the barn door. As I fumbled with the flying suit in the dark, I could hear peels of laughter from the audience as Wallace recounted some of the more comical mishaps encountered during the filming of *Radar Men from the Moon*. Suddenly, my nephew Miko poked his head outside and gave me the cue to strap on the helmet. An instant later, I banged loudly on the door, which slid open slowly to reveal the stunned faces of the crowd and of Wallace himself. I ran to the table in front where he was seated, rattled off my lines, and quickly bolted out the door. A moment later, rousing applause indicated our prank had been a hit with the crowd. I'll never forget the feeling of reentering the room and seeing the confused but smiling expressions of the audience.

We spent the rest of the evening hobnobbing with other attendees who were very much taken with the replica-flying suit. George Wallace even autographed the inside of the helmet, thereby giving it the official Commando Cody seal of approval. Finally, Bob Burns allowed me to examine and try on the original Commando Cody hero helmet. All the countless emails, phone calls, letters, and assorted research had been rewarded at last. My brother and I were more determined than ever to push ahead with our serial film project.

Classic cliffhangers were action-driven cinematic vehicles, and it was decided we needed to focus on this element throughout the remainder of *Thirty Second Doom*. I had, by this time, decided to add another element to the film: a full-sized, wearable replica of the legendary Republic serial robot. Affectionately dubbed the "water heater" by its creators, this clinking, clanking, clattering collection of serial nostalgia would add another vehicle for action to *Doom*. Now, all I had to do was build it.

Once again, I set about the task of assimilating the knowledge and materials needed to complete this rather daunting project. I was fortunate enough to connect with robot collector/builder John Rigg, who had fabricated a static display of the famous automaton. With John's help, along with that of several other movie-robot hobbyists, I was, after seven months, finally able to tinker together a reasonable facsimile of the original. Our villain, Dr. X, now had an "Electronic Assassin" at his disposal.

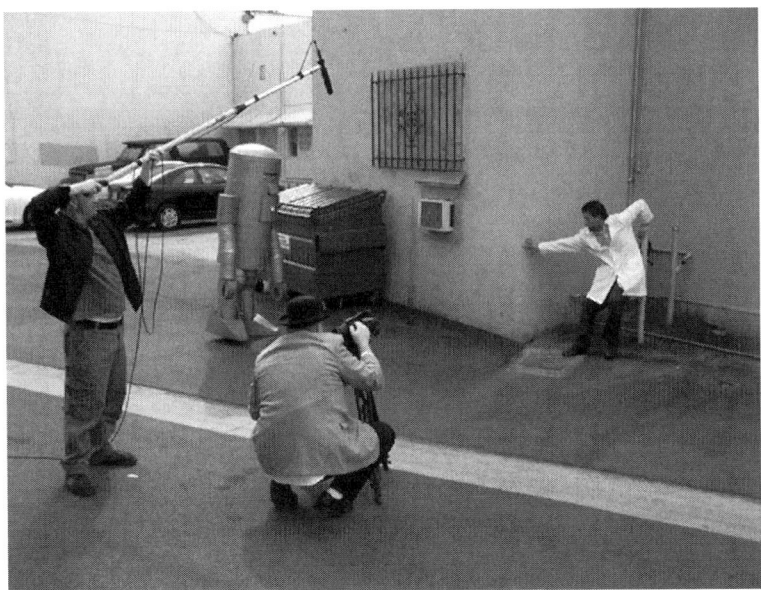

Image 14.4   Shooting a scene with the robot in North Hollywood. [Author's collection]

As this mechanical marvel took shape, we began to concentrate on another essential element of our Commando Cody homage: live-action flying scenes. In the original "flying suit" serials, legendary stunt performer Dave Sharpe hung from a wired harness in front of a process screen to achieve the effect of free flight. If it was good enough for Republic, it was good enough for us.

We had by now become adept at utilizing whatever was available to us; in this case, a heavy-duty electric hoist secured to the roof of a large steel building. I acquired a rock-climbing harness, which was worn backwards beneath the costume, so as to afford being secured from above. Two nylon dog collars were fitted with fishing line and attached to a length of PVC pipe. When fastened to my wrists, brother Bill, perched just off camera atop a tall ladder, could raise and lower my arms, thereby changing the trajectory of flight. Despite being rather excruciating, the entire process went off without a hitch, and we captured several flying shots. When filmed before the green screen, we were able to successfully replicate the original look of "flight" once the background was replaced with stock footage of cloud fly-throughs in postproduction.

As each new piece of *Doom* was edited, we began posting excerpts on The Rocketpage website, as well as YouTube. Viewer feedback was consistently positive as more and more fans began to take an interest in our film. Local Sacramento TV Horror Host Mr. Lobo, whose late-night *Cinema Insomnia* had garnered a large contingent of faithful followers, agreed to do a cameo performance, along with Nashville television's own "Physician of Fright" Dr. Gangrene (Larry Underwood) and Nurse Moan-eek (Linda Wylie). A very talented group of amateur Southern California sci-fi filmmakers, headed by John Garside, also made appearances in

Image 14.5   My Dad Vic gives me a shoulder for support as we test the live-action flying rig for the first time. [Author's collection]

Doom. Garside and Company were currently putting the finishing touches on their own retro sci-fi fan film, *Max Neptune and the Menacing Squid*, with an upcoming theatrical premiere slated for Whittier, California. I was absolutely stunned when John offered to show our new trailer at the event. What started out as a group of seven friends and family had, by this time, ballooned to a cast of nearly twenty.

By now, we had decided to make *Thirty Second Doom* completely our own, which meant composing an original score in lieu of the stock Republic music we'd started with. Thanks to Mr. Lobo, we were introduced to talented local film composer Christopher Crites, also known as Mars, of deadhousemusic.com, who agreed to create original music for *Doom*. Another long-distance friend and fan, Illinois native Don Michals, generously covered the cost of the composition fee. With the help of these and many other newfound comrades, *Thirty Second Doom* was moving ever closer to becoming the film project I'd always dreamed of making.

In the spring of 2010, Bill and I traveled south to Whittier, California, for the premiere of *Max Neptune* and the first-ever screening of our new *Thirty Second Doom* trailer. The Whittier Village Cinema was abuzz on that magical night, packed to capacity. John had made no mention of the *Doom* trailer to the audience beforehand, so no one in attendance expected what they saw when the lights finally dimmed. I sat breathless through the entire preview, more than a little nervous about what sort of reaction our work would elicit. After all, many in attendance were too young to even know what a serial was. The final fade-out was greeted with cheers and a rousing round of applause. We'd thoroughly entertained 200 people with our zero budget pipedream, and I couldn't believe my ears. It was truly an evening I will never forget.

September 2010 marked the seventy-fifth anniversary of the founding of Republic Pictures, the studio responsible for so many classic B-Westerns, adventure films, and, of course, my beloved cliffhangers. During their heyday, Republic was tops in serial excitement with the best fight choreography, music, miniature effects, and fast-paced action.

I immediately contacted Bob Burns regarding the upcoming event scheduled at what is now CBS Studios. He explained that, in addition to appearances and panel discussions with some of the original surviving Western stars, there was to be a presentation on the work of special effects pioneers Howard and Theodore Lydecker, whose amazing pyrotechnics and miniatures set the industry standard for visual effects and scale model work. The panel was to include Bob Burns; author Jan Henderson, who had recently authored the book, *The Legendary Lydecker Brothers*; and George Lydecker, son of Howard.

I told Bob that it was an event I absolutely had to attend, and asked if it would be OK to bring down my replica Commando Cody flying suit. Bob asked if I would care to ride to the event with him and his wife, Kathy, and stop in at the VIP room where the celebrity guests would be checking in. Bob had also made arrangements with the Lydecker Brothers panel coordinator to have me make a walk-in appearance during the discussion wearing the flying suit.

Despite the 100-degree Los Angeles heat that Saturday, I gladly donned the heavy leather jacket and helmet outside the commissary, where the Lydecker panel was being held. On a signal, I entered the room just as the theatrical trailer for *Radar Men from the Moon* was showing on a large TV screen. I was greeted with surprised exclamations and rousing applause as I stepped into the room. Like the earlier George Wallace tribute, the packed room was full of appreciative Commando Cody fans.

Needless to say, I was on cloud nine throughout the entire panel discussion. At the conclusion of the event, I felt a tap on my shoulder as one of the press personnel in attendance casually remarked, "OK, it's time for pictures." I turned to see a large group of attendees with camcorders, cell phones, and still cameras pointed in my direction. One by one, people came up and posed next to me as the cameras flashed. The event coordinator even brought her infant daughter over just to take a picture. I received numerous compliments and questions regarding my flying suit and engaged in spirited conversation with many people young and old. Apparently, I was enjoying the fabled 15 minutes of fame, courtesy of *Thirty Second Doom*.

At this writing, Chapter Three "The Electronic Assassin" is officially wrapped, with work scheduled to begin soon on the fourth and final installment. If all goes according to plan, the entire project will be completed by year's end. With nearly seven years invested in *Thirty Second Doom*, it will indeed be a relief to see it finally come to fruition. What began in 1960, before a small, snowy black-and-white television set, has evolved into a lifelong fascination with serials: their creators, their history, and, in particular, the daring exploits of one of their most memorable heroes, Commando Cody.

Contributors

Jean-Noel Bassior is the author of *Space Patrol: Missions of Daring in the Name of Early Television* (2005). She has written numerous articles for *Filmfax, Redbook, Parade, McCall's* and many other publications, and her work has been syndicated worldwide by the *New York Times* and Knight Features (London). Her writing on *Space Patrol* was nominated for the Rondo Award in 2003 for Best Article, "The Search for the Ralston Rocket," and in 2004, in the Best Book and Best Writer categories. The Rondo Awards are designed to recognize research, scholarship, and creativity in the fields of science fiction and classic horror. She has been a featured guest on numerous talk shows, including *Coast-to-Coast A. M.* with George Noory and Fox News affiliates.

Mick Broderick is associate professor and research coordinator, School of Media Communication & Culture, Murdoch University, where he is Deputy Director of the National Academy of Screen & Sound (NASS). His major publications include editions of the reference work *Nuclear Movies* (1988, 1991) and, as editor, *Hibakusha Cinema: Hiroshima, Nagasaki, and the Nuclear Image in Japanese Film* (1996, 1999). Recent coedited collections with Antonio Traverso include *Interrogating Trauma: Collective Suffering in Global Arts and Media* (2010) and *Trauma, Media, Art: New Perspectives* (2010). He is a media producer and curator, with exhibitions of his Cold War material culture collection displayed in Australia, Japan, and the United States. He is cofounding editor of the praxis-led e-journal *IM: Interactive Media*, an editorial board member of ScreenWorks (UK) and was a West Australia commissioning editor for Realtime.

Gary Coville is a media historian and author as well as a former teacher and reference librarian. He specializes in 1950s radio and television science fiction. Gary has written frequently on the link between radio and early television and their influential impact on American popular culture. Together with Patrick Lucanio, his longtime friend and colleague, they have authored three works on genre history: *American Science Fiction Television Series of the 1950s* (1998); *Jack the Ripper: His Life and Crimes in Popular Entertainment* (2008); *and Smokin' Rockets: The Romance of Technology in Film, Radio and Television, 1945–1962* (2002). Their other collaborations have included a stint as contributing writers for *Filmfax Magazine*, as contributors to the anthology work *Jack the Ripper: Media, Culture, History* (2008), and service together as advisors and onscreen commentators for the documentary film *Monsters From the Id*, based largely on *Smokin Rockets*.

Wheeler Winston Dixon is the Ryan Professor of Film Studies, Coordinator of the Film Studies Program, and Professor of English at the University of Nebraska, Lincoln. He is Editor in Chief, with Gwendolyn Audrey Foster, of the *Quarterly Review and Film and Video*. Dixon's articles on film theory, history, and criticism have appeared in *Cineaste, Interview, Literature/Film Quarterly, Films in Review, Post Script, Journal of Film and Video, Film Criticism, New Orleans Review, Classic Images, Film and Philosophy*, and numerous other journals. His most recent books are: *Death of the Moguls: The End of Classical Hollywood* (2012); *21st Century Hollywood: Movies in the Era of Transformation* (coauthored with Gwendolyn Audrey Foster; 2011); *A History of Horror* (2010), *Film Noir and the Cinema of Paranoia* (2009), and *A Short History of Film* (coauthored with Gwendolyn Audrey Foster; 2008; 2nd rev, ed., forthcoming 2013).

Amy Foster is associate professor of History at the University of Central Florida. Her research interests include the history of the US space program and the interrelationship between gender and technology. She has published several articles on women in the NASA's astronaut corps. Her book, *Integrating Women into the Astronaut Corps: Politics and Logistics at NASA, 1972–2004*, is scheduled for release in fall 2011 by Johns Hopkins University Press. She has held the American Historical Association/NASA Fellowship in Aerospace History, and the Guggenheim Fellowship at the Smithsonian's National Air and Space Museum. She has also appeared as a commentator on National Public Radio, discussing the role of women engineers and managers at NASA.

Gary Hughes is, by day, the operator of a landscaping business. By night, and on most weekends, he transforms into a model maker, prop builder, and amateur filmmaker, as the founder of Randori Productions, a film production company focused on productions of 1950s-style serial films. His essay in this volume chronicles the production and reception of his most recent film, *Thirty-Second Doom*, a four-episode serial homage to the early "rocketmen" series. Along with his production crew—including his wife, Rae Amaral, and daughter, Nikki—Gary fights a never-ending battle for truth, justice, and the preservation of fondly remembered childhood heroes.

Robert Jacobs is associate professor at the Hiroshima Peace Institute of Hiroshima City University, Japan. He is the author of *The Dragon's Tail: Americans Face the Atomic Age* (2010) and the editor of *Filling the Hole in the Nuclear Future: Art and Popular Culture Respond to the Bomb* (2010). He has written extensively on nuclear weapons, nuclear testing, civil defense, and their impact on American culture during the Cold War era, including "Atomic Kids: *Duck and Cover* and *Atomic Alert* Teach American Children How to Survive Atomic Attack" (*Film & History: An Interdisciplinary Journal of Film and Television Studies*); "'There Are No Civilians, We Are All At War': Nuclear War Shelter and Survival Narratives during the Early Cold War" (*Journal of American Culture*), and "Nuclear Culture in Cold War America: Events and Impacts" (*Hiroshima and Peace*, forthcoming).

Contributors

Henry Jenkins is the Provost's Professor of Communication, Journalism, and Cinematic Arts at the University of Southern California. He is the author and/or editor of 12 books on various aspects of media and popular culture, including *Textual Poachers: Television Fans and Participatory Culture* (1992), *Hop on Pop: The Politics and Pleasures of Popular Culture* (2000), and *From Barbie to Mortal Kombat: Gender and Computer Games* (2003). His newest books include *Convergence Culture: Where Old and New Media Collide* (2008) and *Fans, Bloggers, and Gamers: Exploring Participatory Culture* (2006). He is currently coauthoring a book on "spreadable media" with Sam Ford and Joshua Green. He has written for *Technology Review*, *Computer Games*, *Salon*, and *The Huffington Post*.

Roy Kinnard is a freelance writer living in Chicago. His film-history books include *Fifty Years of Serial Thrills* (1983); *The American Films of Michael Curtiz* (1986); *Beasts and Behemoths* (1988); *Comics Come Alive* (1991); *Divine Images: A History of Jesus on Screen* (1992); *The Blue and the Gray on the Silver Screen: More Than 80 Years of Civil War Movies* (1996); *Science Fiction Serials: A Critical Filmography* (1998); *Horror in the Silent Film* (1999), *The Films of Fay Wray* (2008); and *The Flash Gordon Serials, 1936–1940* (2011). He has written numerous articles for magazines such as *Films in Review*, *Classic Images*, and *Starlog*.

Patrick Lucanio holds a doctorate in film and telecommunications from the University of Oregon where he once served as a visiting professor of film history. He has taught film studies at the college level for over 25 years and currently serves as an adjunct instructor in film studies at Lane Community College in Eugene, Oregon. His research interests include 1950s popular culture and science fiction films and television series. He is the author of *Them or Us: Archetypal Interpretations of 1950s Alien Invasion Films* (1988) and *With Fire and Sword: Italian Spectacles on American Screens 1958–1968* (1994). He is also the coauthor of *American Science Fiction Television Series of the 1950s* (1998); *Jack the Ripper: His Life and Crimes in Popular Entertainment* (2002); and *Smokin' Rockets: The Romance of Technology in Film, Radio & Television in the 1950s* (2008). He was an on-camera contributor to the 2008 independent documentary, *Monsters from the Id*.

Howard E. McCurdy is professor of Public Affairs in the Public Administration and Policy department at American University in Washington, DC, and an affiliate professor at the Evans School of Public Affairs at the University of Washington. An expert on space policy, he has published seven books on the US space program, including the recently completed second edition of his award-winning *Space and the American Imagination* (2011), and *Robots in Space*, coauthored with Roger Launius (2008). His volume *Faster, Better, Cheaper* (2003) provides a critical analysis of cost-cutting initiatives in NASA. An earlier study of NASA's organizational culture, *Inside NASA* (1994), won the 1994 Henry Adams prize for that year's best history on the federal government. Among his other publications are books on public administration, the space station decision, and the myth of presidential leadership.

Cynthia J. Miller is a cultural anthropologist, specializing in popular culture and visual media. She is Film Review Editor of *Film & History: An Interdisciplinary Journal of Film and Television Studies*, and her writing has appeared in a wide range of journals across the disciplines. She is a contributing author for numerous edited volumes, including the recent: *Télévision: le moment experimental* (2011); *Learning from Mickey, Donald and Walt: Essays on Disney's Edutainment Films* (2011); *Science Fiction Film, Television, and Adaptation: Across the Screens* (2011); and *Science Fiction across Media* (2012). Cynthia is the editor of *Too Bold for the Box Office: The Mockumentary, from Big Screen to Small* (2012) and is currently coediting two anthologies: *Undead in the West: Vampires, Zombies, Mummies and Ghosts on the Cinematic Frontier*, with A. Bowdoin Van Riper, and *Steaming into a Victorian Future: A Steampunk Anthology*, with Julie Anne Taddeo.

Lawrence R. Samuel is Founder of Culture Planning LLC, a consultancy to Fortune 500 companies. He holds a PhD in American Studies, and was a Smithsonian Institution Fellow. His previous books include *Pledging Allegiance: American Identity and the Bond Drive of World War II* (1997); *Brought to You By: Postwar Television Advertising and the American Dream* (2002); *Rich: The Rise and Fall of American Wealth Culture* (2009); *Freud on Madison Avenue: Motivation Research and Subliminal Advertising in America* (2010); *Future: A Recent History* (2010); *The End of the Innocence: The 1964–1965 New York World's Fair* (2010); and *Supernatural America: A Cultural History* (2011). His next book is *The American Dream: A Cultural History*.

J. P. Telotte is a professor of film and media studies and chair of the School of Literature, Communication, and Culture at Georgia Tech where he teaches courses in film genres, film technology, and animation. Coeditor of the journal *Post Script*, he has published widely on science fiction film and television. Among his books in this area are *Replications: A Robotic History of Science Fiction Film* (1995), *A Distant Technology: Science Fiction Film and the Machine Age* (1999), *The Science Fiction Film* (2001; Spanish translation, 2002), *The Essential Science Fiction Television Reader* (2008), and, with Gerald Duchovnay, *Science Fiction Film, Television, and Adaptation: Across the Screens* (2011).

John C. Tibbetts is associate professor of Film and Media Studies at the University of Kansas. His 18 published books include, most recently, *The Gothic Imagination* (2011), *Robert Schumann: A Chorus of Voices* (2010), *All My Loving?: The Films of Tony Palmer* (2009), and *Composers in the Movies* (2005). His articles on film, literature, painting, theater, and music have appeared in *Journal of the Fantastic in the Arts*, *Film Comment*, and *The Historical Journal of Film Radio and Television*, and *Literature/Film Quarterly*. He has worked as a broadcaster for National Public Radio, the Christian Science Monitor Radio Network, Voice of America, and CBS television. His 15-hour radio series, *The World of Robert Schumann*, has been heard worldwide on the WFMT broadcast network. In 2008, he received the Kansas Governor's "Arts in Education" Award. His hobbies include playing piano for silent films and illustrating his own books and articles.

A. Bowdoin Van Riper is a historian who specializes in depictions of science and technology in popular culture. His publications include *Science and Popular Culture: A Reference Guide* (2002); *Imagining Flight: Aviation and the Popular Culture* (2003); *Rockets and Missiles: The Life Story of a Technology* (2004; rpt. 2007); and *A*

Biographical Encyclopedia of Scientists and Inventors in American Film and Television (2011). He was guest editor, with Cynthia J. Miller, of a special two-issue themed volume (Spring/Fall 2010) of *Film & History* ("Images of Science and Technology in Film,") and the editor of *Learning From Mickey, Donald, and Walt: Essays on Disney's Edutainment Films* (2011). He is currently at work on an anthology coedited with Cynthia J. Miller: *Undead in the West: Vampires, Zombies, Mummies, and Ghosts on the Cinematic Frontier*.

S. Mark Young holds the George Bozanic and Holman G. Hurt Chair in Sports and Entertainment Business at the University of Southern California and is also Professor of Accounting, Management, and Communication. He has current interests in the psychology of celebrity and the sociology of collecting and futurism. His most recent book, *The Mirror Effect: How Celebrity Narcissism Is Seducing America* (coauthored with Dr. Drew Pinsky, 2009), was a *New York Times* best seller. His book *Blast Off! Rockets, Robots, Ray Guns and Rarities from the Golden Age of Space Toys* (with Steve Duin and Mike Richardson, 2001) is a social history of space toys. Mark has also written numerous articles for publications such as *Filmfax, The Old Toy Soldier, Antique Toy World*, and the *British Toy Soldier and Model Figure Magazine*. Mark comments regularly in the business and entertainment presses and has appeared on CNN's *Situation Room*, *The Howard Stern Show*, and *The View*.

Index

20th Century Fox, 22

ABC Network, 5, 39, 42, 93, 101, 134, 141, 150, 163, 165–168, 172, 175, 198
Above and Beyond (film, 1952), 197
Abrahams, Mort, 40
Acme Designs, 241
Across the Space Frontier (1952), 90, 107
Adams, Julie, 72
Adamski, George, 98, 112
Adventures of Superman (radio program), 134, 140
advertising, 4, 9, 41, 131, 133–146, 151–177, 194–195, 197, 200
   see also commercials, sponsors
Aerojet-General Corporation, 109
Agent X, 164
Air Scouts, 53
Air Wonder Stories (magazine), 36
aircraft
   B-17, 62, 235, 241
   Douglas D-558 Skyrocket, 195, 210n40
   Douglas X-F4D1, 202
"Airlords of Han, The" (1929), 2
Akio Ito, Alan, 239
Alexander, Richard, 22
Aley, Albert, 41
Alien Encounter, 88
   see also Disneyland (theme park)
aliens, xxi, 17, 42, 91
   invasion by, 98, 107, 150, 154, 158, 160, 164, 197, 234, 239, 243
All-American Conference to Combat Communism, 59
All-Story (magazine), 86
Alpha Centauri, 42, 68
Alyn, Kirk, 21

amateur filmmaking, 231–247
Amazing Stories (magazine), 2, 17, 86–87, 91–92
American Century, 62, 144, 193, 207n1, 210
American Culture, American Tastes (1999), 135
American dream, 135, 144, 148
American Interplanetary Society, 90
American Legion, 59
American Movie Classics network, 27
American Rocket Society, *see* American Interplanetary Society
American Weekly (magazine), 6
Ames, Dale, 171, 176n6
Anderson, Christopher, 197, 207n3, 209n21, 210
Anderson, Melody, 27
Angelucci, Orfeo, 98, 112
animation, xix, 44, 52, 94, 128n26, 238
Anthenia (fictitious planet), 74–75
archetypes, 54–63, 225–226
archives, 10–11, 34, 52, 175
Arden, Dale (*Flash Gordon* character), 18, 21–23, 25–26, 68, 70, 72, 79
Argosy (magazine), 86
"Armageddon 2419 AD" (1928), 2, 12–13
Armstrong, Neil, 4
Arnold, Kenneth, 150, 161
Around the Moon (1870), 3
art, 91, 158, 162, 231
Ash, Jerry, 23
Asimov, Isaac, 88, 96, 110
asteroids, 41–42
Astounding Science Fiction, see Astounding Stories
Astounding Stories, 86, 90
Astro (*Tom Corbett, Space Cadet* character), 38, 40–42, 121–122, 138

astronauts, xxi, 4, 43, 47, 70, 76, 80n10, 85, 95, 143, 222, 234
Atlasande (character), 184, 189
Atom Man vs. Superman (film serial,1950), 21
Atomic Age, 5–7, 11, 63, 134, 151, 200, 207n4, 211, 222, 233
Atoms for Peace program, 194, 197
audiences, xvi, xxi, 1, 3, 43, 54, 58, 62, 68, 89, 92–93, 107, 115–117, 139, 195
  family, 5–6, 36, 190
  juvenile, 4, 7, 18, 39, 67, 73, 80, 102–103, 213, 215–216, 225, 235
automaton, 244

B-12 (character), 120
Babylon 5 (television series, 1994–1999), 45
badges, 9, 104, 176n4
  see also membership, premiums, uniforms
Bakewell, William, 68
"Ballad of Davy Crockett", 172
Banner, John, 188
Bara, Nina, 165, 169
Barbour, Alan G., 240
Barcroft, Roy, 68
Barnes, Bucky (character), 53
Barrie, J. M., 33–36, 43–44, 46, 49, 51–52
Barry, James A., 196, 209nn16–17, 210
Baruch, Donald, 197, 199, 203–205, 209n24,nn31–32
Bassior, Jean-Noel, 9–10, 11n2, 12, 157, 161, 163–177, 249
Batman (character), 3, 18, 21, 28n11
Battlestar Galactica (television series, 2003–2009), 46
Baxter, Dr. Frank, 109
Beck, Jack, 40–41
Beebe, Ford, 24
Bell, Raymond, 199–205, 209nn38–39, 210
Bell System Science series (television specials, 1956–1964), 109, 127
Bennett, Steve, 242
"Beyond the Curtain of Space" (episode, *Rocky Jones*), 58, 80n5, 81n15, 125, 185, 187
Big Creek Missile Agency, 110
Big Picture, The (television series, 1951–1964), 198–199
Bikini Atoll, 204
Bilson, George, 198–200, 209n28nn33–34,
Blood Tong From Space (amateur film), 239–240

Bobby (*Rocky Jones* character), 53, 55–56, 58, 63, 68–69, 125–126, 183–184, 186–188
Boddy, William, 116, 124, 127n5, 128
Bonestell, Chesley, 91–94
box tops, 6, 168, 194
  see also premiums
Bradbury, Ray, 52, 88, 96–97, 110
Bradford, Brick (character), 101
Brain-O-Graph machine, 123
brainwashing (as plot device), 138
"Brick Moon, The ", 3
Bride of Frankenstein (film, 1935), 22, 25
Bridgeman, Bill, 109
Briskin, Fred, 205
Broderick, Mick, 10, 193–211, 249
Brought to You By: Postwar Television and the American Dream (2002), 135, 148, 252
Brown, Rod, *see* Rod Brown
Brunette, David, 237
Bryce, Ed, 41
Buck Rogers
  Buck Rogers (character), xviii, 3–4, 8, 68, 85, 91–93, 98
  Buck Rogers (film serial, 1939), 5, 25, 67, 92, 100
  Buck Rogers (television program, 1950–1951), 160n5
  Buck Rogers in the 25th Century (comic strip), 2, 18, 68
  Buck Rogers in the 25th Century (short film,1933), 3
Burns, Bob, 241–244, 247
Burroughs, Edgar Rice, 86
Buzz Corry (*Space Patrol* character), 5, 10, 48, 62, 92, 93, 95, 135, 141–143, 163–172, 213
  commercials featuring, 120–121, 133, 141–143
  use of television technology by, 118, 123–124
  toys connected with, 104, 152, 161n19
Buzz Lightyear (character), xix, xx
Byrns, Stu, 41

Cadet Happy (*Space Patrol* character), 118, 123–124, 141–142, 164–167, 169, 172–174, 182, 204, 240
Calkins, Dick, 2, 150

Camel News Caravan (television series, 1949–1956), 107
Cape Canaveral, xvii, 98, 106
capitalism, xviii, 138
Captain America (character), 53
Captain Blast (fictitious television program), xvi-xviii
Captain Galaxy (character), 106
Captain Midnight
   Captain Midnight (character), 3, 133–134, 143–146, 147n31, 193–210
   Captain Midnight (radio serial), 143
   Captain Midnight (television series), 10, 12, 135, 143–146, 181, 189, 191, 193–210
Captain Sacto (character), 231–234
Captain Space (character), 158–159
Captain Video
   Captain Video (character), xx, 1, 4, 5, 8, 9, 19, 40, 53, 54, 59–62, 64n17, 100–105, 107–109, 111, 127n1, 135, 147, 214
   Captain Video and His Video Rangers (television series), xiii–xvi, 4, 5, 8, 19, 39, 54, 64n19, 93, 95, 107–109, 111, 115, 117–120, 123, 134, 136–137, 150, 152–154, 164, 181, 191, 195, 216, 225
Captain Z-Ro
   Captain Z-Ro (character), 5, 7, 10, 53, 62–63, 213–227
   Captain Z-Ro (television series), xxiii, 12, 56, 60, 93, 95, 103, 213–227
Cardoza, Biffen "Biff" (*Rocky Jones* character), 182, 184, 187, 190
Carlisle, Carol (*Space Patrol* character), 123, 164, 165, 166
Carney, Art, xiii, xiv
cartoons, 44, 106, 141, 215, 233
Casetti, Francesco, 116, 126, 127n3, 128
Cass, Maurice, 68, 125, 183–184
catch-phrases, 39, 47, 119, 164
   see also "spaceman's luck"
CBS network, 5, 39–40, 42, 46, 139, 143, 150, 172, 194, 208n6, 210n49, 221, 247, 252
Champlin, Irene, 68
Chaney, Lon, 21, 22
Chaney, Warren, 172
Charon (fictitious planet), 74
Chesterton, G. K., 46, 51n9, 52

Chicago, 3, 19, 20, 21, 143, 170, 241
Chicago Tribune, 19
children's books, xv, 3, 9, 36–38, 46, 47, 104
   Big Little books, 3
   boys' books, 36
children's television programming, xv, xvi, xviii, xix, xxiii
   see also individual programs
China, 73, 185
Chris Conway, Rocket Ranger (character), 105
Churchill, Winston, 185
Cinema Insomnia, 245
Citizen Kane (film, 1941), 21
civic responsibility, 9, 133, 201, 206–207, 215, 223–226
civil defense, 207, 221, 250–251
Clarke, Arthur C., 81n19, 88, 90, 96n4, 106, 110
Clay People, 25
Cleolanta (character), 55, 74, 126, 184–185, 186, 188–189
Cliffhanger (1977), 240
cliffhanger ending, 195, 231, 242, 244, 247
Clifton, Marg, 166
Clutch Cargo (television series, 1959–60), 8, 68, 70, 72, 74
Coker, Rory, 169, 175
Cold War, xiv, xviii, 10, 75, 76, 138, 191, 194, 195, 223, 225
   children in, 1, 5, 7, 11, 75
   culture of, 39, 42, 60–61, 67, 73, 76, 100, 117, 134, 138, 188–190, 191, 194, 213, 217
   heroism in, xxiii, 1, 5, 7, 10, 54, 62, 63, 74, 181, 184, 195, 222
   masculinity, 7, 55, 58, 59–62
   politics of, 10, 73, 106, 117, 181, 185–188, 195–196, 200, 207, 222–225
   triumphalism, 55
Coleman, Don, 241, 244
collectibles, 41, 145–146, 149–162, 168–170, 194
   see also lunch boxes, premiums, rings, toys
Collier's (magazine), 5, 12n17, 13, 90, 93–94, 96n8, 107, 127n1, 128
Collins, Eileen, 70, 76
Columbia Pictures, 21–22, 27, 194, 199, 200, 202, 204, 205
combat film, 57, 64n8

comics
  comic books, 3, 18, 41, 53, 100, 104, 153, 163, 172, 175, 190
  comic strips, 2, 18, 22–23, 41, 68, 100, 150, 202, 215
  Golden Age of, xxi
  Silver Age of, xx–xxi
Commando Cody
Commando Cody (character), 1, 5, 11, 68, 70, 73, 135, 231, 234–235, 237, 238, 239–245, 247
Commando Cody: Sky Marshall of the Universe, 5, 11, 12n22, 67, 103, 136, 239–242
Radar Men from the Moon (film serial, 1952), 68, 70, 73, 231, 234–235, 240–244, 247
commercials, 11, 21, 133, 138–139, 140–144, 190–191, 208n6
  intertextual, 41, 119–121, 139–140, 167–168
  promoting consumerism, 4, 9, 133, 136
Communism, 59, 64n18, 65, 194, 196, 197
computers, xv, xx, xxii, 71, 88, 100, 108, 241–243
conformity, 54, 56–57, 187
Conquest of Space (film, 1955), 88, 98
Conquest of Space, The (1931), 90
Conquest of Space, The (1949), 42, 90–91
Conquest of the Moon, The (1953), 90, 107
consumerism, 4, 9, 119, 133, 136–139
  see also commercials
Contreras, Ruben, 237
Contreras, Victor, 237
Coogan, Richard, 100–101
Cooke, Darwyn, xxi, xxii
Corbett, Tom, *see* Tom Corbett
corporate leader, 54
Corry, Buzz, *see* Buzz Corry (*Space Patrol* character)
Corry, Kit (character), 120
costumes, 5, 6, 9, 23, 48, 51, 93, 102, 117, 144, 168, 181, 183, 191, 199, 239, 242, 243
  see also uniforms
Count Callisto (character), 101
Coville, Gary, 8, 11n2, 12n24, 13, 97–113, 118, 120, 125, 127n1, 128nn19–20, 134, 146n2, 148, 162, 249
cowboys, xviii, 6, 54–55, 57, 102, 110, 115, 140, 154, 158, 215, 233, 236
  see also six-shooter
Coy, Walter, 184
Crabbe, Buster, 3, 18–22, 24–26

Cracker Jack, 140
Crane, Richard, 55, 68, 92, 125, 182, 191
creativity, 4, 46, 142, 154, 157, 175, 234–247
Creature Features (television broadcast), 237–238, 242
Creature from the Black Lagoon, The (film, 1954), 72
Creepy (magazine), 236
Crites, Christopher, 246
Crockett, Davy (character), xx, 172, 191
Crossfield, Scott, 109
Crusade for Freedom, 61
cult films, 191, 237

Dale, Dr. Joan (character), 35, 41, 45, 72, 156
Dark Horse Entertainment, 153, 154, 155, 156, 159, 160, 162, 164
Darley, Dick, 167
Darling, Wendy, 33, 36, 44–46, 49n2
da Vinci, Leonardo (character), 56, 214, 218, 219, 220
Day the Earth Stood Still, The (film, 1951), 150
Days of Thrills and Adventure (1968), 240
DC Comics, xxi–xxii
De Laurentis, Dino, 27
Deadhousemusic.com, 246
Deadly Ray from Mars The (film, 1966), *see* Flash Gordon
Deane, Shirley, 25–26
Death by Television (film, 1935), 116
decoder ring, *see* rings
Deering, Col. Wilma (character), 25
DeMille, Cecil B., 241
democracy, 1, 5, 10, 60, 61, 138, 181–192, 223–224
Dennis the Menace (television series, 1959–1963), xvi–xviii
Desk Set, The (film, 1957), 71
Destination Moon (film, 1950), 33, 49, 91–92, 98, 150
dictators, 8, 23, 74, 138, 184–185
digital age, xvi, xxi, xxii, xiii235, 242
dime novels, 86
diplomacy, 10, 181–182, 188–190
Discatron, 119
Disney, Walt, 8, 43, 44, 49n3, 76, 81, 88, 90, 93–95, 96n3, 107, 127, 128n26, 172, 191, 221, 226n1, 227, 252, 253
Disneyland (television series), 76, 93–95, 107, 172, 221

Disneyland (theme park), 88, 95
Dixon, Wheeler Winston, 10, 50n33, 52, 134–135, 146n1, 148, 181–192, 250
Doolittle Committee, 196
Dr. Aristotle "Tut" Jones (character), 146, 204
Dr. Gangrene (character), 245
Dr. Hans Zarkov (*Flash Gordon* character), 18, 22–26, 68, 74, 81n22
Dr. Knockwurst (character), 70
Dr. Lina Van Horn (character), 71
Dr. Mary Hoganweiler (character), 70, 72
Dr. Pauli (character), 100
Dr. Richard Seaton (character), 2–4, 87
Dr. X (character), 242, 244
Dr. Zavier (character), 233
Dracula (film, 1931), 22, 237
Drake, Secretary, *see* Secretary Drake
Drew, Roland, 25
Duckweather, Ernest P. (character), 120
DuMont, Allen, 100
DuMont network, xiii, 39, 45, 99–102, 109, 111, 113n11, 118, 127n1, 137, 141, 146n9, 150
DuQuesne, Marc "Blackie" (character), 2

Earth Bureau of Investigation's Interplanetary Space Force, 68
Edison, Thomas, 101
education, 67, 107, 112n27–28, 226n17, 227
 edutainment, 126n26, 226n11, 227
 programming, 76–78, 81n24n28, 106, 214–220
 toys, 107
Edwards, Gawain, 90
Edwards Air Force Base, 98
Eerie (magazine), 236
Einstein, Albert, 101, 222, 226n14, 227
Eisenhower, Dwight D., 61, 73, 98, 106–107, 109, 185, 187, 194–197, 220
Ellis, John, 12, 116, 118–119, 121, 127n6n16, 128
Emperor Akio (character), 239
Engelhardt, Tom, 55, 65, 194, 207n4, 210
engineers, aspiration to career as, 8, 62, 70–72, 76–77, 79
 fictional, 68
 real world, 67, 221–222
 TV studio, xxiii, 4
Esquire Theater (Chicago), 21
Explorer I (satellite), 95

Famous Monsters of Filmland (magazine), 236
fans, xiv–xvi, xx, xxiii, 1, 3, 5–11, 17, 20, 21, 25–28, 47, 50n42, 53–54, 59, 70, 74, 79, 103–104, 165, 181, 214, 216–218, 222, 231–247
 clubs, xxiii, 6, 8, 99, 106
 girls, xvi, xxi, 8, 53, 67–80, 104, 121, 141, 145
 hobbyists, 244
fantastic technology, xxiii, 1, 2, 4, 63, 88, 98, 100, 119, 123, 213–215, 216, 223–224
 astrophone, 185
 atomic disintegrator rifle, 100
 cosmic ray vibrator, 4, 93, 100, 101, 125
 "death dust", 26
 electronic strait jacket, 100
 flying suit, 7, 11, 231, 234–235, 240–247
 jet packs, 1, 7
 opticon scillometer, 5, 93, 100, 119, 125, 153
 para-ray gun, 4, 50n44, 225
 positronic brain, 88
 radio scillograph, 153
 rocket suit, 234, 238, 241
 Solenoid Assenuator, 100
 see also ray guns, rockets
Father Knows Best (television series, 1954–1960), 69, 83, 187
Felnagle, Richard, 174–175
Feminine Mystique, The (1963), 78–79
Fifties: The Way We Really Were, The (1977), 136, 148
Firefly (television series, 2005), 46
First Men in the Moon, The (1901), 3
Flash, The (character), xxi
Flash Gordon
 Deadly Ray from Mars The (film, 1966), 27
 Flash Gordon (character), 1, 3, 4, 7, 17–18, 23, 25, 27, 53, 68, 72, 74, 92, 135, 149, 188
 Flash Gordon (comic strip), 2, 18, 22, 101
 Flash Gordon (film serials), 3, 5, 11, 18–28, 67, 92, 100
 Flash Gordon (television series), 8, 12n22, 19–21, 73–74, 77, 81n21, 95, 103, 136, 191
 Flash Gordon Conquers the Universe (film serial, 1940), 25–27
 Flash Gordon in the Caverns of Mongo (novel,1936), 3
 Flash Gordon Serials, The (2008), 13, 21, 28n6n9nn14–17, 29

Flash Gordon—*Continued*
  Flash Gordon's Strange Adventure Magazine, 3
  Flash Gordon's Trip to Mars (film serial, 1938), 19, 24–27
  Mars Attacks the World (film, 1938), 25, 27
  Perils from the Planet Mongo (film, 1966), 27
  Purple Death from Outer Space, The (film, 1966), 27
  Rocket Ship (film, 1936), 24, 27
  Spaceship to the Unknown (film, 1966), 27
Flight (television series, 1958–1959), 198
flight simulator, Kraft, 109
Flight to the Moon
  see Disneyland (theme park)
Flood, Beth, 173
flying saucers, 98, 150, 197–198
Folsom Lake, 239, 242
Forbidden Planet (film, 1956), 17
Forgotten Network: DuMont and the Birth of American Television, The (2004), 111n11, 113, 137, 146n9, 148
Fornax (fictitious planet), 184
Foster, Amy, 8, 67–82, 250
fourth dimension, 123
Frankenstein (film, 1931), 22, 25, 237
Frau im Mond [*By Rocket to the Moon*] (film, 1929), 88
Freedom Scroll, 61
Freeman, Fred, 93
Friedan, Betty, 78
Frigia, 26
From the Earth to the Moon (1865), 3, 89
Fry, Daniel, 98, 112
Fryer, Richard, 23

Gagarin, Yuri, 80n9, 109
Galaxy (spacecraft), 101
Galaxy Bureau of Investigation (fictitious organization), 68, 74, 77
Galaxy Patrol (fan club), 171
Gardner Advertising Company, 168, 170, 176n5, 177
Garland, Margaret, 41, 72
Garside, John, 245–246
GAS Laboratories (fictitious organization), 242
Geraghty, Lincoln, 117, 127n7, 128
Gernsback, Hugo, 2, 6, 12n20, 13, 36, 86
Gilbert, Joan, 68, 70
Gilbert, Willie, 41, 46

Gildea, Harry, 197–198, 209n25
Gleason, Jackie, xiii, xiv
Glenn, John, 4, 95, 160
Goddard, Robert H., 70, 89, 97–98, 106, 160n6
Golden Age of Science Fiction, 17, 28n1, 29, 67, 68, 192
Gotham City Municipal Swing Band, 236
Great Depression, 18, 21, 139, 150
"Greatest Generation", 57
Green Hornet (character), 18, 101
Green Lantern (character), xx–xxi
Greene, Joseph Lawrence, 38
Griffith Park Observatory, Los Angeles, 125
Grippo the Great (character), 140, 147n15
Grossman, Gary H., 96, 111n18, 200, 207n2, 210

Hamburger, Phillip, 104–106, 109, 111n19, 112
Hapgood, Happy (character), 25
Hardy Boys, the (characters), 49n18, 52, 53
Hartnagel, Ralph, Sr., 170, 176
Hawkins, Jim (character), 53
Hawkmen, 17, 23
Hawks, Howard, 197
Hayden Planetarium, New York, 92, 93, 96n7, 106
headquarters, 4, 10, 118, 119, 123, 125, 144, 193, 200
Hearst Newspapers, 18, 20
Hecht, Ted, 188
Hefti, Neal, 236
Heinlein, Robert A., xiv, 37–38, 41, 50n22n26n38, 52, 91, 110
helmets, space, xiii, xvi, xviii, 6, 9, 12n19, 41, 102, 104, 109, 150, 154, 157, 158, 233, 241, 243
  see also uniforms
Henderson, Jan, 247
Herbert, Don, 108
heroism, 1, 54, 57, 181, 225, 227
Hewitt, Virginia, 165, 166, 169, 172, 173
Hickam, Homer H., Jr., 110, 112
Hill, Robert F., 24
Hodge, Al, 59, 60, 100–102, 111n13, 112
Hoganweiler, Dr. Mary (character),
  see Dr. Mary Hoganweiler (character)
Hogling, Eric, 171
Holdren, Judd, 68

Holland, Steve, 19, 68
Hollywood, 18, 20, 27, 28, 57, 59, 91, 92, 125, 150, 175, 196, 197, 198, 244, 245
Hollywood Heritage Museum, 241
Honeymooners, The (television series, 1955–1956), xiii, xv, xxn1
Hoover, J. Edgar, 196
horror, 20, 236, 237, 245, 249, 250, 251
Hughes, Bill, 234–236, 238–240, 242–246
Hughes, Carol, 25, 26
Hughes, Karen, 234, 236
Hughes, Miko, 243–244
Hughes, Nikki, 237, 240, 243, 250
Hughes, Rae, 238–239
Hughes, Vic, 236, 237, 239, 246
Hunchback of Notre Dame, The (film, 1923), 22
Huston, Lou, 166

I Was a Communist for the FBI (film, 1951), 195
Indians Are Coming, The (film serial, 1930), 22
individualism, 54–57, 196
  see also masculinity, role models
innovation, xv, 56, 151, 161n10
  see also role models
Inside the Space Ships (1955), 98, 112
internet, 11, 20, 80n2, 104, 185, 241
Invaders from Mars (film, 1953), 98
Invisible Man, The (film, 1933), 22
Invisible Ray, The (film, 1936), 116
"Iron Curtain" speech, 185
Irvin, Ed, 237

Jacobs, Robert, 7, 53–65, 250
Jemison, Mae, 79
Jenkins, Henry, xiii–xxii, 39, 46, 50n31, 51n61, 52, 251
Jet (*Captain Z-Ro* character), 11, 53, 56, 59–60, 63, 213–224
Jet Jackson, Flying Commando (television series, 1958), 194
  see also Captain Midnight
John Carter of Mars (character), 86–87
Johnny Jupiter (television series, 1953–1954), 103, 120
Johns Hopkins Science Review (television series, 1948–1954), 107
Jolley, Norman, 166, 174
Jones, Dr. Aristotle "Tut" (character), *see* Dr. Aristotle "Tut" Jones (character)
Jones, Rocky, *see* Rocky Jones
Jones, Sam J., 27
Jordan, Hal (character), xxi
Juliandra (character), 184
juvenile delinquency, 101, 134, 194, 214

Kammen, Michael, 135, 146n5, 148
Kemmer, Ed, 48, 51n68, 92, 118, 127n9, 141, 165–169, 172–174
Kennedy, John F., 174
Kerr, Donald, 24
Kimball, Ward, 93–95, 96n10
kinescopes, 41, 45, 47, 167, 175
King, Wright, 120
King Features Syndicate, 19–20, 22
King Kong (film, 1933), 20–21, 27
King of the Rocketmen (film serial, 1949), 231
Kinnard, Roy, 7, 11n2, 13, 17–29, 251
Klep, Rolf, 93
Knight, Damon, 2, 12n6, 13
Kovacs, Bela, 169
Kramden, Ralph (character), xiii, xv–xvi

laboratories, 101, 107, 123, 193, 213, 216, 222, 235, 242
Laemmle, Carl, 22, 24
Lampman, Evelyn Sibley, 104
Lang, Fritz, 37, 87
Lassen, Chuck, 169, 170
Lasser, David, 90, 92
"Laughing Alien, The" (episode, *Space Patrol*), 123
Lauter, Harry, 184
Lavier, Tony, 143, 147n28
Lawson, Judd, 171
Lawson, Priscilla, 22, 26
Leahy, Ed, 106
Leave it to Beaver (television series, 1957–1963), 187
Lensman series, xxi
Lewis, Chuck, 166
Ley, Willy, 42, 43, 50n42, 50n44, 81n19, 89–91, 93–94, 106–107
Life (magazine), 6, 91, 97, 160, 165
Lion Men, 3, 22
live broadcasting, xvi, 4, 33, 40, 43–45, 49n3, 50n37, 51n46, 93, 138, 141, 165, 167–168, 181, 213, 214, 216
  see also television

Lone Ranger, The (character), 3, 18, 134, 164, 195
Los Angeles, 141, 165, 170, 173, 184, 191n1, 198, 200, 216, 247
Lost in Space (television series, 1965–1968), 46
loyalty
   exhibited by fans, 103, 145, 152, 194
   modeled by rocketman characters, 61, 62, 166, 172, 174, 184, 187, 213
Lt. Peep (character), xvi
Lucanio, Patrick, 8, 11n2, 12n24, 13, 97–113, 118, 120, 125, 127n1, 128nn19–20, 134, 146n2, 148, 162, 249
Lucas, George, 19, 20
Lucid, Shannon, 76–77, 80n10, 81n25
Lunar Fleet Base, 156, 157
lunch boxes, 9, 47, 149, 190
   see also collectibles, premiums
Lydecker, Theodore and Howard, 21, 242, 247
Lyden, Robert, 55, 56, 68, 183
Lydon, James "Jimmy", 182, 185, 190, 192

MacDonald, J. Fred, 111n22, 113, 195, 208nn10–12, 209nn19–20, 211
Mace, Crystal (character), 68–70, 72–73, 79
MacRae, Henry, 22, 24–26
mad scientists, xix, 77, 238
   see also science
Magic Wardrobe, The (store), 241
Major Astro (character), 106
Major Matt Mason (character), 160
makeup, 125, 183, 238, 244
Man and the Challenge (television series), 95, 109
Man and the Moon (short film, 1955), 94–95
Man From Planet X, The, 106
Man in Space (short film, 1955), xviii, 76, 94–96n10, 127
Mango-Radar, 119
Manning, Roger (*Tom Corbett, Space Cadet* character, 38–42, 121, 138
Mansfield, Sally, 58, 65, 125, 183
Mariner 4 (spacecraft), 85
marketing, see advertising, commercials, premiums, promotion, sponsors
Markim, Al, 38, 40–41, 46, 121, 138
Mars, xvi, xx, 3, 8, 24–26, 40, 61, 76, 85–90, 93, 97, 121, 142, 147n25, 156, 160, 246

Mars and Beyond (short film, 1957), 8, 95
Mars Attacks the World (film, 1938), see Flash Gordon
Mars Project, The (1953), 90, 96
Martian Chronicles, The (1950), 88
Martian Manhunter (comic), xxi
Martin, Mary, 33, 39, 44, 46, 51n46
Marubbio, M. Elise, 55
masculinity, xiv, xv, 53–65, 182
   blue-collar, 62
   Cold War, 7, 53, 59–63
   Frontier, 54–55
   see also archetypes, role models
Mason, Chris, 241
Massen, Osa, 71
Mauldin, Bill, 58
Max Neptune and the Menacing Squid, 246
Mayer, Ken, 124, 165–166, 168–169
McCloud, Scott, 68–69, 74, 234
McCurdy, Howard, 8, 13, 81n19, 82, 85–96, 106, 112n26, 113, 251
McKirgan, Jack, 170, 174
McLaughlin, Robert B., 98, 111n3, 113
membership cards, kits, and benefits, 103–104, 151–153, 155–156, 167, 176n4, 187, 194
   see also badges, pledges, premiums
Men Into Space (television series, 1959–1960), 46, 95, 109, 234
mentors and mentoring, xxi, 5, 7, 55, 58–59, 184, 222–223, 225
   see also role models
Menzies, William Cameron, 98
merchandizing, see premiums, toys, uniforms
Mercury Men, xx
Meredith, Charles, 68, 125, 185
Merlin, Jan, 38, 40–41, 46–47, 121, 138
Metropolis (1927), 116
MGM (Metro-Goldywn-Mayer), 21–22, 173, 197
Michals, Don, 246
Middleton, Charles, 22, 24–25
military-industrial complex, 10, 193–211
Miller, Cynthia J., 1–13, 213–227, 251–252
Miller, Douglas T., 136, 146n6, 148
Ming the Merciless, 18, 22–27, 53, 188
missiles, 76, 90, 98, 110, 150, 181, 199, 252
   Nike guided missile, 199–200, 205
   V-2 rocket, 50n36, 117, 150

Mission to Mars, see Disneyland (theme park)
Mister X, xx
Mongo (fictitious planet), 3, 23, 26–27
Moore, Constance, 25
morality tales, 10, 54, 187
    see also role models
Moran, Jackie, 25
Morse, Hollingsworth, 182, 190
Morse, Ray, 42
Moser, William "Mike", 166
Motter, Dean, xx, xxiin6
Mr. Lobo (character), 237, 245–246
Mr. Moon (character), 106, 112n24, 113
Mr. Wizard, see *Watch Mister Wizard*
Mueller, Maj. Johanna, 201, 205, 210n50
music, 22, 27, 123, 151, 188, 243, 246–247
    muzak, 123
Music Corporation of America, 190
Mutual Radio Network, 194
Mysteries in Space (comic book), xxi

Name the Planet Contest, 9, 170–171
narration, 100, 121, 221
    voiceover, 11n1, 40, 94, 213, 233
Nash, Joseph, 68
National Aeronautics and Space Administration (NASA), 70, 76–82, 85, 94, 109–110, 160, 208n8, 222, 250–251
National Association for Better Radio and Television, 194
National Conference on Citizenship, 59
National Defense Education Act, 78
National Film Registry, 18, 28
National Science Fair, 76
national security state, 195
    see also military-industrial complex
NBC Network, 5, 39, 46, 51n46n62, 122, 141, 194, 198, 221
Negato (fictitious planet), 188
Nelson, Joyce, 197, 209n22, 211
networks, see ABC, CBS, DuMont, NBC, Turner Classic Movies, USA
Neverland, 34, 36, 38, 44–45, 47, 49nn15–16, 52
New Yorker (magazine), 39, 49n11, 52, 104, 112
newspaper, 3, 7, 18, 22, 25, 34, 45, 86
Nichols, Nichelle, 78–79, 82

Nimoy, Leonard, 241
nitron, 24
Norton, Ed, xiii, xvi
nostalgia, xv, xx, 20–21, 34, 163, 244
    homage, 6, 152, 242, 245, 250
Nowak, Marion, 136, 148
Nowlan, Philip Francis, 2, 12n8, 13
nuclear power, 235
nuclear weapons/war, 10, 38, 73–74, 76, 90, 134, 150, 186, 194–197, 203–205, 206, 209n15, 210n48, 211, 222
Nurse Moan-eek (character), 245

oaths, see pledges
Oberth, Hermann, 87
Off on a Comet (1877), 86
Office of Space Affairs (fictitious organization), 68, 125, 185
Ophiuchus (fictitious planet), 55, 84–85, 87–89
Orbit Jet (spacecraft), 10, 55, 58, 69, 125, 126, 186
ornithopter, 56
Osborn, Lyn, 118, 165, 167, 169, 172–174
Our Gang (short-film series, 1922–1944), 182
Our Mister Sun (television program), xviii
outer space, conceptions of, 3, 41, 86–88, 91–95, 115, 121–122, 126, 150, 160, 162

Pal, George, 38
Paramount (film studio), 21, 22, 44
Parker, Fess, 172
Parks, Adm. Lewis, 202
Parsons, Patsy, 55, 74, 126, 184
patriotism, 59, 64n15, 65, 67
    modeled by historical figures, 218, 224
    promoted by rocketman series, 54, 72, 73, 138, 193, 195, 199
Patterson, Neva, 71
Pendray, G. Edward, 90
Pennington Bread, 157
Pentagon, 10, 107, 193–194, 197–205, 207
Perils from the Planet Mongo (film, 1966), see Flash Gordon
personal appearances, 43, 217
Peter Pan, xiv, 7, 33–52
Phantom, The (character), 18
Phantom Empire, The (film serial, 1935), 116

Pierce, James, 22
pins/pinbacks, 152–154, 190, 253
  see also collectibles, premiums, membership
Pippin, Ed, xxiii, 152, 162
Planet Stories (magazine), 86
pledges, xiii, xv, 5, 38, 60, 64, 103, 105, 146, 152, 195, 208, 225
  see also membership
Poe, Edgar Allan, 86
Polaris (spacecraft), 35, 40–42, 45, 48, 50, 68, 117, 121–122, 139, 150, 157
Posito (fictitious planet), 188
premiums, 103, 158, 161n13, 176
  box-tops exchanged for, 137, 139, 141–142, 145, 151, 153, 168
  space coins as, 170, 172
  use of, in shows, 141, 154
  see also badges, collectibles, lunch boxes, pins/pinbacks, toys
preparedness, 10, 200–201, 206–207
Prince Baccarratti (character), 142, 169, 170, 175
Prince Barin (character), 22–23, 25–26
Princess Aura (character), 22–23, 25–26
production
  cinematography, 21
  of film serials, 21, 240
  green screen, 243, 245
  models, 37, 45, 94, 110, 123, 125, 139, 195, 209n4, 236, 238–239, 247
  quality of feature films, 27, 28
  quality of rocketman television series, 4, 5, 7, 11, 93, 102, 123, 167–168, 182
  sound, reliance on, 121
Professor Cardos (character), 186
Professor Checkerboard (character), 143, 147n30
Professor Mayberry (character), 184
Professor Newton (character), 68, 125, 126, 128n21, 183–184
Project-O-Scope, 155
promotion, 6, 9, 104, 133, 140–142, 151, 158
  contests, 109–110, 143, 170
  cross-promotion, 142–143, 195
  relationship marketing, 143, 145–146
  see also commercials, sponsors
propaganda, 195
props, 6, 8, 119, 137, 237, 241–242, 244

premiums used as, 141
pulp magazines, xiv, xx-xxi, 1–3, 11n3, 12, 17, 18, 36, 53, 86–88, 90–92, 95, 231
Purple Death from Outer Space, The (film, 1966), see Flash Gordon
"Pursuit of the Deep Space Projectile, The" (episode, *Tom Corbett*), 121–122

Queen (band), 27
Queen Azura (character), 24–25
Queen Fria (character), 26

R is for Rocket (1962), 97
Radar Men from the Moon (film serial, 1952), *see* Commando Cody
radio, 3, 18, 38, 48, 91–92, 103, 105, 135–136, 140, 143, 145, 151, 166, 168, 176n3, 177, 185, 193–194, 200, 202, 208n6, 221
  on screen, 53, 200
Ralston Rocket, 9, 104, 109, 143, 157, 171
Ranger Messages
  see Video Ranger Messages
Ratings, 19–20, 137, 143, 151, 172
Ray, Vena (*Rocky Jones* character), 58, 68–70, 72, 79, 125, 183, 187–188
ray guns, 1, 3, 6, 9–10, 17, 39, 47, 102, 104, 116, 151, 154, 157–158, 160n1, 162–163, 233
Raymond, Alex, xiv, 2, 17–18, 21–28
reception, critical, 4, 102, 195, 200
Red Nightmare (film, 1962), xviii, xxiin5
Reed, Roland, 124, 128n19, 182, 190–191
replicas, 11, 104, 109, 139, 176, 241, 244, 247
Republic Pictures, 21, 27, 188, 208n6, 241–247
Retik, Ruler of the Moon (character), 68, 73, 243
retrofuturism, 22
Rex Mars (character), 159, 161
Richards, Ted, 68
Riders to the Stars (film, 1954), 98
Rigg, John, 244
Rin Tin Tin (television series, 1954–1959), 174
rings
  decoder rings, 145
  Hydrogen Ray Gun Ring, 155, 169
  picture rings, 61, 137, 140, 147n14
  as premiums, 61, 137, 140, 145, 147n10, 152–153, 155

see also collectibles, membership, premiums
RKO, 21, 197
Robertson, Cliff, 46
Robertson, Maj. Robbie (*Space Patrol* character), 123, 164–166
Robin, the Boy Wonder (character), 53
Robinson, Ann, 184
robots, 88, 96, 120, 216, 233, 237, 244–245
Rock Men, 26
Rocket Boys (1998), 110, 112
rocket pack, 235, 241
Rocket Ship (1936), *see* Flash Gordon
Rocket Ship Galileo (1947), 38, 50n3, 91
rocket sled, 109
Rocket to the Moon, *see* Disneyland (theme park)
rocketmen, *see* Buck Rogers, Buzz Corry, Captain Midnight, Captain Video, Captain Z-Ro, Commando Cody, Flash Gordon, Rocky Jones, Rod Brown, Tom Corbett
Rocketpage, The (website), 241, 243, 245
rockets, 1, 3, 7–8, 11n2, 12n24, 13, 39–40, 47, 70, 74–75, 79, 89–90, 98, 106, 113, 117, 121, 128n20, 134, 146n2, 148, 150, 158, 160n1n6, 162, 176, 222, 234
Rockets (1944), 42
Rocketship 7 (local television program), 106
Rocketship X-M (film, 1950), 33, 71
Rockwell, Carey, 47
Rocky Jones
    Rocky Jones (character), 1, 5, 7, 10, 53–54, 58, 62–63, 68–69, 72, 74, 92, 105, 135–136, 181–192, 213, 225
    Rocky Jones, Space Ranger (television series, 1954), 8–10, 12n22, 19, 39, 55–56, 58, 63–64, 67, 70, 73–74, 80nn5–6, 81nn15–16, 95, 103, 105, 117, 124–126, 152, 181–192, 195, 234
Rod Brown
    Rod Brown (character), 105, 135
    Rod Brown of the Rocket Rangers (television series, 1953–1954), 46, 103, 117
Rogers, Jean, 21–22, 24
role models, 5, 7–8, 36, 54, 59, 63, 70, 72, 79, 103, 106, 138, 141, 225
    "company man," valorization of, 62
    see also archetypes, masculinity, morality tales
Roy Rogers, 158, 174
"Runaway Rocket, The" (episode, *Tom Corbett*), 121, 141
Rusty's Space Ship (1957), 104

Sacramento, CA, 231–233, 238, 245
Sands of Iwo Jima, The (film, 1949), 195
Sarno, Joe, 47, 147n13, 175
Saturday Afternoon at the Movies (1986), 240
Sawyer, Tom, 53
Saylor, Steve, 243
Schwartz, Julius, xxi
science, xiv, xviii, 1, 4, 42, 70, 72, 87, 99, 100, 115–116, 149, 160, 214
    American dominance of, 67, 76–78, 117
    American fascination with, 106–108, 116–117, 125–126, 134, 146, 169, 221, 225
    "Baccarratti and Black Magic" (episode, *Space Patrol*), 142
    "bad", 89
    in education, 8, 67, 76–78, 93–95, 106–109
    in science fiction television, 18, 33, 38, 39, 42, 77, 88–99, 100–102, 107, 119, 184, 214, 222
    women in, 70–72, 76–77
Science Fiction Theater (television series, 1957–1959), 39, 50, 95
scientists, xviii, 8, 47, 67, 77, 91, 221
    as heroes, 10, 63, 68, 87, 107, 213, 215
    real-world, 47, 62, 70, 77–79, 93–94, 106, 150, 165, 218, 222
    as sidekicks, 18, 23, 38, 68, 70–72, 125, 146, 149, 158, 166, 204
    as technical advisors, 42, 87
    as villains, xiv, 2, 168, 233, 238, 242
    see also mad scientists
Sconce, Jeffrey, 121, 127n16, 128
Scott, Montgomery "Scotty" (character), 104n2
Screen Gems Studios, 143, 194, 198–200, 202, 204, 205, 208n6, 209n27
scriptwriting, 50n44, 78, 101, 102, 166, 174, 243, 250, 252
    Pentagon involvement with, 203, 204, 209n14
    product placement and, 139, 142

scriptwriting—*Continued*
  quality of, 20, 21, 164, 174
  speed of, 166, 190
Seaton, Dr. Richard (character),
  see Dr. Richard Seaton (character)
Secret Squadron, the
  fan club, 135, 144–146, 147n32n35, 194–195, 200–201, 206
  fictitious organization, 10, 195, 207
Secretary Drake, 58, 68–69, 125, 128n21, 185, 187
"Secrets of Eternal Youth" (episode, *Space Patrol*), 118
Secrets of the Saucers (1955), 98, 112
Serling, Rod, xviii
sets/soundstages, 4, 22, 23, 42, 93, 117–118, 123, 127n9, 137, 176, 181, 182, 235, 237, 243
Shadow, The (character), 3, 18
Shannon, Frank, 22, 24, 26
Sharkmen, 17, 23
Sharpe, Dave, 245
Shatner, William, 70, 172
Sheffield, Reginald, 184
Shepard, Alan, 4, 80, 95, 109
Sheriff Woody (character), xix–xx
Shocking Tales (short-film series), 277–278
sidekicks, 53–65
  see also Bobby, Cadet Happy, Jet, Winky
"sight machine", 126
silent films, 17, 22, 23, 88, 251, 252
Silver Dart (aircraft), 135, 194, 195, 201, 209n40
"Silver Needle in the Sky" (episode, *Rocky Jones*), 55, 64n6, 188
Sinestro (character), xxi
Sirius (fictitious planet), 121–122
six-shooter, 3, 236
Sky Captain and the World of Tomorrow, xx
sky marshals, 135
Skylark of Space, The (1928), 2, 11n5, 13, 87
Smith, E. E. "Doc", xiv, xxi, 2, 87
Smokin' Rockets (2002), 11, 12n24, 13, 113, 128n20, 146n2, 162, 249, 251
social networking, 99, 104, 106, 185
Solar Alliance (fictitious organization), 40–42
Solar Guard (fan website), xxiii, 6, 12n23, 152
Solar Guard (fictitious organization), 40, 62, 138

S.O.S.—Tidal Wave (film, 1939), 116
Soule, Olan, 146, 204
Soviet Union, 59, 73, 76–78, 95, 106, 134, 185, 188, 196
Space Academy, xiii, 38, 40, 41, 47, 51n68, 68, 72, 77, 139
Space Age, xiv, 1, 61, 74, 103, 107, 143, 216
Space Angel (television series, 1962–1964), 8, 68–69, 73, 74–75, 80n2, 234
Space Cadet (1948), 38, 50n26, 52
Space Commander 8 (character), 106
space opera, xiii, xvi, xix, xx, xxi, 2, 3, 8, 12n7, 13, 17, 35, 50n33, 87, 101, 115, 117, 120, 123–126, 150, 151, 153, 155, 157, 169, 171, 172, 175, 176
Space Patrol (television series, 1950–1955), 5, 6, 9, 11n2, 12nn21–24, 13, 39, 48, 95, 103–104, 109, 117, 118, 121, 123, 127n9, 134, 136, 141–144, 163–177, 234, 241, 249
  toys associated with, 149, 150, 152, 154, 156, 157–159
space race, xx, 8, 40, 68, 95, 103, 233
Space Ranger Code (*Rocky Jones*), 152
space travel, xviii, 6, 8, 9, 78–80, 150, 160
  in science fiction, 3, 38, 39, 43, 67–75, 86–88
  popular attitudes toward, 75–78, 85–86, 89–95, 99, 110–111, 133–134, 151, 181
  seen as "kid stuff", xviii, 8, 85, 98, 106–107
Spaceballs (film, 1987), 149
"spaceman's luck", 6
Space-O-Phone, 155
spaceport, 41, 117
  play sets, 154, 158–159, 161
Spaceship to the Unknown (film, 1966), 27
Spaceship to the Unknown (film, 1966), see Flash Gordon
spaceships, see rockets
special effects, 1, 20, 21, 42, 91, 93, 100, 166, 167, 168, 181, 242, 247
  see also technology as spectacle
Special Remote Carrier, 115, 119, 126
Spigel, Lynn, xv, xxii
Spinner (character), 68, 70
sponsors, 4, 5, 46, 104, 117, 121, 124, 135–137, 151, 161n3, 167–168, 201, 207
  Bovaro, 188
  Butter-Nutt Bread, 157

cereals, 41, 47, 101, 103–104, 133, 136, 139–143, 149, 151, 153, 157, 167–168, 170, 172
Chex, 9, 121, 141–143, 147nn28–29, 152, 168
Clanky Chocolate Flavor Syrup, 233
Cocomalt, 157
Corn Flakes, 139, 147
Kellogg's, 9, 41, 45, 47, 133, 139–143, 151, 153, 157
Kix, 194, 201, 202, 208n6
Kraft, 41, 46, 109, 112, 138, 141
M&M candies, 120
Mars candy bars, 233
Milky Way candy bars, 233
Nestle, 6, 9, 121, 138, 176
Ovaltine, 143–147, 194, 200–202, 206, 208
Pep, 6, 139–141, 147nn14–18, 153, 157
Post Cereals, 101, 143, 153, 161n15
PowerHouse candy, 9, 119, 137, 153
Purity Bread, 153
Raisin Bran, 139, 153, 161n15
Ralston Purina Company, 104, 121, 141–143, 147nn28–30, 151–153, 156–157, 168, 170
Red Goose Shoes, 41, 121, 141
Silver Cup Bread, 161
Sugar Crisp, 119
Sugar-Frosted Jets, 233
Thom McAn, 141
WeatherBird shoes, 157, 170
Wheaties, 140
Sputnik I (satellite), 7, 77, 78, 81n19, 95, 106–107, 109, 110, 160
Stapp, John Paul, 109
Star Trek (television series, 1966–1969), xix, 48, 134, 139, 172, 182
characters, 48, 68, 78, 80n2, 82
Star Wars (film, 1977), xx, 17, 20, 134, 149
Starduster (spaceship), 70
Stargate SG-1 (television series, 1997–2007), 70
Startling Stories (magazine), 86
Steffens, Roy, 56, 63, 214, 215, 217, 226
Stephani, Frederick "Fritz", 21, 23
Stevenson, Robert Louis, 46, 53
Strange Adventures (comic book), xxi
Streamline Moderne, 154, 157
Strong, Capt. Steve, 41, 42, 45
Suid, Lawrence H., 197, 209n23, 211

"Sulky Sue", 144
Sullivan, Ed, 102
Super 8 camera, 237–238
Super Science Stories (magazine), 88
Superman (character), 3, 18, 21, 28n11, 134, 140, 199, 202, 235
surveillance, 119, 126–127, 195, 206
Swanson, Elliott, 169, 176
Swift, Tom, 36, 38, 53, 100
Sydow, Max Von, 27
syndication, 5, 93, 141, 144, 190, 194, 198, 213, 216–217, 234

Tales of Tomorrow (television series, 1951–1953), 39, 50n32, 52
Target Nevada (short film, 1951), 205, 210n54
Tarzan of the Apes (1912), 3, 22, 86
Taurus (character), 68, 80n2
Taylor, Ray, 22
technology, 69, 70, 91, 107, 127, 166, 213, 238, 242
  American dominance of, 67, 75–78, 107, 117, 146, 195
  American fascination with, 7, 72, 77, 99, 108, 116, 126, 150
  real-world advances in, 93, 95–98, 134, 150
  spectacle, technology as, 17, 116–118, 121–123, 197, 236, 251
  television as, xv, xvi, 4, 8–9, 79, 115, 124–125, 197
  see also fantastic technology
telescopes, xvii, 93, 109, 128, 158
television, 1, 7, 167, 182, 196
  advertising on, 21, 104, 120, 133–148, 150–152
  audience for, xvi, 93–95, 115–116, 121–123, 134, 193
  cultural impact of, 34, 75–76, 85, 95, 101, 102–103, 116–117, 120, 223, 224
  as educational tool, xviii, 107–109, 194–201, 214–215, 221, 227
  electronic hearth, 116
  historical footage, use of, 117
  locally produced TV programs, 103, 105–106, 215–216, 233
  as medium, 1, 106, 119, 121, 136, 167, 196–197
  programming, xiv, xix–xxi, 4, 17, 18, 20, 27, 38–40, 44, 67–68, 70, 73, 76, 86, 91–93, 94–95, 115, 125, 133–135, 182, 191, 195–202, 215, 234–236

television—*Continued*
  reruns, 11, 190
  stations: KCRA-TV, 232–233; KECA-TV, 165; KOIN-TV, 106; KRON-TV, xxiii, 4, 213–215; KTTV-TV, 216; WGN-TV, 19; WKBW-TV, 106
  stock footage, use of, 21, 193, 198–199, 201, 204–205, 240, 245
  as technological spectacle, xv–xvi, xxi, 4, 17, 35, 79, 85, 99, 118–120, 125–127, 215
  see also kinescopes, live broadcasting
Teller, Edward, 62, 63, 106, 222
Telotte, J. P., 8–9, 11n2, 15, 50n27n33, 52, 115–129, 146n1, 148, 252
Tereshkova, Valentina, 70
Terminal City (comic book), xx
"Terminal Dive" (episode, *Thirty Second Doom*), 243
Terra IV (spaceship), 104, 118, 170
Terra IV Rocket Club House, *see* Ralston Rocket
test pilots, xxi, 109, 143, 147, 226n16
Thing from Another World, The (film, 1951), 50, 150, 197
Thirty Second Doom (amateur film serial), 242–247
Thistle, T. J. (*Tom Corbett, Space Cadet* character), 42, 121–122
Thomas, Dave, 106
Thomas, Frankie, Jr., 39, 40, 45, 48, 51, 68, 92, 121, 138, 140, 141
A Thousand and One Delights (1971), 240
Thrill of It All, The (1971), 240
Thrilling Wonder Stories (magazine), 86
Thun, king of the Lion Men, 22
Tibbetts, John C., 7, 33–52, 252
Tichi, Cecelia, 116
Tiger Men, 3
time travel, 88, 116, 222–226
Titan (moon of Saturn), xviii, 91
Tom Corbett
  Tom Corbett (character), 1, 3, 10, 53, 54, 62, 68, 72, 74, 92, 109, 121, 122, 133, 213
    commercials featuring, 138–141, 144
    as a Peter Pan figure, 33–52
  toys connected with, 150, 157–159
Tom Corbett (radio serial) (1952), 103
Tom Corbett, Space Cadet (TV series), 1, 5, 7, 9, 10, 12n22, 33–52, 67, 72, 73, 74, 77, 91, 93, 95, 103, 107, 117, 118, 120, 121–123, 133–147, 149–152, 164, 195, 216
Tom Corbett book series (1952–56), 42
Tom Mix (radio serial), 168, 174n4
Tonga (*Space Patrol* character), 123, 165, 166, 167
Tower Theater, 236
Towne, Aline, 68
toy manufacturers
  Archer Toy Company, 151, 161
  Aurora Toy Company, 236
  Bulova Watch Company, 151
  Daisy Manufacturing, 150, 157
  Ideal Toy Company, 161n17
  Lido Toy Company, 154
  Marx, Louis (Marx toys), 156–157, 159, 161nn17–19, 162, 233
  Premier Toy Company, 151
Toy Story (film, 1995), xix–xx
toys, xx, 6, 9, 41, 107, 117, 139, 142, 149–162, 163, 169, 172, 175, 176n4, 236
  autosonic rifle, 157
  Cosmic Smoke Gun, 142, 147n21, 155
  Great Garloo, The, 233
  "Jet Glow belt", 155
  Magic Space Picture, 142
  Mr. Machine, 233
  Mysto-Coder Brass Decoder, 153
  periscopes, 154, 176
  plastics used in manufacture of, 152
  playsets, 153–154, 157–159, 161n4, 233
  Ray-O-Vac, 155–156
  Rite-O-Lite Gun, 153
  Robot Commando, 233
  rocket flashlight, 155–156
  Rocket Pistol, 150
  space binoculars, 142, 147n22n26, 154–155
  Space Patrol Atomic Flashlite, 157
  Viewmaster, 157
  walkie-talkies, 104, 153, 154
  see also premiums
Trachinger, Bob, 175
trading cards, 154, 156
Tree People, 25

Trisonic Compensator, 125
True (magazine), 98
Trumbull, Roy, xxiii, 4, 214, 215
Tufeld, Dick, 167
Turner Classic Movies network, 27
"Tut specials", 146
TV Forecast (magazine), 4, 12
TV Guide (magazine), 174, 236
Twilight Zone, The (television series, 1959–1964), xviii, 95

UFOs, 112n30, 113, 150
Uhura, Lt, *see* Nichols, Nichelle
Ultraplanetary Transmitter, 119
Underwood, Larry, 245
uniforms, 5–6, 9, 117, 145, 168–169
    homemade, 102, 142
    insignia, 145, 157
    see also badges, helmets
United Nations, 38, 74, 184
United Planets (fictitious organization), 62, 93, 121, 152, 166, 184
United States Government, Atomic Energy Commission, 194, 204, 210n54
    CIA, 75, 196, 210
    Department of Defense, 198, 202, 205, 209n24
    Department of the Navy, 203
    FBI, 196
    House Un-American Activities Committee, 186, 196
    National Security Council, 196
    US Air Force, 109, 198, 205, 210
    US Army, 90, 98, 109
    US Navy, 194, 221
    US Senate, 194
United Worlds of the Solar System (fictitious organization), 68, 182, 184, 187–189
Universal Pictures, 18–27, 28n12, 29, 190, 236–237
Up Front (1945), 57–58, 64n9, 65
Uricchio, William, xvi, xxii
USA Network, 171

values, American, 5, 10, 52n62, 54, 59, 61–62, 73, 134, 138, 144, 182, 196, 213, 223–225
    see also morality tales, role models
Van Horn, Dr. Lina *see* Dr. Lina Van Horn (character)
Van Riper, A. Bowdoin, 1–12, 213–227, 252–253
Variety, 20, 123, 127n13n17, 128n18, 129, 191–192
Venera 9 (spacecraft), 85
Verein für Raumschiffahrt [Society for Spaceflight], 87
Verne, Jules, 3, 70, 86, 89, 101, 110, 160n6
Victory at Sea (television series 1952–1953), 198, 221, 226n10, 227
"victory culture", 65, 208n4, 210
video monitor, 115, 118–119, 122–123, 125, 128
Video Ranger, The (*Captain Video* character), 53, 60–62, 100–102, 115
Video Ranger Headquarters, 118–119
Video Ranger Messages, 60–61
villains, 2, 18, 164, 172, 189, 236, 244
    see also Agent X, Cleolanta, Ming the Merciless, Pinto Vortando
violence, on screen, 42, 101, 189, 194
Virilio, Paul, 126, 128n22, 129
Vizeograph, 125–126, 128
von Braun, Wernher, 8, 43, 50n43, 62–63, 70, 81n19, 90, 93–96, 106–107, 150, 222
von Stroheim, Erich, 22
von Sydow, Max, 27
Vortando, Pinto, 188–189

Wade, Buddy, 25
Walker, Ricky, 104, 171
Walker, Sydney, 56, 219
Wallace, George, 68, 241, 243–244, 248
Walt Disney Studios, *see* Disney, Walt
Wannamaker's Department Store, 99, 102
War of the Worlds (1897), 97, 184
Warner Bros., 22
Watch Mister Wizard (television series, 1951–1965), xviii, 18, 76, 108–109
Waxman, Franz, 25
weapons, 74, 150, 169, 191, 233
    non-lethal, 100–102, 126
    nuclear, 38, 76, 196, 197, 200, 250
    smoke bomb, 238
    toy, 164, 236
    see also ray guns
Webb, Richard, 144, 195, 200

Weinstein, David, 111n11, 113, 127n11, 129, 137, 146n9, 148
Weinstock, Jack, 46
Welch, Col. Patrick, 199, 209n29, 209n37
Wells, H. G., 3, 70, 86, 97, 98, 160n6
Werewolf of London, The (film, 1935), 22
Westerns, xiii, xix, xx, 2, 3, 17, 22, 55, 86, 89, 156, 195, 233, 246, 247
    B-Westerns, 115, 233, 246
    Golden Age of the Cowboy, 54
When Worlds Collide (film, 1951), 151
White Sands Incident, The (1954), 112
White Sands Proving Ground, 98, 106
Wilkins, Bob, 236–237, 242
Williams, Wade, xxiii, 34, 35, 40, 43, 47, 48, 51, 71, 110, 122, 140
Williamson, Al, 25
Willie and Joe (characters), 58
Wilson, Mr. (character), xvi–xviii
Winky (*Rocky Jones* character), 53, 58, 59, 63, 68, 72, 124, 125, 128, 182–184, 186–187
Wolf Man, The (film, 1941), 237

Wolfe, Tom, xxi–xxii, 226n16, 227
Woman's Day (magazine), 6, 12, 102
women, xiv, xvi, xx, 8, 18, 34, 53, 58, 67–82, 104, 108, 111n17, 112–113, 121, 141, 145, 182–183, 186, 218, 224, 250
World War II, 4, 27, 39, 54, 57–59, 62–63, 70–74, 90, 117, 149–150, 166, 168, 175, 194–196, 221, 224, 226
Wornom, Lt. Cdr. Joe, 202, 204, 205, 210nn42–43,
Wylie, Linda, 245

Yeager, Chuck, xxi, 109, 226n16
Young, S. Mark, 9, 149–162, 253
YouTube, 11, 147, 185, 245

Zarkov, Dr. Hans (*Flash Gordon* character), *see* Dr. Hans Zarkov (*Flash Gordon* character)
Zombies of the Stratosphere (film, 1952), 241
Zorovac, 184, 186
ZX-99 (spacecraft), 56, 216, 223